Economic Reform in China

Economic Reform in China
Problems and Prospects

edited by
James A. Dorn and Wang Xi

The University of Chicago Press
Chicago and London

The University of Chicago Press, Chicago 60637
The University of Chicago Press, Ltd., London

© 1989, 1990 by the Cato Institute
All rights reserved. Published 1990
Printed in the United States of America

Library of Congress Cataloging-in-Publication Data
Economic reform in China : problems and prospects / edited by
James A. Dorn and Wang Xi.

    p. cm.
"A Cato Institute book."
Based on a Cato Institute conference, cosponsored by Fudan
University in Shanghai and held in September 1988 at the Shanghai
Hilton.
Includes bibliographical references and index.
ISBN 0-226-15831-4.—ISBN 0-226-15832-2 (pbk.)
1. China—Economic policy–1976– —Congresses. 2. Central
planning—China—Congresses. 3. China—Foreign economic
relations—Congresses. 4. Economic forecasting—China—
Congresses. I. Dorn, James A. II. Wang, Hsi, III. Cato
Institute. IV. Fu tan ta hsüeh
(Shanghai, China)
HC427.92.E37 1990   90-10978
338.951′009′048—dc20   CIP

Cover design: *Kent Lytle*

CONTENTS

FOREWORD

CRISIS AND OPPORTUNITY IN CHINA
Edward H. Crane

In September 1988, the Cato Institute held an historic conference in Shanghai, which was cosponsored with the prestigious Fudan University. During that conference, Milton Friedman received an honorary professorship at Fudan University and there was an openness of discussion about the course of China's economic reform movement. There was also a guarded optimism about China's future, with both Westerners and Chinese generally agreeing that there could be no turning back from the transition to a market-oriented system, which began in December 1978.

At the time of the conference, however, China already was facing difficulties: accelerating inflation, corruption resulting from the mix of free and controlled prices, loss of interest in the Marxist-Leninist ideology, urban discontent at the increasing prosperity of rural areas and Special Economic Zones while urban areas were left behind, and a power struggle to determine whether conservatives or reformers took hold of the helm of China's economy.

The events that followed the conference demonstrated the difficulty of trying to introduce markets and rational prices without establishing private property rights and a constitution of liberty providing for the depoliticization of economic life.

Now China faces both an economic and a political-constitutional crisis of grave proportions. While Eastern and Central Europe and the Soviet Union are moving toward open markets and multi-party governments, China's reform movement is, for all practical purposes, on hold. The government must choose its future path and the choice is clear: either a return to central planning and control or a return to liberalization of prices and the market.

But if the latter route is chosen, which I believe will be the case, China's leaders still face the problem of resolving the contradictions inherent in trying to achieve a market system without at the same time providing the institutional framework for markets to effectively

The author is President of the Cato Institute.

function—namely, private property, freedom of contract, and constitutional safeguards for the rights of persons and property.

The essays in this volume, many of which were first presented at the Cato/Fudan conference but have been revised in light of ongoing events, point to the roots of China's crisis, to the implications of alternative reform paths, and to the opportunities that freedom will bring.

In the press conference that preceded the Shanghai conference, I stated: "The unique confluence of historical events—both internally and external to China's experience—presents an unusual and rare opportunity for a great nation to establish radical reforms in light of these events that will ensure a strong role of leadership for China in the world community as we approach the 21st century." I still believe this is the case, and even more so in view of the radical changes that are now occurring outside of China as socialist countries make the transition to freedom and prosperity.

In making the transition to freedom, however, the real problem is to circumvent the ruling elite who have a special interest in maintaining their monopoly of political and economic power. This "tyranny of the status quo," to use Friedman's term, is clearly the case in the Soviet Union and it is evident from the crisis in China. As Steven Cheung points out in his essay, "the root of the difficulties lies in the deeply entrenched state-controlled monopolies designed to protect vested interests." His solution is to privatize state-owned assets and to demolish the state's monopoly over trade and industry.

Under central planning, there is no real competition and no real freedom of choice for the vast majority of people. Moreover, there is a "fatal conceit," as Hayek put it—a belief that central planners can somehow design a blueprint for social and economic life that is superior to the spontaneous order that arises from freedom of choice and stable government by law.

Today, however, nearly everyone agrees that communism is dead and that economic organization along market lines is more likely to yield stability and prosperity than central planning. Nevertheless, while the "chaos of a closed society," as some Chinese economists at the conference expressed it, seems well understood, the dangers associated with even decentralized government control of economic activity is less well understood.

That is why it is important to gain an appreciation of the role of markets and prices in generating useful information and in coordinating millions of individual plans without central direction. It is also important to recognize that self-interest operates in government as well as in private life, and that without constitutional constraints on the range of government action—whether in China or in the United States—one should not expect individual action on the part of bureaucrats to be socially beneficial.

It was argued at the conference that by joining the worldwide move toward privatization and deregulation, China is positioned to avoid many of the lingering interventions—such as high marginal tax rates and central government manipulation of the money supply—that reduce economic prosperity in many Western nations. China, in fact, has the potential to join and lead the economic miracle that is the Pacific Rim today.

Thus, many of the Western speakers emphasized the importance of rapid and radical reform as opposed to slow and piecemeal reform. The radical-reform approach was best explained by Friedman, who argued that the expected benefits from shifting to a market system are far greater than the transition costs, which, in any event, are likely to be reduced by the rapidity of reform. In Friedman's view, "Peace and widely shared prosperity are the ultimate prizes of the worldwide use of voluntary cooperation as the major means of organizing economic activity."

The doubts expressed concerning rapid and thoroughgoing reform were based on China's unique history and the enormity of the task that confronts China's leaders. The events since 1988, however, have lent credence to the difficulty of step-by-step reform: It has been difficult to remove entrenched interests and impossible to create a viable system of market socialism, which is itself an oxymoron.

In examining the problems associated with moving from a centrally planned economy to a market system, the authors in this volume shed further light on the institutional changes necessary for a market order and reveal the inconsistency of trying to combine plan and market. They also draw on the lessons from regulation in the West to show the dangers associated with government intervention in general.

Focus is placed on how the transition to a market system can be made without creating chaos and without inflation. In addition to considering the question of the appropriate speed and extent of reform, the authors address the problems of privatizing state property, undertaking monetary and fiscal reform, decontrolling prices, and divesting the ruling elite of their monopoly over trade and industry. Running through the discussion is the notion that there is a close connection between economic reform and political-constitutional reform.

Although there is no agreement on the exact steps to be taken, it is widely agreed that without a stable rule of law and protection of

personal and economic liberties, there is little chance that China—
or other socialist countries—will actually move toward a private
market system.

The value of this book is that it paints a clear picture of the roots
of China's crisis, provides a framework for reform, and considers the
future prospects for reform. It does so using sound economic analysis,
which incorporates the insights gained from a study of property
rights, public choice, and constitutional economics. In addition, it
adds depth to the economic analysis by considering the impact of
China's reform on foreign relations.

This is a timely work, one made all the more relevant by the
knowledge that millions of Chinese stand poised to push their home-
land into the worldwide liberal revolution—peaceably if possible,
but by force if necessary. Many of us from the West, myself included,
caught up in the euphoria that enveloped that conference in Shanghai, neglected to appreciate the courage of those Chinese intellectuals who spoke so forcefully for freedom. In retrospect, I am certain
they understood fully the risks they—young and old—were taking.
My admiration for them knows no bounds, and it is my fervent hope
that the policy prescriptions contained in this volume will lead one
day in the not-too-distant future to a China that will, to quote from
George Gilder's speech, "Let a billion flowers bloom!"

EDITORS' PREFACE

The essays in this volume address one of the most significant issues in modern times, namely, the problem of how to make the transition from central planning to a free-market system. China's decade-long, but only partial, attempt to make this transition has been filled with spectacular successes as well as dismal failures. If one takes a careful look at these successes and failures, it is possible to gain a better appreciation of the economic, social, and political forces that operate during the transition period.

The book begins with an examination of China's institutions, the changes that have occurred over the past 10 years, and the further changes required if a private market system is to fully emerge. The key issue is the speed and degree of institutional reform: Radical change toward a market system makes sense from a theoretical viewpoint, but is often difficult in practice.

In setting a framework for reform, it is important to see that the market is a mechanism for social development, as Milton Friedman notes. It is also important to realize that markets require transferable ownership rights and freedom of contract—neither of which exists on a large scale in China. The government still exercises strong monopoly control over trade and industry, and there is a large bureaucracy that opposes change. Steven N. S. Cheung argues that the only way to end the rule of special interests in China is by widespread privatization.

It is argued that with open markets and rational prices to guide resources, the chaos of China's present "mixed economy"—with planning and the market existing side by side—will be replaced by spontaneously generated order. Such a result, however, depends on the adoption of an economic constitution that protects property rights and a rule of law. The challenge is to find a means of moving from what He Weiling calls the "ossified bureaucratic system" to a spontaneous market order without social upheaval.

The second section of the book elaborates on the problem of decentralization and on the relation between decentralization and economic development in China. Issues examined include the problem of decentralizing banking and finance; the problem of implementing and maintaining a sound monetary system to prevent inflation; the problem of ownership associated with the decentralization of agriculture; the concept of property in Chinese development; the question of which government services to privatize; and the differential effect of China's reforms on economic growth among regions, provinces, and cities.

The impact of China's economic reform movement on foreign relations is the subject of section three. As the world's most populous country, a strategic giant, and a potential economic powerhouse, China deserves close study. Any significant change in China's economic conditions and long-term prospects can have worldwide repercussions. In addition to considering Sino-Soviet-American relations, the essays examine the China–Hong Kong connection and the role China might play as a partner in the Pacific Rim's ongoing economic transformation.

In the final section, a closer look is taken at the choices that confront China and the probable consequences of alternative development strategies. Nien Cheng traces the roots of China's crisis to the failure to solve either the ownership problem or power-struggle problem, and she sees a psychological conflict in the choice between capitalism and socialism. Although no one would dispute the superiority of the market as a means of achieving economic success, people often do not welcome the risk of failure that is inherent in the free-market system. By collectivizing risk and providing a cushion for hardship, socialism has a certain appeal. But the idealism of socialism has, in Cheng's view, been overtaken by the harsh realities of communism.

China can learn from the lessons of Hong Kong and from those of the other East Asian tigers, but it can also learn from the experiences of U.S. deregulation in the 1980s. Alvin Rabushka argues that China would benefit by adopting many of the institutions now in place in Hong Kong and by drafting a "free-market" constitution to reflect Hong Kong's Basic Law. In examining the lessons for China from the U.S. experience with deregulation, William Niskanen points out that (1) deregulation is possible even if there is considerable opposition from special interest groups, (2) ideas do matter in determining the direction of public policy, and (3) the net benefits from deregulation are substantial. As he states, "The road to deregulation is not without rocks or detours, but it is the road to prosperity and opportunity."

The Chinese have done remarkably well outside their own country—in the West and elsewhere. A point George Gilder makes in his essay. They also have begun to do well at home, in the Special Economic Zones (SEZs) and in the rural areas that have been opened to competition and to the market by the agricultural reform. The future, says Gilder, will be bright—but only if China pursues the path of openness and opportunity.

The experiences of the Soviet Union and of Central and Eastern Europe teach us that meaningful change is possible. We hope that a better understanding of the forces that shape institutional change and the impacts of alternative institutional arrangements on economic development will serve to open China's door further to the outside world. The future prospects for peace and prosperity will then be much greater not only for China but for the entire world.

Several acknowledgements are in order. First, we would like to express our sincere thanks to all the authors in this volume for the care they took in preparing their papers and comments for publication. In particular, the Chinese authors deserve special thanks given the changes that have occurred over the course of this project. Second, we wish to thank Professor Xie Xide, former president of Fudan University, the excellent staff at Fudan's Center for American Studies, and Ted Galen Carpenter for their help in organizing the September 1988 conference in Shanghai, at which many of the papers in this volume were first presented. We also wish to acknowledge the assistance of the current president of Fudan University, Hua Zhongyi. Our greatest debt, however, goes to the Cato Institute for sponsoring the conference and to Ed Crane for his enthusiasm from start to finish. Third, we wish to thank Barbara B. Hart and Marianne Keddington for their assistance in preparing the manuscript for publication.

Finally, Jim Dorn gratefully acknowledges a grant from the Towson State University Faculty Research Committee and a sabbatical that helped facilitate the completion of this work. Wang XI acknowledges a grant from the Committee on International Relations Studies with the People's Republic of China (CIRSPRC) that enabled him to be in the United States during the preparation of this book.

PART I

CHINA IN TRANSITION:
SETTING A FRAMEWORK FOR REFORM

1

USING THE MARKET FOR SOCIAL DEVELOPMENT*
Milton Friedman

Introduction

An episode during an earlier visit to China impressed me strongly
with the wide gulf of understanding that separates people immersed
in different economic institutions. That gulf makes it extremely
important to stress over and over basic principles and ideas that all
of us simply take for granted with respect to the system to which we
are accustomed. The episode in question occurred when my wife
and I had lunch with a deputy minister of one of the government
departments who was shortly going to the United States to observe
the American economy. Our host wanted help from us on whom to
see.

His first question in that connection was, "Who in the United
States is in charge of materials distribution?" That question took my
wife and me aback. I doubt that any resident of the United States,
however unsophisticated about economics, would even think of asking such a question. Yet it was entirely natural for a citizen of a
command economy to ask such a question. He is accustomed to a
situation in which somebody decides who gets what from whom,
whether that be who gets what materials from whom or who gets
what wages from whom.

My initial answer was to suggest that he visit the floor of the
Chicago Mercantile Exchange where commodities such as wheat,
cotton, silver, and gold are traded. This answer understandably baf-
fled our host, so I went on to elaborate on the fact that there was no
single person—or even committee of persons—"in charge of materials distribution." There are a Department of Commerce and a Department of the Interior that are concerned with materials production
and distribution in a wholly different way. But they do not determine

*Reprinted from *Cato Journal* 8 (Winter 1989): 567–79, with revisions.
The author is Senior Research Fellow at the Hoover Institution at Stanford University
and a Nobel Laureate in Economics.

who gets how much of what. They collect information, examine the situation in various industries, evaluate legislation, and so on. Legislation (for example, tax and foreign trade laws) certainly affects the course of materials prices and distribution, but no single person or political body is "in charge of materials distribution" in the sense in which there is or has been such a person or political body in China or the Soviet Union. In consequence, I was forced to answer in terms that my host found extremely difficult to comprehend. Needless to say, that is not a criticism of him. Given his background, it is almost inconceivable that he could have understood how the market can distribute a variety of materials among millions of different people for thousands of uses untouched, as an ad might say, by political hands.

The miracle of the market is precisely that out of the chaos of people screaming at one another, making arcane signals with their hands, and fighting on the floor of the Chicago Mercantile Exchange, somehow or other the corner store always seems to have enough bread, the bakery always seems to have enough flour, and the miller always seems to have enough wheat. That is the miracle of the way the market coordinates the activities of millions of people, and does so in a wholly impersonal way through prices that, if left completely free, do not involve any corruption, bribes, special influence, or need for political mechanisms.

Let me now turn more directly to the topic at hand. In some ways, referring to "the market" puts the discussion on the wrong basis. The market is not a cow to be milked; neither is it a sure-fire cure for all ills. In literal terms, the market is simply a meeting of people at a specified place and time for the purpose of making deals. Needless to say, "meeting" and "place" are often euphemisms; they do not involve physical getting together. As of the moment, there is a market in foreign exchange that encompasses the world. People get together through satellites, telephones, and other means. Moreover, the deals made in or through a market are not restricted to those involving money, purchases, or sales. Scientists who cooperate with one another in advancing their discipline, whether it be physics, chemistry, economics, or astronomy, are effectively making deals with one another. Their market is a set of interrelated journals, conferences, and so on.

The market is a mechanism that may be mobilized for any number of purposes. Depending on the way it is used, the market may contribute to social and economic development or it may inhibit such development. Using or not using the market is not the crucial distinction. Every society, whether communist, socialist, social democratic, or capitalist, uses the market. Rather, the crucial distinction is private property or no private property. Who are the participants in the market and on whose behalf are they operating? Are the participants government bureaucrats who are operating on behalf of something called the state? Or are they individuals operating directly or indirectly on their own behalf?

That is why, in an earlier paper delivered in China, I advocated the widest possible use not of the market but of "free private markets" (Friedman [1980] 1982). The words "free" and "private" are even more important than the word "market." The wider use of the market that is sweeping the world is better described as "privatization"— transferring government-owned enterprises to private hands and thereby giving greater scope to the invisible hand of which Adam Smith wrote. In 1987 alone, over $90 billion of assets and enterprises were privatized by governments around the world.

In this paper I propose to discuss some of the problems that arise when a society tries to replace a command economy with the invisible hand of the market. Those problems are not restricted to societies that have tried to use command as their basic economic mechanism, such as China and the Soviet Union. The same problems arise in Western economies, such as the United States, Great Britain, and Germany, in which command elements have become more extensive over time and in which there are attempts to reverse that process. Privatizing government-owned enterprises in the West, such as the postal service in the United States and railroads and utilities in other countries, raises problems that are identical with those that arise in replacing command and government ownership by voluntary cooperation and private ownership in China and the Soviet Union. In consequence, China can learn a great deal by studying the experience of privatization in Western countries. At the moment, the most extensive experience of that kind is doubtless in Great Britain. Much has been written about the British experience, and it provides many instructive examples about correct and incorrect ways to privatize.[1]

I shall organize my discussion under three headings: partial versus total decontrol (or deregulation or privatization); gradual versus immediate decontrol; and overcoming political obstacles or, in more technical economic terms, short-circuiting rent seeking. Although the same issues arise whatever the domain in which command is replaced by voluntary cooperation—whether economic, political, or social—I shall restrict my comments to the economic domain. A

[1]An excellent source for Britain and other countries is Hanke (1987).

concluding section discusses the general problem of the tyranny of the status quo.

Partial versus Total Decontrol

Introducing a greater role for private market mechanisms in one sector of an economy may be partially or completely frustrated by the limited scope of the change. Consider what has been regarded as a major move toward wider use of the market, namely creation of the European common market and the attempt to achieve free trade among the common market countries. It has now been nearly 40 years since the Schuman plan for a coal and steel community was adopted, yet no observer will dispute that free trade within the common market is still an ideal rather than a reality. The latest bit of evidence is the recent agreement to *really* eliminate all barriers by 1992. Had the initial common market agreement been successful, that elimination would have been achieved many years ago. What was the problem? Why is there no real United States of Europe? In my view, the answer is that decontrol was adopted even in principle only for goods and services but not for money. The separate countries retained full authority over their national moneys. More important, they refused to adopt a system of freely floating exchange rates—that is, the free exchange of one currency for another at whatever rates of exchange were voluntarily agreed to in free private markets. The refusal to let the private market determine the rates of exchange among currencies was a fatal weakness.

I first reached that conclusion in the fall of 1950 when I spent a few months as a consultant in Paris to the then Marshall Plan agency. My assignment was to assess the likely consequences of the proposed coal and steel community. I concluded that free trade within a common market could not be achieved unless currencies as well as goods and services were freed from government control. That analysis was the basis for my article on "The Case for Flexible Exchange Rates" published in 1953. As I stated in that article (p. 157):

> A system of flexible or floating exchange rates—exchange rates freely determined in an open market primarily by private dealings and, like other market prices, varying from day to day—[is] absolutely essential for the fulfillment of our basic economic objective: the achievement and maintenance of a free and prosperous world community engaging in unrestricted multilateral trade. . . . Liberalization of trade, avoidance of allocations and other direct controls, both internal and external, harmonization of internal monetary and fiscal policies—all these problems take on a different cast and become far easier to solve in a world of flexible exchange rates and its corollary, free convertibility of currencies.

Experience during the 35 years since that article was published has, I believe, provided much additional evidence for the validity of this proposition.

Currently, China is faced with precisely the same problem. But my purpose in discussing it here is not to present again the case for a system of freely floating exchange rates but rather to give a striking illustration of how limiting decontrol or privatization to one area, while not extending it to closely related areas, can largely frustrate the basic objective.

A second example is from the United States. Although nominally private, U.S. airlines were subject to extensive government control with respect to the prices they could charge and the markets they could serve. Deregulation of the airlines in 1978 has enhanced competition, resulted in widespread and substantial reductions in prices, and increased the range of services. In consequence, there has been a major expansion in the volume of air traffic. However, while U.S. airlines were deregulated or, as I would prefer to put it, privatized, airports were not. They remain government-owned and operated.[2] Private enterprise has had no difficulty in producing all the planes the airlines find it profitable to use, and private airlines have had no difficulty in finding pilots or attendants. On the other hand, planes are often delayed because facilities or provisions for landing them at government-run airports are inadequate, at great inconvenience to passengers. Naturally, the government responds by trying to blame the private airlines: It has started requiring them to report delays in meeting their scheduled arrival times and publishing summary reports on the on-time performance of the several airlines. Repeated proposals have been made that—even if government retained the ownership and operation of the airports—rights to gates, both with respect to number of gates and to the times at which they are to be used, should be auctioned off. Unfortunately, the opposition of airlines, which have vested interests in the gates and times assigned to them by government agencies, has prevented the adoption of even such incomplete reforms. Of course, a far better solution would be to privatize the airports.

A third example is privatizing some areas of manufacturing while keeping the production or pricing of the raw materials under government control. The failure of the prices of the raw materials to conform to their market value means that private operation, however efficient privately, may be socially wasteful. Let me illustrate with an extreme

---

[2]In Britain, however, the British Airports Authority, which controls some airports, has been privatized.

example that I came across in India many years ago. It had to do with the manufacture of bicycles in a small community in the Punjab. The government of India controlled the production of steel and rationed the output to users, rather than auctioning off the steel produced at whatever prices the market would yield. As a result, the producers of bicycles could not get the amount of steel they were willing to buy at the officially set price of steel. However, there was a private market in finished or semifinished steel products. The bicycle manufacturers supplemented their government ration of steel by buying semifinished steel products and melting them down—hardly an efficient way to convert iron ore and coal into bicycles.

Let me cite some obvious examples for China. Introduction of a considerable element of privatization in agriculture has produced a remarkable increase in agricultural output and productivity—the most dramatic manifestation of China's success in widening the use of the private market. But it is clear that the very success has created a real problem. The overwhelming majority of the Chinese population is employed in agriculture. Even a relatively small improvement in agricultural productivity means the release from agriculture of workers who can now be more usefully employed in industry. Yet, the bulk of industry remains in the command economy; it has not been privatized, deregulated, or fully subjected to the competitive market process.

There has been a real attempt to change the way government-owned enterprises operate in China. The people in charge have been told to use market mechanisms, and an attempt has been made to provide incentives for them to do so. However, as long as industrial enterprises are government-owned, there are severe limits to the ability of politically sensitive managers (bureaucrats) to respond effectively to market pressures. The most serious limitation is on flexibility, that is, on the willingness or ability of managers in state-owned enterprises to be venturesome, to undertake risky projects that are likely to fail but have a real, if small, chance of spectacular success. Again, the problem is universal. Every study of the United States or Great Britain demonstrates that small enterprises—not the mega-corporations that are household names—are responsible for most of the new jobs. In China, the opportunity for such private enterprises is narrowly limited.

A much wider privatization of economic activity would greatly reduce the difficulty of absorbing the workers released from agriculture. That is precisely what happened in the United States and in the rest of the world during the 19th and 20th centuries. The fraction of the American population employed in agriculture in the early 19th century was over 90 percent—not far from the fraction currently employed in China—but it is now 2 or 3 percent. True, the transition in the West took much longer and proceeded at a more gradual pace than either should be or can be hoped for in China. Nonetheless, if the command sector of the economy had been as extensive in the United States then as it is now, let alone as extensive in China, the transition would never have occurred to anything like the same extent. The experience of Russia over the past 70 years is persuasive evidence. The way to expedite the transition in China is to proceed with privatization as rapidly and on as wide a scale as possible. Private enterprises would then spring up all over the place to absorb the working force.

A second example for China is similar to the problem I described for the common market: the difference between the extent of freedom in the production and distribution of goods and services and in the production and distribution of money. The substantial freeing of many prices, particularly those of agricultural and similar goods, has not been accompanied by the privatization of the banking system. As I understand it, the Chinese government indirectly determines what happens to the money supply through the credits it grants state enterprises. One result has been a rapid increase in the quantity of money and, not surprisingly, rapid upward pressure on prices, so that inflation, both open and repressed, has reared its ugly head.

It is much easier to point out the problems raised by partial use of the market than it is to draw any explicit implications for policy. It is easy to say that the best thing to do is to go all the way. However, in many really interesting and important cases, it is simply not politically feasible to do so. It would be clearly helpful in such cases to have some maxims that would suggest a way to draw the boundaries. However, it is not easy to do so in the abstract. I suspect that the only possible way to proceed is to analyze each case separately in light of the general economic principles embodied in price and monetary theory.

Gradualism versus Shock Treatment

When should reform be gradual, and when is radical and immediate change appropriate? One alternative is illustrated by the tale of the tortoise and the hare, when the "slow but steady" tortoise reaches the finish line ahead of the much speedier but more erratic hare; the other is illustrated by the maxim, there is no sense in cutting a dog's tail off by inches. This is one of the most difficult problems encountered in widening the scope of the market. Let me illustrate

9

with foreign trade. Suppose a country that has had high levels of tariffs decides to move to a free trade position. The case for moving gradually is clear. Capital has been invested in ways that will no longer represent an effective use of private resources under the new conditions. Much of that capital is in the form of machinery, buildings, human skills, and the like. Is it not clearly both more equitable and more efficient to reduce the tariffs gradually? That would give the owners of specialized resources the opportunity to withdraw their capital gradually and thus would reduce the costs imposed on them by the change.

The case for eliminating the tariff in one fell swoop, that is, for shock treatment, is more subtle, yet at the level of economic efficiency, compelling. Insofar as it is economically efficient to use the specialized resources in the absence of a tariff, they will be used. If any return over marginal cost can be obtained by continuing to use the specialized human and other resources, it is better to get that return than to get nothing. The burden would be imposed on the owners of the specialized resources immediately, but technical disinvestment would proceed only as rapidly as the specialized labor and other resources could be employed more productively elsewhere. On the other hand, gradual reduction in the tariff makes it privately profitable to continue using the specialized resources at a higher level than is socially efficient, thereby imposing unnecessary costs on the community.

The possibly valid arguments for gradualism are not technical and economic but equitable and political, and neither of these is clearcut. The individuals who invested in the protected industries did so with the full knowledge that the authorities that imposed the tariffs could eliminate them. The existence of such a possibility kept down the amount of capital invested in the industry and permitted the owners of such capital to earn a higher return than otherwise. Why is it now equitable for consumers to bear part of the owners' costs of adjustment? Politically, gradualism encourages the protected industries to spend resources to reverse the decision.

The analysis is complicated even further by considering the activities that will tend to expand under the new circumstances, that is, the industries that will replace the former so-called protected industries. Here, too, issues about efficiency, equity, and politics require attention.

Ending an on-going inflation raises similar problems. Eliminating inflation in one fell swoop, if not anticipated long in advance, may cause widespread capital losses. Long-term contracts entered into with one expectation about the likely rate of inflation may now suddenly be rendered inappropriate. The case on equity grounds for a gradual transition is far stronger for moderate degrees of inflation than for tariffs. The effects of both the prior inflation and its unanticipated ending are more pervasive and affect more people who have not only been harmed rather than benefited by the prior inflation but would be harmed again by its abrupt end. Reducing inflation gradually eases the transition and reduces the cost of achieving noninflationary growth.

However, much depends on the height of the inflation. If inflation is extremely high—at annual rates in triple digits—the situation is very different. Almost all participants in the market will have adjusted their arrangements so that any longstanding commitments are fully indexed. Abrupt disinflation will impose few costs because financial and other institutions have been adapted to radical changes in the rate of inflation. Indeed, such adaptations represent a major cost of high and erratic inflation. Gradual elimination is sometimes not even feasible because there is not time enough—the dog will be dead before its extra long tail can be cut off by inches.

Direct controls over prices—whether general or specific, for example, on rents or exchange rates—are almost always best ended at once. Margaret Thatcher properly ended exchange rate controls in Britain overnight and completely. Gradual adjustment only prolongs the harm done by controls and provides unjustified benefits to "insiders." The shortages and queues and other distortions produced by trying to hold prices below their market level would continue though they might get shorter, and additional problems arise because gradualism encourages speculation about reversal and encourages opponents to seek reversal. A similar proposition holds for attempts to keep prices above market levels—as is so amply demonstrated by the agricultural policies of the United States, Japan, and the common market.

Overcoming Political Obstacles

This subject has already inevitably intruded into the preceding section. The general issue here is how to overcome political obstacles to widening the market. The danger is not alone that these obstacles will frustrate the attempt to free the market but equally that overcoming political obstacles will destroy the advantages of freeing the market. The challenge is to find ways to overcome obstacles that do not have those effects. The experience of the West with privatization is particularly helpful in this connection. Perhaps the most extensive body of experience and the experience that has been most widely analyzed is the British experience with privatization, and I strongly recommend to our Chinese friends seeking to widen the market that they examine the evidence of privatization in Britain.

A simple case from the United States that illustrates the problem is privatizing the post office. The U.S. Postal Service has a monopoly in first-class mail because of the private express statutes, which make it a crime for individuals to offer common-carrier first-class service. Various attempts to do so have only succeeded in prosecution, which has ended the attempts. Privatization has been creeping in at the margin, first in the form of alternate parcel service. The United Parcel Service, a strictly private enterprise, and other parcel delivery companies have taken over the bulk of the Postal Service's prior business. In addition, private messenger services have developed, of which the best known is Federal Express, which has been so successful that numerous competitors have emerged. Developments that technological advances would have encouraged, no matter how postal service was organized, have doubtless been speeded up. Examples are electronic mail via computers and telephones, and facsimile service, again over telephones. These examples illustrate the ingenuity of private markets in exploiting the opportunities offered by the inefficiency of government enterprises.

Repeated attempts have been made to seek the repeal of the private express statutes so that private individuals and enterprises could compete with the U.S. Postal Service. However, such attempts always bring violent protests from the postal employee unions, from the executives of the Postal Service, and from rural communities that feel they would be deprived of postal service. On the other hand, few people have a strong and concentrated interest leading them to favor repealing the private express statutes. Entrepreneurs who might in fact enter the business if it were open to private entry do not know in advance that they would do so. Hundreds of thousands of people who would doubtless obtain employment in a privately developed postal system do not have the slightest idea that they would do so.

I recall a personal experience. I urged a congressman who believed as strongly as I did that it would be desirable to repeal the private express statutes to introduce a bill to that effect. He said, "You and I know the powerful groups who will testify and lobby against such a bill. Can you give me a list of people who will be equally willing to testify and work in favor of such a bill? People who will have some influence on Congress? People with a strong personal interest other than academic economists?" I admitted that I could not do so and he never introduced the bill. Vested interests have been built up in the postal monopoly. Few vested interests have been built up in opposing the postal monopoly, though there are some. That situation may be changing as corporations such as Federal Express and United Parcel Service begin to see the possibilities open to them.

One way to overcome the opposition to privatization, widely used in Britain, is, as described by Robert Poole (1988, p. 25),

> to identify potential opponents and cut them in on the deal, generally by means of stock ownership. Two specific applications of the principle are employee stock ownership and popular capitalism. . . .
>
> The opportunity to become shareholders can dramatically change the incentives of unionized civil servants, as illustrated in the case of British Telecom. Union officials denounced the planned privatization of Telecom, telling their members not to purchase the shares which were being offered to them at a discount. Yet in the end, sensing the chance to make money, some 96 percent of the workforce bought shares.

Poole also uses British Telecom to illustrate the second technique, popular capitalism: "To encourage telephone customers to buy shares, they were offered vouchers granting them a discount on their phone bills if they held their shares for at least six months. And to prevent institutions and large firms from buying up the lion's share, initial purchases were limited to 800 shares per buyer."

A pitfall to be avoided in adopting such expedients is to sweeten the deal by converting a government monopoly into a private monopoly—which may be an improvement but falls far short of the desirable outcome. The U.S. Postal Service illustrates that pitfall as well as the fallacy that mimicking the form of private enterprise can achieve the substance. It was established as a supposedly independent government corporation that would not be subject to direct political influence and that would operate on market principles. That has hardly been the outcome, and understandably so. It remained a monopoly and never developed a strong private interest in efficiency.

My own favorite form of privatization is not to sell shares of stock at all but to give government-owned enterprises to the citizens. Who, I ask opponents, owns the government enterprises? The answer invariably is, "The public." Well, then, why not make that into a reality rather than a rhetorical flourish? Set up a private corporation and give each citizen one or one hundred shares in it. Let citizens be free to buy or sell the shares. The shares would soon come into the hands of entrepreneurs who would either maintain the enterprise, for example, the postal system, as a single entity if it was most profitable to do so or break it up into a number of entities if that seemed most profitable. I know only one major case in which this procedure was followed, namely in British Columbia (see Ohashi and Roth 1980, part 1). Unfortunately, the collapse of energy prices made this venture less than an outstanding success. Nonetheless, it is well worth studying.

A final example illustrates the point in another way. The Russians have permitted small private plots in agriculture. Those private plots are estimated to occupy about 3 percent of the arable land in the Soviet Union, and roughly one-third of all domestic food products in the Soviet Union are sold as coming from those private plots. I have chosen my words carefully. I did not say that one-third were "produced on those private plots," because in my opinion that would not be correct. Much of the food sold as coming from the private plots has indeed been produced on them, but I strongly suspect that much has also been diverted from collective farms.

For decades, it has been clear to the rulers of the Soviet Union that they could increase the domestic output of agriculture substantially by increasing the size and role of the private plots. Why have they not done so? Surely not because of ignorance. The answer clearly is that privatization would tend to establish independent centers of power that would reduce the political power of the bureaucracy. The rulers regarded the political price they would have to pay as higher than the economic reward. As of the moment, largely I suspect under the influence of the extraordinary success of such a policy in China, President Gorbachev is talking about a considerable expansion in private plots. It is by no means clear whether he will succeed.

Tyranny of the Status Quo

The problems of overcoming vested interests, of frustrating rent seeking, apply to almost every attempt to change government policy, whether the change involves privatization, or eliminating military bases, or reducing subsidies, or anything else. The resulting "Tyranny of the Status Quo," as my wife and I entitled a recent book (Friedman and Friedman 1984) discussing a range of such cases in the United States, is the major reason that political mechanisms are so much less effective than free-market mechanisms in encouraging dynamic change, and in producing growth and economic prosperity.

Few simple maxims exist for overcoming the tyranny of the status quo. But there is one that ties in closely with the earlier discussion of gradual versus abrupt change. If a government activity is to be privatized or eliminated, by all means do so completely. Do not compromise by partial privatization or partial reduction. That simply leaves a core of determined opponents who will work diligently and often successfully to reverse the change. The Reagan administration repeatedly attempted, for example, to privatize Amtrak (the railroad passenger service) and to eliminate the Legal Services Corporation. In each case, it settled for a reduction in budget, achieving a fairly transitory victory. On the other hand, the complete abolition of the Civil Aeronautics Board gives far greater hope that airline deregulation is here to stay.

In conclusion, there are better and worse ways to privatize a command economy, but there is no magic formula for shifting painlessly from a command to a voluntary exchange economy. Nonetheless, the potential rewards are so great that, if the shift can be achieved, transitional costs will pale into insignificance. The Chinese people would be the main, but by no means the only, beneficiaries of the success of this shift. All the peoples of the world would benefit. Peace and widely shared prosperity are the ultimate prizes of the worldwide use of voluntary cooperation as the major means of organizing economic activity.

References

Friedman, Milton. "The Case for Flexible Exchange Rates." In Friedman, *Essays in Positive Economics*, pp. 157–203. Chicago: University of Chicago Press, 1953. Reprinted in *The Essence of Friedman*, pp. 461–98. Edited by Kurt R. Leube. Stanford, California: Hoover Institution Press, 1987.

Friedman, Milton. "How to Use Market Mechanisms in Connection with Central Planning." Lecture no. 4, presented in Beijing on 30 September 1980 and in Shanghai on 4 October 1980 under the auspices of the Chinese Academy of Social Sciences. Translated into Chinese and published in *On Inflation: Four Lectures in China*, pp. 50–67. Beijing: Chinese Social Sciences Publishing House, 1982.

Friedman, Milton, and Friedman, Rose D. *Tyranny of the Status Quo.* New York: Harcourt Brace Jovanovich, 1984.

Hanke, Steve H., ed. *Privatization and Development.* San Francisco: Institute for Contemporary Studies Press, 1987.

Ohashi, T. M., and Roth, T. P. *Privatization: Theory & Practice.* Vancouver, B.C., Canada: The Fraser Institute, 1980.

Poole, Robert W., Jr. "Stocks Populi, A Privatization Strategy." *Policy Review*, no. 46 (Fall 1988): 24–29.

COMMENT

PLANNING AND THE MARKET*
Pu Shan

Socialism in Theory and Practice

In economic literature, the question has long been raised whether the socialist system that is based on public ownership of the means of production could effectively organize economic activities. One point of view is that the socialist system is incompatible with the market mechanism and, therefore, cannot rationally allocate resources and organize economic activities. As early as the 1920s, Ludwig von Mises had argued strongly for this viewpoint. Oscar Lange, Abba Lerner, and others, however, offered the counterargument and demonstrated that in theory the socialist system could also make use of the market principle. Although their argument has sometimes been labeled "playing the game of competition" or "playing at capitalism," the theoretical question is basically resolved.

Another point of view is that although the socialist system could in theory make use of the market mechanism, public enterprises lack the incentive to observe the market principle and, therefore, cannot respond effectively to market pressures. Friedrick Hayek has long been of that opinion. Milton Friedman's argument seems to belong to the same category. The practical problem does exist. Since no socialist country has yet had a completely successful experience in making use of the market, it should be recognized that this practical problem remains unresolved.

The Direction of China's Economic Reform

The direction of China's economic reform is toward the development of a planned commodity economy that is based on socialist public ownership and not toward what Friedman calls "free private

*Reprinted from *Cato Journal* 8 (Winter 1989): 581–84, with revisions.
The author is President of the Chinese Society of World Economy.

markets." After the founding of the People's Republic in 1949, a vast amount of manpower, materiel, and financial resources were mobilized for large-scale economic development. Under a planned economy, with a relatively comprehensive industrial structure, China met the basic needs of the masses and achieved remarkable success. Nevertheless, the neglect of the role of the market mechanism, the overcentralization of the planning system, and the lack of production units with autonomous decisionmaking power affected more and more seriously the vitality of the economy. One of the important tasks of the current economic reform is to allow full play to the positive role of the market mechanism. Mandatory planning, therefore, is to be replaced by "guidance planning," the scope of prices set by the state is to be reduced, and the scope of prices determined by the market expanded. Moreover, even mandatory planning and state-set prices should take full account of market responses and the role of the law of value. The overall direction is "the state regulates the market and the market guides the enterprises."

Economic reform also bears on the question of ownership. The socialist economic system is based on public ownership of the means of production, including state ownership (mainly in the form of state enterprises) and collective ownership. In the past, however, there was an overemphasis on state ownership and a neglect of collective ownership, especially the necessary supplementary role of individual private ownership. A major component of the reform is to develop actively collective and individual economies while maintaining the basis of public ownership, and to develop extensively various forms of contractual management and cooperative management among the state, collective, and individual economies on a voluntary and mutually beneficial basis. China does not intend to privatize extensively its state enterprises. But in these enterprises, there will also be a separation of ownership and management, and through such measures as the management contract system the interests of the managers will be directly related to the economic efficiency and the profits and losses of the enterprises. Under these provisos, China is experimenting with stock ownership. The purpose is to render the state enterprises more responsive to market adjustments.

In this connection, Friedman mentioned the very important problem in China of transferring agricultural workers to industry. The actual situation is that during the process of economic reform in China, the rapid development of rural village and township enterprises has played a remarkable role in absorbing surplus agricultural workers. In recent years, the number of workers absorbed in village and township enterprises has been increasing by close to 10 million annually. These enterprises are mainly collective enterprises established by towns and villages.[1] In 1987, the number of workers in village and township enterprises amounted to 88 million, and their output value accounted for one-fourth of the total value of industrial output of the whole country. It is noteworthy that the large-scale transfer of agricultural labor to industry has been accomplished amid unprecedented prosperity in the rural economy, unlike many other countries that went through the painful process of widespread bankruptcy of farmers during the 19th and 20th centuries.

The economic efficiency of China's state enterprises is still far from being satisfactory. China's economic reform is also faced with many difficulties. There is still no sufficient factual evidence, therefore, to prove that the planned commodity economy based on Chinese-style public ownership will necessarily be superior to an economic system based mainly on "free private markets." On the other hand, judging from the actual evidence, any opposite conclusion seems also unwarranted.

The Extent and Rapidity of Reform

Friedman also raised the problems of "partial versus total decontrol" and "gradual versus immediate decontrol" in economic reform. These are very pertinent issues in the economic reform in China. "Partial versus total" and "gradual versus immediate" are, of course, relative concepts and closely related concepts. Relative to complete "free private markets," a planned commodity economy based on public ownership might be considered as a kind of partial reform. But no significant reform can be accomplished overnight, and any gradual reform inevitably creates continuous situations of partial reform.

China's economic reform has adopted the approach of gradual implementation. Judging from the actual situation in China, this approach has avoided irretrievable mistakes in the reform and serious volatility in economic activities. Moreover, through continuous demonstration of the practical benefits of economic reform, the gradualist approach has reduced resistance to reform. But this approach also has created the coexistence of the old and the new system and has created many new difficulties. For instance, at the present time, there are different prices for many of the same products, which has led to

---

[1]According to 1985 statistics, collective enterprises accounted for about 60 percent of the workers in village and township enterprises, whereas other cooperative enterprises accounted for 13 percent and individual or private enterprises for 27 percent.

serious malpractices. As such, price reform is increasingly becoming the key to the whole economic reform. Yet price reform is seriously hampered by such constraints as inflationary pressures.

Price reform concerns the whole economic structure and there is no simple choice among "partial or total" and "gradual or immediate" approaches. What is important is to have a comprehensive and coordinated program, and the steps and speed of the implementation of this program should take into consideration the actual situation in various fields as well as their interrelationship. The State Council has already put forward a preliminary program of price and wage reform, and the program is under extensive discussion and examination.

The Question of Political Reform

The deepening of reform will inevitably involve adjustments of economic rights and benefits and will, therefore, inevitably meet with political resistances and obstacles. This is why it is necessary to carry out political reform alongside economic reform. At the present time, the foremost task of political reform is to ensure the correct and successful implementation of the economic reform. But this task can rely only on the evolution and development of socialist democracy, rather than on such devices as "to identify the potential opponents and cut them in on the deal." From a long-run point of view, it is of vital importance that at the same time as material production is developed, the ideological and moral standards of members of society be raised—so as to establish gradually a new type of social relation among humankind. This is indeed the essence of socialism.

2

PRIVATIZATION VS. SPECIAL INTERESTS: THE EXPERIENCE OF CHINA'S ECONOMIC REFORMS*

Steven N. S. Cheung

When China opened her doors to the world in 1978, a period of great economic change was begun. In the span of a decade, China experienced economic changes of a magnitude and speed that are simply awesome. Remembering what China was like in 1978, we are compelled to think that her declared growth statistics, impressive though they certainly are, must be understated. Whatever the future holds, China's decade of growth (1978–88) will be remembered as one of the most significant economic events in history.

In 1981, I predicted China would go "capitalist" (Cheung 1982). With the single exception of Ronald Coase, all my friends objected that this judgment was far too optimistic. My prediction, stated in no uncertain terms, was that China, although probably never officially endorsing "private property," would nonetheless adopt a system akin to private property in practice. Unfortunately, recent events confirm another judgment call I made four years ago: The easy part of China's economic reforms was coming to pass, and high hurdles that could not be overcome without bold actions would soon follow.

Outsiders and Chinese authorities alike identify the same baffling difficulties. Mounting inflation is coupled with ever-rising government spending. The government finds price controls increasingly difficult to finance, yet to relax them without a sharp rise in the wages of state employees beyond the government's budget constraint may lead to social unrest. This view of a two-sided problem is not wrong. However, I shall argue that the root of the difficulties lies in the deeply entrenched state-controlled monopolies designed to protect vested interests.

In this paper I begin with a brief discussion of China's success in promoting private property rights in land and in labor. I then turn to

*Reprinted from *Cato Journal* 8 (Winter 1989): 585–96, with revisions.
The author is Professor of Economics at the University of Hong Kong.

the difficulties likely to face any attempt to privatize state enterprises. Finally, the relationship between these issues and China's inflation and financial problems will be considered.

The Creation of Private Property via Contracting

Whereas it took a revolution to abolish private property, the process in reverse may be done through peaceful contracting. It is not clear whether authorities in China were aware that the end result of the agricultural reforms initiated at the turn of the decade, is, for all practical purposes, a system of private property rights. Certainly the word "private" was avoided like a plague until March 1988. But as it turns out, the so-called responsibility contract, with all its modifications and refinements, is a Chinese version of the deed of trust.

"Responsibility" means that an individual household, or a set of households, assumes the task of production and payment to the government. In principle, the state imposes few additional restrictions, although in the industrial and business sectors numerous interventions remain. The development of the responsibility contract, with its attendant obstacles as well as implications for resource allocation, deserves a thorough study beyond the scope of this paper. It suffices here to quote from my 1986 "Postscript" to *Will China Go 'Capitalist'?* to pinpoint its nature (Cheung 1986, p. 67).

> The so-called "responsibility contract," if reduced to its simplest and therefore most perfect form, is equivalent to the granting of private property rights through a state lease of land. The duration of the lease may be any number of years or, in principle, it may be in perpetuity. Ownership is not relinquished by the state, but the rights to use and to obtain income are exclusively assigned to the lessee. The right to transfer or to sell the leased resource may take the form of sub-letting. Various dues exacted by the state may be lumped together in the form of a fixed rent, and since this rent is paid to the state it becomes a property tax. If indeed a perpetual lease is assigned, the land-holding becomes fee simple, and if the lease is freely transferable, the land is held in fee simple absolute— or private property in its perfect form!
>
> In ancient China, as in medieval Europe, there was no distinction between the meaning of "rent" and of "tax." A feudal lord who collected "rent" became a collector of "tax" when he assumed the role of a "government" in providing services such as justice and protection. From this point of view, the evolution of the responsibility system in China has come close to repeating in three astonishing years the course of several centuries of development in medieval Europe.

Yes, the responsibility contract as applied in agriculture comes very close to what in the Western world is a grant of private property in land. The clear, if minor, departure is that the Chinese version takes the form of leasehold instead of fee simple; that is, the contract is not in perpetuity. The length of the responsibility contract varies considerably across different regions or for different types of crops, and there is a tendency for contracts of a more recent vintage to have longer terms. In some regions, local authorities stipulate no time limitation at all: Confidence in the leasehold, therefore, varies with political climate. With the passage of time the contract holders gradually assume the view that they have an implicit perpetual right.

The use of the leasehold method finds its counterpart in Hong Kong, where practically all land belongs to the Crown. Although in this and in other developments in China the influence of Hong Kong is unmistakable, there is no doubt that a contract falling short of a deed serves a vital political function. With a leasehold the ownership of land remains with the state, thereby excluding private property in title and permitting the preservation of an image of socialist ownership. Early on, the transfer of the contract—equivalent to selling land—was forbidden as a way to suppress capital gain, but even this restriction has been relaxed and in some localities it is entirely ignored.

The public auction of land for nonagricultural uses, which occurred for the first time on December 1, 1987, also falls short of fee simple. Here again the exclusion of outright sale preserves the title of state ownership. Yet in a true economic sense, private property in land had been created, and with the recent explicit allowance of capital gain, not only Karl Marx has been forgotten but also Henry George. Significantly, in a public auction in Shanghai in July 1988, a Japanese firm was the winner. For the first time since the communist revolution, a foreigner had openly gained a private interest in China's soil We may suppose that ultimately the protection of private property of land will be generally strengthened: With any degree of foreign participation, any backward step is likely to have broader repercussions.

The establishment of private property rights in labor is even more prevalent than in land, although it has received much less attention. Unlike land, which itself makes no decision, every worker is a decisionmaking unit. Therefore, as soon as the government relaxes its control over labor, individuals would automatically assume responsibility for themselves. In other words, labor becomes private property the moment it is not manipulated and controlled by the government.

The privatization of labor became evident about six years ago, when the authorities relaxed the requirement that all employment be assigned by the state. The unemployed (described as "waiting to be employed") were far too numerous, and the pressure from Hong Kong investors to hire labor by private contracting was far too great. The experiment of letting state employees take their chances with the market began in the Pearl River basin and gradually spread northward. Today, the state control of labor still found in Beijing is nonexistent in Southern China.

Individual households running their own small enterprises can now be found everywhere, and in Southern China even state-owned enterprises now refuse to hire state employees; rather, they opt for contract workers. In the South, the survival of the state-employee system in trade and industry is sustained by only three factors. First, state employees have guaranteed security and retirement benefits. Second, contract workers employed by state enterprises are subject to wage ceilings. And third, with most sizeable enterprises still owned by the state, employment opportunities are limited. Still, in a number of localities, particularly in areas where Hong Kong investors are popular, the state-employee system is quite literally falling apart.

Difficulties Confronting Trade and Industry

By 1985 the responsibility contract was well established in agriculture and China began to extend the system to state-owned enterprises in trade and industry. I noted in 1986 five problems encountered in trade and industry (Cheung 1986, pp. 68–69):

> First, productive assets such as a desk, a machine, a brand name, or know-how are not physically divisible like land, so the productive assets in a corporation are not owned exclusively by any specific member of the corporation. With many individuals working in a group, as in a typical state enterprise in China, rights over productive assets obviously cannot be delineated in the way lands are divided among individual peasant households. In the absence of any clearly delineated exclusive rights, the collective holders of a responsibility contract are, not surprisingly, prone to argue over the division of the income generated by their joint efforts.
>
> Second, virtually all productive assets other than land tend to have finite usable lives. Depreciation of equipment and buildings might be thought to justify the government laying down the amount of re-investment, the kind of goods to be produced, and the type of business that must be maintained. In deciding these matters, conflicts of interest arise between the government and the joint holders of responsibility contracts. Of course, there is simply no way the government could be expected, in a wide diversity of trades and industries, to rival the wisdom or expertise in decision-making of those actually engaged in the enterprise.

Third, the production process in trade and industry is generally far more complex than in agriculture. Contracting, sub-contracting, and sub-sub-contracting are common, and these have led to responsibility arrangements in complex, multi-stage forms. When the holders of an original responsibility contract—responsible directly to the government—sub-contract to others, the terms of performance and the division of income are difficult to negotiate because both the contractor and the sub-contractor lack the option of refusing to cooperate and of seeking competitive bidding elsewhere. Further, the government often wants to maintain a say over the terms of sub-contracting.

Fourth, because of changing market conditions, profits and losses fluctuate more sharply in trade and industry than in agriculture. Responsibility contracts therefore tend to have a much shorter life (typically one year). Holding to the labour theory of value, the government tends in renewing contracts to increase or reduce its "take" depending on the results of performance, and contractors who have performed above expectations naturally feel unjustly deprived of any reward.

Finally, productivity in trade and industry, far more than in agriculture, depends on the quality of human capital. An entrepreneur with creative ideas may be worth a fortune, but his innovation cannot be fully rewarded within the short duration of a responsibility contract. Indeed, a prime target for common condemnation of the responsibility system is the average wage ceiling of 250 RMB (about US$50) per month, imposed both to effect a desired distribution of income and to force an increase in investment.

I argued that to tackle these problems, three requirements are in order (Cheung 1986, p. 70):

First, state ownership of depreciating productive assets must be relinquished, either to the highest bidder or simply as an endowment to members of the existing state enterprise. This must be done because these assets, or their values, unlike land, will disappear in time.

Second, if several or many individuals own the assets, shares should be issued against the asset value and assigned to the individuals. If necessary, this division of wealth might be done by voting, as baseball players in the United States vote to divide the income from the World Series.

Third, the shares must be freely transferable.

Of these recommendations, the only one the authorities remain reluctant to accept is the first, namely, relinquishing state ownership of depreciating assets. The impression I obtained at the time is that for political reasons state ownership of resources must be preserved. That is, private property may be practiced in nature, but not in name, and this dichotomy is far more easily resolved in agriculture than in trade and industry.

In September 1987, therefore, I suggested to my Beijing friends a new solution that, following Mao's terminology, may be called a "thorough" responsibility system. Thinking of a private individual borrowing from a bank to buy an automobile in the United States, in which the legal owner (the bank) and the registered owner (the individual) are separate, I proposed that the assets of a state enterprise be assessed and converted into a monetary value. The state would then "loan" this capital value to the individuals running the enterprise, with dues in the form of interest payments. The state would relinquish all controls as long as interest payments were met. With the issuance of transferable shares, the nature of private enterprise will be practiced while preserving the legal title of state ownership.

My proposal would have worked perfectly if the only concern were to preserve the image of a socialist system. There is no inherent conflict between the economic nature of private property and socialism. (After all, each individual is a social entity.) However, recent events suggest that the real problem of reform in trade and industry does not rest so much with the preservation of an image, or what the system should be called. Rather, the main problem lies in something most of us working on the theory of the state have known all along, namely, the protection of privileges associated with special rights. And it appears that special interests are far more easily defended in trade and industry than in agriculture.

Why Price and Wage Controls?

As early as 1981, I predicted that in China's movement toward private property, the last and most stubborn redoubt standing in the way of reform would consist of those state enterprises in which monopoly can be maintained most easily. This observation has become self-evident.

In agriculture and in household enterprises, competition is severe, and it is difficult for special interest groups to protect their rights. Similarly, in industries such as hotels, restaurants, or handicrafts in which entry is free, special rights dissipate readily with the onset of competition. A state-owned hotel surrounded by private hotels must follow what the market dictates or face defeat. The right to control is valueless if competitors are exempt from that control. In China there is no question that businesses subject to open competition have blossomed.

On the other hand, it is to be expected that sectors such as public transportation, public communication, utilities, petroleum, and mineral rights will not readily go private. But the list does not end there. Banking, foreign exchange, international trade, the steel industry, products with successful trademarks, and industries with trade secrets or with effective barriers to entry such as heavy machinery, drugs, and silk are all candidates for persistent state manipulation and control because of their monopoly status.

Authorities in charge of these monopolistic industries benefit from price and wage controls. From price control, the officials with the right to allocate or ration goods, along with those who have special rights to receive them, stand to gain at the expense of government subsidies as well as costs to consumers. From wage control, workers' income is reduced in favor of those in command.

While price and wage controls are easily enforced with state ownership, they are difficult in the case of private enterprise. For example, if fish is sold in a state-operated market in which profit and loss are not the concern of anybody, it can literally be marked at any price. But an individual who gets up before dawn, rides a bicycle to the village to buy a few fish with his own money, and then rushes back to sell in the market is likely to grow violent if a government official tries to restrict his pricing.

It is easy to give reasons for controls: wage control to promote a desirable income distribution; price control to check inflation, to assist the needy, to encourage industrial development, and so on. These justifications are both trite and wrong, but they are used routinely all the same. Even in our modern times, politicians seem to be running out of imagination.

The Chinese experience is the most telling. State ownership of monopolistic ventures is maintained because it is relatively easy to do so, and with state ownership, price and wage controls are relatively easy to enforce because no private party has a vested interest to object, and these controls generate income to individuals with special rights.

Supporting evidence is strong. Domestic plane tickets used to be sold at one-third the market price, allowing privileged officials to preempt blocks of them for sideways dealing. However, sometimes planes would fly almost empty. Steel for construction work is sold at less than half the market price, allowing those with the right to ration to capture handsome "rents." It is absurd that at a time when the whole of China requires rebuilding, the import of rebars is severely restricted. The foreign exchange rate (a price) is "controlled," so to speak, but special exchange centers are officially allowed to deal at near black market rates. That is, black market foreign exchange dealing is prohibited for private citizens, but not for government officials. The interest rate (again a price) is pegged at a level far below the rate of inflation. The result is that households or small state-owned enterprises cannot hope to borrow money, while officials with proper connections borrow to relend subtly, to invest carelessly, or to consume lavishly. And the list goes on.

A Collision at Last

We are all aware that proponents of market-oriented reforms in China have had their fair share of opposition. Yet with numerous reports of political infighting, China's progress over the 1978–88 period was so fast that it would have been unthinkable in an earlier period. We have felt all along that vested interests cannot be dismissed lightly, that there is no pay-off or buy-out which can be conveniently executed, and that a free-enterprise economy cannot be developed without bold actions. A reform program that benefits the society at large does not mean all its members will benefit. Some special interests, somewhere, somehow, will have to bear the cost of change.

On a number of occasions I have pointed out that China cannot remain long at this balance point without turning into another India. The Indian syndrome of government regulations, state-controlled monopolies, and massive corruption is certainly seen in China today. But unlike India, China's reform process has both mass and acceleration. A collision of reform and special interests, therefore, must come with great force at some point in time. From an optimistic point of view, it is a relief that this collision comes so soon. Yes, what China will turn out to be depends on what will happen in the next two or three years.

Observers concur on what they see. In 1989, China had mounting and near runaway inflation; officials or state employees of ordinary status found their purchasing power declining with sticky wages. To print more money means more inflation. Yet inflation is apparently fueled less by increases in the money supply than by tight control of interest rates. With these rates being pegged significantly below the rate of inflation, people have a strong incentive not to hold renminbi (RMB). But to let the interest rate float would mean decontrol in a vital government monopoly.

As my whole argument implies, since price control exists primarily in state-owned monopolies, the freeing of prices would strip down the rights of the privileged groups. Furthermore, so long as enterprises are owned by the state, increased prices will not lead to increased production of goods and services as would be the case with private enterprise.

In 1988, Deng Xiaoping and Zhao Ziyang announced that it was essential for price controls to be bulldozed away. Their statement was bold and admirable. Some prices have since risen sharply, including those of liquor, cigarettes, and plane tickets. Unfortunately, the coverage does not extend to interest rates and exchange rates—which hints at powerful vested interests in these areas. It is equally regrettable that taxes, dues, and duties have also been increased. The great *sine qua non* now is to set right the fundamental source of the difficulties. China's deep and basic needs now are the privatization of state-owned enterprises and the demolition of state-created monopolies.

The Nature of the Problem

China has reached a point where piecemeal tactics are not likely to be effective in advancing her economic reforms. In the past such tactics have served China well, often brilliantly. While cadres and citizens alike agree that the "common rice wok" and the "iron rice bowl" are detrimental to productivity and must be discarded, they have little understanding of how a market system based on private property rights operates. With the Marxian doctrine nearly dead, there was, and still is, an ideological vacuum in China. The piecemeal approach thereby adopted is impressively pragmatic, using common sense rather than theory to correct the economic ills that have become all too evident. Indeed if any people can be called experts on the shortcomings of a communist system, the Chinese have no peers. Piecemeal tactics guided by common sense and the economic forces at work have, by and large, been the policy guideline. And in spite of the political opposition and occasional backslidings that often occupied news headlines over the 1978–88 period, economic progress was phenomenal.

In the process, a substantial number of comrades lost their privileged status. The more astute ones have turned to trade and industry and do well because of connections. Others have become ordinary citizens or have gone into retirement. In areas subject to intense competition, previous hierarchical rights that are based on rank regardless of productivity have become valueless. In other areas, however, these privileges are transformed into monopoly and regulation rights. An attempt to protect a state monopoly or to protect a regulation is an attempt to protect "a right."

I can cite numerous instances to support this view. But if we must single out one example of prime importance, then the financial sector would be a natural choice because of the wide ranging implications involved, and because its problems make the headlines almost every day.

Take Wenzhou, for instance, where any impartial observer must stand in awe of its economic success. A number of small private savings-and-loan institutions cropped up to finance small businesses, with brilliant success. But this booming enterprise was soon restrained by the banking authority, which imposed interest and licensing regulations. Again, in the area of foreign exchange, it has been a monopoly long enjoyed by the Bank of China, reaping handsome profits through exchange controls and rationing. But when black market activity became prevalent and hard to control, the authorities themselves started exchange centers dealing in near free-market rates. It is difficult to say in what sense exchange control now exists in China. Certainly, all arguments in favor of it have been flatly contradicted by the government's own behavior.

Indeed the pattern is replete that where competition is severe and monopoly power can hardly be maintained, the authorities routinely opt for a freer market and more private property protection. But where monopoly is protected, the policies adopted always tend to benefit special interest groups and, along with price and wage controls, the superiority of socialist ownership is again upheld as unquestionable.

Nothing can be further from the truth. The arguments for freer markets and for the necessity of maintaining controls, often heard from the same authorities, reveal such glaring contradictions that one must infer that the prime motivation of controls is to benefit privileged groups. There is no conceptual difference among the monopoly and controls in silk, steel, heavy machinery, foreign trade, foreign exchange, and banking. The problem is general, although inflation and the difficulty of feeding state employees (as well as students) are placed in the spotlight, they tend to obscure the nature of the problem.

Monopoly protects; state ownership facilitates controls; the right to control generates income to the privileged. This is as true in the production of goods and services as in the banking and financial sectors, although the latter has broader implications for the economy as a whole. The piecemeal tactic of decontrolling a few prices, of restraining the growth in money supply, or of curbing government expenditure does not get to the heart of the matter. A general problem calls for a general solution: Privatize state enterprises and allow free entry for all.

Conclusion

It is somewhat puzzling that the 25 to 30 percent annual increase in the money supply of RMB, reported for 1989, could have caused a near 30 percent annual rate of inflation. A number of localities in China have experienced real growth rates in excess of 25 percent per year, and goods and services that were previously self-consumed or bartered are now transacted in the marketplace. These things are not recorded in the official statistics. Still, one may argue that a 15 to 20 percent monetary growth per annum would be more appropriate. However, I surmise that inflation in China is prompted mainly by controls on interest rates, by government restrictions on savings and loans or small private banks, by the fact that even major foreign banks are not allowed to perform the essential functions of banking, and because output in state-operated enterprises are not elastic to increases in price.

The financial difficulties of China so often discerned are real. But how are these possible? How is it possible that a nation with citizens rushing to buy gold has more financial problems than when they could not even afford to buy vegetables? Why should the Chinese government now find it necessary to impose heavy taxes on practically everything, as compared to the earlier starvation period when taxes were unheard of?

No, China should not have any financial problems at all! She has all the "lands under heaven" to sell, all the mineral rights to sell, numerous state enterprises to sell, and an army of officials who could be relieved and turned to more productive employment. If these things are done, China would have a budget surplus with a tax system as simple as that of Hong Kong, and even at lower tax rates.

More fundamentally, therefore, my view is that whereas the formation of private property via contracting has been relatively smooth in areas subject to active competition, the process fails when it comes to areas where monopolies are fostered. It is time for China to consider the creation of private property by mandate. And whereupon they may follow one simple rule: For state-owned resources that are salable, sell. This is the most straightforward way to create private property, and the selling prices as well as the forms of payments may be adjusted as special cases demand—in the initial sale to distribute and define property rights, the market price need not be applied. The proceeds may be used to compensate individuals who suffer

31

greatly from the changes; to invest in the infrastructure (or better still, to loan out to private parties for such investment); and above all, to establish a judicial system that is based firmly on the principle of equality before the law.

Reference

Cheung, Steven N.S. *Will China Go 'Capitalist'?* London: Institute of Economic Affairs, 1982; 2d ed. with "Postscript" published in 1986.

COMMENT

ESTABLISHING A NEW ORDER OF THE SOCIALIST COMMODITY ECONOMY*
Xu Pengfei

Steven Cheung has freely and candidly described and analyzed the situations, controversies, and contingencies of our economic reform. In the old days the rigid economic mechanism had pulled the leg of our productivity. That is why reform is needed. Our ultimate aim is to build socialism with Chinese characteristics, in conformity with which we are to decide what reforms should be carried out and where they should lead to. We need to learn from the experience of other countries, but not necessarily follow their footsteps.

Price Reform and Wage Reform

Until recently, China's economic situation was far better than anybody could have imagined when the reform movement began more than a decade ago. Such indexes as the total output value of the entire society, the total industrial and agricultural output value, and national income were shooting up by dazzling percentages. Statistics show that the actual take-home pay of the peasants and the city dwellers, even though we incorporate the inflation rate, steadily increased from 1978 to 1988. All enterprises, with Party guidance separated from management, were rapidly becoming independent commodity producers and operators. It must also be pointed out that although during recent years a "double-track system" combining the mechanisms of a planned economy and a market economy has been initially introduced, this combination has not attained perfection either in terms of theory or practice. The new order of the socialist commodity economy has to evolve from a highly centralized old order that excludes market mechanisms. Therefore, the establishment of

*Reprinted from *Cato Journal* 8 (Winter 1989): 607–11, with revisions.

The author is Chairman and President of Lesterian Technical Consultants in Shanghai.

a new economic order in China is a painful and relatively long process. At present, China is in the midst of a transitional period during which the new and old systems are interwoven with the new replacing the old step by step. In particular, there now exist two systems, two price structures, two social psychologies, and both positive and negative factors typical of the initial period of growth of a commodity economy. The direct results of this kind of coexistence have been dwelled upon by Cheung. China's economic reform is an unprecedented undertaking for which various blueprints can be drafted. But whatever blueprint is drafted must conform to the actual conditions of China. What, then, is the way out for China?

The 10th Plenary Session of the Central Political Bureau of the Communist Party of China, held in August 1988, pointed out that the crux of economic reform lies in price and wage reform. Undoubtedly, this was a timely, wise decision based on previous practice and suggestions by economists both at home and abroad. According to this decision, while the prices of several major commodities and the cost of labor would remain regulated by the state, the prices of the majority of commodities would be decontrolled and subjected to the adjustments of a fluctuating market. Fluctuating prices would then form a system of their own, leading step by step to the goal that "the State adjusts and controls the market which, in turn, leads and guides the enterprises." The immediate objective is to gradually systemize more reasonable price relations and solve those problems seriously affecting economic expansion and market growth. The overall aim of the wage reform is to ensure that there is no drop in the actual living standards of the majority of working citizens by wage adjustments and hikes plus necessary allowances and, furthermore, to help improve living standards alongside the development of production. Meanwhile, the principle of distribution according to work will be further put into practice, to solve the problem of unfairness in distribution.

The basic direction in which China's economic reform is going is to establish a hitherto unknown new order of the socialist commodity economy. In other words, we aim at a macro-market appropriately guided by state plans. The core issue is prices. Therefore, if we succeed in the price reform, we can achieve a breakthrough that serves to coordinate the relations of the state, the enterprise, and the individual by well-regulated price and market mechanisms. This is a highly complex undertaking; many things remain to be experimented and theoretically crystallized.

Reform in the Ownership of Enterprises

The pivotal task for China's economic reform is to modify the system of management and administration of our enterprises so as to

3

PRICING AND PROPERTY: THE CHINESE PUZZLE

James A. Dorn

The proportion of private persons who are prepared to try new possibilities, if they appear to them to promise better conditions, and if they are not prevented by the pressure of their fellows, is much the same everywhere. The much lamented absence of a spirit of enterprise in many of the new countries is not an unalterable characteristic of the individual inhabitants, but the consequence of restraints which existing customs and institutions place upon them. This is why it would be fatal in such societies for the collective will to be allowed to direct the efforts of individuals, instead of governmental power being confined to protecting individuals against the pressures of society. Such protection for private initiatives and enterprise can only ever by achieved through the institution of private property and the whole aggregate of libertarian institutions of law.

—Friedrich A. Hayek (1978, pp. 189–90)

A Problem of Constitutional Economics

The idea that property rights matter in shaping incentives and behavior is central to understanding economic reform in China. Ownership rights in land, labor, and capital and the status of the entrepreneur's claim to residual income are important determinants of economic development. At the root of any economic reform, however, is a certain conception of policy, that is, a certain ideology. If the prevailing ideology clashes with the economic and social institutions necessary for promoting wealth creation and satisfying consumers' preferences, then political considerations may well dominate any rational attempt to decentralize a socialist economy.

China's leaders have mistakenly perceived their problem as how to introduce markets without establishing effective ownership rights.

The author is Vice President for Academic Affairs at the Cato Institute and Professor of Economics at Towson State University. An earlier version of this paper was presented at the Third Hayek Symposium on Knowledge, Evolution, and Competition in Freiburg, West Germany.

Their deeper conceptual problem is how to achieve economic and social order without central planning. The clue to solving the puzzle as a whole is to recognize that markets cannot exist without private ownership rights and that once such rights are established, a spontaneous economic order can emerge. Thus, at the heart of any effective reform in China is the necessity of understanding what James Buchanan (1979, pp. 81–82) has called the "most important central principle in economics," namely, "the principle of spontaneous order"—and recognizing that this order critically depends on what Friedrich Hayek (1960) has called a "constitution of liberty." By limiting the influence of politics over economics, self-interest can be directed toward realizing mutual gains from market exchange. In this sense, then, the problem of economic reform under socialism is a problem of constitutional economics, that is, a problem of how to change the rules of the game (the effective economic constitution) to increase freedom and wealth.

Stable government by law, private ownership, and freedom of contract—all of which are necessary for establishing a viable market price system in which individual plans can be coordinated without central direction—have yet to gain widespread support among China's ruling elite. Communist party bureaucrats recognize the dangers that a free-market system and a rule of law pose to their privileged position, and they have little incentive to depart from the status quo. But the institutional inertia that is characteristic of all socialist regimes also stems from a lack of vision. The eyes of socialist leaders are typically focused on distributive justice and ignore the commutative justice inherent in a free-market process. Moreover, socialist leaders have not fully appreciated the information and incentive functions of prices and profits in solving society's economic problem, "a problem of the utilization of knowledge which is not given to anyone in its totality" (Hayek [1945] 1948, p. 78).

The impossibility of centralizing the vast array of information spread throughout society and the continual changes in the information available to different individuals point to the necessity of relying on markets and prices to efficiently utilize existing information and to rapidly disseminate new information.[1] To think that central plan-

---

[1]On the so-called Hayekian knowledge problem, see Hayek ([1945] 1948, pp. 83–84), where he states:

> If we can agree that the economic problem of society is mainly one of rapid adaptation to changes in the particular circumstances of time and place, it would seem to follow that the ultimate decisions must be left to the people who are familiar with these circumstances, who know directly of the relevant changes and of the resources immediately available to meet them.

See also Hayek ([1937] 1948).

ners, in China or elsewhere, can duplicate the competitive market process without allowing for private ownership and price competition is a fatal conceit, as Hayek puts it.[2]

A legal system that effectively protects economic and civil liberties is a necessary condition for a spontaneous market order within which individuals will be able to pursue their own interests while also serving the interests of others. When the rule of law is eroded by catering to special interests, the market process will become politicized. The information and incentive functions of market prices will then be weakened as "rent seekers" attentuate private property rights and redistribute national wealth.

Although the modern redistributive state is recognizable in democratic governments in the West, it is pervasive in all socialist countries including China, where there are no effective constitutional limits on governmental takings. Nevertheless, China's experience with social engineering is widely regarded as a dismal failure, and over the past decade China's leaders have demonstrated a willingness to move toward a more open society and a more market-oriented economic system. Since 1978, the search has been under way to discover a new set of rules that provide greater economic stability, make individual decisionmakers more responsible for their use of scarce resources, and set the basis for long-run economic growth. It is generally understood that unless allowance is made for the possibility of loss whenever individuals or firms fail the market test, the redirection of resources required for increased efficiency and wealth will not take place.

Rational economic calculation requires competitive markets and prices supported by a system of private property rights providing individuals with exclusive rights to use their property, to sell it, and to capture the increase in value from prudent use or to bear the loss from mismanagement.[3] The problem of rational economic calculation under socialism and the difficulty of piecemeal reform are clearly recognized in China. The recognition of these problems, in turn, has led to the call for price reform, intended to make prices more fully reflect the underlying forces of demand and supply. Reporting on an article by Wang Guiwu, the *China Daily* stated: "Reasonable prices, reasonable price parities and a rational price composition are formed in the course of market exchanges in line with the requirements of

---

[2]Hayek (1988) uses the phrase "fatal conceit" in a comprehensive way to undermine all of socialism, but the expression seems particularly appropriate to characterize the fallacy of economic calculation under socialism and the knowledge problem.

[3]On the requirements for rational economic calculation, see Hayek ([1935] 1975) and Mises ([1936] 1974).

the law governing supply and demand. . . . Intense market competition and changes in the supply-demand relationship and prices are not subject to the subjective will of government officials."[4] The *China Daily* went on to quote Wang as saying, " 'The more the government controls, the more it is likely to depart from the requirements of the law governing supply and demand.' " The article concluded by noting that "it is imperative to apply that law [of supply and demand] to the formulation of China's price policies and the introduction of a price managerial system."

The efficient use of resources stemming from competitive markets requires that individuals bear responsibility for their actions. As Hayek ([1940] 1974, p. 156) observed, "to assume that it is possible to create conditions of full competition without making those who are responsible for the decisions pay for their mistakes seems to be pure illusion." This fact too is gaining attention in China. Reporting on an article by Ruan Bin, the *China Daily* noted: "The private economy is the most economical in China. . . . In private businesses, both owners and workers pay the closest attention to thrift and saving, because waste means their own loss."[5] The newspaper cited Ruan as saying, " 'Private businesses regard the customer as king.' " And the major finding of the study, according to the *China Daily*, was that "market-led decisions force private businesses to operate in a pioneering spirit, which is the powerful driving force for the expansion of the private economy."

The problem of ownership has also been openly acknowledged in China as one of the fundamental difficulties in moving toward a market system. Changing the ownership system in China to allow for rational price calculation and responsible decisionmaking at all levels is a problem that China's future leaders cannot afford to ignore. Although China has some 225,000 private enterprises that employ nearly four million people,[6] state-owned enterprises continue to dominate the economic landscape. In September 1988, however, Zhao Ziyang announced a major plan to convert state enterprises into publicly owned enterprises under a "shareholding system," designed to help reduce the nearly $11 billion that the government pays in subsidies to support state-owned enterprises (Southerland 1988b). Unfortunately, the abrupt policy shift following the May-

[4]"Lift of Price Controls in Focus," *China Daily*, 13 July 1988, p. 4. (The *China Daily* is an English language summary of key articles in the Chinese press.)
[5]"Private Economy Praised," *China Daily*, 16 July 1988, p. 4.
[6]Ibid.

June 1989 demonstrations has forestalled any further ownership reform.

As the events surrounding Tiananmen Square illustrate, the major difficulty in reforming the Chinese economy is that under the present system economic questions are necessarily political questions.[7] The widespread corruption in state enterprises attests to the politicization of economic life in China and to the consequent failure of the "contract system," which was supposed to allow managers of state-owned enterprises greater autonomy after satisfying a governmentally determined profitability target. As Julia Leung (1989) observed, many state enterprises remained unprofitable under the contract system and the monies used to prop up inefficient state enterprises were often "squandered on grandiose construction projects, inappropriate equipment and fancy state housing" or found their way into the pockets of "corrupt officials." Again, the basic problem, writes Leung, is "the failure of the contract system to distance government from the running of enterprises."[8]

The politicization of economic life is nowhere more evident than in the sphere of finance and banking, where the state controls the bulk of investment resources. The lack of a private capital market has handicapped economic development in China and hampered rational investment decisionmaking. Moreover, the extension of bank credits to cover the losses of inefficient state enterprises has led to serious inflation. The austerity program, initiated in September 1988, dampened state investment spending and slowed the growth of bank credit. As a result, inflation has been reduced from a peak of 27 percent in 1989 (an official estimate; the actual inflation was reportedly much higher) to about 4 percent for the first half of 1990 (again an official estimate; see Leung 1990). But the program did nothing to change the basic structure of China's economic system—a system characterized by state monopoly of trade and industry, a rigid material-supply system, and state control over prices and property. Indeed, Zheng Hongqing, an adviser to the State Commission for Restructuring the Economy, recently observed that after more than 10 years of attempted reform, the "traditional economic

---

[7]Cf. Hayek ([1940] 1974, p. 158): "In a planned system all economic questions become political questions."

[8]In commenting on the failure to stabilize the Chinese economy and prevent corruption, Hua Sheng, Zhang Xuejun, and Luo Xiaopeng contend that "the root cause lies in our failure to separate political power from economic management. The Chinese economy today is, to a significant extent, manipulated by political power." Quoted in "China Reforms Said Snarled by Politics," *Washington Times*, 11 January 1989, p. A9.

framework has remained essentially intact" (*China Daily* 26 July 1990; cited in Ellingsen 1990, p. 3).

If anything has been learned from China's experience with reform over the last decade, it is that effective economic reform requires constitutional change to protect persons and property against political opportunism by those who control government. In short, economic decisionmaking must be insulated from political decisionmaking as much as possible if a *private* market system is to develop and prosper. To accomplish this objective, a sound legal system will have to be developed—one that limits the massive state bureaucracy and the ruling elite who will lose their power and privilege as China's economic and political systems are opened to the forces of competition. In this vein, Nien Cheng (1988, p. 543) wrote: "Unless and until a political system rooted in law, rather than personal power, is firmly established in China, the road to the future will always be full of twists and turns."

Pricing, Property, and Reform

Until the summer of 1989, China's leadership seemed intent on reform and it was generally felt that there could be no turning back. This sentiment was expressed by Zhao in 1988 when he said, "Without reform there will be no way out for China. If reform is not carried out today, it will have to be carried out in the future, but that will only prolong China's backwardness."[9] How fast China moves toward markets and prices, however, will depend on how fast and how far China's leaders are willing to extend and protect property rights.

Li Yining, an economist at Beijing University, has argued that effective price reform is impossible without reforming the system of ownership, and has recommended slowing price reform until a shareholding system can be introduced to transform state-owned enterprises into more efficient units. However, Wu Jinglin, also an economist, has argued that price reform should not be divorced from other reforms and should not be delayed. Until the May-June 1989 reversal, Deng Xiaoping managed to keep price reform on the political agenda, arguing that such reform involves "very big risks," but holding that China "can accomplish it." As he noted, "even if a big risk appears, the sky won't fall down."[10] The challenge to Chinese leaders is to keep the economic reform movement alive by coupling price reform with ownership reform so that a spontaneous market

---

[9]Quoted in Abrams (1988).

[10]The views of Li, Wu, and Deng on price reform are presented in Southerland (1988a).

order can emerge to replace the ossified order of Soviet-style central planning.

In gaining an appreciation for the contradiction inherent in trying to stimulate competitive pricing under socialism, China's leaders could learn from G. Warren Nutter (1968, pp. 144–45) who wrote:

> Markets without divisible and transferable property rights are a sheer illusion. There can be no competitive behavior, real or simulated, without dispersed power and responsibility. And it will not do to disperse the one without the other. If all property is to be literally collectivized and all pricing literally centralized, there is no scope left for a mechanism that can reproduce in any significant respect the functioning of competitive private enterprise.

The central role of property rights in pricing resources and commodities has also been elegantly stated by Armen Alchian (1967b, p. 6):

> Every question of pricing is a question of property rights . . . . In essence, economics is the study of property rights. Without scarce resources property rights are pointless. The allocation of scarce resources in a society is the assignment of rights to uses of resources. So the question of economics, or of how prices should be determined, is the question of how property rights should be defined and exchanged and on what terms.

In his work (e.g., 1965, 1967a, 1967b), Alchian has shown that competition is inescapable in a world of scarcity, where resources have to be allocated among alternative uses. The type of competition chosen, however, dictates the corresponding price and ownership system. Differences in ownership forms necessarily imply differences in the type of competition and pricing mechanism used to coordinate economic activity. Abolishing private property as a social institution, therefore, does not abolish competition and the need to assign rights to scarce values.[11] Rather, in shifting from private ownership, nonprice competition substitutes for price competition and political decisionmaking replaces impersonal market forces in determining the allocation of resources and products. As Alchian (1967b, p. 13) noted: "Departures from private property . . . induce two kinds of behavior. One is to charge prices below market-clearing levels more frequently. The other is to let business costs increase to absorb revenues." Both types of behavior appear in China's socialist enterprises (see Cheung 1989).

China cannot ignore the necessity of instituting a rational price system without disregarding the reality of the marketplace. By choos-

---

[11]See, for example, Hallowell (1943) and Moore (1943).

ing state ownership and central planning, Mao Zedong chose politics over the free market in setting relative prices. It was the failure of Mao's political economy and the adverse reaction to the "cultural revolution" that laid the basis for economic reform in China. The major obstacle to continued liberalization, however, is the coupling of political and economic power. Those politicians and bureaucrats who run China's state enterprises refuse to release their iron grip on the socioeconomic system. As long as Communist party bureaucrats control the bulk of investment resources and dominate the interests of the newly emerging enterpreneurial class, private individuals will lack the freedom to decide where to invest their savings for the highest return and resources will be locked into unprofitable uses.

To think that China can develop an efficient financial system without an effective legal system that effectively curtails the self-interest of party chiefs, safeguards freedom of contract, and provides for security of private property is to disregard reality and to miss the true nature of China's dilemma. The real Chinese puzzle has been aptly expressed by Steven Mosher (1988):

> China's economic crises are the crises of all totalitarian states. To be efficient, information, capital and goods must flow freely throughout an economic system. But with economically illiterate bureaucrats manning checkpoints and stop valves throughout the system, the channels are clogged.
>
> The Chinese Communist Party, while marginally curbing its appetite for ubiquitous economic control, continues to insist on its myth of infallibility and repress criticism of its policies. Far too little reliable information, both of an economic and noneconomic variety, reaches Beijing for it to achieve economic growth without inflation, or successfully deregulate prices without causing further unemployment. This is the ultimate Chinese puzzle, and it may prove insoluble.

The detrimental effects of the Chinese Communist party's monopoly over a large part of economic life and the lack of an effective legal system have been carefully examined in an important article by Steven N. S. Cheung (1989). In South China where Special Economic Zones (SEZs) have been set up and in the agricultural sector where more effective rights to use land have been created, economic life has been vibrant. But in the North and in state enterprises powerful state interests continue to rule, retarding economic development in the process. For Cheung, the source of the so-called Chinese headache is the failure to overcome special interest groups that continue to benefit from state control and that oppose thoroughgoing price reform and the privatization of state enterprises.

Chinese bureaucrats, like others who face the soft budget constraint of state or social ownership, prefer the status quo of nonprice competition to the dynamic discovery process of market price competition. However, in conjunction with their economic reform, Chinese leaders would be well advised to trace out the implications of alternative types of competition on incentives and behavior. With regard to price competition, the insights of Hayek (1978, p. 189) should not be overlooked:

> One of the chief reasons for the dislike of [price] competition [is] that it not only shows how things can be done more effectively, but also confronts those who depend for their incomes on the market with the alternative of imitating the more successful or losing some or all of their income. Competition produces in this way a kind of impersonal compulsion which makes it necessary for numerous individuals to adjust their way of life in a manner that no deliberate instructions or commands could bring about. Central direction in the service of so-called "social justice" may be a luxury rich nations can afford, perhaps for a long time, without too great an impairment of their incomes. But it is certainly not a method by which poor countries can accelerate their adaptation to rapidly changing circumstances, on which their growth depends.

Resolving the Chinese Puzzle

If the Chinese puzzle is a problem of exposing the internal contradiction of pricing under socialism and of developing a legal system that solves the problem of creating economic and social harmony without state intervention, then it is useful to consider, in turn, the relation between ownership rights and responsibility, the constitutional changes required for achieving a spontaneous market order, and whether China's cultural heritage offers guidance for reform.

Ownership Rights and Responsibility

The waste that is often reported in the Chinese press and by those who have studied state-run enterprises indicates a need for making those who control resources directly responsible for their actions. Ending state subsidies and reinstituting the disciplinary force of bankruptcy would help promote enterprise efficiency and responsibility. Greater enterprise autonomy and market pricing, however, need to be reinforced by a system of enterprise ownership rights that provides managers with an incentive to lower costs and increase profitability. Establishing transferable shares that reflect changes in expected profits would be a major step in restoring responsible use of enterprise assets. Moreover, the development of a competitive capital market that allowed the general public greater opportunities to invest their savings in productive enterprises would increase the mobility of resources and make China's economy more robust.

Until the policy reversal following Tianamen Square, steps were being taken to establish a rudimentary capital market. China's leaders announced their intention to experiment with alternative ownership forms during the "primary stage of socialism." This openness to new ownership forms encouraged economists such as Li Yining and Hua Sheng to offer proposals for converting state-owned enterprises into shareholder enterprises.

Li, for example, advocated creating a Chinese stock market in which the shares of the new publicly held enterprises could be traded. However, he would still have the central government retain a controlling ownership interest. Hua Sheng, an economist at the Chinese Academy of Social Sciences, in a bolder plan, argued that all state enterprises should be converted into shareholding organizations and that the central government should not retain a majority interest. As an incentive for workers to forgo the so-called iron rice bowl (a promise of permanent employment by state-owned enterprises), Hua would offer workers shares in their firms in the form of "asset certificates." According to Hua, Marx wrongly opposed private property and "the problem with many socialist reforms is that they try to reduce government intervention without creating an owner for each company." Li and Hua favor changing state-owned enterprises to shareholding firms because they expect the ownership change to make the new owners and managers more responsive to market prices and profits, and hence more prudent in utilizing enterprise assets.[12]

Once it is recognized that individual responsibility depends in large part on the structure of property rights, it will be more difficult for politicians to hide behind ideological banners. Actual economic systems will have to be examined and the implications for responsible resource usage compared. It will then be seen that as individuals bear more of the costs of their actions, less waste and more responsible action will be observed. The characteristic feature of private ownership is precisely that it concentrates decisionmaking costs and rewards on the owner, who has a strong incentive to be resourceful or suffer the losses. Under public ownership, on the other hand, no one has effective rights to capture expected changes in value by

---

[12]The proposals by Li Yining and Hua Sheng for a shareholding system are discussed in Kristof (1988, 1989a, 1989b). Hua's proposal was drawn up in collaboration with two other economists, Zhang Zuejun and Luo Xiaopeng.

selling ownership shares. The absence of capitalization and residual claimancy in state-owned enterprises means that the consequences of failure are more widely dispersed than under private ownership.[13] Managers of socialist enterprises, therefore, can be expected to shirk more often than managers of private for-profit firms, and the evidence is consistent with this hypothesis.[14] In a recent article in the *China Daily*, for example, Bian Yi (1988) reported that "in a TV factory in Shanghai, quality examiners sit down and turn on the TV sets in front of them; not to check the quality but to watch their favourite programmes." Much the same behavior can be found in government-run enterprises the world over.

Investment decisions and other economic decisions in China are necessarily political decisions. Centralized investment planning and the lack of transferable enterprise shares have led to the socialization of risk. Socialist managers respond more to political directives than to market price signals, which are suppressed. As a result, rational risk taking is diminished and large-scale mistakes are more likely to occur than in a decentralized market price system with its automatic feedback mechanism that helps coordinate individuals' saving and investment plans and prevents errors from accumulating. In particular, the competitive price system with its profit and loss signals provides an internal guidance system that moves resources "in the right direction" without central authority.[15]

The proclivity for large-scale error under socialism and central planning stems from the sluggishness of adjustment compared to an economic system based on private property and open markets. Insofar as individuals are free to adjust prices in response to changes in wants, resources, and technology, the market price system will work reasonably well in allocating resources to their highest-valued uses. Moreover, the enormous information requirements of a dynamic economic system will be met by allowing individual freedom and by relying on entrepreneurial foresight and price competition.[16] Under

---

[13]According to Alchian (1967b, p. 12):

> Marketability implies *capitalisation* of future effects on to present values. Thus, long-range effects are thrust back on to the current owner of the marketable value of the goods. He will heed the long-run effects of current decisions more carefully than if the rights were not transferable.

For a discussion of the importance of transferability in differentiating between private and public ownership, see Alchian ([1965] 1977, especially pp. 137–48).

[14]See Furubotn and Pejovich (1972, pp. 1154–57) for a survey of some of the relevant literature.

[15]See Hayek ([1945] 1948, pp. 85–87).

[16]See, for example, Kirzner (1973).

socialism and state investment planning, on the other hand, there is no automatic feedback mechanism—no competitive price and profit system—that can inform the authorities of the opportunity costs of moving resources in one direction rather than another, and authorities have little incentive to move resources in directions consistent with consumers' preferences. Thus, the fundamental flaw of socialist planning is to think that responsibility is enhanced and error minimized by central decisionmaking. Rather, as Benjamin M. Anderson (1922, p. 7) recognized:

> If a government or a collective system undertakes to regulate the business of a country as a whole and to guide and control production, there is required a central brain of such vast power that no human being who has yet lived, or can be expected to live, can supply it. When millions of people are working, each at his own special problem, studying his own special market, making his readjustment piecemeal, under the guidance of market prices, the problem is manageable. If a central brain must do the thinking for all of them, chaos is inevitable. Great mistakes are made and these mistakes are carried much further than would be possible under the competitive system, controlled by free prices.

China has tried to increase efficiency in agriculture by instituting a "responsibility system" and by extending new ownership rights to peasants, allowing them to benefit directly from more productive use of the land at their disposal. Taking the success of the agricultural reforms as a signal, Cheung (1989, p. 590) has suggested creating a " 'thorough' responsibility system" in trade and industry. The capital values of state enterprises would be determined and then loaned out to the individuals operating the enterprises, who would acquire transferable ownership rights to their firms' assets. Meanwhile, to satisfy political demands, the legal appearance of socialism would be preserved by requiring private shareholders to pay the state interest on the "loan" of capital value. In this way, argues Cheung, "the nature of private enterprise will be practiced while preserving the legal title of state ownership."[17]

---

[17]According to Cheung (1989, p. 590), "There is no inherent conflict between the economic nature of private property and socialism." See also Bajt (1968) who argues that economically meaningful property relations depend on the rewards an individual can capture from existing ownership rights, and that the effective rights structure need not parallel the nominal legal rights structure. Cf. McKean (1972, p. 177) who defines "property rights" in terms of appropriability, that is, as "one's effective rights to do things and his effective claims to rewards (positive or negative) as a result of his actions."

Unlike "social ownership" in Yugoslavia, where workers have the right to use enterprise assets but no right to sell,[18] Cheung's privatization scheme would vest shareholders with the right of transferability. As such, shareholders could specialize in ownership and control, and they could capitalize future income streams into their present values by selling ownership shares, which is the essence of "capitalism."[19] Cheung's privatization scheme, therefore, would thrust most of the future value consequences of resource usage and investment decisions onto current owners, and this increased bearing of responsibility for success and failure would have an immediate impact on enterprise efficiency.

In making his proposal for the transfer of state assets to private owners by first loaning the capital value of state enterprises to current employees and then establishing transferable shares, Cheung was thinking of a way to introduce effective private ownership while maintaining "the image of a socialist system." Recent events, however, have convinced Cheung (1989, p. 590) that "the real problem of reform in trade and industry does not rest so much with the preservation of an image," but rather with "the protection of privileges associated with special rights." According to Cheung (p. 593), "China's deep and basic needs now are the privatization of state-owned enterprises and the demolition of state-created monopolies."[20] The fundamental problem is how to circumvent China's ruling elite who oppose the dismantling of state monopolies and who benefit from price fixing and nonprice rationing. For Cheung (p. 595), it is time for China to take a more radical and direct route to privatization, namely, "it is time for China to consider the creation of private property by mandate." And the "simple rule" should be: "For state-owned resources that are salable, sell." The proceeds could then be used to ease the adjustment process and "to establish a judicial

[18]On the nature and implications of social ownership in Yugoslavia, see Furubotn and Pejovich (1970).
[19]Alchian (1967a, p. 11) has suggested that the term "capitalism" may have been derived from the fundamental characteristic of a capitalist economy, namely, " 'capitalization' of resource values." Relating capitalism to this feature and its implications might disarm ideologues and help shed light on one of the essential differences between private and public enterprise. It is interesting to note that Alchian early on recognized that "if public ownership rights were separable and exchangeable, they would soon be 'privatized' by a movement toward specialization of ownership" (p. 12).
[20]The state monopoly in industry and trade—coupled with the two-tier price system, subsidies, and the presence of double-digit inflation—has led to widespread speculation and scalping. Dorinda Elliott (1988), for example, reported in *Newsweek* that "scalpers, called 'yellow cows' in Shanghai, buy up cheap state-subsidized goods direct from the factory—often by bribing the plant manager—then sell them at premium prices to consumers."

system based firmly on the principle of equality before the law"
(p. 596).

Cheung's call for direct privatization in trade and industry, like the
proposal of Li Yining and Hua Sheng for a shareholding system, is a
bold plan. The phenomenal success of SEZs and the auctioning off
of several state-owned enterprises in 1988 point to the possibility of
further privatization in China.[21] However, the more general application of privatization and market pricing will have to await further
political reform in which meaningful constitutional change occurs.
Although officials have shown a willingness over the last decade to
experiment with private ownership, they have never embraced it. Li
Peng made the official position clear when he stated that China
would "never return to the old economic order characterized by
overcentralized, excessive and rigid control. Nor shall we adopt private ownership, negating the socialist system."[22]

Adopting Cheung's proposal for loaning the capital value of state
enterprises to current employees, however, would provide leaders
like Li Peng with an escape valve, since the state could retain legal
ownership while passing effective economic ownership and control
to private parties. Some movement toward this escape valve was
evident in 1988 when those calling for the expansion of China's
nascent stock system argued that such expansion would not necessarily clash with socialist principles—because stocks, after all, would
be owned by the public (shareholders). Thus, Nicholas Kristof (1988,
p. D8) reported: "The enthusiasts say, stocks are just another form
of public ownership, not so different from the existing system in
China where almost everything nominally belongs to everybody."
And Yuan Mu, speaking for China's State Council, remarked, "We
will adhere to public ownership, not privatization." As interpreted
by Kristof, "the distinction appears to be that privatization involves
selling off all the shares of state-owned companies, while in China
the Government will retain an interest." Taking a longer run view,
Yang Peixin, also an adviser to the State Council, has argued that a
"shareholding system will lead to a dwindling of the state's controlling interests, and gradually all state concerns will be privatized and
socialism will be finished."[23] But this is precisely the reason China's

---

[21]State-owned enterprises have been auctioned off to the highest bidder in Xiamen and
Fuzhou, and foreigners have been permitted to enter the bidding on a selected basis.
Although state-owned enterprises supplied roughly two-thirds of industrial output in
1988, their share had been as high as 78 percent just four years earlier. For a discussion
of these and other aspects of privatization in China, see Ignatius (1988).

[22]Quoted in Southerland (1989, p. A16).

[23]Quoted in Leung (1989).

ruling elite fear any large-scale privatization drive. Nevertheless, if China's leaders really want to avoid the chaos of central planning and desire economic progress for China's vast population, they must come to appreciate the self-organizing forces of a private market system based on transferable property titles. In particular, they will have to gain a better understanding of the linkage among pricing, property, and constitutional choice.

Constitutional Choice and Economic Order

Spontaneous order, not chaos, is the result of a competitive price system resting on private ownership, freedom of contract, open entry and exit, and a legal system that enforces these rights. Enforcement is crucial in determining who can get what for what behavior, and appropriability of rewards is central to the question of whether economic reform will be socially beneficial.[24] With private property rights, the owner or residual claimant bears most of the consequences of his decisions affecting resource usage. He therefore has an incentive to utilize all relevant information and to direct resources to those uses valued most highly by consumers. Moreover, in a price system driven by the profit motive and voluntary exchange, economic coordination will occur smoothly as individuals cooperate and realize mutually beneficial gains from specialization and trade. An effective constitution that limits the power of government and protects the private domain is therefore indispensable for the emergence of a spontaneous market order.[25] Without limits on the discretionary power of government, including limits on the monetary authority, the market and the monetary system will become politicized, leading to uncertainty in relative price formation and in future price-level stability. Moreover, without secure claims to either current or future income flowing from present investment decisions, incentives to work, save, and invest will diminish.

A constitution protecting the rights of persons and property along with a strong judiciary to safeguard these rights against political opportunism and special interests is therefore essential for the maintenance of a free and prosperous society. By increasing the security of persons, property, and contracts, a nation's wealth will immediately increase—even without any corresponding increase in physical resources or technology. In the long run, new capital, both human and nonhuman, will be attracted into the system as resource owners and investors search for higher rates of return. This is why Cheung

[24]See McKean (1972).
[25]See, for example, Hayek (1960, 1982).

is so insistent on improving the legal and judicial system in China. "The Chinese Constitution," writes Cheung (1986, p. 25), "rather than establishing a structure of rights for social and economic interaction, merely serves to confuse. If . . . economic progress depends on constitutional law, China's plans for modernisation would undoubtedly be best advanced by a total rewriting of the country's Constitution."[26]

The upshot is that political reform is ultimately inseparable from economic reform. As Deng Xiaoping (1987, pp. 147–48) observed: "The reform of the political structure and the reform of the economic structure are interdependent and should be coordinated. Without political reform, economic reform cannot succeed." Deng's statement certainly rings true in light of the recent events in China. But for economic and political reform to occur it is also necessary to proceed from a sound understanding of economic and constitutional principles as they relate to actual events.

To avoid chaos and to bring about a stable social and economic order require a constitutional setting in which all individuals are treated equally under a just rule of law protecting individual rights to life, liberty, and property. In this sense, a just and legitimate government is one that secures an individual's right to noninterference and enforces the correlative obligation that each individual refrain from interfering with the equal rights of others.[27] In such a system of natural liberty, as Adam Smith expressed it, the exploitation of man by man has a better chance of being abolished—provided trade is voluntary and contracts are enforced—than under a politicized socioeconomic system where everyone is subservient to the state's ruling class and the rule of law is nowhere to be found.

The need for constitutional change in promoting price reform has not escaped the attention of China's leaders. Zhao Ziyang (1987, pp. 58–59), in his speech at the Thirteenth National Congress of the

---

[26]Rabushka (1989) recommends that in any constitutional rewriting, the Chinese could turn to Hong Kong for guidance.

[27]See, for example, Dorn (1986, pp. 1–6) and Pilon (1979, pp. 1340–41). James Madison (1792, p. 174), the chief architect of the U.S. Constitution and Bill of Rights, expressed the notion of an *unjust* government when he wrote:

> That is not a just government, nor is property secure under it, where the property which a man has in his personal safety and personal liberty, is violated by arbitrary seizures of one class of citizens for the service of the rest . . . . That is not a just government, nor is property secure under it, where arbitrary restrictions, exemptions, and monopolies deny to part of its citizens that free use of their faculties, and free choice of their occupations, which not only constitute their property in the general sense of the word; but are the means of acquiring property strictly so called.

Communist Party (October 25, 1987), called for "strengthening the socialist legal system." And in discussing the benefits of a sound legal system, Zhao stated that such a system is "a fundamental guarantee against a recurrence of the 'cultural revolution' and for lasting political stability in the country" (p. 59). In addition, he emphasized that "to rationalize the structure of production and the organizational structure of enterprises and to achieve the optimal distribution [allocation] of resources, we should give play to market forces and free competition" (p. 25). On institutional reform, he noted: "Efforts should be made to develop new types of institutions for commodity circulation, foreign trade and banking as well as networks of agencies to provide technology, information and service, all of which have full authority for management and full responsibility for their profits and losses. This is the way to promote the development of a market system" (p. 36).

The resiliency of the market and the spontaneous emergence of thousands of small-scale enterprises that followed in the wake of the agricultural reforms caught China's leaders by surprise. According to Deng Xiaoping (1987, p. 189):

> Our greatest success—and it is one we had by no means anticipated—has been the emergence of a large number of enterprises run by villages and townships. They were like a new force that just came into being spontaneously. . . . If the Central Committee made any contribution in this respect, it was only by laying down the correct policy of invigorating the domestic economy. The fact that this policy has had such a favourable result shows that we made a good decision. But this result was not anything that I or any of the other comrades had foreseen; it just came out of the blue.

The lesson is simple: If government is limited to the enforcement of rational rules that do not interfere with private rights and production, then there is no need for a complex state planning apparatus and political elite to monitor every move of the economic system.[28] Individual self-interest will promote the nation's wealth, as Adam Smith envisioned, once the appropriate institutions are in place, whether in Hong Kong or the People's Republic. Foremost among these institutions is an economic constitution that safeguards property and maintains a sound monetary and fiscal regime within which rational economic calculation can proceed.

Under the present system in China, whereby the major part of trade and industry are controlled by the state bureaucracy and enterprises remain the "people's property," corruption is inevitable. The lack

[28]See Hayek ([1976] 1982, vol. 2, chap. 8).

of private. ownership of capital assets and the absence of residual claimants responsible for enterprise efficiency imply that losses from theft and misuse will be socialized. As such, individuals are likely to rationalize the use of state property for their own ends, especially if wages are relatively low. Moreover, since monitoring is costly, officials are likely to tolerate a certain level of abuse, especially if they are bribed. It is not surprising, therefore, that in a recent study the Chinese Academy of Social Sciences found that "more than 83 percent of China's urban dwellers believe that the country's bureaucracy is corrupt," and "more than 63 percent of the cadres surveyed admitted that they were involved in corrupt practices."[29]

Ending corrupt practices requires more than exhortations for good behavior on the part of state officials; it requires effective constitutional constraints on the state's economic empowerments. As long as most of the economic cards are held by the state, politics will continue to dominate economics. When prices are set in Beijing, they must be monitored and enforced; when prices are set by the market, the forces of demand and supply serve to automatically bring individual plans into consistency without a coercive state planning agency. In the open market, therefore, there is no need to bribe suppliers to ensure delivery; the prevailing market price provides the necessary information and incentive.

The politicization of economic life in China has frustrated reform efforts. Hua Sheng, Zhang Xuejun, and Luo Xiaopeng, for example, point to the state's monopoly over the material supply system and argue that officials "have shown no scruples about illegal speculation or taking bribes." The authors conclude that such officials "must be stripped of their monopoly, otherwise they will continue to exert a negative influence, despite the lifting of price controls."[30]

Placing constitutional limits on state monopoly power and freeing up prices and property will lead to a more efficient use of knowledge and the evolution of a free-market order, but only if monetary and price-level stability is also achieved. If the money supply is kept on a noninflationary growth path and productive forces are encouraged by the proper incentives, then decontrolling relative prices will not

---

[29]Reported in Salem (1988). On the problem of corruption in state enterprises, Nien Cheng (1988, p. 390) states:

Pilfering was common in Communist China's state-owned enterprises, as the Party secretaries were slack in guarding properties that belonged to the government and the poorly paid workers felt it fair compensation for their low pay. The practice was so widespread that it was an open secret. The workers joked about it and called it "Communism," which in Chinese translation means "sharing property."

[30]Quoted in "China Reforms," p. A9.

cause a persistent rise in the general price level. Rather, price decontrol (within a stable monetary environment) will tend to increase output, reduce transactions costs, and move resources to higher-valued uses, increasing the wealth of society. If, on the other hand, China fails to exercise monetary restraint, does not stem the flow of state bank loans to inefficient enterprises, and fails to abandon piecemeal reform and to introduce thoroughgoing ownership and price reform, the economic system will continue to be prone to inflation, corruption, and inefficiency.

The Cultural Factor in Development

The notion of spontaneous order and the idea that a nation is better ruled by law, in the sense of "rules of just conduct" (see Hayek [1976] 1982, vol. 2, chap. 8), than by force are part of China's cultural heritage, as expressed in the writings of Confucius and Lao Tzu. Both taught that the state should be subservient to the individual and that the best state is the one in which the ruler does not interfere with the natural order—the order that emerges spontaneously if individuals follow the principle of noninterference, broadly interpreted as respect for life, liberty, and property. Thus, Wing-Tsit Chan (1969, pp. 136–37) notes:

> In its doctrines on government, on cultivating and preserving life, and on handling things, Taoism is fully the equal of Confucianism. . . . It teaches submission, but strongly opposes oppressive government. The philosophy of the *Lao Tzu* is not for the hermit, but for the sage-ruler, who does not desert the world but rules it with noninterference. Taoism is therefore not a philosophy of withdrawal. Man is to follow Nature but in doing so he is not eliminated; instead, his nature is fulfilled.

In contrast, the Legalists wanted to use the power of government to control individual action. Instead of using the law as a basis for a Smithean system of natural liberty, the Legalists sought to use the force of legislation to limit freedom and enhance the ruler's power.[31] The significant difference between Legalism and Confucianism is further evidenced in the following passage from Chan (p. 251):

> The Confucianists were dedicated to the cultivation of virtue, the development of individual personality, government for the people, social harmony, and the use of moral principles, moral examples, and moral persuasion. On the contrary, the Legalists were primarily interested in the accumulation of power, the subjugation of the individual to the state, uniformity of thought, and the use of force.

[31]See Chan (1969, p. 251). On the difference between law and legislation, see Hayek ([1973] 1982, vol. 1).

Although China has taken on a legalistic mentality at various times in its long history, Chan (p. 251) observes that "there has been no continuous Legalist tradition comparable to that of the Confucianists and Taoists."

The importance of China's cultural background as the basis for guiding modern-day constitutional reform and economic development is illustrated by the following passages from the *Lao Tzu* or *Tao-te ching:*

> Administer the empire by engaging in no activity . . . . The more taboos and prohibitions there are in the world, the poorer the people will be . . . . The more laws and orders are made prominent, the more thieves and robbers there will be . . . . Therefore the sage says: I take no action and the people of themselves are transformed. . . . I engage in no activity and the people of themselves become prosperous.[32]

These ideas reappeared centuries later in the works of Adam Smith and his contemporaries and in the discussions shaping the U.S. Constitution. It is to this body of thought and to their own cultural heritage that China's leaders can now turn to find a sound basis for thoroughgoing reform. Armed with the logic of constitutional choice and the logic of the price system, China can move forward into the 21st century confident of its place in the world economy. For once the institutional basis is laid for a stable government by law, a spontaneous market order can emerge that will release the creative energy of the Chinese people.

References

Abrams, Jim. "Great Risks, Greater Rewards Mark 10 Years of Economic Reform in China." *The Sun* (Baltimore), 11 December 1988, p. 15C.

Alchian, Armen A. "Some Economics of Property Rights." *Il Politico* 30, no. 4 (1965). Reprinted in Alchian, *Economic Forces at Work*, pp. 127–49. Indianapolis: Liberty Press, 1977.

Alchian, Armen A. "Prices, Markets, Incentives." Paper presented at IV Seminario Internazionale, Rapallo, Italy, 12–14 September 1967a. (The seminar was part of the CESES series.)

Alchian, Armen A. *Pricing and Society.* Occasional Paper 17. London: Institute of Economic Affairs, 1967b.

Anderson, Benjamin M. "Capitalism versus Socialism in the Light of the Present World Economic and Financial Situation." *Chase Economic Bulletin* 2, no. 3 (23 June 1922): 3–12.

Bajt, Aleksander. "Property in Capital and in the Means of Production in Socialist Economies." *Journal of Law and Economics* 11 (April 1968): 1–4.

---

[32]Quoted in Chan (1969, pp. 166–67).

Buchanan, James M. "General Implications of Subjectivism in Economics." In Buchanan, *What Should Economists Do?* pp. 81–91. Indianapolis: Liberty Press, 1979.

Chan, Wing-Tsit. *A Source Book in Chinese Philosophy.* First Princeton Paperback Edition. Princeton, N.J.: Princeton University Press, 1969.

Cheng, Nien. *Life and Death in Shanghai.* New York: Penguin Books, 1988.

Cheung, Steven N. S. *Will China Go 'Capitalist'?* 2d ed. Hobart Paper 94. London: Institute of Economic Affairs, 1986.

Cheung, Steven N. S. "Privatization vs. Special Interests: The Experience of China's Economic Reforms." *Cato Journal* 8 (Winter 1989): 585–96.

"China Reforms Said Snarled by Politics." *Washington Times,* 11 January 1989, p. A9.

Deng, Xiaoping. *Fundamental Issues in Present-Day China.* Translated by the Bureau for the Compilation and Translation of Works of Marx, Engels, Lenin, and Stalin under the Central Committee of the Communist Party of China. Beijing: Foreign Languages Press, 1987.

Dorn, James A. "The Transfer Society." Introduction. *Cato Journal* 6 (Spring/ Summer 1986): 1–17.

Ellingsen, Peter. "Chinese Economic Reform 'a Sham.'" *Financial Times,* 27 July 1990, p. 3.

Elliott, Dorinda. "High Price of Reform: Beijing Battles Inflation." *Newsweek,* 30 May 1988, p. 42.

Furubotn, Eirik G., and Pejovich, Svetozar. "Property Rights and the Behavior of the Firm in a Socialist State: The Example of Yugoslavia." *Zeitschrift für Nationalökonomie* 30 (1970): 431–54.

Furubotn, Eirik G., and Pejovich, Svetozar. "Property Rights and Economic Theory: A Survey of Recent Literature." *Journal of Economic Literature* 10 (December 1972): 1137–62.

Hallowell, A. Irving. "The Nature and Function of Property as a Social Institution." *Journal of Legal and Political Sociology* 1 (April 1943): 115–38.

Hayek, Friedrich A., ed. *Collectivist Economic Planning.* 1935. Reprint. Clifton, N.J.: Augustus M. Kelley, 1975.

Hayek, Friedrich A. "Economics and Knowledge." *Economica* 4 (n.s., 1937). Reprinted in Hayek, *Individualism and Economic Order,* pp. 33–56. South Bend, Ind.: Gateway Editions (by arrangement with University of Chicago Press), 1948.

Hayek, Friedrich A. "Socialist Calculation: The Competitive 'Solution.'" *Economica* 7 (n.s., May 1940). Reprinted in *Comparative Economic Systems: Models and Cases,* pp. 140–59. 3rd ed. Edited by Morris Bornstein. Homewood, Ill.: Richard D. Irwin, 1974.

Hayek, Friedrich A. "The Use of Knowledge in Society." *American Economic Review* 35 (September 1945). Reprinted in Hayek, *Individualism and Economic Order,* pp. 77–91. South Bend, Ind.: Gateway Editions (by arrangement with University of Chicago Press), 1948.

Hayek, Friedrich A. *The Constitution of Liberty.* Chicago: University of Chicago Press, 1960.

Hayek, Friedrich A. *Law, Legislation and Liberty.* Vol. 1: *Rules and Order.* Chicago: University of Chicago Press, 1973. Reprinted in Hayek, *Law,*

Legislation and Liberty (3 vols. in 1), chaps. 1–6. London: Routledge & Kegan Paul, 1982.

Hayek, Friedrich A. *Law, Legislation and Liberty.* Vol. 2: *The Mirage of Social Justice.* Chicago: University of Chicago Press, 1976. Reprinted in Hayek, *Law, Legislation and Liberty* (3 vols. in 1), chaps. 7–11. London: Routledge & Kegan Paul, 1982.

Hayek, Friedrich A. "Competition as a Discovery Procedure." In Hayek, *New Studies in Philosophy, Politics, Economics and the History of Ideas,* pp. 179–90. Chicago: University of Chicago Press, 1978.

Hayek, Friedrich A. *Law, Legislation and Liberty.* Reprint (3 vols. in 1). London: Routledge & Kegan Paul, 1982.

Hayek, Friedrich A. *The Fatal Conceit: The Errors of Socialism.* London: Routledge & Kegan Paul, 1988.

Ignatius, Adi. "China Turning Increasingly to Auctions in Its Bid to Privatize State Enterprises." *Wall Street Journal,* 19 February 1988, p. 16.

Kirzner, Israel M. *Competition and Entrepreneurship.* Chicago: University of Chicago Press, 1973.

Kristof, Nicholas D. "China, Seeking More Efficiency, Looks to a Stock Market System." *New York Times,* 5 December 1988, pp. A1, D8.

Kristof, Nicholas D. "Selling China on a 'Public' Privatization." *New York Times,* 8 January 1989a, p. 8F.

Kristof, Nicholas D. "In Beijing, a Bold New Proposal: End State Ownership of Industry." *New York Times,* 10 January 1989b, pp. A1, A6.

Leung, Julia. "China Faces Huge Ideological Hurdles in Plan to Sell Shares in State Concerns." *Wall Street Journal,* 2 March 1989, p. A12.

Leung, Julia. "China Eases Harsh Austerity Plan to Avert Potential Worker Unrest." *Wall Street Journal,* 27 July 1990, p. A8.

"Lift of Price Controls in Focus." *China Daily,* 13 July 1988, p. 4.

[Madison, James]. "Property." Unsigned article in *National Gazette* 1, no. 44, 29 March 1792, pp. 174–75.

McKean, Roland N. "Property Rights within Government, and Devices to Increase Governmental Efficiency." *Southern Economic Journal* 39 (October 1972): 177–86.

Mises, Ludwig von. "Economic Calculation in Socialism." 1936. Reprinted in *Comparative Economic Systems: Models and Cases,* pp. 120–26. 3rd ed. Edited by Morris Bornstein. Homewood, Ill.: Richard D. Irwin, 1974.

Moore, Wilbert E. "The Emergence of New Property Conceptions in America." *Journal of Legal and Political Sociology* 1 (April 1943): 34–58.

Mosher, Steven. W. "China's Economic Puzzle." Letters to the Editor, *Wall Street Journal,* 8 January 1988, p. 19.

Nutter, G. Warren. "Markets without Property: A Grand Illusion." In *Money, the Market and the State,* pp. 137–45. Edited by Nicholas Beadles and Aubrey Drewry. Athens: University of Georgia Press, 1968.

Pilon, Roger. "On Moral and Legal Justification." *Southwestern Law Review* 11 (1979): 1327–44.

"Private Economy Praised." *China Daily,* 16 July 1988, p. 4.

Rabushka, Alvin. "A Free-Market Constitution for Hong Kong: A Blueprint for China." *Cato Journal* 8 (Winter 1989): 641–52.

Salem, Ellen. "Fighting Sticky Fingers: Corrupt Cadres Erode Support for Economic Reforms." *Far Eastern Economic Review,* 16 June 1988, p. 22.

Southerland, Daniel. "China's Leaders Wrestle with Key Reform—Changing the Pricing System." *Washington Post*, 29 July 1988a, pp. A13, A15.

Southerland, Daniel. "China Plans to Sell Stock in State-Owned Enterprises." *Washington Post*, 21 September 1988b, pp. F1, F5.

Southerland, Daniel. "Chinese Are Told to Prepare for New Austerity Measures." *Washington Post*, 21 March 1989, pp. A1, A16.

Yi, Bian. "Enterprises Reorganize Workforces." *China Daily*, 14 July 1988, p. 4.

Zhao, Ziyang, "Advance Along the Road of Socialism with Chinese Characteristics." Report Delivered at the Thirteenth National Congress of the Communist Party of China on October 25, 1987. In *Documents of the Thirteenth National Congress of the Communist Party of China (1987)*. Beijing: Foreign Languages Press, 1987.

4

ECONOMIC CHAOS OR SPONTANEOUS ORDER? IMPLICATIONS FOR POLITICAL ECONOMY OF THE NEW VIEW OF SCIENCE*

Don Lavoie

Introduction

Ideas about political economy, like other products of human culture, are liable to being profoundly influenced by underlying conceptions of the nature of science. Socialist political economy was not just influenced by the 19th-century view of science, it was modeled on it. Marxism has been widely interpreted as a "scientific socialism" in a strictly Newtonian sense, a study of the "laws of motion of the capitalist system" analogous to the physical laws of motion of planetary systems. I will later take up the question of whether this is the best way to read the essential message of Marx, but in any case it would certainly be understandable if many aspects of the Marxian system of thought were tainted by the mechanistic model of the universe in which 19th-century culture was embedded. The great successes of Newtonian mechanics made them a natural object at that time for emulation in the study of human society. But other, non-Newtonian, sciences have by now been successful too. Even thermodynamics and organic chemistry exhibit features that do not fit well in the mechanistic Newtonian view of the universe, and if we consider biology, anthropology, intellectual history, or psychology, we find fields that have made enormous accomplishments over the past century without coming close to the Newtonian model. The argument from success no longer makes a good case for the mechanistic view of the world.

There is now a wide body of explicit philosophical literature that, for want of a better label, I will simply call the new view of science, which develops a way of coming to terms with the nonmechanistic

*Reprinted from *Cato Journal* 8 (Winter 1989): 613–35.

The author is Associate Professor of Economics at the Center for the Study of Market Processes at George Mason University.

nature of the universe.[1] This literature constitutes, among other things, a radical reinterpretation of the nature of order, and a powerful critique of the Newtonian vision. It carries important implications for a variety of scholarly disciplines, from mathematics to the natural and social sciences, to the humanities, and it has begun to serve as an inspiration for practical proposals in everyday life.

In the contemporary work on "chaos theory" in mathematics, things that would appear to be utterly disorderly by Newtonian standards are seen to nevertheless possess great intelligibility, even mathematical elegance and beauty. The theory is misleadingly named because what is being celebrated here is not really utter disorder but a new kind of order. Scientists have found applications of these ideas in a remarkably wide range of phenomena that exhibit what Erich Jantsch (1980) calls a "self-organizing" process and Ilya Prigogine and Isabelle Stengers (1984) call "order out of chaos." Michael Polanyi, a physical chemist and philosopher of science, coined the phrase "spontaneous order" to describe this kind of process, and he has elaborated on how scientific discovery is itself a spontaneous order. Friedrich A. Hayek, an economist and social theorist, has elaborated on this idea in reference to the ordering processes at work in law and the economy.

One thing all of these spontaneous order theorists have in common is an emphasis on the creative aspect of ordering processes. The processes are not merely "equilibrating" in the Newtonian sense, where there is a deducible "target" toward which forces are pulling. An equilibrating mechanism, like a clock winding down, contains from the outset everything necessary to bring about its conclusion. A spontaneous order exhibits essentially novel changes and needs to work itself out through time. The direction things take may be completely unpredictable, and yet an overall pattern emerges and is systematically discernible.

Just as 19th-century socialists constructed a radical vision based on that century's view of science, so the economic reformers in the People's Republic of China are taking the views of science of our own time as their starting point. The philosophers who seem to have been serving as the inspiration for these reformers, such as Nobel Prize winning physicist Ilya Prigogine, are some of the most articulate spokesmen for the new view of science. The Chinese reformers have already been using this new view of science to revise their interpretation of socialism into a more humanistic and decentralized vision. In this paper I will be endorsing the humanistic revision of

[1]For a useful summary of the new view of science, see Gleick (1987).

socialism and elaborating on how I think one of the classic critiques of orthodox socialism is consistent with the new view of science. The older views of socialism, I will be arguing, have been subjected to criticisms along essentially the same lines as the older views of science have been. These criticisms suggest that all the world's governments, whether called socialistic or capitalistic, have been trying to centrally control their economies in a manner that is utterly futile.

Beyond Traditionalism and Modernism

> Do we really have to make this tragic choice? Must we choose between a science that leads to alienation and an anti-scientific metaphysical view of nature? We think such a choice is no longer necessary, since the changes that science is undergoing today lead to a radically new situation. This recent evolution of science gives us a unique opportunity to reconsider its position in culture in general. Modern science originated in the specific context of the European seventeenth century. We are now approaching the end of the twentieth century, and it seems some more *universal message* is carried by science, a message that concerns the interaction of man and nature as well as of man with man.
>
> —Prigogine and Stengers (1984, p. 7)

The orthodox view of science that is sometimes called "modernism" arose in reaction to pre-scientific attitudes called "traditionalism." Traditionalism holds truth to be timeless and discoverable through revelation and by the dogmatic interpretation of sacred texts. It bestows unquestioned authority on a priestly caste, who act as a political elite as well as guardians of social mores. Within this world view, political economy is taken to be largely outside the domain of human choice, the product of supernatural forces guided by the gods. The order we find in the natural world is also intelligible as the conscious design of its creator, within this perspective, so that there is no great chasm separating the study of man from the study of nature. Both can be understood as teleological, as a matter of reading a text. We can read god's purposes in natural events just as we can read them (or perhaps a combination of man's and god's purposes) in human history.

Modernism is a useful label to tag the pro-scientific world view that arose against traditionalism because, to use the words of Donald McCloskey (1985, p. 5), it helps "to emphasize its pervasiveness in modern thinking well beyond science." According to McCloskey:

> In a preliminary way [modernism] can be said to be, as the literary critic Wayne Booth has put it, the notion that we know only what

we cannot doubt and cannot really know what we can merely assent to. It is the attitude that the only real knowledge is, in common parlance, "scientific," that is, knowledge tested by certain kinds of rigorous scepticism. Philosophically speaking, modernism is the program of Descartes, regnant in philosophy since the seventeenth century, to build knowledge on a foundation of radical doubt.

The enlightenment represented a major break with traditionalist thinking and led to a radically different view of nature, man, and their relationship to one another. It opened the way for science, which in turn liberated many people from some of the constraints of traditional society. The astonishing successes of science, especially Newtonian physics, led to a momentous transformation of modern thinking. Nature is seen to be the outgrowth of predictable laws that are not the design of any conscious entity, but in principle are subject to human mastery. Natural forces are like mechanisms we invent, so that, to the extent we comprehend their systematic elements, we can expect to subject them to our purposes. Political economy too can be rendered as a systematic mechanism that can be mastered if we only learn its principles of operation. A central part of the enlightenment was the undermining of established authority and its claims to dogmatic access to the truth. The fruit of this challenge to traditional authority was a new defense of the independence and autonomy of individual human beings, and the realization of greater freedom through the bourgeois revolutions. Society was to be modeled after science in the sense that it was to be universal principles, discoverable by a systematic study of political economy, that would rule, rather than the arbitrary desires of traditional authorities. The rights of man were declared inviolate, just as the laws of nature were. The rulers were to be as much subject to the principles of freedom as their "subjects." The creative powers of free minds have now been unleashed on the world. We find ourselves trying to cope with changes in our everyday lives more rapid than any period in human history. The rise of the enlightenment gives birth to the "modern" world with its dizzying array of new technologies. And of course all this change has given us an accompanying set of new problems.

The enlightenment has led to great advances, but it can also be seen to have led to some shocking catastrophes. The attitude of "modernism" that it spawned leaves a dangerous gulf between our everyday understanding of the humanly meaningful world around us, and our scientific developments. This has had the inevitable consequence that, as science advances, our society becomes increasingly dehumanized. Within the modernist world view there is no way to make a rational case for any sorts of "rights," and political policy is thus reduced to a problem of social engineering, of using the population as resources for scientific planning. The very gains made by the enlightenment over traditional society, involving respect for the freedom and autonomy of the individual, are now seriously undermined by the philosophical prejudices of modernism.

The gains secured by the enlightenment cannot be simply reversed. Conservative philosophies that essentially wish we could return to the more fixed world of traditional society are still with us, but they are hopelessly utopian. There is no turning back to the (supposedly noble) days when every person was in his place and when we were content to leave our fate to the gods. We cannot address the new problems we face in the modernist age by reversing the great transformations that got us here. We cannot "forget" what we have learned in the advancement of science, nor can we expect people who have tasted freedom to go back to blind obedience to traditional authority.

The new view of science may help us to find a way to retain our modern society's respect for scientific progress without sacrificing our respect for the rights of individual human beings. It may help us to escape from the anti-humanistic attitudes of modernism without reverting to the anti-scientific attitudes of traditionalism.

Time, Complexity, and Humanity in Science

> The ambition of Newtonian science was to present a vision of nature that would be universal, deterministic, and objective inasmuch as it contains no reference to the observer, complete inasmuch as it attains a level of description that escapes the clutches of time.
>
> —Prigogine and Stengers (1984, p. 213)

Modernism can be summarized by reference to the way it deals with time and complexity, and the way it fails altogether to deal with humanity, in its conception of science. Time is reduced to a fourth dimension, fully analogous to spatial dimensions, and thus loses an aspect that, in our everyday experience, seems essential to it: its irreversibility. Complexity is treated not as an inherent feature of the world but as a temporary problem of our insufficient knowledge, to be overcome by reductionist methods. Humanity is to be either kept outside the scientific process as if it were a source of contamination, or reinterpreted so that it too is a timeless and ultimately simple mechanism. Each of these concepts would, if it were taken seriously, pose a challenge to the universality of the modernist world view, and thus each is diminished and transformed by modernism into a pale imitation of what we mean by it in everyday life.

67

Modernism would like us to believe that it is merely our pre-scientific illusion that time is irreducible to space, that complexity is irreducible to simple and controllable causes, and that humanity is irreducible to mechanism. Thus it forces on us a dangerous dichotomy between science and life. Nature appears to be a timeless mechanism entirely foreign to our human experience of the world as "in time." It is supposed to be comprehended by reducing it to more basic and simple forces, by dissecting it into its elementary parts, whereas our human world seems explicable only in terms of complex wholes. Everyday experience and the humanities, which take that experience as real, are both "scientifically suspect" in the modernist culture. And it works the other way too: Many outside the scientific community find science itself "humanistically suspect." The much lamented split of our society into two deeply separated cultures is the result of a particular view of science.

The point of the new view of science is precisely to show that modernism does not only fail to do justice to everyday life and the humanities; it fails to do justice to most of the natural sciences themselves. Except for certain parts of classical mechanics, most of science today constitutes a challenge to the modernist view. Little of the natural world exhibits the kind of pure deterministic mechanism to which modernism sought to reduce everything. Even in physics, indeed in the very heart of physics, we find irreversible processes that defy the modernist view of time and complexity. Thermodynamics and physical chemistry are filled with processes that are irreducible to simple elements and relationships, and are in principle irreversible in time.[2] And the impossibility of removing the observing subject from the scientific study of objects has been reinforced from within quantum mechanics by the work of Heisenberg. One does not have to be an anti-scientific metaphysician to question modernism.

As one moves up what we might call the scale of complexity from those simple phenomena that are amenable to Newtonian modeling through the more complex physical sciences and into the sciences of life, we find a greater and greater scope for nonmechanistic ordering processes, that is, processes that are intelligible but not predictable.[3] These processes take place in time as irreversible changes so that the question "When did it happen?" is not optional but central to

[2]See Polanyi (1958) and Prigogine and Stengers (1984).
[3]There is a long scholarly tradition of defending the human sciences against encroachment by the modernist view of science, but this methodological-dualist position concedes too much to modernism with respect to the natural sciences. On the idea that the differences between the natural and human sciences are of degree rather than of kind, see Polanyi (1959) and Hayek (1955, 1964).

understanding what it was that happened. Such complex processes can be understood not in the sense that they can be simulated by simple models, but in the sense that they can be explained as resulting from general principles that have been found to govern this kind of process. We cannot deterministically model the biological process by which the human brain evolved, for example, nor can we predict where evolution will take us in the future, yet I think it is fair to say that we understand a great deal about this evolutionary process. And, of course, the place of man within science changes too as we move closer along the evolutionary path to the higher forms of living intelligence, and ultimately to ourselves, perhaps the most complex things we find in nature. The new perspective on science finds all the sciences and humanities on a continuum, all involving time, complexity, and humanity, varying only in degree, not in kind.

One of the great controversies of philosophy at the turn of the century was over whether the historical and human sciences are philosophically legitimate in light of the (then) obvious fact that they bear so little resemblance to the methods of the natural sciences. The procedure of simply telling a plausible story that fits the evidence seemed inadequate to give historical research scientific legitimacy. Today the tables have turned. The irreducible complexity and irreversible processes of history and the room that history gives to the human subject no longer make history scientifically suspect. In short, the change from modernism to the new views on science is the change from the "scientization" of human beings to the humanization of science.

Mechanism and Order; Control and Cultivation

> Even if we cannot control the external circumstances at all, we may adapt our actions to them. And sometimes, though we may not be able to bring about the particular results we would like, knowledge of the principle of the thing will enable us to make circumstances more favorable to the kinds of events we desire. . . . An explanation of the principle will thus often enable us to create such favorable circumstances even if it does not allow us to control the outcome. Such activities in which we are guided by a knowledge merely of the principle of the thing should perhaps better be described by the term *cultivation* than by the familiar term "control"—cultivation in the sense in which the farmer or gardener cultivates his plants, where he knows and can control only some of the determining circumstances, and in which the wise legislator or statesman will probably attempt to cultivate rather than to control the forces of the social process.
>
> —F. A. Hayek ([1955] 1967, p. 19)

If what was orderly about the world was only that in it which was pure mechanism, essentially timeless and simple, it would make sense to confine science to the search for strict Newtonian predictability. Anything, however complex, that we could not reduce to a fixed mechanism, to an underlying simplicity, we would sensibly label chaotic. Either something is "known" in the sense that it can be deterministically modeled as a predictable system like the orbiting planets, or it is unknown. The new view of science liberates us from this situation. Things that would appear chaotic to the modernist seem quite orderly to the proponents of the new view of science.

As Polanyi's work on science as a spontaneous order shows, the modernist conception of the nature of knowledge is fundamentally flawed. Modernism treats the process of science as if it were a matter of an isolated mind confronting and mastering the natural world. A single scientist follows given methods to bring nature under his rational control. The new view of science urges instead that it is the *dialogue* taking place in the scientific community as a whole which is the proper locus of analysis for the philosophy of science. It is the uncontrolled "dialogical" process that brings knowledge to the participants, not the strictly controlled "monological" methods of any particular scientist.[4] The process of mutual interpretations and criticisms going on in the scientific community is a good example of an order that emerges out of an apparently haphazard chaos. The process works best precisely when it is *not* under any one mind's control but is allowed to evolve by its own logic, taking advantage of the variety of perspectives it contains. A healthy scientific community cannot be designed in detail, it can be cultivated only by setting up conditions where the freedom of individual scientists to pursue their own hunches is protected.

The "order" we find in a spontaneous order process may be closely akin to that of a story whose plot we can "follow" without claiming to be able to anticipate it from the outset. Here the theory of narrative as it has been developed in the study of history and fiction is relevant to scientific explanation. As the philosopher Paul Ricoeur has shown, the articulation of history has an irreducibly narrative character, and good history shares many of the attributes of good fiction.[5] Essentially to impart the subjective meaning and significance of events in history involves us, not in a mechanistic search for determinate laws, but in

[4]For a useful summary of the contemporary philosophy of science literature in terms of this contrast between monological and dialogical processes, see Bernstein (1983).
[5]See Ricoeur (1983, 1984).

the uniquely human act of storytelling. As Ricoeur (1981, p. 277) put it:

> To follow a story is to understand the successive actions, thoughts, and feelings as displaying a particular directedness. By this I mean that we are pushed along by the development and that we respond to this thrust with expectations concerning the outcome and culmination of the process. In this sense, the "conclusion" of the story is the pole of attraction of the whole process. But a narrative conclusion can be neither deduced nor predicted. There is no story unless our attention is held in suspense by a thousand contingencies. Hence we must follow the story to its conclusion. So rather than being predictable, a conclusion must be acceptable. Looking back from the conclusion towards the episodes which led up to it, we must be able to say that this end required those events and that chain of action.

It is this kind of intelligibility of the process that we can aspire to in trying to understand complex orders. If we implicitly identify all scientific explanation with the standards applicable to understanding mechanisms, we will never see anything "out there" in the universe but the relatively timeless and simple mechanisms. For example, we will not see ourselves or our accomplishments. When we can find only cold mechanism in nature, our own creative achievements in science and elsewhere appear to us as inexplicable mysteries.

A machine is understood when it is fully under the control of its user. A philosophy that sees everything as a machine will naturally put the idea of control at the very center of its view of reason and science. By contrast, spontaneous order analysis prefers a notion such as cultivation. A spontaneous order is not designed and never really under our control, since it evolves according to a logic all its own. This does not mean, however, that we are utterly helpless to exert influence over the workings of such ordering processes. Its order may be intelligible in terms of general principles, and these principles may well show us that some environments are more conducive to its self-ordering process than others. Understanding a spontaneous order may enable us to tailor the general conditions for its flourishing. But if we persist in trying to control the detailed working of this kind of process, we are more likely to interfere with its own logic and obstruct its self-ordering, than to intelligently "guide" it in any sense. Attempting to control a spontaneous order is like trying to fix a complex machine, whose detailed workings we do not know, by throwing a monkey wrench at it.

The sociopolitical consequences of modernism's view of knowledge as control are suggested when we consider that other people are part of what we want to know about. The more the modernist view of science advances into the human sciences, the more threatened we find our freedoms. The modernist notion that understanding something means controlling it leads to the attempt to control our own society as we might control a machine we built ourselves. Social engineering in turn has led not only to a loss of freedom for those not in control of the social "steering" mechanism, but, to the surprise of many, it has led to a loss of social order. The great paradox of modernism is that while born in the aspiration of freedom and control over our world, it has brought us now to a position where we seem to have neither. The more bold and ambitious the attempts to control our world, the more irrational "chaos" we seem to generate, and the less freedom we seem to enjoy.

Scientific Socialism: Old and New

> For more than half a century the belief that deliberate regulation of all social affairs must necessarily be more successful than the apparent haphazard interplay of independent individuals has continuously gained ground until today there is hardly a political group anywhere in the world which does not want central direction of most human activities in the service of one aim or another. It seemed so easy to improve upon the institutions of a free society which had come more and more to be considered as the result of mere accident. . . . To bring order to such a chaos, to apply reason to the organization of society, and to shape it deliberately in every detail according to human wishes and the common ideas of justice seemed the only course of action worthy of a rational being.
>
> —F. A. Hayek ([1935b] 1948, p. 119)

In many respects Marx's critique of capitalism already involves an embryonic critique of modernism. It points to a vision of a society where persons are treated as beings in control of their own lives rather than resources to be manipulated by others. Marxism might even lay claim to being the first systematic attempt at a social critique of modernism. Philosophically it contains suggestions of the radical significance of time and genuine novelty in its dialectical approach. Economically it is concerned with disclosing the dynamic and historical forces of social change and not some fixed, eternal structure. It contains a vigorous critique of the attitude of naturalism and insists that there are profound methodological consequences from the fact that in the social sciences man studies himself and not an alien objective world. It condemns bourgeois ideology for its failure to dig beneath the simple and static appearance of social reality and to see the more complex and dynamic processes going on in society. In these and other respects Marxism can be said to be a social theory that is in the spirit of the new view of science, indeed amazingly so in light of when it was first developed.

But Marx and his followers in the late 19th and early 20th centuries could not have anticipated the momentous transformation of science that has taken place by now. Orthodox Marxism implicitly retains many elements of unmistakably modernist thinking, and I would like to argue that it is these very elements which have led to the main difficulties in this century's experiments with socialism. I will focus on the central theme by which Marx engages in a radical critique of capitalism: his analysis of its chaotic and undemocratic form of organization. The ultimate emancipatory goal of Marxism, to build a more rational and more democratic society, is inhibited by defects in the critique of capitalism, and the new conceptions of science enable us today to find a way to correct these defects.

The point of correcting what I consider defects in the traditional Marxian critique of capitalism is not to try to rescue historical capitalism from the critique, but to help reconstruct a better alternative to both historical capitalism and socialism. I would not deny the fact that there are serious difficulties in the way state capitalism works, for example, in the recurrent business cycles, stock market crises, unemployment and inflation problems, and so on.[6] Of course, historical socialist regimes have their own share of difficulties, but contemporary socialists have good reasons not to want their reforms to aim at nothing better than what historical capitalism has accomplished. My purpose here is not conservative but radical. I want to explore how we might update the critique of capitalism in such a way as to improve our vision of an alternative to both it and the versions of socialism we have seen so far.

It is well known that Marx said little directly about how socialism was supposed to work, and he devoted his attention to a critique of capitalism. This procedure is misunderstood if it is taken as an opportunity to freely invent any model of socialism, however foreign to Marx's own way of thinking, and graft it onto his critique of capitalism. The critique of capitalism is not an alternative to the study of socialism but a means of conducting that study. Implicit in the critique is a vision of a society that transcends the problems the critique identifies with the capitalist system. If Marx's critique of the capitalist

[6]I would argue that attempts to centrally control the money supply are responsible for introducing unnecessary chaos into the market process, and that those relatively rare instances in which money and banking were left decentralized and unregulated are also among the most orderly episodes of modern economic history. See White (1984) for a discussion of the experience with relatively unregulated money and banking in Scotland in the early 19th century.

system needs revision today in light of our new views of science, so must our vision of the alternative system.

While I consider it a perfectly legitimate analytical procedure to develop a vision of social change indirectly by way of a critique, there are likely to be costs to this approach.[7] It is hard to see how socialist institutions might work when they are not "thematized" specifically. I believe that one result of this lack of attention to the institutional details of socialism is a serious tension in Marx's implicit vision of the socialist society, a tension that suggests there is room for some *re-vision*.

Marx was on the one hand asking us to conceive a form of democracy more extreme than advocates of capitalist democracy can usually imagine, a democracy in which the basic direction of social change is a topic for all members of society to have their say about, and thus the form has a radically decentralized character. This aspect of Marx's work is most vivid in his earlier and more philosophical writings. On the other hand he was suggesting that this democratic process should culminate in society settling on a common plan by which the entire economy is to be ordered, and thus the vision has a radically centralized character. The centralized aspect is suggested more strongly in Marx's later and more political-economic writings, and especially in his critique of market institutions as "anarchic."

In his economic critique of capitalism, Marx charged that this form of social organization was an "anarchy of production," a system of organization that was "out of control." He was not denying that this system exhibits some degree of orderliness, indeed his whole analysis of the theory of value is an attempt to describe the order that does emerge in this system. But he stressed that the order that arises is brought to the system only haphazardly in the form of periodic crises, which forcefully correct for the disorder that continuously accumulates throughout the system.

The orthodox interpretation of Marxism seeks to correct the undoubtedly chaotic difficulties of historical capitalism by means of a wholesale rejection of market institutions, prices, money, and the profit and loss system. If the whole productive system is to be taken

---

[7]I have used this procedure myself in my critique of national economic planning (1985b), which was really aimed at a reconceptualization of the nature of a free-market society. I am convinced that it is often necessary to approach one's ideal society indirectly by developing a critique of the features of modern society that one would like to overcome. One should still try to get around eventually to a more constructive institutional analysis, however. Advocates of free-market institutions, like advocates of socialism, might do well to spend more of their time directly on how their proposed ideal institutions might work, and less on deconstructing the ideals of one another.

over and rationally controlled, then it will not do to permit isolated agents in the economy to act on their own initiative and spend their cash balances wherever they please. It will not do for investments to flow haphazardly in whatever direction profits attract them, regardless of the (democratically decided) plan. It will not do for competitors to struggle against one another for these profits under risk of losses, to bid prices up against one another on the demand side, or to bid them under one another on the supply side. The price system does work as an ordered anarchy, and it seems reasonable—at least for a modernist—to visualize its radical alternative as a system that dispenses with all this chaotic competitiveness and brings the diverse projects of separated decisionmakers into a unity under a common plan.

Marx did occasionally suggest that the way to overcome this chaotic system was to bring the socioeconomic system as a whole under the deliberate control of "the associated producers." He used the phrase "dictatorship of the proletariat" (which includes, at the moment of revolution, not just one social class, but virtually the whole of humanity) in an ironic way, which certainly hints at centralized control, but also suggests that somehow everyone would participate democratically in this plan. This approach, like most of Marx's allusions to how socialism might work, is tantalizingly ambiguous. The idea of bringing the whole economy under the control of somebody sounds like extreme centralization, yet the phrase "associated producers" suggests a radically decentralized and democratic form of organization.

Unfortunately, Marx's ambiguous vision of socialism has historically been elaborated in a one-sided way that makes it nothing more than a system of hierarchical central planning. In Lenin's words socialism is organized as a "democratic centralism." That is, a democratic process would first take place by which the goals of society would be determined, and then these goals would be translated into a general plan that would design economic production as if it were a single, gigantic engineering problem. Once the plan was settled, there would be no room for democratic differences. If the society was to be organized "rationally," the plan must be obeyed diligently.

This centralized interpretation has the advantage that it fits well with some of Marx's economic writings, especially his wholesale condemnation of market institutions, but it has the disadvantage that it fails altogether to fit Marx's political vision of human beings in control of their own lives. Centralized economic planning on the orthodox socialist model has been a complete failure in the democratic dimension, and this failure has spawned a renewed focus within the Marxist tradition on the decentralized aspects of Marx's vision. Within the Marxian tradition there are powerful intellectual currents that constitute a critique of the social-engineering view of politics that comes from the orthodox Marxists.[8]

Spontaneous Order and the Critique of Orthodox Socialism

> That we have been able to achieve a reasonably high degree of order in our economic lives despite modern complexities is only because our affairs have been guided, not by central direction, but by the operations of the market and competition in securing the mutual adjustment of separate efforts. The market system functions because it is able to take account of millions of separate facts and desires, because it reaches with thousands of sensitive feelers into every nook and cranny of the economic world and feeds back the information acquired in coded form to a "public information board." What the marketplace and its prices give most particularly is a continuing updating of the ever-changing relative scarcities of different commodities and services. In other words, the complexity of the structure required to produce the real income we are now able to provide for the masses of the Western World—which exceeds anything we can survey or picture in detail—could develop only because we did not attempt to plan it or subject it to any central direction, but left it to be guided by a spontaneous ordering mechanism, or a self-generating order, as modern cybernetics calls it.

> F. A. Hayek (1976, p. 237)

[8] I am thinking of the Frankfurt School of Marxism, and particularly its contemporary leader Jürgen Habermas, whose work on the idea of a communicative ethic involves a radical critique of the modernist view of rationality, and of its corollary, the social-engineering view of politics. See, for example, Habermas's essay "Dogmatism, Reason, and Decision: On Theory and Praxis in Our Scientific Civilization" (1973, pp. 254–55) where he writes:

> The social potential of science is reduced to the powers of technical control—its potential for enlightened action is no longer considered.... Emancipation by means of enlightenment is replaced by instruction in control over objective or objectified processes. Socially effective theory is no longer directed toward the consciousness of human beings who live together and discuss matters with each other, but to the behavior of human beings who manipulate....

> Yet even a civilization that has been rendered scientific is not granted dispensation from practical questions; therefore a peculiar danger arises when the process of scientification transgresses the limit of technical questions, without, however, departing from the level of reflection of a rationality confined to the technical horizon. For then no attempt at all is made to attain a rational consensus on the part of citizens concerning the practical control of their destiny. Its place is taken by the attempt to attain technical control over history by perfecting the administration of society, an attempt that is just as impractical as it is unhistorical.

The most important critique that has been raised by economists against the traditional, centralized view of socialism is the challenge that was first issued in the 1920s by the Austrian school economist, Ludwig Mises, and substantially elaborated by his leading student, F. A. Hayek.[9] This critique concerns the difficulty, perhaps the utter impossibility, of rationally organizing an economy according to a central plan. The "calculation argument" is essentially an application of spontaneous order analysis to economics. The process by which order emerges in the economy is one that can be cultivated but not controlled.

The Mises/Hayek critique of socialism is well known to this day in the field of comparative economic systems and is often credited with having refuted the orthodox Marxian central planning position. I do not think it is generally understood, however, exactly *why* this centralized model fails, and as a result the alternative direction the critique suggests is also misunderstood. All too often economic reformers reject orthodox socialism only to endorse a form of orthodox capitalism that is subject to virtually the same criticism. One form of modernist thinking, one kind of social engineering, is simply replaced by another.

Properly understood, the critique of orthodox socialism is not a conservative defense of the state-capitalist systems prevalent in the West, but a basis for criticizing both traditional capitalism and social-ism. The Austrians' challenge is widely thought to have been circum-vented by one or both of two standard neoclassical approaches, each of which fundamentally misunderstands the critique it is supposed to answer. The microeconomic answer reduces the problem to a matter of pure, abstract equilibrium theory and thus fails altogether to meet the practical challenge.[10] The macroeconomic answer pro-

---

[9]The "calculation argument" was formulated, and so named, by Mises in his 1920 essay "Die Wirtschaftsrechnung im sozialistischen Gemeinwesen" and his 1922 book *Die Gemeinwirtschaft* (1936). Mises's original essay, along with similar formulations of this argument by Halm, Hayek, and Pierson, are included in English in Hayek's *Collectivist Economic Planning* (1935a). Hayek's rejoinder to Lange and other relevant essays on the role of knowledge in the economy are included in Hayek's *Individualism and Economic Order* (1948). Summaries of the debate include Armentano (1969); Hoff (1949); Lavoie (1981, 1985a, 1987b); Murrell (1983); and Vaughn (1980). For interpretations of Soviet economic experience in light of this theoretical critique, see Brutzkus (1935), Lavoie (1987a), Polanyi (1951), and Roberts (1971).

[10]The micro answer to the critique of orthodox socialism embodies a new model of socialism, devised by the well-known Polish economist Oskar Lange ([1936] 1964), which is supposed to consist of an ingenious combination of centralized planning with a decentralized price system. Although Lange's answer to this argument is right insofar as it insists that socialism needs to accommodate itself to the price system, it fails to realize the implications of this important change in the vision of a socialist society. Lange thinks socialism can still be centrally planned in some meaningful sense, and

poses a kind of partial planning that has led to serious difficulties of inflation and unemployment throughout the Western world, for reasons the Austrians had warned about long ago.[11] The upshot of both of these interpretations is a simple endorsement of the idea of the "mixed economy," that is, a defense of the status quo economic systems of the West, systems that involve a substantial mixture of markets and state intervention.

I would like to suggest that this complacent defense of interventionism is due to a confusion that is rooted in the very philosophical prejudices I have been calling modernism. Interventionism does not represent either an advancement over traditional Marxism or an effective answer to the Mises/Hayek critique of centralized planning. Thus I would like to offer my own interpretation of this classic critique in order to show both how it represents an instance of spontaneous order analysis and how it points not in a conservative but in a radical direction for economic reform.

The problem the calculation argument raises for the economics of socialism can be described as an application of the new view of science to the study of economic institutions. It depicts these institutions as working in a self-organizing way, establishing order by means of apparently disorderly processes. The argument emphasizes that the production process is fundamentally complex and that its adjustments take place through time by way of irreversible, evolutionary processes.[12] And it is central to the argument that what makes the "structure" of production hang together is the *meaning* that gets conveyed through the price system. The goods produced in the economy are not viewed as objective, physical things, but as intimately connected to human subjects and their purposes.[13]

he is still ready to condemn the anarchy of capitalist production for being unguided. He has essentially reverted to a conservative defense of interventionism, to a policy of state interference into a market-organized economy. His market-socialist model manages to reconcile planning with markets only by failing to deal with the real problem the critique raised about socialism in the first place. The Langean world is based on the perfect competition equilibrium model from Walrasian economics, and as such fails to grapple with the complexity of the real economy, or with the existence of uncertainty in economic decisionmaking. He depicts the economic problem as if it were a matter of monologically performing an objective calculation, instead of dialogically discovering subjective meaning.

[11]The ideas about "fine-tuning" the economy by management of the money supply and fiscal policy, which have come to be known as Keynesian, were vigorously criticized by the Austrian economists at the same time as they were formulating their critique of orthodox socialism, and for similar reasons. The fine-tuners know as little about what they are doing as do the central planners.

[12]For summaries of the Austrian tradition in economics and the way it grapples with time and complexity, see Rizzo (1979) and O'Driscoll and Rizzo (1985).

[13]For a summary of the Austrian approach to economics that stresses this point about

ECONOMIC CHAOS OR SPONTANEOUS ORDER?

The Mises/Hayek critique of socialism contends that any system of common ownership of the means of production is inherently unable to generate and disseminate the scattered and largely tacit knowledge, including knowledge of the relative scarcities of various consumers' and producers' goods, upon which advanced technological production depends. Separate owners actively contending with one another for money profits are able to (undeliberately) impart knowledge to the system of relative prices, and in turn to orient their own actions by reference to their "economic calculations" in terms of these prices, in such a way as to enable the millions of independent decisionmakers to coordinate their actions with one another. Without these prices to serve as "aids to the mind," as Mises called them, the planner would not know how to organize his or her commonly owned means of production with anything close to the degree of efficiency attained spontaneously by the rivalrous workings of the market process. Thus the argument is that there is a practical problem involving the use of knowledge facing any society that attempts to deliberately (and thus non-rivalrously) plan its economic order.

Hayek's later restatements of this argument (1935b, 1935c, 1940, 1976) make increasingly clear the importance of the nature and uses of knowledge to the whole critique of socialism. The problem with centralized planning is a problem in the social use of knowledge. Participants to the market process contribute to the discovery and conveyance of knowledge by imparting their local information to prices and in turn receiving from others useful information that is digested in prices. The challenge shows why socialism cannot afford to completely abolish the price system, as orthodox Marxism intended. Prices represent vital signals that each market participant needs in order to act intelligently.[14]

Now if proponents of socialism take seriously Hayek's argument that the complexity of the planner's task exceeds the capacity of any single mind or organization, the natural response would seem to be to greatly simplify this complex task. Instead of trying to plan the whole economy down to its every detail, as orthodox Marxians had ambitiously proposed, a more modest planning policy might be to just plan major sectors or aggregate categories or particular aspects of the economy. Many proponents and critics of socialism in the 1920s and 1930s assumed that the Central Planning Board would actually keep track of all the intimate details of the individual organi-

---

meaning, see Mises (1949).
[14]See also Hayek's related papers on knowledge and competition: Hayek (1937, 1942, 1945, 1946, and 1978b).

zation of each factory. Such a view of comprehensive planning is implicit in the traditional interpretation of Marxian socialism, but today it seems so far from the real experience of Soviet-type economies that it sounds almost like a straw man.

The attempts, however, to withdraw from comprehensive planning to more moderate forms of partial planning or interventionism are illusory. The appraisal of the efficacy of an economic plan can be made only in the context of a specific choice between real alternatives whose opportunity costs can be ascertained. The choices that together impart rationality to economic processes are meaningful only in certain specific contexts. It is not possible arbitrarily to separate out choices about prices from all the other aspects of choices, allocating decisions about price changes alone to the planning board. Neither is it possible for the central planners to decide on overall macroeconomic aggregates while leaving the microeconomic details to be worked out by decentralized decisionmakers. In both cases an artificial division of decisionmaking is being proposed in which the partial decision that the planners are supposed to make is in fact a meaningless one.

The planning board cannot intelligently decide on the price to charge for, say, a new computer program without detailed knowledge of the qualitative characteristics of this good and the costs of its production. For exactly the same reason, the planning board cannot decide on the total "quantity" of all computer programs needed by society without first having detailed knowledge of all the specific programs that make up this aggregate. To pretend to plan the price alone or the aggregate alone and leave the rest to others is to retreat from rational planning as the society's organizing mechanism to arbitrary intervention in a market-organized system. Thus the whole rationale of planning is undermined unless it can be shown how the planners' task could possibly be parceled out or delegated to subordinates without also relinquishing the meaningfulness of the decisions being made.

How, then, is the "intellectual division of labour," as Mises ([1920] 1935, p. 102) put it, accomplished in the market? Here each rival is able to focus his mental capacity on but a part of a complex network of economic relationships whose overall structure no market participant knows. Yet by allowing its participants to adjust their activities to one another through prices, the overall system exhibits an unintended order that makes advanced technological production possible.

The practice of accounting, that is, of the calculation of profit/loss accounts in terms of money outlays and receipts, both *ex ante* and *ex post,* has enabled human beings to orient their productive activities to one another in such a manner as to permit social production as a whole to be carried on with a very high degree of complexity. The calculation argument contends that in fact this complexity has, in the case of the advanced economies of the modern world, come to far exceed that which could possibly be consciously planned by any single mind or agency. By taking account of one another's decentralized plans indirectly, as mediated through relative price signals, which are continuously registering the competitive tugs and pulls of market participants, we are able to attain a complexity that is unattainable in any noncompetitive and centralized way. Thus the traditional socialist ideal of abolishing the "anarchy" of capitalist production to be replaced by central planning is impossible.

The crucial issue for Mises and Hayek was not primarily how the relative demands for consumers' goods were to be registered without competition, but rather how these consumers' goods evaluations, however determined, could be imputed through the complex network of relationships known as the capital structure. The defining characteristic of socialism throughout the period of the calculation debate was its ambition of abolishing separate ownership of the means of production. Whether we assume the state arbitrarily decides what everyone needs for consumer goods, as Maurice Dobb was to suggest during the debate, or a free market in consumers' goods was to prevail, as advocated by the market socialists, the real problem lies in translating these consumer evaluations into evaluations of producers' goods. Producers' goods prices are not "derived" logically from consumers' goods prices; they are "imputed" through a historical process of competition.

If the means of production are commonly owned, then plant managers cannot openly bid against one another for factors in the kind of competitive discovery process that imparts information to producers' goods prices in a capitalistic market economy. They cannot "play at competition" without putting their own wealth commitments at stake. It is precisely through rivalrous contention by separate and independent owners that market participants are able to impart information to the prices of factors of production, prices that in turn allow them to intelligently appraise alternative avenues of production. Thus the critique of socialism leads directly to the case for shifting the attention of economic policy from the attempt to control specific outcomes to the attempt to cultivate a system of rules in the form of "property rights."

Now there are many conservative economists who will think this critique of orthodox socialism constitutes a case for the status quo of

Western economies. These economies, however, have been sub-jected to ambitious attempts to control them, attempts that are no more justified than are orthodox central planning policies. Among the tools of control, for example, is the effort to control money, the very life-blood of market institutions, by means of central banking and monetary policy. Yet the very same reasons why an economy cannot be intelligently planned suggest that its supply of money and credit cannot be either. The severe problems with inflation and unemployment that plague most Western capitalist economies are not due to the fact that they have relied too much on spontaneous market forces, but rather to the fact that they too have tried to control rather than cultivate the economic order.[15]

Conclusion

> We stand at the beginning of a great new synthesis. The correspon-dence of static structures is not its subject, but the connectedness of self-organization dynamics—of mind—at many levels. It becomes possible to view evolution as a complex, but holistic dynamic phe-nomenon of an universal unfolding of order which becomes mani-fest in many ways, as matter and energy, information and complex-ity, consciousness and self-reflection. It is no longer necessary to assume a special life force (such as Bergson's *elan vital* or the *prana* of Hinduism) separate from the physical forces. Natural history, including the history of man, may now be understood as the history of the organization of matter and energy. But it may also be viewed as the organization of information into complexity or knowledge. Above all, however, it may be understood as the evolution of con-sciousness, or in other words, of autonomy and emancipation.
>
> Erich Jantsch (1980, p. 307)

Critics of the current reformers in the People's Republic of China have charged that the attempt to borrow from the new view of science is merely another form of "scientism," or "science worship," which fails to leave room for the human element. They also warn that market reformers in Yugoslavia and Hungary have brought those countries a new set of difficulties, including inflation and unemployment, and

---

[15]The Austrian economists Mises and Hayek have pointed to the problems with efforts to control an economy by manipulating the supply of money and credit, and they have argued that not only inflation but also much unemployment is traceable to this policy. See Mises (1981) and Hayek (1931). For a useful overview of Hayek's work on econom-ics that shows the common basis of both his critiques of orthodox socialism and of orthodox capitalism in his theory of spontaneous order, see O'Driscoll (1977). The contemporary work on free banking by White (1984) and Selgin (1988) is particularly important in this regard in that it shows specifically how a decentralized monetary system can be more orderly than one that is controlled by central banking policy.

that freeing up the price system necessarily implies condemning socialism to all the vices familiar to Western state-capitalist economies. Both of these criticisms fail to appreciate the new synthesis that is emerging in science in general and within political economy in particular. The choice between being pro-science and pro-human is a false one, a legacy of modernist thinking that is being overcome in the new view of science. There is a third alternative that is at once humanistic and scientific. Similarly the choice between socialism and conservatism is a false one. There is no necessity that when prices are freed up, problems of inflation and unemployment will result. There is a third alternative, namely, a truly free society that minimizes the overall role of government and allows the spontaneous forces of the competitive market process to produce social and economic order.

References

Armentano, Dominick T. "Resource Allocation Problems under Socialism." In *Theory of Economic Systems: Capitalism, Socialism, and Corporatism*, pp. 127–39. Edited by William P. Snavely. Columbus, Ohio: Charles E. Merrill, 1969.

Bernstein, Richard J. *Beyond Objectivism and Relativism: Science, Hermeneutics, and Praxis*. Philadelphia: University of Pennsylvania Press, 1983.

Brutzkus, Boris. *Economic Planning in Soviet Russia*. London: Routledge, 1935.

Gleick, James. *Chaos: Making a New Science*. New York: Viking Penguin, 1987.

Habermas, Jurgen. "Dogmatism, Reason, and Decision: On Theory and Praxis in Our Scientific Civilization." In *Theory and Practice*, pp. 253–82. Boston: Beacon Press, 1973.

Halm, Georg. "Further Considerations on the Possibility of Adequate Calculation in a Socialist Community." Translated by H. E. Batson. In Hayek (1935a, pp. 131–200).

Hayek, Friedrich A. *Prices and Production*. London: Routledge and Kegan Paul, 1931.

Hayek, Friedrich A., ed. *Collectivist Economic Planning, Critical Studies on the Possibilities of Socialism*. London: George Routledge & Sons, 1935a.

Hayek, Friedrich A. "The Nature and History of the Problem." 1935b. Reprinted in Hayek (1948, pp. 119–47).

Hayek, Friedrich A. "The State of the Debate." 1935c. Reprinted in Hayek (1948, pp. 148–80).

Hayek, Friedrich A. "Economics and Knowledge." 1937. Reprinted in Hayek (1948, pp. 33–56).

Hayek, Friedrich A. "The Competitive 'Solution.' " 1940. Reprinted in Hayek (1948, pp. 181–208).

Hayek, Friedrich A. "The Facts of the Social Sciences." 1942. Reprinted in Hayek (1948, pp. 57–76).

Hayek, Friedrich A. "The Use of Knowledge in Society." 1945. Reprinted in Hayek (1948, pp. 77–91).

Hayek, Friedrich A. "The Meaning of Competition." 1946. Reprinted in Hayek (1948, pp. 92–106).

Hayek, Friedrich A. *Individualism and Economic Order*. Chicago: University of Chicago Press, 1948.

Hayek, Friedrich A. "Degrees of Explanation." 1955. Reprinted in Hayek (1967, pp. 3–21).

Hayek, Friedrich A. "The Theory of Complex Phenomena." 1964. Reprinted in Hayek (1967, pp. 22–42).

Hayek, Friedrich A. *Studies in Philosophy, Politics, and Economics*. Chicago: University of Chicago Press, 1967.

Hayek, Friedrich A. "The New Confusion about 'Planning.'" 1976. Reprinted in Hayek (1978a, pp. 232–46).

Hayek, Friedrich A. *New Studies in Philosophy, Politics, Economics, and the History of Ideas*. Chicago: University of Chicago Press, 1978a.

Hayek, Friedrich A. "Competition as a Discovery Procedure." 1978b. In Hayek (1978a, pp. 179–90).

Hoff, Trygve J. B. *Economic Calculation in the Socialist Society*. London: William Hodge, 1949.

Jantsch, Erich. *The Self-Organizing Universe: Scientific and Human Implications of the Emerging Paradigm of Evolution*. New York: Pergamon Press, 1980.

Lange, Oskar. "On the Economic Theory of Socialism." 1936. Reprinted in Lippincott (1964, pp. 55–143).

Lavoie, Don. "A Critique of the Standard Account of the Socialist Calculation Debate." *Journal of Libertarian Studies* 5 (1981): 41–87.

Lavoie, Don. *Rivalry and Central Planning: The Socialist Calculation Debate Reconsidered*. New York: Cambridge University Press, 1985a.

Lavoie, Don. *National Economic Planning: What Is Left?* Cambridge, Mass.: Ballinger, 1985b.

Lavoie, Don. "Political and Economic Illusions of Socialism." *Critical Review* 1 (1987a): 1–35.

Lavoie, Don. "The Accounting of Interpretations and the Interpretation of Accounts: The Communicative Function of the Language of Business." *Accounting, Organizations, and Society* 12, no. 6 (1987b): 579–604.

Lippincott, Benjamin E., ed. *On the Economic Theory of Socialism*. 1938. Reprint. New York: McGraw-Hill, 1964.

McCloskey, Donald N. *The Rhetoric of Economics*. Madison: University of Wisconsin Press, 1985.

Mises, Ludwig von. *The Theory of Money and Credit*. Translation by H. E. Batson. 1912. Reprint. Irvington-on-Hudson, N.Y.: Foundation for Economic Education, 1981.

Mises, Ludwig von. "Economic Calculation in the Socialist Commonwealth." Translated by S. Alder. 1920. Reprinted in *Collectivist Economic Planning, Critical Studies on the Possibilities of Socialism*, pp. 87–130. Edited by F. A. Hayek. London: George Routledge & Sons, 1935.

Mises, Ludwig von. *Socialism: An Economic and Sociological Analysis*. Translated by J. Kahane, London: Jonathan Cape, 1936.

Mises, Ludwig von. *Human Action: A Treatise on Economics*. London: William Hodge, 1949.

Murrell, Peter. "Did the Theory of Market Socialism Answer the Challenge of Ludwig von Mises? A Reinterpretation of the Socialist Controversy." *History of Political Economy* 15(1983): 92–105.

O'Driscoll, Gerald P. *Economics as a Coordination Problem: The Contributions of Friedrich A. Hayek*. Kansas City: Sheed, Andrews and McMeel, 1977.

O'Driscoll, Gerald P., and Rizzo, Mario J. *The Economics of Time and Ignorance*. New York: Basil Blackwell, 1985.

Pierson, Nikolaas Gerard. "The Problem of Value in the Socialist Community." Translated by G. Gardiner. 1902. Reprinted in Hayek (1935a, pp. 41–85).

Polanyi, Michael. "The Span of Central Direction." In *Logic of Liberty*, pp. 111–37. Chicago: University of Chicago Press, 1951.

Polanyi, Michael. *Personal Knowledge*. Chicago: University of Chicago Press, 1958.

Polanyi, Michael. *The Study of Man*. Chicago: University of Chicago Press, 1959.

Prigogine, Ilya, and Stengers, Isabelle. *Order Out of Chaos: Man's New Dialogue with Nature*. New York: Bantam, 1984.

Ricoeur, Paul. *Hermeneutics and the Human Sciences*. New York: Cambridge University Press, 1981.

Ricoeur, Paul. *Time and Narrative*, vol. 1. Chicago: University of Chicago Press, 1983.

Ricoeur, Paul. *Time and Narrative*, vol. 2. Chicago: University of Chicago Press, 1984.

Rizzo, Mario J., ed. *Time, Uncertainty, and Disequilibrium*. Lexington, Mass.: Lexington Books, 1979.

Roberts, Paul Craig. *Alienation and the Soviet Economy*. Albuquerque: University of New Mexico Press, 1971.

Selgin, George A. *The Theory of Free Banking*. Totowa, N.J.: Rowman & Littlefield, 1988.

Vaughn, Karen. "Economic Calculation under Socialism: The Austrian Contribution." *Economic Inquiry* 18 (Summer 1980). 535–54.

White, Lawrence H. *Free Banking in Britain: Theory, Experience, and Debate, 1800–1845*. New York: Cambridge University Press, 1984.

COMMENT

THE IMPACT AND INFLUENCE OF THE NEW VIEW OF SCIENCE ON CHINA'S REFORM*
He Weiling

Great changes have taken place since the economic system reform was introduced in China in 1978. The reform covers a wide field with different outcomes and significances, predominated by a change in the ways of viewing and ways of thinking. Don Lavoie points out that today in China the economic reformers are taking "the new view of science" as their starting point.

The so-called new scientific methodology—such as control theory, catastrophe theory, and dissipative structure theory—was introduced progressively and extensively to the study of social science, and it greatly enlightened people's outlook and thinking. This change is the result of China's reform on the one hand and the driving force for the reform on the other hand.

The significance of the new view of science, or rather the new way of thinking, is profound. It is a powerful tool that helps us in analyzing the issues concerning social-economic development and reform, and it makes people's way of thinking more identical and practical—especially as it creates a condition for the dialogue between policy-makers and young researchers. On the other hand, the new scientific methodology is also an appropriate way to deal with, to combat, to eliminate, and to renovate the traditional and classical dogmatism.

The new view of science—the new way of thinking—has been applied throughout all the processes of the reform, during which the reform has been penetrating into every corner of the society.

In consideration of the nature of Lavoie's paper, I will focus my comment on two subjects: (1) the implications of the new view of science for China's reform, especially the new view of order and

*Reprinted from *Cato Journal* 8 (Winter 1989): 637–40, with revisions.
The author is President of the China-U.S. Liaison Committee for International Enterprises and Senior Fellow at the National Economic System Reform Institute of China.

chaos, and (2) a review of China's reform over the 1978–88 period in light of the new view of science.

A New View of Order and Chaos

The new view of science, as Lavoie points out, adopts a new category of order and chaos. In turn, this change gives rise to a very important perspective in exploring and analyzing social-economic development, and social-economic laws in terms of order and chaos. The new view explains especially how the social and economic order develops.

The old way of thinking exaggerated and overemphasized Marxist criticism of the capitalist market economy, overlooking the decisive role the market mechanism plays in economic development. As such, the old view led to state-monopolized planning. When Newton's way of viewing the world was universally acknowledged, all laws (both natural and social) were regarded as absolute, and no one could change them. Adversely, the old view overlooked the importance of human knowledge and reflection; it did not recognize that the participation of human beings in the social-economic process will influence their perceptions as they learn and acquire new information.

The old way of thinking has served as the philosophical basis for the theory of comprehensive planning. As a result, like all socialist countries, China made a detour on its way to economic development, during the founding of the new China, because of the theory of comprehensive planning.

Two Kinds of Order

According to the new scientific view of Prigogine's theory (dissipative structure theory), there are two kinds of order: ossified and alive order. The planning order actually belongs to the ossified order that cannot meet the need of rapid development, which depends on an efficient division of labor and intelligence and on the incessant emergence of new technology and new productivity. Therefore, the planning order is only a primitive order in accordance with a simple economic system.

The centrally planned order will totally collapse in the progress of new technological development and new social subdivision of labor and intelligence. The chaos arising from excessive central planning is self-evident, and has been especially visible during the progress of China's economic reform. And to make matters worse, the planning system could do nothing for resolving the chaos problem by economic means because it could not regulate automatically; that is, under central planning there is no spontaneous self-organizing process. So every time chaos arose, only political movements followed. (In this sense, the question addressed in Lavoie's recent book *National Economic Planning: What Is Left?* is clearly relevant.)

The Problems of Knowledge and Democracy

According to Lavoie, there are two problems that the planning system cannot solve: the knowledge problem and the democracy problem.

As to the first problem, it is not the lack of information, per se, that leads to the ill-practice of planning. It is because the planning system does not align itself with the drive for modernization. Under the planning system, the plan is made by a small number of people or organs. It therefore cannot perform in the same manner as a highly integrated mechanism. Under the planned economy, it is difficult to make any new adjustment and allow for new economic activity. The adjustment problem can be solved only by introducing a market mechanism that can automatically and spontaneously adjust itself by using all kinds of economic measures, including competitive prices, a stock market, and a bond market, as well as by introducing sound monetary and fiscal measures. By doing so, a type of collective social intelligence can replace individual intelligence, and the social-economic structure could be transformed into a new order, a higher-level order that can stand the test of time.

One point needs to be emphasized: The market mechanism is not only a key measure for maintaining the balance of demand and supply, but also an important measure for promoting the transformation of the economic system from a lower level of integration to a higher level.

The second problem, the problem of democratic rule, is very clear. Under the old planning system only a small group of people, operating in a hierarchical way, administer and manage the system. Such an arrangement will undoubtedly brew and produce a cumbersome and ossified bureaucratic system.

Theoretically and practically, the establishment of a market-oriented economic system is the prerequisite for modern economic development. This conclusion is quite obvious from the process of the reform as well as from the new view of science, including the concept that the formation of a highly self-adaptive and self-regulating social structure stems from the opening of the system.

China's Reform Process

Since 1978, newly born ideas were often subject to much criticism. New ideas always take shape along with any reform drive. New ideas also serve as a pathbreaker for changing and developing an economic system.

During China's reform process, there have been three stages in the development of the new way of thinking about and viewing economic organization. First, those who accepted the new view of science would not question classical dogmatism directly. They avoided any confrontation with orthodox views, and only advocated a new scientific method, applied new concepts, new technology, and new ways of expression. In the second stage, advocates of the new view reassessed and challenged the analysis of the classical theory of Marxism. Finally, in the third stage, which has yet to be fully developed, there has been an open discussion of the market order, ownership, and the role of a stock market in China's socialist system.

Cultivating a Spontaneous Order

Another important concept offered by Lavoie is "cultivation." When we regulate the economic system, cultivation is better than control. In the process of undertaking reform, policymakers should keep two concepts in mind: graduation and cultivation. In that process, the most important thing is not control but cultivation.

We have to liberalize and cultivate but not control the social economic realities in light of the application of laws and principles of economic development by means of the new view of science—using the new concept of spontaneous order, the new methodology, and the new terminology. Only by openly acknowledging the spontaneous and self-organizing process can we fully understand and accept the basic laws in our way toward a higher social-economic order. Otherwise we will be thrown back into chaos and suffer another big setback.

PART II

DECENTRALIZATION AND DEVELOPMENT
IN CHINA

5

THE IMPORTANCE OF REORGANIZING MONEY, CREDIT, AND BANKING WHEN DECENTRALIZING ECONOMIC DECISIONMAKING

Peter Bernholz

Introduction

In a centrally planned economy, money and prices—and thus the monetary regime, the banks, and the monetary authority or central bank—are in a subordinate, subsidiary position. Investment, production, and consumption decisions are mainly taken by central authorities and executed by production plants, firms, and wholesale and retail distributors. The monetary system is passively obliged to supply necessary funds and money to implement the plans, and it is not allowed to interfere with them. Prices do not provide information and have no function in motivating the decisions of economic agents.

If a formerly centrally planned economy tries to invigorate and to harness individual and group initiative by decentralizing economic decisions to production plants, firms, households, and communities, then the role of money, credit, and banking changes drastically. Prices now inform and guide decisions: They tell producers and consumers how scarce goods are, and they redirect labor and production efforts toward activities where higher incomes and profits can be earned.

But individual decisions of firms and consumers, of saving and investing, and of buying and selling somehow have to be coordinated. Thus, the coordination of decentralized decisions by markets and prices becomes the more important the fewer decisions are taken centrally. A precondition for well-functioning markets is, moreover, a sound monetary and credit system. The monetary regime has to be organized in a way that individual agents can expect the money they earn to remain stable in value until it is disbursed for purchases.

The author is Professor of Economics at the University of Basel.

Otherwise, they will take decisions leading to a less-efficient allocation of resources.

These facts have been clearly seen by the German neoliberals. Their ideas about the economic order were developed from the 1930s to the 1950s and were decisive in shaping the new economic regime in West Germany after 1948 (Bernholz 1989)—a regime that proved extremely successful in rebuilding the German economy and in leading it on the path of rapid growth. For example, Walter Eucken (1952) clearly expressed the idea that a well-functioning monetary order is a precondition for using the free and competitive formation of prices as a steering mechanism for the efficient allocation of resources in a decentralized economy. Eucken (1952, p. 256) pointed out that "the efforts to realize a competitive order are in vain as long as a certain stability of money has not been secured."

The Importance of Financial Assets, Financial Markets, and Financial Intermediaries for an Efficient Use of Resources

In a decentralized economy, intertemporal plans of consumers for consumption and of producers for production have to be coordinated by markets and prices to allow an optimal use of the means of production and to efficiently coordinate production and consumption over time. This task is taken care of if claims can be bought and sold on developed and competitive money, credit, and futures markets. Firms and the government make net real investments, which implies that the final goods and services that are produced with these investments are available only later. Thus, a great part of the costs of producing these goods has to be expended a long time before the proceeds from sales are available.

It follows that adequate credits are necessary to cover this gap. Consequently, it is necessary for firms and the government to incur debt, that is, to sell claims. If households are free to decide how much of their incomes to spend on consumption and how much to save, they will be the final creditors or buyers of claims. In doing so, they transfer for some time the real resources not needed for the production of consumers' goods to the business firms who use them to produce investment goods. Obviously, households sometimes also make real investments. They buy houses or durable consumption goods and thereby incur debt. It is also possible that firms and the government sometimes enjoy greater revenues than outlays, so that they buy claims issued by others. But, generally speaking, firms and the government are net investors in decentralized economies and thereby incur debt, whereas households as a group are net savers and thus creditors. This can be clearly seen, for example, in the figures for the Federal Republic of Germany in Table 1. Corresponding financial flows can be found for other countries, such as the rough estimates for Switzerland in Figure 1.

Claims or financial assets originating from events in the real sphere (that is, from consumption, production, and real investments) are called primary financial assets (Gurley and Shaw 1960). Primary assets are often not suited to directly coordinate consumption and production plans, since potential creditors and debtors have quite different needs concerning the characteristics of claims. Thus, firms that undertake long-term investments prefer to indebt themselves by holding financial assets that are due only after a corresponding period. Households, on the other hand, prefer to give short-term credit because of unpredictable future expenditures. Production firms need substantial credits, whereas individual households save only small sums. An individual household would have to get information about several producing firms. Moreover, it might be too expensive for these firms to get numerous small credits from the many households. Consequently, households find that buying different financial assets to diversify risks is too costly and too time-consuming.

All these problems are obstacles to an efficient intertemporal allocation of resources and limit the development of the economy. Thus, in market economies many different types of financial intermediaries and financial markets have developed to overcome these problems. Financial intermediaries such as banks, investment and pension funds, and insurance firms buy primary financial assets (for example, from producing firms) and finance these credits by producing secondary assets and by selling them to households. In this way, secondary financial assets with characteristics adapted to the needs of creditors concerning maturity, interest, and risk can be created. Financial intermediaries transform the time structure of debts and destroy risk, to the advantage of firms, governments, and households. The creditor with a savings deposit has only to form an opinion on the creditworthiness of his bank. The bank itself can diversify its great portfolio by extending credit to several firms, since it is relatively cheaper for the bank than for households to judge the firms' ratings as debtors because of the greater amount of credit given.

The development of capital markets leads to similar advantages. It is true that in this case households also buy primary assets such as bonds issued by producing firms or the government. But bonds have a long maturity and thus protect the debtor, whereas the individual creditor can sell them at any time. And secondary financial assets produced

TABLE 1
WEALTH FORMATION AND SAVINGS
IN THE FEDERAL REPUBLIC OF GERMANY

Position	Billion DM			Share in %	
	1984	1985	1986	1985	1986
Wealth Creation in the Whole Economy					
Formation of Real Assets[a]	138.2	136.0	139.1	78.1	65.4
All firms	109.1	107.0	106.8	61.5	50.2
Producing firms	40.8	52.1	54.7	29.9	25.7
Building industry	62.6	49.9	48.0	28.7	22.6
Financial institutions	5.7	5.0	4.1	2.9	1.9
Government	29.2	29.0	32.3	16.7	15.2
Changes of Net Foreign Position against Rest of the World[b]	15.7	38.1	73.5	21.9	34.6
Total	153.9	174.1	212.6	100.0	100.0
Total Savings[c]					
Private Households	110.5	113.9	127.2	65.4	59.9
All firms	47.9	50.9	77.0	29.2	36.2
Producing firms	13.5	18.4	36.3	10.5	17.1
Building industry	8.8	10.1	20.7	5.8	9.7
Financial institutions	25.6	22.4	20.1	12.9	9.4
State	−4.5	9.3	8.3	5.4	3.9
Total	153.9	174.1	212.6	100.0	100.0
Total in % of Net National Product at Market Prices	10.0	10.8	12.4	—	—

TABLE 1 (cont.t)

WEALTH FORMATION AND SAVINGS
IN THE FEDERAL REPUBLIC OF GERMANY

				Change against last year in billion DM	
Balance of Financial Flows					
Private Households	110.5	113.9	127.2	+3.4	+13.4
All firms	−61.2	−56.1	−29.7	+5.1	+26.4
Producing firms	−27.4	−33.7	−18.4	−6.4	+15.4
Building industry	−53.7	−39.8	−27.3	+13.9	+12.5
State	−33.7	−19.7	−24.0	+14.0	−4.3
Total[d]	15.7	38.1	73.5	+22.4	+35.5

[a]Net investment in fixed capital and inventories.
[b]Corresponds to difference between savings and domestic real asset formation.
[c]Includes transfers.
[d]Corresponds to change of Net Foreign Position against Rest of the World.
SOURCE: Deutsche Bundesbank.

FIGURE 1

FINANCIAL FLOWS IN SWITZERLAND 1985
(BILLIONS OF SWISS FRANCS)

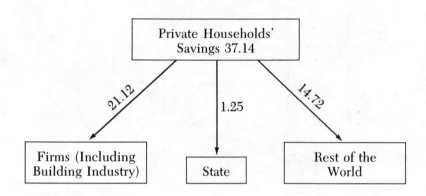

by financial intermediaries are also sold in the capital market. These relationships are schematically represented in Figure 2.

It is obvious that the whole financial system serves to obtain a better intertemporal coordination of production and consumption plans. This includes a transformation of the time structure of claims, a destruction of risk, and a lowering of information and transaction costs. We should note that futures and options markets are also means to remove or decrease the risk of uncertain future prices, whereas insurance markets help to limit the risk of uncertain future events, the probability of which can be calculated.

The Functions of Stable Money in a Decentralized Economic System

We have just explained the functions of financial assets, of financial markets, and of financial intermediaries for the efficient coordination of production and consumption over time, for reducing risk, for lowering transaction and information costs, and for creating a greater productivity of the whole economy. But what is the relationship of all this to the function of money in a decentralized economy?

To answer this question, we will recall that in a decentralized market economy prices (and interest rates) not only clear markets but also aggregate information about the present and expected scarcity of goods and services. Prices inform those who strive to make profits, to earn income, or to prevent losses about the rational use or the saving of resources. Prices inform individuals about unused opportu-

FIGURE 2
Relationships among Primary Creditors and Primary Debtors

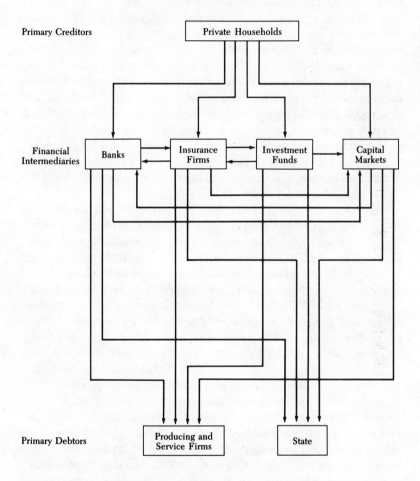

nities, motivate agents to reallocate resources more efficiently according to the degree of scarcity expressed by prices, and guide individuals in search of new, valuable information (Hayek 1945). Interest rates are formed in financial markets and are paid for credits. They serve, together with futures markets, to direct and inform savings and investment decisions concerning the future production and consumption of goods. These credit and capital markets, as well as interest rates and prices in futures markets, provide information that is essential to coordinate the decisions of decentralized agents.

Prices and interest rates in a competitive environment must adapt to changing degrees of scarcity of goods to perform their functions. But changes in relative prices and interest rates brought about by unpredictable changes in the money supply—and, thus by changes in the absolute price level—disturb the smooth operation of the price system, since such changes have nothing to do with changes in the degree of scarcity. Theoretically, we could argue that changes in the absolute price level caused by changes of the money supply do not influence relative prices and real interest rates, and thus do not distort the allocation, information, and motivation provided by them. But this proposition is empirically refuted. We know quite well that relative prices and real interest rates are influenced by inflation because of incomplete information on the part of individuals about the reasons for changes in market demand and supply and because of transaction costs. (For the case of the German hyperinflation of the 1920s, see Bresciani-Turroni 1937.)

Relative prices and real interest rates, not distorted by monetary factors, are also required to prevent too costly, inefficient, or even shrinking financial markets. Money serves as a unit of account and financial assets are thus denominated in money. But agents are prepared only to extend credit and to borrow if the future real value of the financial assets at maturity is reasonably predictable. A strongly increasing real value of debts might ruin debtors, whereas a strongly falling real value of extended credits would decimate the fortune of creditors. Under these unpredictable conditions that are usually connected with deflation or inflation, people are less and less willing to incur debt or to buy financial assets. Financial intermediation is less efficient and may shrink sizably, thus damaging the efficient coordination of intertemporal production and consumption plans. Experience teaches us that with even moderate inflation, not to speak of advanced inflation and hyperinflation, financial markets tend to shrink strongly or even to vanish, especially at the long end of the market. We should also note that unexpected changes in the value of financial assets because of monetary factors causes a substantial redistribution of wealth in developed economies.

The stability of money is also important for bookkeeping and for rational calculation by firms and public authorities if money is used as a unit of account. With price-level instability, it becomes very difficult to adequately calculate the value of depreciation for plants, machinery, and other real capital assets—a calculation that is necessary to replace such real assets adequately at the time of obsolescence. The same is true for the correct calculation of the real value of future tax receipts and expenditures.

Finally, modern money is itself, for good or bad, a monetized financial asset that suffers from unpredictable value changes brought about by monetary factors. As a medium of exchange, money needs stability of value to be held by individuals and firms in adequate amounts. People reduce their real demand for money during inflationary periods, which is itself a factor in the misallocation of resources. Moreover, during periods of advanced inflation or hyperinflation, the function of money as a unit of account is usually abolished and the economy may even partially return to barter. Also, the less developed a country is financially, the more money serves as a store of value, a function that is hurt again by unpredictable changes in its value.

The damages brought about by unpredictable changes in the value of money can, of course, be mitigated by indexing. But the search for adequate indices and their application itself increases transaction costs and wastes resources. Nor can indexing be extended to everything, least of all to the value of money holdings themselves. Indexing must, by necessity, remain an inadequate surrogate for stable money.

Characteristics of Some Historical Monetary Regimes

It follows from the above discussion that economic reforms, which seek to decentralize the economy and to use markets to coordinate, motivate, and inform the actions of economic agents, have to be complemented by the development of financial markets, financial institutions, and a sound monetary regime. The monetary regime has to provide money that is as stable in value as possible. It has, moreover, to provide a framework to exclude as far as possible, or to minimize, disturbances of real economic activities caused by monetary factors.

To judge the respective characteristics of different monetary regimes or constitutions, we have to look at the historical experiences under different regimes. In doing so, we will first concentrate on the question of value stability (in this section) and then turn to midterm movements of real exchange rates (in the following section).

Historical evidence during the past 200 years is limited to pure commodity standards such as the pure gold and silver standards (roughly until 1914, or in the United States until 1933; see Table 2); to the gold exchange standard (roughly 1925–33, 1958–71); and to the pure fiat money or paper money discretionary regimes with fixed (1971–73) and with flexible exchange rates (1914–25 and since 1973).

TABLE 2
PERIODS OF DISCRETIONARY MONETARY MANAGEMENT[a]

Country	From[b]	To	From	To	Comment
Argentina	1824	1867	1885	1899	
	1876	1881	1914	1927	
			1930		
Austria	1797	1819	1914	1923	
	1848	1892	1933		
France	1789	1796	1914	1928	Return to old parity in 1928
			1936		
Russia	1786	1839	1914		
	1854	1899			
Switzerland	1914	1925	1936		Return to old parity in 1925
United Kingdom	1797	1821	1914	1925	Return to old parity in 1821 and 1914
			1931		
United States	1861	1873	1933		Return to old parity in 1873

[a]Countries in Figure 3 were off the gold or silver standards since 1790.
[b]The listed dates should be viewed with caution. Periods of legal and of de facto convertibility used here have sometimes differed. Austria had a one-sided convertibility only in 1892; full convertibility followed in 1896. The United States kept gold convertibility for monetary authorities until 1971.

It should be mentioned that widespread exchange controls and bilateral trade were present even between many developed Western market economies during and after World War I and from 1931–58. Moreover, it is unclear whether the monetary regime from 1958–71 should be listed as a gold exchange standard, since it did not provide gold convertibility of bank notes at a fixed gold parity for everybody at each central bank. Convertibility was limited during this period to monetary authorities at the U.S. Treasury. Even there, the U.S. government put increasing pressure on several governments, especially during the last years of the Bretton Woods system, not to convert dollars into gold. One can argue that the monetary regime after World War II became, in fact, more and more a fiat paper money regime with discretionary management, especially as far as the United States was concerned. This implied, of course, that other developed countries maintaining a fixed dollar parity did not have much leeway for discretionary policies. On the contrary, their policies strongly reflected the discretionary monetary management of the U.S. Federal Reserve Board, which soon proved to be inflationary.

From time to time several countries freed themselves for a while from these limitations by revaluing or devaluing their currencies. Finally in August 1971, President Richard Nixon abolished gold convertibility of the U.S. dollar, even for foreign monetary authorities. This action turned the world monetary order into a pure exchange standard resting on the dollar as a reserve currency. But other industrialized countries were no longer willing to subordinate their own currencies to discretionary U.S. monetary policy. Therefore, fixed exchange rates were abolished vis-à-vis the dollar by most developed countries in early 1973. Let us now turn to the question of the degree of long-term monetary stability reached in different monetary regimes during the past 200 years.

Monetary regimes that leave decisions concerning the supply of fiat money to governments or to more or less dependent central banks are characterized by two rather negative traits. First, if these regimes are combined with flexible exchange rates, they exhibit strong midterm swings of real exchange rates, a fact that will be discussed below (see the section on controlling the money supply). Second, they are biased in favor of inflationary developments.

Let us examine the second of these characteristics. If we look at the evidence for "relatively" stable currencies like the Swiss franc and the West German mark, we find their values shrank from 1950 to 1980 by 61.5 percent and 60.6 percent, respectively (in terms of the cost-of-living index). If this depreciation was true for so-called stable currencies, we should not be surprised at the far greater depreciation recorded by other currencies. Indeed, a study of about 30 currencies shows that there has not been a single case of a currency freely manipulated by its government or central bank since 1700 which enjoyed price stability for at least 30 years running. This instability has been true even for "autonomous" central banks, although their currencies fared better than those manipulated by central banks that were more subservient to their governments (Parkin and Bade 1978).

The picture would be quite different if governments and central banks were controlled by strict monetary constitutions such as gold or silver standards. Such systems allow public authorities hardly any discretion to control the money supply if bank notes and (indirectly) demand deposits have to be exchanged at the will of the holder, and at a fixed parity, into gold or silver.

Figure 3 illustrates this thesis clearly. The wholesale price index shows no trend between 1790 and 1914 for Great Britain, France, or the United States. The same was true for Germany, Switzerland, and other countries that were also on gold or silver standards. After 1914, or after 1931–36 (compare Table 2), when these countries went off the gold or gold exchange standard in favor of paper money standards freely manipulated by monetary authorities (fiat money), the situation changed dramatically. (Note that no hyperinflations are present in Figure 3.) The impression is reinforced if we look at the development of the value of fiat monies in the 19th century. Russia, Austria, and Argentina were off the gold or silver standard for decades during that period (see Table 2). The inflationary consequences are obvious.

China also had wide-ranging experiences with the inflationary bias of discretionary paper money regimes. We are referring not only to the hyperinflation during and after World War II (Kia-Ngau 1958, Chou 1963) but also to the subsequent inflation that developed after the communist victory. Since the Chinese were the first to invent paper, ink, and printing and were the first to invent paper money, it is not surprising that they were also the first to experience paper money inflation. It is well known that from about A.D. 1000–1500 all Chinese dynasties in time overissued paper money and brought about inflations that were usually ended only by stopping the circulation of the paper money (Tullock 1956). Around 1500, however, the Chinese ended their use of paper money. It is still an unresolved question as to why and how this fundamental change of the monetary regime could have happened, given the inflationary bias of governments.

A look at the historical evidence shows two points that should be remembered. Gold and silver standards need not be the only infla-

FIGURE 3
Development of Wholesale Prices
in Several Countries, 1790–1980

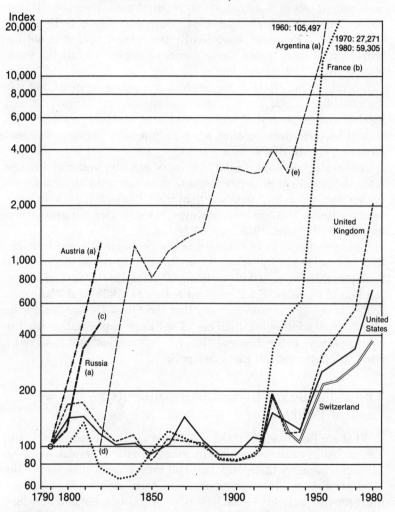

(a) Exchange rate on Amsterdam for Russia, on Hamburg for Austria, gold price until
    1929, and exchange rate on US$, since then for Argentina.
(b) 1796 = 100.
(c) 1814.
(d) 1826 = 100.
(e) 1929.
Source: Mitchell 1976, pp. 735–47); U.S. Department of Commerce (1975,
Part 1, pp. 199–202); Bernholz (1982, p. 15); Olarra Jiménez (1968, pp.
181–84).

tion-free monetary regimes. For instance, there have been proposals for other potentially inflation-free systems, such as anchoring a monetary growth rule in the constitution (Friedman 1968), or having free competitive private banking with no central bank monopoly (Hayek 1976; Campbell and Dougan 1986; Dorn and Schwartz 1987). All such systems, however, have hardly been tried, and it is not my purpose to discuss their relative merits vis-à-vis each other or vis-à-vis the gold or silver standard.

Second, not only the inflationary bias of monetary systems, but also the variability of real factors such as real growth rates of gross national product and employment, real interest rates, and real exchange rates should be taken into account when judging the merits of different monetary constitutions.

Concerning unemployment, business activity, and real interest rates, the empirical evidence seems to show that their variances were higher under the gold standard than from 1950–80 (Bernholz 1983; Meltzer 1986). The opposite, however, is true for the variance of real exchange rates after 1973.

A final factor to be considered is the problem of grave mistakes that can be made by monetary authorities in times of crisis (for example, during recessions or financial crises) if the authorities are not bound by rules. Friedman and Schwartz (1963) and Warburton (1966) have argued convincingly that the Great Depression in the United States following 1929 could not have happened, at least in such severity, if the Federal Reserve System had not followed a strongly contractionary monetary policy.

The Inflationary Bias of Governments and Central Banks

What are the reasons for the inflationary bias of governments and central banks in democracies? In trying to give an explanation, we have to remember that politicians and their parties compete for the support of voters, interest groups, and party members. Thus, they must provide benefits in the form of public goods, income transfers, subsidies, and regulations without excessive increases in the tax burden as perceived by the population.

Increasing the supply of money to finance such benefits is precisely such a method of taxation because it is not easily discerned by the people, at least not in the beginning. Even later, most citizens will not hold the government or central bank responsible for the ensuing inflation for a fairly long time. Moreover, by creating money, real interest rates are kept lower, as long as inflation remains moderate and people do not anticipate the full consequences. In the first phase of the inflationary process, growth rates of real GNP and employment even increase, and inflation reduces the real government debt. Revenues from progressive taxes grow imperceptibly. Obviously, in this phase the party (parties) in power will gain more votes than they will lose. Therefore, there will be a definite preference for expansionary monetary policies. True, an autonomous central bank is less dependent on political support than the politicians. But central bankers need to be appointed and reappointed by the political authorities. These bankers are usually obliged by law to cooperate with the government. Last but not least, they, too, are influenced to a certain degree by interests expressed in their environment and they enjoy wielding discretionary powers for the so-called public good.

The political pressures on politicians and central bankers change when the inflation rate accelerates. Price and tax increases brought about by inflationary financing will be seen as substantial by more and more voters. An increasing number of people will perceive the devaluation of their nominal assets, expectations will become inflationary, and the positive influences of unanticipated inflation on unemployment will vanish. As a result, more voters will vote against than for the incumbent party. The (new) government and central bank will proceed to restrict the growth rate of the money supply to get inflation under control. But this policy change does not mean that politicians will persist in their stabilization efforts until an inflation-free situation has been reached. Quite the contrary. Stabilization leads to a short-term increase in unemployment and real interest rates, as well as to further consequences to be discussed below (in the section on additional features of inflation). Thus, in time another about-face to more expansionary policies must be expected. The system shows a long-run inflationary bias.

The political forces just described for democracies are also present in other political regimes with more or less decentralized economies. The ruling elite must, at least to a certain degree, react to dissatisfaction or unrest among broad segments of the population. Moreover, rulers will certainly be influenced by the situation in different sectors of the economy. It follows that political pressures leading to a long-run inflationary bias of discretionary monetary regimes may be weakened in nondemocratic systems, but these pressures are certainly present. A good example of this truth is provided by Yugoslavia, a socialist market economy where inflation reached about 58.8 percent per month between November 11 and December 21, 1989, and led to a monetary reform on December 18, 1989.

Problems in Controlling the Money Supply and Inflation during the Period of Transition

During the period of transition from a more or less centrally planned to a decentralized market-oriented economic system, there seems to be a systematic bias for inflation if the change is not brought about in one stroke. (For a general discussion of China's reform movement, see Perkins 1988.) Such inflationary tendencies are, however, a danger for the reform movement itself, a movement that the population sees as responsible for the adverse effects of inflation. Functionaries, bureaucrats, and managers who are afraid to lose their privileged political or economic positions, or who are unable to face the new entrepreneurial tasks, grasp and kindle the resulting dissatisfaction. They use the precarious situation to ask for a rethinking of reforms, for a step-by-step reintroduction of direct government interventions, and, finally, even for an abolition of the reform experiments. It is thus of great importance to know the reasons for the inflationary bias of the transition period, so that the inflation can be brought under control as soon as possible.

The dangers just mentioned have become obvious in China. According to a report of the *China Daily* (13 September 1988, p. 2), a "serious inflation panic occurred" in Shanghai at the end of August 1988 "as hundreds of thousands of local citizens," who had withdrawn their bank deposits, "rushed to snap up durable goods and manufactured commodities for daily use." This panic was the consequence of an official inflation figure of about 18 percent and probably of the fact that the older generation still remembers the ravages of hyperinflation under the Kuomintang Regime until 1949.

Events such as these put strong political pressure on political reformers to postpone the freeing of prices still regulated by the government. Even the vice mayor of Shanghai promised, according to the article in *China Daily*, that his government "will organize inspections on prices, finance, and taxes to curb indiscriminate price rises and overcharging." Moreover, "Tianjin leaders visiting local people . . . promised to stabilize prices and punish traders making illegal profits."

Such moves are a setback to reforms, since they result in repressed inflation and a further distortion of relative prices. These tactics are politically understandable, but they hinder the functioning of markets and the efficient allocation of resources. The confusion of stabilizing *relative* prices instead of the price *level* also stands behind such decisions.

It is comforting that the People's Bank of China, the central bank, has taken more constructive steps in response to the above-mentioned events, to "cut back on lending and to tighten the money supply." It linked "interest rates on savings deposits to inflation in a move to quell bank runs." Xinhua (the official news agency) said, "Lending should be restricted to organizations needing funds for key state projects or for buying daily necessities such as grain" (*Mainichi Daily News* 6 September 1988). Moreover, the State Council, China's Cabinet, besides announcing "that the government would hold prices in check for the rest of the year," and that "there would be no radical reforms in prices next year" (*Mainichi Daily*), announced new regulations on holding cash. The regulations took effect on October 1, 1988, and included "setting a ceiling on the amount of cash an institution can keep on hand and on the scale and scope of cash transactions" (*China Daily* 13 September 1988). Though these latter measures are certainly problematic, since they try to limit the growth of money and credit by doubtful regulations instead of higher interest rates, they are preferable to fixing the prices of individual goods.

Let us now consider the institutional reasons behind the inflationary bias during the transition period. Economic reforms, such as those undertaken in China, imply an ever-stronger decentralization of economic decisionmaking and coordination of decisions by markets with freely formed prices. Economic scarcity, as reflected in market prices, determines the direction of production and the use of savings and investment. The decisions of firms, individuals, and managers have to be increasingly motivated by expected profits and incomes. This implies the possibility of losses, of losing one's job, and even of bankruptcy. In the transition period, especially if it is executed in a cautious experimental trial-and-error approach, as in the People's Republic of China, all the necessary elements of a well-functioning decentralized economic system will not have already been introduced. (See Feltenstein and Farhadian 1987 and Herrmann-Pillath 1988 for a discussion the monetary reforms undertaken in China, their background, and the resulting problems.)

In several sectors of the economy, the rights of individuals to make decentralized decisions and the responsibility of these individuals for these decisions are still weak. Prices of essential goods are still fixed by the government and are not allowed to fluctuate according to scarcity (that is, according to excess supply or demand). Financial markets are underdeveloped; firms and cooperatives are not allowed to go bankrupt. Since wages and other input prices may already, under certain conditions, be determined by firms—whereas this condition is not true for prices of essential products—losses of firms may result. These losses must be covered by public subsidies. Thus, in

1983 prices subsidies in China amounted to about 20 percent of total government expenditures (Feltenstein and Farhadian 1987, pp. 142–43). In cases of artificially low prices, bankruptcy would not be warranted since losses are not a symptom of inefficiency. Finally, central and provincial governments, as well as communities, are still accustomed to making plans in terms of real targets, regardless of their abilities to cover the implied expenses out of ordinary revenues. This situation may be worsened by the losses of state- or community-owned firms that must be subsidized; thus, deficits may occur that have to be financed. We are confronted with what Janos Kornai (1971) has called "soft budget restraints," if such losses and deficits are financed by credit expansion and money creation.

Two important facts should be kept in mind concerning these relationships. First, subsidies are inescapable if one wants to keep prices of important goods below equilibrium prices and to prevent queuing, rationing, and black markets. Second, if firms, collectives, and communities are not faced by the threat of bankruptcy, then there is no reason for them to restrict their credit demands and to be cautious with their investments (that is, to keep within their financial means). Even the pressure to work efficiently and to innovate is weakened.

A similar statement holds true for politicians, bureaucrats, and functionaries shaping the decisions of central and provincial governments. Unless they are threatened with sanctions when incurring deficits that do not serve warranted investments that can be financed in free-capital markets, then little fiscal responsibility can be expected.

We have seen many reasons to expect losses of firms and collectives, as well as deficits of communities and of central and provincial governments during the period of transition. During this period, however, capital markets are still underdeveloped and savings may be too small to cover the credit demand resulting from these losses and deficits and from normal net investments. The consequence is an unbearable pressure on the banking system to extend credit not covered by savings, and finally this pressure extends to the central bank, which has to refinance the banks to create money above the needs corresponding to GNP growth. We should note that this pressure is caused by financial requirements stemming from losses, deficits, subsidies, and unwarranted investments (that is, investments that would be unprofitable if prices and interest rates reflected the true scarcity of resources).

It is understandable that banks will succumb to pressures exerted by firms, communities, and governments. If they are not allowed to go bankrupt themselves, and if they are in real need of refinancing by the central bank, why should banks resist the credit demands of influential local and provincial politicians, bureaucrats, and managers? And what else could be done if bankruptcy is not allowed, if the survival of firms and cooperatives is at risk, and if the functioning of local and regional governments and if employment are at stake?

The views of China's leading monetary expert Yang Peixin support our analysis. According to Yang, "The swelling credit, another factor in inflation, exists because banks have issued excessive loans for investment and for operation of the enterprises" (*China Daily* 13 September 1988).

The central bank is in a similar position. How can it resist the demand for refinancing if banks are not allowed to go bankrupt and if deficits of the central government have to be financed? Scarcely any hope exists for such a policy if no strong sanctions against its directors are available when they overshoot monetary targets. But such sanctions rarely are used during the period of transition. On the contrary, members of government and bank members may be sitting on the board of directors of the central bank and pleading for some compromise to save the finances of their governments and banks. This analysis is again in tune with the views of Yang Peixin who stated: "The more the State spends on investment, the more budget deficit there may be. When there is deficit, the Ministry of Finance has to ask for an overdraft from the central bank and the bank has to issue more currency" (*China Daily* 13 September 1988). But if this is true, then inflation and its obnoxious consequences for the reform seem to be inescapable.

What can be done, given these relationships? The above analysis suggests that an immediate introduction of strict monetary control together with freely determined prices for all goods—and the possibility of bankruptcy and tough sanctions against politicians and bureaucrats who are responsible for government deficits and against central bankers who overshoot monetary targets—would be preferable to piecemeal reform.

During my youth I witnessed exactly such an immediate transition in West Germany. After World War II, I observed the breakdown of a planned economy and the transition to a free-market order that laid the foundation for what has been called the German economic miracle. The ideas put into effect in 1948 had been prepared by German neoliberals during the late 1930s. The neoliberals recommended removing price controls at one stroke, together with installing currency reform to stabilize the value of money (Bernholz 1988). This shock treatment was carried out by Ludwig Erhard on July 20,

1948, against the wishes of the Western Allies' military government and the concerns of many Germans. The deregulation of prices, together with sound money, proved to be a resounding success. Black markets, rationing, queuing, and shortages vanished overnight.

If a once-and-for-all approach (as in West Germany in 1948) is not feasible in a country like China where private property rights and decentralized management scarcely existed before the reforms, then subsidies necessitated by price controls and losses of firms stemming from such controls should be covered by ordinary government revenues. Bankruptcies of firms, whose prices are not controlled, should be allowed. For other firms and collectives, sanctions against managers should be introduced in cases of unwarranted losses and investments. Similar sanctions would be necessary for politicians and bureaucrats making decisions leading to deficits of communities and governments, and for directors of the central bank and its branches who overshoot monetary targets and extend credits to cover public deficits. No ministers, government bureaucrats, members of provincial and communal governments, or members of other banks should be allowed on the board of directors of the central bank and of its branches. Board members should not be removable by the government except in case of violation of monetary targets set forth in the monetary constitution.

Some Additional Features of Inflation under Flexible Exchange Rates

This paper has already mentioned that strong medium-term swings of real exchange rates are characteristic of discretionary monetary regimes with flexible exchange rates. The reasons may be manifold. Especially under flexible exchange rates, monetary policies that are more expansive than those of other countries have consequences that are also politically relevant. These consequences can be appreciated by looking at the example of Czechoslovakia in 1914–27 (see Figure 4). After the money supply in Czechoslovakia began expanding relatively more strongly than in the United States, the exchange rate of the dollar moved up more strongly and more rapidly between 1914 and 1921 than did the Czech cost-of-living index compared to that of the United States. Thus, an undervaluation resulted that stimulated exports and discouraged imports, obviously to the advantage of the export sector and domestic industries competing against imports, as well as to the benefit of their employees. Indirectly, the whole economy was stimulated, a fact that explains the political interest in expansionary monetary policies.

FIGURE 4

Inflation and Stabilization in Czechoslovakia, 1914–1927

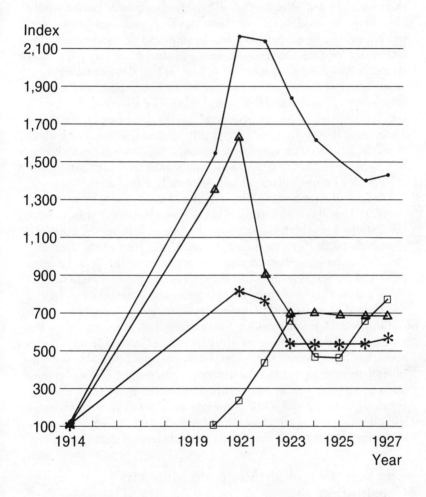

- — Currency in circulation in Czechoslovakia relative to the United States.
- △ Exchange rate for US$.
- ✻ Cost-of-living index for Czechoslovakia relative to the United States.
- ☐ Gold and foreign exchange reserves.

SOURCE: Statistisches Reichsamt (1928 and 1921/22–1934).

The situation changes when the relatively more expansionary policies are ended or (as in the case above) reversed. The exchange rate fell more rapidly than the relative price level (which in other cases can even increase further for some time) from 1921 to 1923. The undervaluation diminished, and purchasing power parity would have been reestablished had these developments not been interrupted, as will be discussed later. In some cases, an overvaluation may result for a time as a consequence of strict monetary policies or strong deflationary expectations. It is clear that developments such as these offset the advantages enjoyed by the export- and import-competing industries and their employees. The advantages can even turn into disadvantages when overvaluation takes place. The adverse effects on foreign trade and the resulting unemployment are additional factors working politically against a continuation of stabilization policies and in favor of introducing another round of expansionary policies before inflation has been totally eliminated.

The case of Czechoslovakia (as depicted in Figure 4) is not exceptional. In fact, about 20 historical cases from 1700 to the present have been studied in which the same qualitative pattern can be observed (Bernholz 1982, 1986; Bernholz, Gärtner, and Heri 1985). Recently the U.S. dollar has followed a similar path against the West German mark and the Swiss franc. After the shift to flexible exchange rates in 1973, and with a relatively more expansionary monetary policy in the United States, the dollar was devalued more strongly in terms of the West German mark or Swiss franc than corresponds to the movement of the relative cost-of-living indices. A sizable undervaluation developed. When the Federal Reserve Board turned to stabilizing inflation after 1979, the dollar recovered strongly. The undervaluation even gave way to an overvaluation of the American currency. From February 1985, U.S. monetary policy became much more expansionary again, which resulted in another strong decrease in the exchange rate of the dollar during the subsequent three years.

The Selection of an Adequate Monetary Constitution

We will now consider the question of which kind of monetary regime to select, if a country such as the People's Republic of China wants to move to a more decentralized and market-oriented system.

At first glance, one might be inclined to propose the introduction of a pure gold or silver standard, or of another commodity standard (which could also consist of a basket of commodities), with the right for everybody to convert bank notes into the commodity (or commodity basket) at a fixed parity. After what has been said before, such a solution would bind and control the monetary policies of the central bank and the government by very specific and definite rules. Long-term value stability in terms of the commodity (or commodity basket) would thus be guaranteed.

Some people might argue that free banking without any regulation by the government and without a central bank would lead to stable money and might even prevent the fluctuations of real magnitudes observed under the gold standard before 1914.

Unfortunately, however, such solutions have to be rejected for countries of small or medium economic weight, given the present situation of the international monetary system. With other countries still using discretionary monetary regimes, a country with less economic weight would have to adopt flexible exchange rates with the outside world. But, as we have shown, in a regime with flexible exchange rates, a more stability-oriented monetary policy compared to the main trading partners will result in overvaluation of the country's own currency, thus hurting export- and import-competing industries. This situation is also true for free banking, since the historical evidence implies that such a system works well only in combination with a commodity standard. Moreover, since important foreign countries such as the United States change the growth rate of their money supply strongly and unpredictably from time to time, the real exchange rates would show wide midterm swings in spite of stable domestic monetary policies implied by the commodity standard. Last, we must expect that a country of small or medium economic weight could not stabilize movements in the relative price(s) of the monetary commodity(ies) by using it (them) as a monetary standard. From these deliberations we see that the international system could move only to a commodity standard with convertibility at a fixed parity if such a step were taken by the United States or the European Monetary System.

Another proposal for a stable monetary regime has been made by Friedman (1968). According to his proposal, there should be a rule for the annual growth rate of the money supply in tune with the growth of real GNP, which would bind the behavior of the monetary authorities. It is well known that some central banks (such as those of the United States, Germany, and Switzerland) have experimented with such pre-announced, but self-imposed targets for monetary growth over the past 15 years. These experiences, however, have not been encouraging, which perhaps is not surprising considering the political-economic forces previously discussed. Respective central banks have, in fact, often changed the kind of money supply to which the growth rate had to be applied. Moreover, they went from point targets to target zones, changed the targets from year to year, and missed targets without later correcting them. This experience is ample proof that they actually did not want to give up their discretion.

But even if an adequate rule that binds monetary authorities could be written into the constitution or into a central bank law, severe difficulties would remain. First, the public would, in contrast to the convertibility rule at fixed parity of a commodity standard, be able neither to test the monetary growth rule nor to determine whether that rule had been actually followed. Second, even if the relevant monetary aggregate, the base period, and the growth rate were explicitly fixed, difficulties would remain. What would happen if the money aggregate selected became less and less relevant because of financial innovations? Moreover, the observance of the rule still could not be monitored by the public. Who then should control a central bank? Another government agency? Or would individuals have a right to sue the government or the central bank and its directors for violating the rule? Given these practical experiences and the connected political problems, it is not surprising that Friedman (1987) has now given up his original proposal.

We conclude that monetary regimes that are based on a commodity standard or on a money growth rule are, at least at the moment, not feasible because of domestic or international difficulties. We seem to be thrown back to a discretionary regime with a central bank whose independence from the government is guaranteed by the constitution or a specific law, and which is obliged legally to guarantee the stability of money. But we have already mentioned that though such a system seems to show a smaller inflationary bias than discretionary systems with dependent central banks, it does not get rid of this bias. These difficulties were foreseen by several German neoliberals even before West Germany accepted the idea of an independent central bank in the early 1950s. Walter Eucken (1952, p. 257), for example, stated that discretion by central bankers should not be allowed "for experience shows that a monetary order allowing managers of monetary policy a free hand trusts them more than is generally warranted. Lack of knowledge, weakness against interest groups and public opinion, false theories, all influence these managers, greatly damaging the task entrusted to them." Friedrich A. Lutz (1935, p. 233) sees one of the advantages of the gold standard in the fact "that an important condition for social life is fulfilled, not although but because little is principally demanded of the human intellect."

What monetary regime can be proposed given these difficulties and the present international disarray of the monetary order? Since recently proposed monetary regimes such as a private competitive monetary system (Hayek 1976) have not been tested in reality, these schemes should not be attempted in a country like China. Otherwise, the far-reaching economic reforms already undertaken or planned could be endangered. A pragmatic second-best proposal has to be envisaged. One such proposal would be to establish an independent central bank and a currency bound by constitutional or legal rules to the least unstable foreign currencies. Therefore, the central bank would be obliged by law to maintain free convertibility of the domestic money for everybody at a fixed exchange rate into one or several foreign currencies. Practically speaking, this arrangement implies selection of a fixed parity vis-à-vis the U.S. dollar, the European Monetary System, or the Japanese yen. The first and the last currencies can, however, scarcely be chosen because of the poor record of U.S. discretionary monetary policies and because of historical reasons. The alternative of pegging the value of Chinese currency to the ECU (or the DM) may be inadvisable, since the volume of trade between China and the European community may be too small to warrant such a decision. Given these difficulties, I would like to propose an approach that has been successfully taken by Finland, Norway, and Sweden. These Nordic countries presently maintain a fixed parity with a basket of the currencies of their main trading partners, which are weighted according to their shares in total trade with these Scandinavian countries.

One remaining difficulty concerns selection of the initial parity. Here it might be advisable to approach such a parity with flexible exchange rates at full convertibility during a limited time. Another possibility would be to begin with a clearly undervalued initial parity. This possibility would imply the risk of some limited inflation in the beginning but would extend some help to export- and import-competing industries.

My proposal also would deal with the possible variation of variables such as real GNP, employment, real interest rates, and real exchange rates caused by monetary factors. According to the monetarists, such fluctuations of real variables are often caused by the discretionary changes of monetary policy of the central bank. In the proposed monetary regime, the central banks' discretion would be strictly limited, since the money supply would be determined mainly by the central bank's obligation to intervene in the foreign exchange market to maintain parity with the basket of foreign currencies. Monetary discretion of the central banks in controlling these currencies might, of course, remain a disturbing factor. But since, and as long as, these policies usually move in different directions, their influence on domestic real magnitudes is weakened. Medium-term overvaluations and undervaluations are also mitigated for the same reasons. Finally, if no devaluations or revaluations of the national money in foreign exchange markets have to be expected because of the fixed parity, then variations of real interest rates resulting from expected devaluations and revaluations are absent.

Exchange Controls, Multiple Exchange Rates, and the Monetary Regime

The monetary constitution binding the value of domestic currency, and thus monetary policy, to a fixed currency basket of the main trading partners requires the absence of exchange controls and multiple exchange rates. Otherwise, no full convertibility would be present for everybody at one legally determined parity with the basket of foreign currencies.

But would abolishing foreign exchange controls and multiple exchange rates be in the national interest, since it means forgoing tight control over the movements of goods, services, and capital? Most economists agree that such a restriction on national sovereignty is warranted from the point of view of national welfare. One of the oldest theorems of economics is that international trade and the resulting international division of production enhances the welfare of the participants. Trade is better than autarchy; and trade protection, exchange controls, and multiple exchange rates decrease welfare, since they lead to a distortion of relative prices and therefore to a misallocation of resources. There are a few exceptions, especially if the dynamics of economic development are taken into account. For example, it may be necessary and even beneficial to protect an industry or consumers against dumping or a foreign monopoly, or to protect infant industries for some initial period. But these are exceptions of limited validity and can be handled better by specific tariffs than by multiple exchange rates or by exchange controls.

It is less well known that strong arguments also exist for free capital movements (that is, selling and buying of claims to and from foreign agents). First, net capital movements are necessary to finance surpluses and deficits in the current-account balance. Second, and more important, only net capital movements allow an intertemporally efficient international allocation of resources, as well as an international coordination of saving and investment and of consumption and production plans. (For example, if saving is high in one country and if the marginal return on investment is higher in another country, then the resources set free from producing consumers' goods in the first country can be used with greater benefit in the latter country than in the former.) With free international capital markets, a net capital inflow would result, bringing about a real transfer of goods and thus a current-account deficit. Similarly, international capital movements allow more efficient consumption plans, which increase the welfare of participating nations.

The absence of barriers to trade and capital movements is also important from a public choice perspective. Krueger (1974) has shown that import restrictions, as well as exchange controls, imply rents for those who have the privilege of importing or receiving foreign exchange. Thus, strong interests are created that work politically to maintain import barriers. Resources are also spent to obtain the privileges and, therefore, are not available for productive uses. In addition, the use of these resources to corrupt politicians and bureaucrats is a strong possibility. Finally, industries protected by trade barriers often do not face enough competition to force them to work efficiently, to become more productive, and to innovate.

German neoliberals in the late 1940s and 1950s were quite adamant in their demands for the removal of trade barriers and the introduction of free convertibility. As Wilhelm Röpke (1950, p. 84), put it:

> To ask for multilateral trade and for free convertibility is thus not just a postulate of liberal ideology but only a different expression for the demand for international integration, as bilateralism and exchange controls are, on the other hand, nothing but a different name for the international disintegration of the economy. The greater the region integrated by multilateralism and convertibility, the greater are the advantages of economic cooperation, which everybody is ready to admit for individual national economies.

Another article by Röpke (1954) is especially interesting because of the public choice perspective taken. He stresses the opposition of vested interests, of the relevant bureaucracy, and of specialists of exchange controls against the introduction of free convertibility. According to Röpke (1954, p. 82):

> The faster and the more decisive a totally new situation is created by abolishing exchange controls, the smaller will be the danger that after the lapse of the period of four years the total economic system, which is decisively determined by convertibility, will be questioned again. . . . If exchange control has once been abolished and if this fact has become part of a new international monetary system, it will be very difficult for a later, more leftist government to question again what has been accomplished by returning to a "left-leaning" course of economic and monetary policy. . . . It follows not only that establishing the market economy securely . . . is the best

basis for convertibility, but *that the passage towards convertibility is the most secure way to anchor the market economy.*

Röpke (1954) stresses the importance of free capital movements and of a system of fixed exchange rates under full convertibility. His final ideal is the return to the gold standard. The road toward this aim is, however, endangered if no actions toward convertibility are taken at this critical juncture. Otherwise, "we are threatened to get back into the vicious circle, in which inflation, exchange controls, and paralysis of international capital movements further each other" (Röpke 1954, p. 80). He concludes with the remark (p. 122), "The abolishment of foreign exchange controls is thus not mainly a question of monetary technique, but a question of social and economic philosophy and the corresponding total economic order."

Sometimes it is argued that the abolition of exchange controls and the deregulation of capital movements would lead to capital flight, devaluation, and inflation because of the higher prices of imported goods. No doubt these problems do pose a real danger in an inflationary situation with a too-generous increase of the money supply as it exists in China today. But ample empirical evidence is available showing that no capital flight and no devaluation and imported inflation result if property rights are safe and if the money supply is under control. In fact, the empirical evidence shows (see, for example, Figure 4) that a stabilization or a reduction of the money supply makes itself first felt in a fall of foreign exchange rates.

When West Germany in the early 1950s rapidly began to dismantle foreign exchange controls so that full convertibility, restored in 1958, was only a last formal step, many people—including some well-known economists—made gloomy predictions about the future. These predictions proved to be unfounded, however, given the security of property rights and the stable monetary policies of the German Bundesbank.

Conclusion

This paper has discussed the role of financial assets, financial intermediaries, financial markets, and stable money for the efficient (intertemporal) coordination of production and consumption plans, the saving and investment, and the efficient allocation of resources. A precondition for these markets and institutions is a stable and predictable value of money and as few disturbances as possible stemming from monetary factors. Given the present disarray of the international monetary order, a monetary regime with an independent central bank and a currency that is freely convertible at a fixed parity with a currency basket has been proposed for countries like China. This basket should contain the currencies of the main trading partners with relatively stable currencies. Since this is only a second-best solution, the task remains to work in the international field for a better monetary order, possibly built on a commodity standard with free convertibility.

A precondition for the introduction in China of a fixed parity and for the removal of import quotas and controls on capital flows and on foreign exchange is the defeat of the present inflation. As mentioned before, between A.D. 1000 and 1500, China experienced several inflationary cycles. But in the 16th century it returned to noninflationary commodity money. Let us hope that China will once again recover its historical capability for monetary reform. Sound money is not sufficient for economic reforms leading to a decentralized market order, but is a necessary condition to complete them successfully.

References

Bernholz, Peter. *Flexible Exchange Rates in Historical Perspective.* Princeton Studies in International Finance no. 49, Princeton University, 1982.
Bernholz, Peter. "Inflation and Monetary Constitutions in Historical Perspective." *Kyklos* 36(1983): 397–419.
Bernholz, Peter. "Ordo-Liberals and the Control of the Money Supply." In *German Neo-Liberals and the Social Market Economy*, pp. 191–215. Edited by Alan Peacock and Hans Willgerodt. Basingstoke and London: Macmillan, 1989.
Bernholz, Peter. "The Implementation and Maintenance of a Monetary Constitution." *Cato Journal* 6 (Fall 1986): 477–511.
Bernholz, Peter; Gärtner, Manfred; and Heri, Erwin. "Historical Experiences with Flexible Exchange Rates: A Simulation of Common Qualitative Characteristics." *Journal of International Economics* 19 (1985): 21–45.
Bresciani-Turroni, Constantino. *The Economics of Inflation.* 1st ed. in Italian, 1931. London: Allen & Unwin, 1937.
Campbell, Colin D., and Dougan, William R., eds. *Alternative Monetary Regimes.* Baltimore: Johns Hopkins Press, 1986.
Chou, Shun-Hsin. *The Chinese Inflation, 1937–1949.* New York: Columbia University Press, 1963.
Deutsche Bundesbank. *Monatsberichte.* 1987.
Dorn, James A., and Schwartz, Anna J., eds. *The Search for Stable Money.* Chicago: University of Chicago Press, 1987.
Eucken, Walter. *Grundsätze der Wirtschaftspolitik.* Edited by Edith Eucken and K. Paul Hensel. Bern and Tübingen: A. Francke and J.C.B. Mohr, 1952.
Feltenstein, Andrew, and Farhadian, Ziba. "Fiscal Policy, Monetary Targets, and the Price Level in a Centrally Planned Economy: An Application to

the Case of China." *Journal of Money, Credit, and Banking* 19, no. 2 (1987): 137–56.

Friedman, Milton. "The Role of Monetary Policy." *American Economic Review* 58 (March 1968): 1–77.

Friedman, Milton. "Monetary Policy: Tactics versus Strategy." In *The Search for Stable Money*, pp. 361–82. Edited by James A. Dorn and Anna J. Schwartz. Chicago: University of Chicago Press, 1987.

Friedman, Milton, and Schwartz, Anna J. *A Monetary History of the United States 1867–1960.* Princeton, N.J.: Princeton University Press, 1963.

Gurley, John G., and Shaw, Edward S. *Money in a Theory of Finance.* Washington, D.C.: Brookings Institution, 1960.

Hayek, Friedrich A. "The Use of Knowledge in Society." *American Economic Review* 35 (September 1945): 519–30.

Hayek, Friedrich A. *Denationalization of Money.* 2nd ed., Hobart Paper no. 70. London: Institute of Economic Affairs, 1976.

Herrmann-Pillath, Carsten. "Das Grundproblem der Geldverfassung in den jüngsten wirtschaftspolitischen Erfahrungen der Volksrepublik China." Unpublished manuscript. Köln: Universität Köln, 1988.

Jiménez, Rafael Olarra. "Evolución Monetaria Argentina." Editorial Universitaria de Buenos Aires, Eudeba, 1968.

Kia-Ngau, Chang. *The Inflationary Spiral. The Experience in China 1939–1950.* New York: MIT Press and John Wiley & Sons, 1958.

Kornai, Janos. *Anti-Equilibrium.* Amsterdam: North-Holland, 1971.

Krueger, Anne O. "The Political Economy of the Rent-Seeking Society." *The American Economic Review* 64 (June 1974): 291–303.

Lutz, Friedrich A. "Goldwährung und Wirtschaftsordnung." *Weltwirtschaftliches Archiv* 1 (1935): 224–51.

Meltzer, Allan H. "Some Evidence on the Comparative Uncertainty Experienced under Different Monetary Regimes." In *Alternative Monetary Regimes*, pp. 122–53. Edited by Colin D. Campbell and William R. Dougan. Baltimore: Johns Hopkins Press, 1986.

Mitchell, Brian R. *European Historical Statistics, 1750–1970.* New York: Columbia University Press, 1976.

Parkin, Michael, and Bade, Robin. "Central Bank Laws and Monetary Policy. A Preliminary Investigation." In *The Australian Monetary System in the 1970s*, pp. 24–39. Edited by M. A. Porter. Melbourne: Monash University, 1978.

Perkins, Dwight Heald. "Reforming China's Economic System." *Journal of Economic Literature* 26 (June 1988): 601–45.

Röpke, Wilhelm. *Ist die deutsche Wirtschaftspolitik richtig?* Stuttgart and Köln: W. Kohlhammer, 1950.

Röpke, Wilhelm. "Wege zur Konvertibilität." In *Die Konvertibilität der Europäischen Währungen*, pp. 67–122. Edited by Gottfried Haberler et al. Erlenbach-Zürich and Stuttgart: Eugen Rentsch, 1954.

Statistisches Reichsamt. *Die Wirtschaft des Auslands 1900–1927.* Berlin: Reimar Hobbing, 1928.

Statistisches Reichsamt. *Statistische Jahrbücher für das Deutsche Reich.* Berlin: Reimar Hobbing, 1921/22–1934.

Tullock, Gordon. "Paper Money. A Cycle in Cathay." *Economic History Review* 9 (June 1956): 237–45.

U.S. Department of Commerce. Bureau of the Census. *Historical Statistics of the United States*. Bicentennial ed. Washington, D.C.: Government Printing Office, 1975.
Warburton, Clark. *Depression, Inflation, and Monetary Policy. Selected Papers 1945–1963*. Baltimore: Johns Hopkins Press, 1966.

COMMENT

FINANCIAL REFORM: A PREREQUISITE FOR DEVELOPMENT
Liu Funian

Banks, currency, and credit play vital roles in a market economy. Over the past few decades, these mechanisms have effectively been used in the West to promote the development of the national economy with recognized success. However, in China and some Eastern European countries, a variety of reforms and trials are being conducted to find a new financial structure, with banks and monetary credit as the main instruments for meeting the needs of the market.

Peter Bernholz's paper provides a systematic treatment of the importance of restructuring the financial system when moving toward a market economy. His paper draws on the historical record of different monetary systems and presents ideas for controlling inflation while decontrolling prices. As such, his study is a useful contribution to the discussion on how to conduct reforms in currency, credit, and banking for a socialist commodity economy.

Shortcomings of the Existing Financial System

For a long time, China has been seeking ways to achieve a balance between supply and demand in the process of developing its economy. Yet, restricted by the traditional confines, the focus seemed to fall on the financial capability of the government and hardly any other footholds were possible. In this respect, we need to examine the experiences of countries with a decentralized financial system in which banks are allowed to play roles of their own.

China's existing financial structure is incompatible, in many respects, with economic development. The main problem is that the mechanism for raising, distributing, and managing capital funds is

The author is Director of the Financial Management Section at the People's Bank of China in Beijing.

outdated. Despite reforms since the founding of the People's Republic, the traditional financial structure is still with us and poses the following problems:

1. There has been rigidity and overcentralization in the management of credit, as shown in the vertical jurisdictional control and the lack of indirect means for managing credits. The structure of capital circulation is suffering from the rigid administrative patterns, which are obvious and are violently clashing with the nascent market economy in this country.
2. The existing structure of financial institutions is not very rational. The state bank's monopoly position is in contradiction to the necessity for competition in the development of our economy.
3. There are too few financial instruments, and financial services are sadly lacking. Little progress has been made in the practice of honoring notes, discounting promissory notes, or forming real markets for stocks and bonds.

All these deficiencies in the existing financial system are holding back the development of the national economy.

Problems of Reform

China faces several difficulties in reforming its financial sector under the conditions of its socialist commodity economy. The first one is the realization of effective macro-management in finance. Since the reform began, there has been some success in employing macrocontrol mechanisms, such as readjusting deposit funds and special deposit accounts. But, on the whole, little has changed. Second, banks for various specialized purposes need to be operated as independent enterprises. At present, these banks are "eating out of the big rice pot" of the central bank, and individual enterprises are "eating out of the big rice pot" of the specialized banks. Third, raising capital from the market has not been realized. Some progress has been made in developing and coordinating financial markets, but no effective market mechanisms for issuing shares and bonds, or for borrowing short-term capital, have been developed.

The goal for us to achieve, under the conditions of a socialist commodity economy, is the establishment of a socialist financial system that has vigor, flexibility, and operationability. In other words, it should be one with a central bank as the leader and with specialized banks forming the main body, including insurance and other financial institutions with a clear division of labor.

As a prerequisite for financial reform, China will have to reinforce and perfect its finance laws. I readily share the view of Bernholz that the independence of the central bank from the government must be guaranteed by the Constitution and special laws. Moreover, the central bank must be held accountable by law for maintaining stability of the currency. Only by so doing, I think, can the financial regulating bodies at various levels get rid of the interference from the government. These bodies can then function normally to guarantee the relative stability of currency and to decrease and alleviate inflation. It, therefore, looks more urgent and indispensable for us to study earnestly how the Western countries, under the conditions of the market economy, make good use of currency, credit, and banks, and for us to draw on their experiences.

COMMENT

ON THE IMPORTANCE OF DECENTRALIZING MONEY
George A. Selgin

Peter Bernholz argues convincingly that a decentralized economy without sound money cannot be expected to function well. His claim is of crucial importance because it is all too easy for economic instability coming in the wake of liberal reforms to be blamed on the market, when the real culprit is a faulty monetary system. China's current economic reforms are threatened by this very misunderstanding: The deregulation of prices has been accompanied by inflation, which in turn has been pointed to by conservatives as an argument for restoring price controls.[1] The real cause of inflation—the failure of China's monetary institutions to limit adequately the supply of credit—remains unaddressed.

Indeed, I would take Bernholz's claim even further and argue that central planning itself has been embraced by so many countries partly because market systems have been plagued by monetary instability, which has wrongly been seen as the inherent weakness of such systems. The truth is that, rather than being a defect of the marketplace, monetary instability arises whenever money, instead of being managed by market forces, is centrally administered. An economic system with a centrally administered money supply is not a pure market system.

This realization is why I think it necessary to go beyond the recommendations made by Bernholz. For although I fully share his opinion that markets cannot function without sound money, I question his suggestion that sound money can be secured by nonmarket means,

The author is Assistant Professor of Economics at the University of Georgia and formerly a Lecturer in Economics at the University of Hong Kong.

[1]Misunderstanding is not the only problem. Many persons in China also have a vested interest in continuing price controls and cheap credit. These persons may understand that price reform is not the root cause of inflation, but it is not in their interest to admit this.

that is, by a central bank issuing currency convertible into a "currency basket" unit. If we are to reject the idea of central planning in general in favor of markets, then ought we not to reject central planning of the money supply as well?

The Inherent Instability of Central Banking

It is important in facing this question to step back for a moment to consider the historical origins and functions of central banks. They are not a free-market institution but a remnant of mercantilist policy. As such, they are designed to serve the interests of a ruling elite, and not those of the public as a whole, by allowing the government to transfer resources to itself by means of currency debasement and inflation. The story behind China's first central bank, erected by the Nationalist government, illustrates well the overriding concern for state finance (at the expense of monetary stability) that has been the true essence of central banking throughout most of the world even in the 20th century.[2] Whether a central bank is nominally private or is government owned makes, in this regard, very little difference. Either way, it amounts to a dangerous and unjustified form of monopoly privilege.

That privilege is the reality of central banking. The popular view of central banks as essential vehicles for monetary stability is, on the other hand, a rationalization after the fact, with only the flimsiest connection to the historical record. It is true that central banks must occasionally serve as lenders of last resort. But it is by no means clear that they would have to do so if numerous banks participated as equals in the issuance of (convertible) notes. The peculiar strength and confidence that central banks often enjoy is a consequence of special privileges that they have usurped from would-be rivals, which have been rendered correspondingly weaker. Moreover, central banks are capable of far more serious *mismanagement* of the money supply than would take place in any system of competing banks of issue. It is at least an open question whether their presence makes any net contribution to stability; my own view, which I have defended at length elsewhere (Selgin 1988), is that it does not.

Even if one disregards such considerations, the evidence provided by Bernholz himself is sufficient to show why no one should continue to place confidence in central banks. I refer in particular to his obser-

[2]After this paper was presented in Shanghai, an elderly gentleman in the audience made a long comment in which he stated that "it must be conceded that the main purpose of central banks has been to exploit the people." The speaker, it turns out, was a deputy minister of finance during the Nationalist era.

130

vation that "there has not been a single case of a currency freely manipulated by its government or central bank since 1700 which enjoyed price stability for at least 30 years running. This has been true even for 'autonomous' central banks." Nor do I think that any simple monetary rule can be relied on to keep a central bank in line. To take the case of a price-level stabilization rule, which Bernholz favors, the tendency of the authorities to abandon such a rule will occasionally be overwhelming and even justified, as during a severe negative supply shock.

If a price-stability rule must be abandoned periodically, it is unlikely to remain in force for very long. A theoretically better alternative, I think, would be for the monetary authority to stabilize a measure of the aggregate, final demand for goods. But this rule would be placed under tremendous political pressure at times of rapidly improving productivity when it would lead to falling prices of goods, which many would (wrongly) interpret as a symptom of depression. My point is that no simple monetary central plan (for that is what a monetary rule really is) can be relied on to provide sound money in the long run. This point becomes even more apparent if one considers other sources of monetary instability that exist only because currency is not competitively supplied, including instability stemming from unaccommodated changes in the public's relative demand for currency.

Toward a Free-Market Monetary Regime

Thus, if free markets are to work properly, money itself must be denationalized and decentralized. Private, competing banks must be allowed to issue notes in place of government currency, and no bank should have such powers and privileges as would allow it unilaterally to alter the aggregate money supply. Bernholz claims that such systems "have hardly been tried." But a number of recent studies show that this is not the case. The Scottish free-banking system is the most famous example (see White 1984). Canada, New England, Sweden, and New Zealand should also be mentioned as places where freedom in banking and note issue contributed to monetary regimes of remarkable stability, even relative to other gold standard systems.

China also had a free-banking era. Not coincidentally, this era was during the Ch'ing Dynasty from 1644 to 1911, which was the only extended period in China's history during which it did not experience substantial depreciation of its currency. The Ming dynasty abandoned the use of fiat money midway through the 15th century and—except for two brief episodes in the 1650s and 1850s—the

Manchus also refrained entirely from issuing their own paper money, while leaving private banks entirely free to do so. In some places (such as Shanghai and Fuzhou), the private currency systems that developed were quite sophisticated.

It is still, as Bernholz says, "an unresolved question why" China should have temporarily abandoned using the printing press.[3] But what is resolved, in my opinion, is that present-day governments in China and elsewhere will not abandon using the printing press unless it is taken away from them entirely and the business of producing currency is divided among competing, private banks.

The need for China to resist slavishly imitating economic arrangements and institutions of the capitalist West is often stressed by various commentators on China's economic reforms. Central banking should be high on the list of such institutions of Western origin that policymakers in China should unhesitatingly reject.

References

Selgin, George A. *The Theory of Free Banking: Money Supply under Competitive Note Issue.* Totowa, N.J.: Rowman & Littlefield, 1988.

White, Lawrence H. *Free Banking in Britain: Theory, Experience, and Debate, 1800–1845.* New York: Cambridge University Press, 1984.

[3]A tentative explanation is that previous administrations abused the power of paper money finance to the point where the economy became demonetized. This demonetization rendered inflation impotent as a means for gaining revenue, while also making it necessary for taxes to be collected in kind. The encouragement of sound money was necessary to remonetize the economy and to permit an efficient form of taxation.

6

RECENT DEVELOPMENTS IN CHINA'S FINANCIAL SECTOR: FINANCIAL INSTRUMENTS AND MARKETS

Christine I. Wallich

Introduction

Since 1978 China has undertaken a bold process of reform of its economic system. Reforms began first in the rural economy, with the comprehensive restructuring of rural institutions and the introduction of a "production responsibility system" for farming. This initial reform made the household the fundamental unit responsible for management and production in agriculture, as distinct from the pre-reform period when the commune had this role.

Since 1984, significant reforms have also been undertaken in urban areas. These reforms stress changes in enterprise management, the financial sector, and management of the macroeconomy. The reform program has stressed decentralized decisionmaking and the need to increase economic efficiency. Its major elements consist of the development of state enterprises as independent units with financial accountability; a shift in emphasis in the form of the planning mechanism from mandatory planning to indicative planning; and the development and reforms of the tax, financial, and banking systems.

Development of the reforms and of the institutional changes and institutional building required to underpin the reforms remains incomplete, but significant changes have already been made. A system of enterprise income taxation was introduced in 1984 in lieu of the previous system in which enterprise earnings were transferred to the state. In the financial sector, the first steps were also taken in 1984, with the separation of China's mono-bank system and its commercial and central banking functions. The People's Bank of China was established as China's central bank and three other spe-

The author is the Principal Economist in the China Department at the World Bank. The views and interpretations in this article are those of the author and should not be attributed to the World Bank, to its affiliated organizations, nor to any individual acting on its behalf.

cialized state-owned banks were established to undertake commercial banking business. These were the People's Construction Bank of China (PCBC), the Industrial and Commercial Bank of China (ICBC), and the Agricultural Bank of China (ABC). The Bank of China, the country's specialized foreign exchange bank, was established some three decades ago. Rural and urban cooperative banks have also emerged. A number of Chinese-style investment banks have been established to sponsor foreign investment and to attract equity investments. Finally, a small number of foreign banks have been licensed and are now permitted to undertake a limited range of banking business such as foreign exchange lending, discounting of bills, and limited deposit taking. Each activity represents a step toward the emergence of a broader financial market to provide alternative financing sources for the government, enterprises, and financial institutions themselves.

Further development of the financial sector along these lines is seen as helping to bolster economic growth and efficiency. In the banking sector, to further the trend toward more decentralized decisionmaking and "self-responsibility" of banks—a reference to the need to make banks more commercially oriented—the emphasis on improvement of credit analysis, loan-structuring, and financial management is expected to continue. The government has also begun to liberalize interest rates for purposes of macroeconomic management, a change from the previous system of administered rates. As this trend develops, it will increasingly lead financial institutions to be able to compete for funds at market-related levels and to lend at competitively determined spreads.

In the nonbank financial sector more generally, reforms are likely to mean a growing number of financial intermediaries such as the aforementioned investment banks that have been licensed by provincial governments, as well as pension funds and insurance companies. These institutions will increasingly compete for funds among themselves and with the banking system, helping to reduce the costs of intermediation as specialization takes place. The larger number of intermediaries can help to facilitate a more efficient allocation of credit and investment as elements of an integrated financial system that offers competing options for savers.

This article highlights the reforms that are taking place in one small part of China's financial sector—the nonbank market sector. The first section describes some of the new financial intermediaries, the nature of their operations, and the scope of their business. The second section describes the market for nonbank financial instruments and outlines the issuing activity, the characteristics of the market, the issue procedures, and the instruments themselves and how they differ from similar forms of the same security in foreign markets. Finally, the article offers some hypotheses regarding the future development of China's financial markets. It concludes with a discussion of some major requisites for the continued smooth development of China's financial markets.

Emerging Nonbank Institutions

Most financial sector activity in China is still accounted for by the banking system. As is the case in many developing countries, banks were the first financial institutions to emerge. The banking system may dominate the financial sector for extended periods, with virtually all financial activity in the economy intermediated by the banking system; however, a nonbank financial sector has emerged in China and is growing rapidly. While the market share of the four specialized banks is very large, nonbank institutions are increasingly important.[1] Such nonbank financial institutions include the People's Insurance Company (PIC), the Chinese-style investment banks or trust and investment companies (TICs), and the recently established pension and social security funds. Leasing companies, most of them partly foreign owned, but some also sponsored by provincial governments, have also sprung up. Figure 1 indicates the broad outlines of the market share (in terms of percentage of total assets of domestic intermediaries) between 1985–87 by type of financial institution.

In terms of market share, the TICs are perhaps the most important of the new nonbank financial sector institutions. By the end of 1988, more than 700 of such institutions existed at the local and national level, with different charters, ranges of activity, and scopes of business. These institutions have been developed to act as intermediaries for lending and investment activities outside the banking system. Most are sponsored and wholly owned by central, provincial, or local governments. Some are subsidiaries of specialized banks. Most significant of these institutions are the international trust and investment companies (ITICs), which raise foreign resources through bond issues, foreign borrowing, and foreign exchange deposits from the enterprise sector. They also raise domestic resources through loans from specialized banks, through domestic bonds, and by other means. The objective of the ITICs is to identify and to finance foreign direct investment projects and to attract equity capital to China. They

[1]Estimates are that the specialized banks including the state development bank, People's Construction Bank of China, and the rural and urban cooperative banks mobilize 90 percent or more of the financial savings generated in China.

FIGURE 1
MARKET SHARE OF FINANCIAL INTERMEDIARIES
(1985–87 AVERAGES)

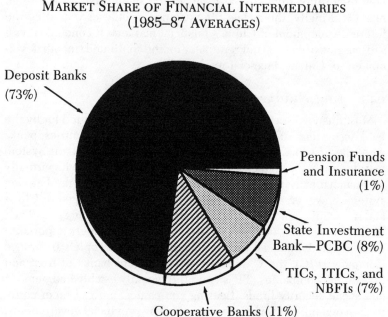

Deposit Banks
(73%)

Pension Funds
and Insurance
(1%)

State Investment
Bank—PCBC (8%)

TICs, ITICs, and
NBFIs (7%)

Cooperative Banks (11%)

SOURCES: Chinese Financial Press; *Statistical Yearbook of China, 1987;*
"Assets and Liabilities of People's Banks in China."

achieve this through participation in joint ventures and through
direct lending.

The best known of the TICs are the ones with an international
orientation such as China International Trust and Investment Company (CITIC), founded in 1979; the Shanghai International Trust
and Investment Company (SITCO); and the China Investment Bank
(CIB), established in 1981. The CIB finances primarily small- and
medium-sized domestic ventures, while CITIC and SITCO focus
more on Chinese-foreign joint ventures. The ITICs do not at present
undertake investment banking activities such as underwriting (their
activities in this area are largely confined to brokering private place-
ment-type financings on behalf of enterprise clients). Balance-sheet
assets are broadly limited to bank deposits, loans, bonds, and equity
investments in Chinese and joint-venture enterprises and in owned
real estate. However, as their market share and role in intermediation
grow, these institutions represent a potentially important channel of
funds to the securities markets (as well as to users of this market).

The market share and financial intermediation of the insurance sector remain very small at present. The People's Insurance Company is not, strictly speaking a new financial institution. It was originally established in the early 1960s but emerged in the 1980s as a force in providing insurance of various types, including investable long-term insurance such as life insurance. Pension insurance is another of its products and was developed for nonstate enterprises that are not governed by the state-sponsored system of retirement pensions provided by enterprises. This insurance is essentially an annuity, under which PIC collects monthly premiums from collective enterprises and undertakes to pay the enterprises' subsequent pension expenses. Until recently, PIC's assets were held only as deposits in the banking system. As a major institutional investor, the role of the PIC is, therefore, still limited. More recently, however, the investment guidelines of the PIC have been broadened to include enterprise bonds. In the future, the PIC and other similar institutions will be potentially more significant intermediaries.

Another emerging institutional intermediary is represented by the, as yet, small pension or social security funds. These funds are organized on a municipal basis under local government supervision and have emerged as enterprises have sought to pool the risks (and the demographic burden) of their social security responsibilities. Until recently, China's social security system operated by requiring each state-owned enterprise to be responsible for paying the retirement pensions of its retired employees. Since the pension obligation represents a differential burden across old and new enterprises—or across enterprises according to the skill and age composition of their workers—this pooling of risks has tended to equalize risks. These pension funds collect resources from enterprises in their jurisdiction and undertake to pay the enterprises' pension expenses. The funds now appear to operate on a pay-as-you-go basis with few investable resources. Over time, however, the pension funds could become more important, with the potential for a larger role as intermediaries.

In sum, China's financial sector is now more diversified than in the past. The market share of these new intermediaries is still small overall; however, as their resource mobilization potential deepens, these institutions could play a growing role in financial intermediation. Potentially, they can become major intermediaries and channelers of funds in the financial market.

The Market for Financial Instruments

In China the dominant role of banks in the financial sector is also evidenced in the composition of financial assets, with the bulk of all financial assets having their source in the banking system and with very little in the way of equity, fixed income, or other types of securities existing in the market. Thus, the financial market consists largely of deposit-type instruments. Experimentation has been considerable, however, and a still-narrow but broadening range of nondeposit instruments exists in China's financial market. Most of these instruments could be characterized as fixed-income securities, not unlike bonds. Since 1981, the central government has issued Treasury bonds, local governments have raised funds using bonds, and state-owned enterprises have issued fixed-income securities. State-owned enterprises have also issued so-called stocks, but these have only limited characteristics of equities, given the need to clarify ownership issues. Finally, China's banking and financial institutions have issued so-called financial bonds. Within the money market, an increasing number of short-term instruments have been introduced. Trade bills, which can be discounted in some of the financial centers in China's major cities, have begun to circulate, reflecting the need for trade credit. In addition, commercial paper—with 3- to 6-month maturities—has been issued. Figure 2 shows the approximate share of these financial instruments, and the following paragraphs describe them in more detail.

Government Securities

First to emerge, and certainly the most well-known type of security, are central government bonds. First issued in 1981, Treasury bonds are also quantitatively the most important fixed-income security in China's financial market. Government bonds are available as the result of the changing manner in which the government's fiscal deficit is financed. In the past, as in many developing countries, the government's fiscal deficits were financed almost entirely by borrowing from the central bank or the domestic banking system. In 1981, more than 85 percent of the overall budget deficit was financed in this way. Since then, however, reliance on the central bank and the banking system has become more limited, as Treasury bonds were introduced to provide nonbank domestic financing. The government now increasingly issues bonds and finances its fiscal deficit through the bond market. Thus, in 1985 Treasury bonds covered just under half of the government's financing requirement. By 1987 there was a further decline in central-bank borrowing, with Treasury bonds covering more than half of the government's total financing needs.

As the government has increased its use of bond financing, it has also broadened its vehicles for placing these securities. In 1981, the first year they were introduced, the government issued about ¥4

FIGURE 2
FINANCIAL ASSETS BY TYPE OF INSTRUMENT
(1985–87 AVERAGES)

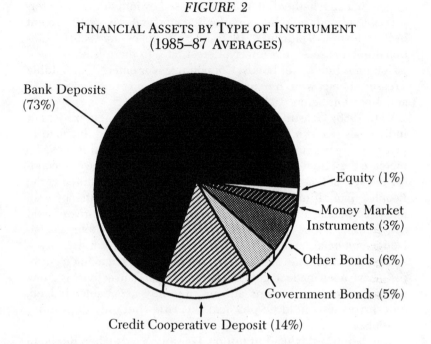

Bank Deposits (73%)

Equity (1%)

Money Market Instruments (3%)

Other Bonds (6%)

Government Bonds (5%)

Credit Cooperative Deposit (14%)

SOURCE: *China Daily* (selected issues); *State Statistical Yearbook, 1987;* "Receipts and Payments of People's Banks."

billion of Treasury bonds. These bonds were sold entirely to government institutions and enterprises; purchases were mandatory and were allocated according to purchase quotas on the basis of each institution's net income after tax. Individuals were first permitted to purchase Treasury bonds in 1982. Purchases were made from the allotment to an individual's enterprise, so that, in effect, enterprises reallocated their purchase quota among their staff. By 1984 such individual holdings accounted for about 50 percent of the total volume outstanding. Since then the issue volume has been increased and individuals now hold about two-thirds of the total volume of bonds issued.

Finally, as the government has sought to broaden the placement of Treasury securities, it has also taken steps to make Treasury bond operations more flexible and to increase the attractiveness of government securities. In 1985 the bonds' maximum maturity was shortened from 10 years to 5 years, while the 1988 issue had a maturity of 3 years. Coupon rates have been increased and continue to differ depending on whether bonds are purchased by individuals or enterprises. For bonds held by individuals, coupon rates were 10 percent in 1988, up from 9 percent in 1985 and 8 percent before 1985. Institutional holders receive a lower interest rate, so there is an implicit tax on their holding of bonds. Coupon rates for enterprises holding Treasury bonds were 6 percent in 1988, up from 5 percent in 1985 and 4 percent before 1985.

Until 1988, Treasury bonds were nonnegotiable for enterprises or individuals out of a concern, in part, that these would fluctuate in price and leave households with unexpected capital losses. To increase their liquidity and to compensate for the absence of secondary markets at that time, Treasury bonds could be discounted at the People's Bank if individuals holding them had an emergency cash need. To increase the bonds' effective liquidity, enterprises could use Treasury bonds as collateral when borrowing at the four specialized commercial banks. Since 1988, certain Treasury bill issues—such as the 1985 issue maturing in 1990 and expected to trade above par—have been made negotiable for individuals and activity is growing. Enterprise-held bonds are not presently negotiable; indeed, enterprises now hold no physical securities but only depository receipts.

Simple interest is paid in full on Treasury bonds when the bond matures, with no interim interest payments. The bonds are thus not unlike zero-coupon bonds or discount securities, with the distinction that they are sold at par and redeemed with cumulative simple interest. Simple interest makes the effective compound yield to maturity well below the quoted coupon rate.[2]

Local Government Bonds

To date, the use of debt finance by local governments in China has been limited, and until 1984 local government borrowing appears to have been prohibited. Very few local governments, either municipalities or provinces, have thus far issued bonds directly. Local governments more typically borrow through provincially owned investment companies. Among those that have done so directly is Guangzhou Municipality,[3] whose Finance Department first issued bonds in 1984 to raise some 30 percent of the funds required for a key electricity

[2]A 5-year bond with a 10 percent coupon (paying 10 percent simple interest) would sell at par and mature at 150. This is akin to a zero-coupon bond selling at 66 and maturing at 100, for an (annual) yield to maturity of 8.2 percent.
[3]Guangzhou Municipality is one of the cities in China with the status of a province, which enables the city to undertake activities normally reserved for provincial government and gives it special tax status.

project in the public investment program. Financial characteristics of the bonds were similar to those of Treasury bonds, with the additional feature that besides the fixed coupon, enterprise bond holders also received an entitlement to an electricity quota. This quota enabled bond holders to obtain electricity—a commodity subject to allocation under the state plan and typically in short supply—in larger amounts than those allocated to them under the plan. Purchased competitively, these bonds were bought primarily by enterprise users of electric power. A second bond, issued by the municipality, raised funds for the expansion of a cement plant, with bond holders receiving a combination yield comprising a fixed coupon and a quota for ensured supplies of cement. This structure of coupon plus quota has some of characteristics of a bond-cum-warrant, where the warrant (which may or may not be detachable) entitles the holder to goods, rather than purchases of additional securities, at a set price.

More commonly, as noted, it is not the local government itself but an investment company or other financial institution associated with the local government that issues bonds. Frequently these bonds support government-sponsored projects and are guaranteed by the corresponding level of government. One such example is the Guangdong International Trust and Investment Company (GITIC)—the ITIC, or investment bank, owned by Guangdong Province raising funds for major projects in the province. As in the case of Treasury bonds, the interest and principal on these bonds is paid at maturity, and coupon rates depend on whether bonds are held by individuals or enterprises. Typically, provincial or local bonds may be purchased by any resident of the locality and by Chinese who live overseas. The bonds may be registered (at the request of the purchaser) and, if registered (like Treasury bonds), can be replaced if lost. When these bonds were introduced, there was no formal secondary market in local government securities. To provide liquidity, these financial bonds typically could be sold back (put) to the issuing institution at face value. Thus, the issuer did not have guaranteed access to the funds for the duration of the maturity under this arrangement. With the development of financial markets and with secondary market trading by individuals being permitted since 1988, this practice appears to have been discontinued, with liquidity being provided through secondary markets.

Enterprise Securities

In the period before 1984 the assortment of financial instruments that Chinese collective and state enterprises could use to raise money for new projects was very limited. Essentially, Chinese enterprises were limited to bank finance and funds supplied to them through the government budget. Since 1984, however, the financing sources of enterprises have become substantially more diversified. Retained earnings now play an important role, accounting for about 50 percent of investment financing in China. This development is a result of the tax reforms that allow enterprises to retain their net-of-tax profits instead of turning profits over to the budgetary authorities. Supplementing these retained earnings and bank loans, enterprises also are now able to use an array of different financing instruments, including bonds and bond-like "share" instruments. While no data are currently available on the share that such instruments represent in financing for enterprises, these securities have been issued by state enterprises as well as by rural and urban collectives.

Enterprise shares are typically a hybrid type of security. Although known in China as "shares," these securities have few of the more common characteristics of shares in the Western financial markets—such as voting rights, ownership status, or a claim on the liquidated value of the enterprise. In essence, these shares are entitlements to participate in the profitability of an enterprise, but only as a junior claimant (that is, after taxes, bank loans, and other obligations are met). Except for the latter, the securities are not unlike nonvoting, preferred shares. Unlike common stock, these shares are usually dedicated to financing a specific enterprise project, and interest payments are made out of the project's cash flow, not the cash flow of the enterprise as a whole. Usually such shares pay a fixed base return (for example, at 8 percent) and an excess return related to the profitability of the project that was financed.

These bonds or shares typically have a short maturity (2 to 3 years) and pay an interest rate considerably higher than the rate on 1-year individual savings deposits, but less than the rate on 3-year deposits. A ceiling of 15 percent was fixed in 1985 by the regulatory authorities on the interest or dividend payable and this ceiling remains in place. Enterprise bonds or shares may be bought by the employees of the enterprise itself; these bonds have elements of employee profit-sharing and stock-ownership programs. Bonds also may be purchased by the public and by other enterprises, often with a view toward gaining access to guaranteed input supplies in exchange for their equity stake. Individuals trade their bonds or shares in an informal secondary market and these bonds appear to be negotiable.

Financial Institution Bonds

Financial institutions in China—specialized banks as well as investment and trust companies—generate the bulk of their domestic resources for lending both from deposits and from loans from the central bank. For some specialized banks, budgetary loans continue to play a role. Increasingly, however, specialized banks have issued bonds as an alternative way of mobilizing funds. These bonds, called "financial bonds," represent 5 percent or less of the banks' total liabilities. Financial bonds have many traditional characteristics of a fixed-income security, with a coupon that is usually payable annually.

Bonds issued by financial institutions traditionally offered significantly higher interest rates than those institutions paid on their sight deposits, which is consistent with the lesser liquidity and generally longer maturity of such deposits. However, in September 1988 the central bank authorized interest rates on deposits held longer than 3 years to be indexed to the rate of inflation, a step that raised the rates carried on such deposits to 17 percent for 1988. Whether bond rates and share yields will be permitted to rise above this level is uncertain. Like enterprises' bonds, funds raised by bond issues tend to be dedicated or segregated for specific uses. For example, the proceeds of ABC's bond issues go toward financing projects of rural and village enterprises, and borrowers pay a correspondingly higher interest rate than ABC's normal lending rate for long-term loans. The People's Construction Bank of China, the bank specialized in lending to state enterprises, also issued key construction bonds in 1987 and 1988 to finance major infrastructure projects of national importance.

Institutional Features

At this stage of development in China's security markets it may be useful to analyze the characteristics and features that distinguish China's approach from that of more traditional bond and share markets. An unusual feature of China's financial system is that short-term instruments—money market instruments and the like—until recently were almost non-existent. Unlike other countries, where the bond markets develop from the gradual extension of maturities of short-term instruments as conditions ripen for financial deepening, in China the reverse can be observed. The reasons may include the following: the liquidity of the banking system, plus the banks' consequent flexibility in providing short-term and trade-related credit as well as working capital; the liquidity of the enterprises themselves; and, until recently, the near absence of inflation, which made long-term markets relatively free from the risk of inflation. Among other distinguishing features are the limits on the transferability of securities, the segmentation of securities markets, the dedicated financing approach, and the issue methods and underwriting mechanisms.

Negotiability

Until 1987 there were strong restrictions on the transferability of most financial instruments in China, including bonds. Except for securities issued by the government, financial instruments issued by enterprises or financial institutions could not formally be bought and sold after their original issue. That restriction, however, began to change in 1988. As noted, the 1985 Treasury bond issue is formally negotiable for individuals. In addition, individuals can transfer seasoned enterprise and financial bonds between themselves in a variety of over-the-counter markets. Enterprises' holdings of securities are not formally tradable at present. Even if they were, transfers between individuals and enterprises would be difficult to envisage as long as the differing coupon rates and the price floor prevail and as long as the use of depository receipts is continued.

The transactions described above take place in a dealer or face-to-face market. Many TICs and specialized banks have set up a trading counter, and some 60 of China's major cities now have exchanges. Although the bulk of the transactions taking place appear to be sales and new-issue activity (new securities issues are advertised in the Chinese financial press, TV, and radio, and by flyers), trading is now growing. Buyers and sellers may be brought together by an agent, and buy-and-sell orders for securities can be held by an agent if no opposite party is immediately found. Agents do not currently hold a "book." Thus, what appears to be emerging is a combination of a face-to-face market operating in and around an exchange, along with a localized dealer network. In view of the communications difficulties, this approach is likely to continue for some time.

Market Segmentation

Interest rate ceilings are a second feature of China's bond securities. Most bonds have been issued subject to a 15 percent ceiling on the coupon rate offered. With inflation relatively stable until recently (at between 7 and 9 percent), this ceiling represented a generous return in relation to deposit instruments. Indeed, one reason for such ceilings was to prevent bonds from being excessively attractive when compared to bank deposits, thus drawing funds from or disintermediating the existing banking institutions. With interest rates on longer-term deposits indexed since 1988 to inflation, these financial instruments are increasingly noncompetitive. While the thinness of markets makes representative prices difficult to observe, in markets where trading can be tracked (such as the Treasury-bond market for individuals), there are indications that bond prices have fallen to bring yields up—if not to a level of deposits, then to well above their nominal coupon level.

Market activity is, therefore, increasingly leading to the emergence of an integrated spectrum of interest rates in the market with the clear, albeit slow, emergence of a yield curve. As recently as 1986 the securities markets were strongly segmented, with very limited integration of rates across maturity sectors or across financial instruments. Yield spreads based on sector, issuer, or issue type, however, have not emerged in a consistent fashion.

Dedicated Financing

A third characteristic of China's financial instruments is that, except for securities issued by the central government, bonds are often issued for and associated with a specific project. Whether the Agriculture Bank's bonds finance projects of rural enterprises, municipal governments' bonds finance a public utility, or an enterprise's bonds finance expansion of its plant, in most cases the cash-flow from the project at hand is earmarked and dedicated to generate resources for repayment of the bond. Bond issues thus tend to be project specific (although no formal mortgages are set up and bonds are not collateralized) rather than enterprise specific. Although there are no precedents to look to, the implication of this financing structure is that if the project performs poorly, the bond holder may lose, even though the enterprise's overall financial health remains good. Similarly, this project-backed approach allows a state enterprise, which may be incurring losses on some activities because of China's distorted price system, to protect its bond holders' interests. Indeed, this kind of segregated finance is usually associated with a firm whose credit may not be good and which, on the strength of its overall financial position, may not be able to obtain financing. In municipal financing, for example, revenue bonds, which commit the income stream of a project, are a way of raising resources when the municipality might not otherwise be able to obtain financing on acceptable terms through general obligation bonds. In the long run, however, bonds that commit the entire income stream of an enterprise are usually a more powerful way of raising funds.

Issuing and Underwriting

A final characteristic of the market for financial instruments that may be of interest is its issue procedures. Financial bonds in China are frequently sold directly by the issuing entity. All major banks issue their own securities. In the past this practice was also true of enterprise securities. Because these securities were sold, in most cases, to employees of the enterprise, intermediaries such as an underwriter or sales agent were not required. Thus, the issue procedures are similar to commercial paper issuance—which bypasses the underwriter. Increasingly, however, the same financial institutions are getting into the underwriting business, placing bonds on behalf of enterprise clients and collecting a small fee. The service is more accurately characterized as "placement on a best-efforts basis." The issuing entity typically sets both price and yield; since the issue price is not competitively determined, the issuer accepts the subscription level that emerges. Auction-style issuance is as yet unknown.

Future Market Directions

Further expansion of the securities market can be envisaged along a number of lines. Greater use of bond finance could be made by all entities outlined in the first section of this paper. Local governments could use bonds to finance revenue-earning infrastructure projects such as roads, bridges, water supply, housing development, and the like. To ensure that these projects will be adequately structured, governments could set up earmarked revenue accounts such as would be established for revenue bonds. User fees could be charged to defray capital and operating expenses, and these fees could be set at levels sufficient to meet interest and repayment requirements.

Enterprises currently issue a hybrid security with characteristics of both bonds and equities; true equity finance does not yet exist. The need for risk capital in China is clear. It is equally clear that the government budget cannot be the sole source of funds for enterprises that (along with retained earnings) effectively represent equity or risk-cushioning finance in market economies. It is not possible to deal with the complex subject of ownership in this brief article; however, in this context the institutional investors such as the PIC and others could be compatible with the socialist concept of ownership by the whole people and could support equity development. Chinese enterprises clearly also need bond finance as both an alternative and a supplement to bank borrowing and equity in enterprise capital budgets.

Financial institutions could also further use fixed-income securities to enhance their liability structure, to mobilize more resources than is possible with deposits and government loans, and to limit the risks of maturity transformation. For them and for the TICs, longer-maturity bonds can finance increased long-term lending. Finally, the central government can continue to use bonds to finance deficits in a non-inflationary way.

Demand for such financial instruments can derive from the emergence of new intermediaries and from further development of the financial institutions described. In most developing countries, as income rises the breadth as well as the depth of the financial system grows in response to savers' needs and borrowers' requirements. Such a phenomenon could be expected in China as well. Thus, institutions such as the TICs, the leasing companies, the PIC, and the emerging pension funds are potentially important long-term suppliers of finance to the economy. The traditional banking system, as it develops, may also look to marketable liquid securities as a means of portfolio diversification.

To function effectively, the financial sector, the emerging institutions, and their activities will need supervision. Bank supervision regulations have already been drafted and the supervisory role of the People's Bank, China's central bank, has been considerably strengthened. While previously PBC's focus had been on economic supervision—supervision to ensure that bank's lending was consistent with the Plan—its orientation is now increasingly, and more appropriately, one of prudential supervision, designed to confine banks' risk-taking and to define their scope of business. Supervision along with a legal infrastructure for supervision of the nonbank sector, however, is still in its infancy. PBC is considering the establishment of a securities regulatory and enforcement agency as one possibility. These steps to strengthen supervision of the banks and financial markets are significant because the experience of all countries shows that a sound legal system that defines property rights, an accounting system that provides for transparency, and market supervision that generates faith in markets and their fair operation play an essential role in financial development.

Conclusion

The reform process in China led to the transformation in the late 1970s of China's financial sector from a virtual mono-bank system to today's increasingly decentralized—although by no means fully competitive—financial system. In addition to the four major state-owned banks, the emergence of rural and urban credit cooperatives has helped to create a more diversified banking system.

The TICs, pension funds, and insurance companies now have the potential to become significant intermediaries. In addition, the macroeconomic reforms of tax, budget, and credit policy have led to a change in the nature of intermediation in the economy. The government's role in financing investment has been reduced, with a concomitant increase in the importance of retained earnings, bank finance, and new financial instruments such as bonds and shares. These instruments represent a vehicle of growing importance for the issuers and a potential source of competition to the banking system.

Ultimately, a shrinking proportion of intermediation will take place through the banking system. Nonbank funding represents a potentially important source for enterprises, municipalities, and local governments, as well as for the financial institutions themselves. The issuance of securities by government financial institutions and by enterprises (the latter on the basis of segregated cash flows) can be expected to continue. As information disclosure requirements are improved, the noncollateralized securities sector can grow, providing yet further flexibility to issuers and better quality to bond holders.

References

"Assets and Liabilities of Peoples' Banks in China." Beijing: People's Bank of China, various years.

China Daily. Various issues, 1986–88.

"Receipts and Payments of Peoples' Banks." Beijing: People's Bank of China, various years.

State Statistical Yearbook, 1987. Beijing: China Statistics Press, 1988.

World Bank. *Finance and Investment: A World Bank Country Study*. Washington, D.C.: World Bank, 1988.

7

INSTITUTIONAL REFORMS IN CHINESE AGRICULTURE: RETROSPECT AND PROSPECT

Justin Yifu Lin

Introduction

As Dwight Perkins and Shahid Yusuf (1984, p. 73) have noted: "What sets China apart from many other developing countries is not that it has increased the use of chemical fertilizer, but how much it has relied on organizational reform to achieve rural development." Since the socialist takeover in 1949, China's agricultural system has swung between the individual household system and the collective system. During the collective period of 1952–78, China was acclaimed for her ability to feed more than one-fifth of the world's population with only one-fifteenth of the world's arable land.[1]

Although some well-known economists (e.g., Robinson [1964] 1973) recommended China's system of collective farming as a development model for densely populated underdeveloped countries, the growth rate of grain in 1952–78 was 2.4 percent per year, only 0.4 percent above the population growth rate. The per capita availability of grain, therefore, increased only 10 percent over a quarter century (see Table 1). Really remarkable achievements in Chinese agriculture did not occur until the institutional reform in 1979, which restored the individual household as the unit of production and accounting in rural areas. Between 1979 and 1984, agricultural output and grain output, respectively, grew at 11.8 percent and 4.1 percent annually while population grew at 1.3 percent in the same period (see Table 1).

The author is Associate Professor of Economics at Beijing University. This article draws on his paper "Farming Institutions, Food Policy, and Agricultural Development in China," which was presented at the Smithsonian Institution's World Food Colloquium on "Sharing Innovation: Global Perspectives on Food, Agriculture and Rural Development," held in Washington, D.C., October 17–18, 1989 (see Lin 1990c).
[1]The world and the Chinese populations in 1986 were 49.16 billion and 10.51 billion, while the arable lands were, respectively, 13.76 billion hectares and 0.96 billion hectares (State Statistical Bureau 1989, pp. 993–94).

TABLE 1

POPULATION, AGRICULTURAL OUTPUT, AND GRAIN OUTPUT
IN CHINA

Year	Population (Millions) (1)	Agricultural Output (1952 = 100) (2)	Grain Output (Million Tons) (3)
1952	574.8	100.0	164.0
1953	588.0	103.1	167.0
1954	602.7	106.6	170.0
1955	614.7	114.7	184.0
1956	628.3	120.5	193.0
1957	646.5	124.8	195.0
1958	659.9	127.8	200.0
1959	672.1	110.4	170.0
1960	662.1	96.4	143.5
1961	658.6	94.1	147.5
1962	673.0	99.9	160.0
1963	691.7	111.5	170.0
1964	705.0	126.7	187.5
1965	725.4	137.1	194.5
1966	745.2	149.0	214.0
1967	763.7	151.3	218.0
1968	785.3	147.6	209.0
1969	806.7	149.2	211.0
1970	829.9	157.8	240.0
1971	852.3	162.9	250.0
1972	871.8	161.2	240.0
1973	892.1	174.5	265.0
1974	908.6	180.7	275.0
1975	924.2	186.3	284.5
1976	937.2	185.5	286.0
1977	949.7	184.8	283.0
1978	962.6	199.8	305.0
1979	975.4	214.8	332.0
1980	987.1	217.9	320.6
1981	1,000.7	230.5	325.0
1982	1,015.9	256.5	355.0
1983	1,027.6	276.5	387.0
1984	1,038.7	310.4	407.0
1985	1,050.4	321.0	379.0
1986	1,065.3	331.8	391.0
1987	1,080.7	351.0	403.0
1988	1,096.1	364.9	394.0

SOURCE: Columns 1, 2, and 3 are from State Statistical Bureau (1989, pp. 87, 45, 198).

Although agriculture as a whole still grew at a respectable rate of 4.1 percent per year after 1984, grain production has, nevertheless, stagnated after reaching a peak of 407 million tons in 1984 (see Table 1). Over the many dynastic transitions in the several thousand years of Chinese history, the political leaders in China learned the crucial importance of food production to the political and social stability.[2] Optimism about agricultural development accumulated during the first five years of rural reforms, but it has been swiftly replaced by pessimism.[3] There even has emerged a call for recollectivization of the individual household-based farming system under the guise of pursuing economies of scale in agricultural production. The institutional reform of Chinese farming is at a crossroad.

In this paper I will argue that the poor performance of grain production during the past four years did not arise from the small size of household farms. The main reason was the failure of government to implement a market-oriented price reform for grain. Therefore, a food policy reform that is market-oriented should be the focus of further economic reforms in rural China. My discussion will be organized as follows: The relations between China's development strategy and collectivization are investigated in the next section, followed by a section discussing the motivation and achievements of the 1979 institutional reform of farming. The penultimate section briefs the main cause for current agricultural stagnation, and the final section provides some concluding remarks.

Development Strategy and Collectivization

Before the 1979 institutional reform, China's agricultural policy was shaped by the development strategy that the Chinese government adopted in the early 1950s. The Chinese economy inherited by the socialist government in 1949 was a war-torn economy in which 89.4 percent of the population lived in rural areas and industry accounted for only 12.6 percent of national income (State Statistical Bureau 1989, pp. 50, 89). With the intention of quickly building up national power, the government adopted a Stalinist heavy-industry-oriented development strategy in 1952 (after the economy had recovered from the destruction of the war). This development strategy

[2]This political wisdom is capsuled in an often-cited motto *"wu nong bu wen"* (without a strong agriculture, the society will not be stable) in the agricultural policy debates in China.

[3]In China both the general public and most economists often regard grain as the whole sector of agriculture. Despite a respectable growth rate for agriculture as a whole in the past four years, agriculture is often regarded as stagnated and declining because of the grain situation.

resulted in a rapid growth in the demand for food and other agricultural products. Since scarce foreign reserves were held mainly for importing capital goods, the increasing demand for agricultural products had to be satisfied by domestic production. Because agricultural stagnation and poor harvests would have an almost immediate and direct impact on industrial expansion,[4] collectivization was promoted as a strategy for the simultaneous development of agriculture and industry. The dual core of this agricultural development strategy was the mass mobilization of rural labor to work on labor-intensive investment projects such as irrigation, flood control, and land reclamation, plus the increase of unit yields through such traditional methods and inputs as closer planting, more careful weeding, and more organic fertilizers.[5]

The independent family farm was the traditional form of institution in rural China for thousands of years before the Communist takeover in 1949. Farmland was not only small but also fragmented. Before the revolution, nearly half of the land in rural China was owned by landlords and leased to peasants for cultivation. Rent was often as high as 50 percent of the output of the main crops. Starting in the 1940s, a land reform program was implemented in areas under the Communist party's control, whereby land was confiscated from landlords without compensation and was distributed to tenants. The land reform program continued after the success of the revolution and was completed in 1952.

Experiments with various forms of cooperatives began even before completion of the land reform program. Of the three major forms of cooperatives up to 1955, the most common one was the "mutual-aid team" in which four or five neighboring households pooled their labor, farm tools, and draft animals during peak seasons on a temporary or permanent basis. In this way, resource ownership was not altered and crop decisions remained the responsibility of the individual household.

The second form was the "elementary cooperative" in which 20–30 neighboring households combined their assets in a unified scheme. The net income of a cooperative was shared in two ways: dividend payments for land, draft animals, and farm tools; and remu-

---

[4]This argument is supported by the fact that the heavy-industry-oriented development strategy had to give way temporarily to the agriculture-first strategy in 1962, after the failure of harvests caused by the collectivization movement in 1959–61.

[5]Of course, the reasons for collectivization were numerous. The desire of the Communist party to consolidate its control over the countryside, to eliminate income disparity in rural areas, and to enable the government to increase the rate of extraction of agricultural surplus are the most frequently mentioned.

152

neration for work performed. The land, draft animals, and farm tools were still owned by individual member households.

The third form was the collective farm, or the "advanced cooperative," in which all means of production were collectivized. Remuneration in a collective was based solely on labor contribution and took the form of work points. The income of a household depended on the amount of work points earned by the family members and on the average value of a work point. The latter in turn depended on the net income of the collective farm. The size of an advanced cooperative initially consisted of about 30 households, and later evolved to consist of all households (150–200) in a village.

The official approach to collectivization was initially cautious and gradualist. Peasants were encouraged and even actively induced to voluntarily join various forms of cooperatives. However, the proponents of collectivization won the debate within the party in the summer of 1955. While there were only 500 advanced cooperatives at the end of 1955, 753,000 advanced cooperative farms with 119 million member households had been established by the winter of 1957.

This collectivization was surprisingly successful in its initial stages. It encountered no active resistance from the peasantry and was carried out relatively smoothly (Eckstein 1975, p. 251). Although population increased 14.8 percent between 1952 and 1958, the gross value of agriculture measured in 1952 prices increased 27.8 percent, and grain output increased 21.9 percent in the same period (see Table 1).

This experience greatly encouraged the leadership within the Communist party and caused leaders to take a bolder approach. The main rationale for collectivization was rooted in the notion that mobilizing rural surplus labor would increase rural capital formation and, hence, increase production. However, although a collective farm of 150 households provided a basis for mobilizing labor for work projects within the collective, the collective farm did not solve the problem of mobilizing labor for large projects, such as irrigation canals, dams, or the like. These kinds of projects would, in general, require the simultaneous participation of laborers from several dozen collective farms. The obvious solution for a large-scale labor mobilization was to pool 20–30 collective farms of 150 households into a larger unit.[6]

[6]In addition to constructing irrigation projects, mechanization was used as another rationale for increasing the size of a collective. The document titled "Opinions Concerning the Mechanization of Agriculture," which was approved and issued by the Politburo in April 1958, argued that for purposes of mechanization, the size of collectives should be increased. The document also set the goal of achieving total mechaniza-

For this reason, a new policy was imposed in 1958 as part of the Great Leap Forward in industry. From the end of August to the beginning of November 1958 (i.e., within only three months), 753,000 collective farms were amalgamated into 24,000 communes, consisting of 120 million households, or more than 99 percent of the total rural households in China in 1958. The average size of a commune was about 5,000 households, 10,000 workers, and 10,000 acres.[7] Remuneration in a commune was based mainly on subsistence needs and only partly on work performed by a peasant. Working on private plots and trading at rural fairs, which existed in the other forms of cooperatives, were prohibited. As planned, billions of worker-days of labor were thus mobilized. The communal movement, nevertheless, resulted in the profound agricultural crisis that occurred between 1959 and 1961. The gross output of agriculture fell 14 percent in 1959, 12 percent in 1960, and another 2.5 percent in 1961. Most devastatingly, grain output plunged by 15 percent in 1959, dropped another 16 percent in 1960, and remained at the same low level for another year (see Table 1). It is estimated that crop failures resulted in 30 million excess deaths in 1958–61.[8]

The commune system was not abolished after this crisis; however, its functions were reduced to administration and coordination. Starting in 1962, resource ownership, responsibility for production man-

tion or semimechanization in agriculture within five years. (See Agricultural Cooperativization in China Editorial Office 1987, pp. 4–12.)

[7]The term "people's commune" first appeared in July 1958 in the article "A Totally New Society and a Totally New Man" carried in the party's theoretical journal, *Hongqi* (*Red Flag*). The author, Chen Boda, was a personal secretary of Mao. The first commune, Weixing People's Commune, was established during that same month in Henan Province. By the end of September, 112 million households were organized into communes, and by the beginning of November, 120 million households were in communes (Chen 1958).

[8]For the estimation of extra deaths, see Ashton et al. (1984, pp. 613–45). The commonly accepted explanations for this crisis were bad weather, poor management, and disincentive for working in a commune. If these explanations were the main causes of this crisis, agricultural productivity should have returned to precrisis levels by 1962 or shortly thereafter, because the size of the production unit was reduced to precrisis levels after 1962. However, the total factor productivity in Chinese agriculture in 1962 was less than three-quarters of the 1957 level and remained at that low level until the early 1980s. These explanations can thus be rejected.

An explanation consistent with empirical evidence was the switch in 1958 from voluntary to compulsory collectivization. Because of the difficulty in supervising agricultural work, the success of an agricultural collective depends on a self-enforcing contract of self-discipline, which can be sustained only in a repeated game. The nature of the collective farm was changed from a repeated game to a one-time game when the principle of the movement was changed from voluntarism to compulsiveness. As a result, the self-enforcing contract could not be sustained and the agricultural productivity collapsed (see Lin 1990a).

154

agement, and accounting for purposes of income distribution were delegated to the small production team of 20–30 households. This new institution, in essence, was a hybrid of the elementary cooperative and the advanced cooperative of the 1950s. Remuneration, which was based on work points earned by each member, resembled the compensation scheme of the advanced cooperative, but the size and production management were similar to the elementary cooperative. After 1962, some experiments were made in improving the evaluation of work points; nevertheless, the production team system was maintained as the basic farming institution until reform of the household-based farming system was instituted in 1979.

A more realistic approach toward agricultural development was also adopted after the 1959–61 crisis. Efforts to mobilize rural labor for public irrigation projects continued. More emphasis, however, was given to modern inputs after the agricultural crisis. The irrigated acreage increased gradually after 1962. Most additional irrigated acreage came from the increase of powered irrigation instead of from constructions of labor-intensive canals and dams. The use of chemical fertilizer was accelerated after 1962, accompanied by the promotion of modern varieties of crops that are very responsive to fertilizer. Dwarf varieties of rice and wheat were introduced in the early 1960s. By the end of the 1970s, about 80 percent of the traditional varieties of rice and wheat had been replaced by modern dwarf varieties. Starting from 1976, dwarf varieties of rice started to be replaced by hybrid rice. Modern varieties of corn, cotton, and other crops were also introduced and promoted in the 1960s and 1970s. The pace of mechanization accelerated after 1965, especially during the 1970s.

Despite dramatic increases in modern inputs in the 1960s and 1970s, the performance of agriculture and grain production was disappointing. Although great emphasis was given to self-sufficiency, China changed from a net grain exporter in the 1950s to a sizable grain importer after 1961; per capita consumption of food grain in 1978 was no higher than it was in 1957. The poor performance has its origin in the collective farming system.

The Household Responsibility System Reform

The main defect of the production team system as an institution for agricultural development is its incentive structure. Members of a production team, working under supervision of a team leader, were credited with work points for jobs they performed. At the end of a year, net team income was first distributed among members according to some basic needs; then the rest was distributed according to the work points that each one accumulated during that year. Work points were supposed to reflect the quality and quantity of effort that each member performed. Theoretically, the work point system is not inherently an inefficient incentive scheme. If the monitoring of each peasant's work is perfect, the incentives to work will be excessive instead of suboptimal. This is because the return for a peasant's additional effort has two components. First, each peasant will get a share of the increase in team output. Second, he will get a larger fraction of the total net team income, because he contributes a larger share of total effort and thus has a larger portion of work points. The former is itself insufficient to make a worker offer the optimal amount of effort, but the latter overcompensates as long as the average product per unit of effort is greater than the marginal product of effort. Since the relevant region of production, in general, is located where the average product is greater than the marginal product, a peasant has incentives to overwork.

On the other hand, if there is no monitoring of effort, a peasant will not get more work points for an additional contribution of effort. In this case, the return on an increased effort has only one component, namely, a share of the increase in team output. The incentives to work are thus suboptimal. How much the increase in the work point share is for an additional unit of effort depends on the degree of monitoring. Therefore, the incentives to work in a production team are positively correlated with the degree of monitoring in the production process. The higher the degree of monitoring, the higher the incentives to work, and thus the more effort contributed.

However, monitoring is costly. Management of the production team needs to balance the gain in productivity resulting from the increase in incentives and the rise in monitoring costs. The monitoring of agricultural operations is particularly difficult because of agricultural production's sequential nature and spatial dimension. In agricultural production, the process typically spans several months over several acres of land. Farming also requires peasants to shift from one job to another throughout the production season. In general, the quality of work provided by a peasant does not become apparent until harvest time. Furthermore, it is impossible to determine each individual's contribution by simply observing the outputs because nature causes random impacts on production. It is thus very costly to provide close monitoring of a peasant's effort in and contribution to agricultural production. Consequently, the optimum degree of monitoring of a team engaging mainly in agricultural production must be very low. The incremental income for each additional unit of effort will be only a small fraction of the marginal product of effort. Therefore, in a production team the incentives for peasants to work must also be low.

The commune, brigade, and production team system of production management, with its work point system of compensation, has been challenged ever since its establishment. After the disaster in 1959–61, land was reallocated to individual families, and households were restored as production units in many parts of China, especially in Anhui Province. Production soon recovered in those areas. Nevertheless, this practice was prohibited and criticized as capitalistic, and the people responsible were oppressed. Although reallocation of land to individual households, secretly or sometimes openly, was never totally extinguished in some areas, the real change was not made possible until 1978 when moderate leaders came into power again after the chaos of the Cultural Revolution and the death of Mao.[9]

At the end of 1978, the government proposed a sweeping change in rural policies.[10] In place of a lopsided stress on grain production, the new policy encouraged the development of a diversified economy. Better prices were set for the state purchase of farm produce. Production teams were granted more freedom in making decisions about their own affairs. Private plots and the country fairs in which farm people sold their surplus products were revived and expanded. Although it had been recognized at that time that solving the managerial problems within the production team system was the key to improving low incentive, the household-based farming system reform was considered the reverse of the socialist principle of collective farming and was prohibited. The official position at that time maintained that the production team was to remain the basic unit of production, income distribution, and accounting.

Nevertheless, a small number of production teams (first secretly and later with the blessing of local authorities) began to try out the system of contracting land, other resources, and output quotas to individual households toward the end of 1978 in Feixi County and

[9]It was found recently that a village in Guizhou Province had adopted this practice secretly for more than 10 years before the recent reform. The villagers did not dare to admit it until the new policy was announced (Du 1985, p. 15).

[10]The policy changes were proposed in the Third Plenary Session of the 11th Central Committee of the Communist Party of China, held in December 1978. The session adopted the "Decisions of the Central Committee of the Communist Party of China on Some Questions Concerning the Acceleration of Agricultural Development (Draft)." The draft was promulgated nine months later (in September 1979) by the Fourth Plenary Session of the CPC Central Committee. For the text of the decision, see the Editorial Committee on the Agricultural Yearbook of China (1981, pp. 56–62).

also in Chuxian Prefecture in Anhui Province, which were both areas frequently victimized by flood and drought. A year later these teams brought in yields far larger than those of other teams. The central authorities later conceded to the existence of this practice and named it "the household responsibility system," but required that this practice be restricted to the poor agricultural regions, mainly to the hilly, mountainous areas and to poor teams in which people had lost confidence in the collective. This restriction, however, could not be put into effect at all.

Rich regions welcomed the household responsibility system as enthusiastically as the poor regions. Full official recognition of the household responsibility system as universally acceptable was eventually given in late 1981. By the end of 1983, almost all households in China's rural areas had adopted this new system. Under the arrangement of the household responsibility system, land is contracted to individual households for a period of 15 years. After fulfilling the procurement quota obligations, farmers are entitled to sell the surplus on the markets or retain it for their own uses.

In the household-based farming system, the difficulty of monitoring does not exist. By definition, peasants become residual claimants. They do not need to meter their own efforts. The marginal return to their efforts is the marginal product of effort. Although the economies of scale are sacrificed in the household-based system, it can be proved that the incentive structure in the household-based system dominates that of the team system (Lin 1988). Therefore, the incentives to work are improved by shifting from the production team system to the household responsibility system. Peasants feel happier and contribute more effort to production in the household responsibility system.

The change from the production team system to the household-based farming system is found empirically to have improved the incentive for adopting new technology, which will have a dynamic impact on long-run agricultural growth (Lin 1990b). The most conspicuous effect, however, is the one-time discrete impact on productivity arising from the increase in the incentive to work. It is estimated that total factor productivity increased 15 percent as a result of the improvement in the incentive structure caused by changing from the production team system to the household responsibility system (Lin 1989). The household responsibility system reform was started in 1979 and completed in 1984. During this period, agricultural output increased 45 percent (see Table 1). About one-third of the output growth between 1979 and 1984, therefore, can be attributed to the household responsibility system reform alone.

Causes of Current Stagnation in Grain Production

China's agriculture as a whole still grew at a respectable rate of 4.1 percent per year after the household responsibility system was fully implemented in 1984. The rapid growth of crop output, nevertheless, came to a sudden halt and the output of grain declined slightly. The optimism about China's agriculture, as a result, was replaced by pessimism. Some Chinese officials, scholars, and Western observers now claim that the agricultural reforms are no longer succeeding (Johnson 1989). Because most prominent Chinese leaders are grain fundamentalists, the disappointing performance in agriculture, especially grain production, has endangered the future of market-oriented reforms. A call has emerged for recollectivization as a means to increase grain output. The rural institutional reform in China is at a crossroad. However, the main reason for stagnation of grain production after 1984 was the failure of government to implement a market-oriented price reform for grain. A market-oriented grain price reform, therefore, should be the focus of further economic reform.

At the beginning of the 1979 reforms, there was a consensus among the political leaders in China that farm income was too low and grain output was barely sufficient to meet subsistence needs. As a measure to increase farm income and to boost grain production, procurement prices of grain and other major crops were increased by a big margin in 1979. The basic-quota price of grain was raised 20 percent, and the above-quota price was raised from 130 to 150 percent of the basic-quota price (the weighed-average increase was 33 percent). Furthermore, the state monopoly on the grain marketing was gradually lifted. Private as well as collective traders were allowed to handle grain marketing alongside the state marketing agency.

The household responsibility reform and the significant price raise caused an upsurge of grain production. Annual growth of grain production increased from an average rate of 2.4 percent in 1953–78 to 4.1 percent in 1979–84. Since the growth rate of grain production was about twice as large as the growth rate of consumption in 1979–84, China became a net grain exporter in 1985, after being a net importer for a quarter century. The sudden success, nevertheless, also brought with it new issues that the Chinese government had never handled before. According to the regulation at that time, the government was obliged to buy all grain at the above-quota price after a farmer fulfilled his quota obligation. Consequently, the faster the output growth, the larger the government's financial burden. Food subsidies (including edible oils) increased from ¥5.6 billion in 1978 to ¥32.1 billion in 1984, or 21 percent of the government's 1984 budget (State Statistical Bureau 1989, p. 763). Furthermore, a serious shortage of storage facilities existed. The government was unable to buy all the grain farmers wanted to sell and, as a result, the market price of grain dropped substantially across the country. In some grain surplus areas, the market price at harvest time even approached the basic-quota price set by the government.

As a measure to reduce government's financial burden and to increase the role of the market in the production and distribution of grain, the mandatory-quota procurement system was changed to a contract procurement system at the beginning of 1985. According to the new design, the procurement quantity was to be stipulated by contracts on the basis of mutual agreements between the government and individual farmers. The contract price was fixed; it was calculated as a weighed average of the original basic-quota price (30 percent) and the above-quota price (70 percent). This price was 135 percent of the original basic-quota price and about equivalent to the market price in major grain production areas at the harvest time in 1984. However, it was 10 percent lower than the above-quota price. As a supplement to the contract procurement, the government would also purchase a certain amount of grain on the market at the market price.[11]

The contract procurement system, however, met with a number of problems. First, the management costs of signing contracts with millions of agricultural households were tremendous, and the means to enforce contracts were limited. Second, the contract price did not provide enough incentives to farmers, especially in areas where the contract price was lower or even roughly equal to the market price. Third, the enforcement of contracts was made difficult because of a 6.9 percent drop in grain output during 1984. As a result of the drop in output, the market price of grain registered a 10 percent increase in 1985. Thus, the gap between the contract price and the market price was widened. Farmers were reluctant to fulfill contracts.

As a reaction to the experiences in 1985, the *contract* procurement system was reversed to the original *compulsory*-quota procurement at the end of 1985, even though the name "contract" was not abolished. The quantity of procurement, however, was reduced and the quantity of market purchase was increased. To minimize administrative costs, the procurement quota in each region was generally allocated to each household in proportion to the cultivated land that each

[11]The amounts purchased on the market were 19.64 million tons in 1985, 32.32 million tons in 1986, and 42.28 million tons in 1987, which were, respectively, 17.0 percent of the total procurement in 1985, 24.0 percent in 1986, and 30.0 percent in 1987.

household operated under the household responsibility system. To compensate for losses, the government promised to provide farmers with fertilizer, diesel gas, and credit at subsidized prices. Farmers, nevertheless, often complained that these promises were not realized.

Local governments enforce procurement contracts. The central government's policy obliges a local government to use its budget to purchase the deficient amount of grain at the market in case some contracts are not fulfilled. Since the market price of grain is clearly higher than the contract price, enforcing contracts is a very demanding job. To overcome the difficulty, a local government often blockades the grain market under its jurisdiction until compulsory procurement is completed. During the blockade, all sales of grain by farmers and purchases of grain by traders, other than the local state grain station, are prohibited. In places with two harvests per year, the blockade can last as long as four or more months each year. As a result of the blockade, the market price of grain varies greatly from region to region.[12]

The markets for most other agricultural products have been liberated. The relative prices of those liberated agricultural products to the price of grain, in general, increase substantially. The forced grain procurement quota and the many limitations on grain markets thus place grain in a disadvantageous position when compared to other crops. Farmers with a profit motivation are induced to divert resources from grain production to the production of more profitable crops and products. Therefore, grain production stagnated after 1984 in spite of a sizable growth in other sectors of agriculture.

Conclusion

China's experiences, both successes and failures, in agricultural development provide many valuable lessons for other developing countries. These lessons are remarkable in the sense that China has been able to feed over one-fifth of the world's population with only one-fifteenth of world's arable land. But China paid a very high price for this achievement before the 1979 reform. The collective farming system was detrimental to work incentives. Therefore, despite sharp increases in modern inputs in the 1960s and 1970s, grain production in China barely kept up with population growth.

[12]For example, in December 1988 the market price of rice in the five rice-surplus provinces (Jiangsu, Jiangxi, Anhui, Hunan, and Hubei) was ¥1,161 per ton, while in the three rice-deficit provinces (Guangdong, Guangxi, and Fujian), the price was ¥1,839 per ton.

The individual household-based farming system reform in 1979 greatly improved the peasant's work incentives. Agriculture as well as grain production registered an unprecedented growth between 1979 and 1984. The increase of work incentives derived from the institutional reform of farming, however, was a once-and-for-all discrete jump and was depleted by 1984. Compared to the agricultural growth rates in other developed, as well as developing, countries, the average growth rate of 4.1 percent per year in 1984–88 is remarkable. Grain production in China, however, has stagnated after reaching its peak in 1984. This stagnation is mainly because the reform in food policy lags behind the institutional reform in farming. An individual household was given more autonomy in production decisions after the household responsibility system reform. A peasant in a household farm will allocate more resources to crops that command higher profits. After the household responsibility system reform, marketing of most crops has been liberated. Grain is among the exceptions. Farmers are still required to meet the grain quota obligations at government-set prices. In addition, local governments often impose blockades on grain markets. This measure reduces the price of grain in areas with a comparative advantage in producing grain. The stagnation of grain production in the post-reform period, which contrasted with a sizable growth of agriculture as a whole, can be attributed mainly to the decline in profitability of grain compared to other crops.

Most people in China, including political leaders and economists, are grain fundamentalists. Because grain production stagnated, the optimism about Chinese agriculture developed in the first five years of reform has been quickly replaced by pessimism. The small farm size and the fragmentation of cultivated land in the household-based farming system are often wrongly blamed for the poor performance of grain production after 1984. In the guise of pursuing economies of scale in agricultural production, some areas have begun to recollectivize the household-based farming system.[13] This practice is especially appealing to local officials because it makes easy the fulfillment of obligatory grain procurement. The market-oriented reform in China is at a crossroad.

The lessons before the 1979 reform have demonstrated that collectivization is not a solution to the increasing demand for grain arising from population growth and industrial expansion. The ultimate way to break the current stagnation of grain production is to let the price carry the right signal to farmers. As long as the grain price offers

[13]See the report by Jiang (1988).

farmers a competitive return, comparable to the return on other crops, the individual household-based farmers in China will be able to produce enough grain to feed the Chinese population.[14] This outcome, of course, requires a market-oriented reform of food policy. The success of a market-oriented reform in a socialist economy, however, depends more on the determination of political leaders than on the wisdom of economists.

References

Agricultural Cooperativization in China Editorial Office. "Chronicle of Events in Agricultural Cooperativization in China II." *Zhongguo Nongye Hezoushi Ziliao (Historical Material of Agricultural Cooperativization in China)* 3 (1987): 4–12.

Ashton, Basil; Hill, Kenneth; Piazza, Alan; and Zeitz, Robin. "Famine in China, 1958–1961." *Population and Development Review* 10 (December 1984): 613–45.

Chen, Boda. "A Totally New Society and a Totally New Man." *Hongqi (Red Flag)* (July 1958).

Du, Runsheng. *China's Rural Economic Reform.* Beijing: Social Science Press, 1985.

Eckstein, Alexander. *China's Economic Development: The Interplay of Scarcity and Ideology.* Ann Arbor: University of Michigan Press, 1975.

Editorial Committee on the Agricultural Yearbook of China. *Zhongguo Nongye Nianjian, 1980 (China Agriculture Yearbook, 1980).* Beijing: Agriculture Press, 1981.

Jiang, Yaping. "Wo men bu gou yao zhong di: Beijing shungyixian yiqi chengbao tudi hetong jiufeng jishi" ("All we want is to cultivate land: An on-the-spot report of a dispute in land contract in Shungyi County, Beijing"). *Renmin Ribao (People's Daily),* 26 October 1988.

Johnson, D. Gale. "Economic vs. Noneconomic Factors in Chinese Rural Development." Paper no. 89:13, Office of Agricultural Economics Research, University of Chicago, 1989.

Lin, Justin Yifu. "The Household Responsibility System in China's Agricultural Reform: A Theoretical and Empirical Study." *Economic Development and Cultural Change* 36 (April 1988): S199–S224.

Lin, Justin Yifu. "The Household Responsibility System in China's Rural Reform." In *Agriculture and Governments in an Interdependent World: Proceedings of the XX International Conference of Agricultural Economists.* Edited by A. Mander and A. Valdes. Aldershot, England: Dartmont, 1989.

Lin, Justin Yifu. "Collectivization and China's Agricultural Crisis in 1959–1961." *Journal of Political Economy* 98 (December 1990a) forthcoming.

[14]Since grain is a land-intensive product and China's land endowment is extremely scarce, it is economically rational for China to produce other labor-intensive crops in exchange for grain through international trade. However, this practice may not be acceptable to the government until the ideology of grain fundamentalism is abandoned.

Lin, Justin Yifu. "The Household Responsibility System Reform and the Adoption of Hybrid Rice in China." *Journal of Development Economics* (1990b) forthcoming.

Lin, Justin Yifu. "Farming Institutions, Food Policy, and Agricultural Development in China." In *Sharing Innovation: Global Perspectives on Food, Agriculture and Rural Development*. Edited by Neil G. Kotler. Washington, D.C.: Smithsonian Institution Press, 1990c.

Perkins, Dwight, and Yusuf, Shahid. *Rural Development in China*. A World Bank Publication. Baltimore: Johns Hopkins University Press, 1984.

Robinson, Joan. "Chinese Agricultural Communes." *Co-Existence* (May 1964): 1–7. Reprinted in *The Political Economy of Development and Underdevelopment*. pp. 209–15. Edited by Charles K. Wilber. New York: Random House, 1973.

State Statistical Bureau. *Zhongguo Tongji Nianjian, 1988 (China Statistical Yearbook, 1988)*. Beijing: China Statistics Press, 1989.

8

PROPERTY IN CHINESE DEVELOPMENT: SOME HISTORICAL COMPARISONS

John P. Powelson

What arrangements for property rights are most conducive to economic development? Although possibilities are numerous and complex, they generally fall within two categories: centralized (government) or decentralized (private) rights. This paper addresses this question in the light of the historical experience of China, contrasted with the experiences of Japan and northwestern Europe.

What Is Property?

In the widest sense, property includes all assets, real and personal, tangible and intangible. Real property consists mainly of land and buildings, but it also includes infrastructure, such as roads, ports, and power plants. Industrial property includes real property devoted to industry, plus machinery and equipment. Personal property includes all things that individuals might own. Tangible property can be seen and touched. Intangible property covers rights to inventions (patents), writings and compositions (copyrights), leases and tenancy, and other values that are legally protected.

Property can also be divided according to whether it is physical or financial. Physical property consists of the goods themselves, whether real or personal, tangible or intantible. Financial property consists of claims to physical property that can be exercized as stocks, bonds, promissory notes, and even money.

In an agrarian society, the principal property is land, and much of the historical background of property rights must be considered with that in mind. In an industrial society, property rights become more diverse.

Freedom of Property versus Central Control

Reforms in property rights usually refer to a change in the focus of decisions over the use of property and the claims to its product. In

The author is Professor of Economics at the University of Colorado.

a socialist reform, the focus and product pass from a wider constituency to the government. In a liberalizing reform, they move in the opposite direction. The advantages of either reform are debated between proponents of Adam Smith–type laissez faire and those who advocate centralized economic planning.

It is often said that governmental ownership of property is equitable, since land and industrial assets ought to belong to all the people. No one deserves to own land, some say, because it was provided free, and other assets, often inherited, do not arise from the efforts of the heirs. But someone must decide how property is used, and someone must enjoy its product. It is not possible for all the people to stand on a given piece of land or for all to decide what to grow on it or to use it for, nor can everyone sit at a table and eat the crop. These things must be done by some people and not by others. The crucial question, therefore, is who has the power to make the decisions and who has the right to the product. The same questions can be asked about claims to industrial assets. In this paper, I will accept the Adam Smith–type argument for the economic efficiency of laissez faire, for it is impossible for a small group of people to efficiently deploy the entire assets of a large nation.

I will also argue that the widespread dispersion of both income and decisions over the use of assets, as opposed to their concentration in either private or public hands, is not only economically efficient but also ethically desirable. Only the degree to which assets and decisions should be collectivized within smaller units, such as a company or group of companies, should be debated. How large should a venture be? How many decision points should it include? Is it desirable to collectivize several ventures? These topics are currently under serious consideration in the United States.

The long-run success of freedom of property rights, however, is not unqualified. I will argue that its success depends on two forces, both of which are historically determined: (1) the security of those rights, that is, whether a powerful group, either private or governmental, can take them away; and (2) other institutions of decentralization, such as the market and the legal and monetary systems that evolve alongside property rights.

I will also show that the history of property rights in China and other parts of Asia except Japan are markedly different from the corresponding history of property rights in northwestern Europe and Japan. Curiously enough, since the 11th century, the experiences of northwestern Europe and Japan have been similar in ways that could hardly be coincidental. Yet, these two areas did not communicate with each other until the 16th century, and thereafter the Tokugawa isolation reduced communication until the late 19th century. Are the economic advances of these areas to be explained, at least in part, by their similar histories in property rights?

Unlike personal property, which can be owned absolutely, real property constitutes a collection of rights that have historically belonged to different people with respect to the same land or other asset. One person may have the right to live on a piece of land, another the right to farm it, and still another the right to hunt or cut wood on it. The possessor of any of these rights might have obligations stemming from that possession, such as to the state or a feudal lord. One person (a feudal lord) might own superior rights while someone else (a freeman) owns lesser rights to the same land; each may or may not alien (sell, buy, give, mortgage, or transfer) his rights at his level. The historical evolution of these rights is more complex than the evolution of rights over personality. I will argue that security of property rights depends not so much on how they are defined as on how they have evolved.

In northwestern Europe and Japan, the present system of fee simple ownership evolved out of centuries of negotiations among different classes of people—peasants, businessmen, city fathers, clerics, military officers, nobility, princes, kings, shoguns, emperors—in ways that are startlingly different from the evolution of such rights in China and the rest of Asia. This negotiation placed these plural groups in a condition of relative balance of power, and in that balance lies their security.

Although China possessed a system of private property earlier and over more centuries than northwestern Europe and Japan did, this system was subject to decisions by the emperor (later the Republic and still later the People's Republic) far more than it was in northwestern Europe and Japan. Lacking the historical negotiations among plural groups and the balance of power that might have arisen out of it, Chinese peasants, businesspeople, and others do not hold the same power over their government as do corresponding groups in northwestern Europe and Japan. Even though decisions on land use and the right to its product have been liberalized in China, Chinese tenants of land are still not as secure in these rights as are their counterparts in northwestern Europe and Japan. This lack of security may portend problems for Chinese economic development.

China

Under the Shang dynasty, (c.1562–1066 B.C.), land was owned in common but at different levels. The "king's domain" was the

167

"territorial unit within which the Shang king had direct access to economic resources" (Chang 1975, p. 216). The lords received their domain in exchange for loyalty and obligation to defend the frontiers. Chang (1975, p. 220) found "no evidence that land was privately owned during any of the Shang period." Slaves or serfs did all the agricultural work.

The Chou, who overthrew the Shang in about 1122 B.C., confiscated the land of their enemies and formed a rigid feudal system based on land (Hsu 1965). They established the well-field system, with land allocated in three-by-three matrices, with each of the outer eight fields going to a serf-farmer to feed his family, and with the eight serfs collectively farming the ninth (center) field on behalf of their lord. Mencius (c.372–279 B.C.) later praised this system as adhering to Confucian principles of loyalty (Fairbank et al. 1978, p. 52).

Officially, this hierarchical system continued during the Spring and Autumn (Chun Qu) period (722–481 B.C.), when the Chou still held the imperial title but shared power with five Hegemons (the number is traditional), or princes. During this period, the concepts of loyalty attributable to Confucius (551–479 B.C.) emerged. By the fifth century B.C., the princes were constantly fighting each other. The period when three of the princes dominated (Qi, Qin, and Chu) is known as the Period of Warring States, or Chan Kuo (453–221 B.C.).

As the Qin became more powerful, Duke Hsiao (r.361–338 B.C.) of that clan appointed Shan Yang as chief minister. Shan Yang persuaded the duke "to institute a series of wide-ranging reforms to promote state control, centralization of power, and economic and military expansion" (Li 1977, p. xiii). Feudalism and the well-field system were abolished, and private property and free alienation (buying, selling, inheriting, mortgaging, and so forth) of land were legalized. Serfs became "free" landowners, responsible to the emperor rather than to a feudal prince. This system triumphed along with the Qin, whose decisive victory in 220 B.C. has earned them the distinction of being called the founders of a unified China.

Private property in China has always been different from private property in Europe. The sovereign authority in China, whether emperor or Republic or People's Republic, has always held the right to confiscate or transfer property. In an earlier century, the emperor claimed the right to move peasants wholesale, and sometimes he did so.

Not only was China's centuries-old system of private property always subject to sovereign intervention, but other interruptions occurred as well. Under the theory of the dynastic cycle, expounded about A.D. 70 by Ban Gu, the official historian of the Han dynasty (221 B.C.–A.D. 220), each dynasty would begin its sovereignty vigorously and uncorrupted, influenced by Confucian morals and eager to promote popular welfare. Lands would be confiscated from owners under the previous dynasty and reallocated equitably among the people. Each farmer would be assigned a quota, or tax in-kind, and communities were collectively responsible for its payment. Because landownership was widespread among small farmers, the tax burden on each was not great.

This idealized beginning, however, applied to only part of the land. Ineluctably, the new emperor had to reward those who had helped him defeat the former dynasty. A new nobility was created as these lords were granted extensions of land, for which they did not pay taxes. In a variation of Gresham's law ("bad money drives out good"), untaxed land drove out taxed land: The taxpaying peasants—for both protection and economy—commended their lands to one noble or another. As the domains of the nobility were extended, the tax burden fell more heavily on the remaining free peasants, whose position became less and less tenable.

Furthermore, the dynasty itself became less secure. The powerful enriched themselves through taxes and extortion, and others became envious of their power. They would be challenged either by a foreign foe, such as the Xiong Nu, the Juchen, the Mongols, or the Manchu, or from within, as by An-Lu Shan during the Tang dynasty (A.D. 756). Wars ultimately led to a military collapse, a new dynasty took over, and the cycle started afresh (the cycle is described in detail by Wu 1952, pp. 7–8).

Even though peasants possessed private property in principle, property was not freely alienable in the same sense as it was in Western societies and in Japan. There are several reasons for this. First, the peasantry could be dispossessed by the emperor at any time. Second, those peasants who were forced into commendation to lords for financial stress or military protection lost control over their lands. Sometimes the financial stress derived from increased taxes to the legitimate emperor and sometimes it derived from tribute to foreign powers, such as to the Juchen to prevent harassment of the Southern Song dynasty after A.D. 1127. In larger estates, ownership by peasants often gave way to ownership by the gentry, only to be returned to the peasantry under another dynasty.

The third reason is that, under some of the dynastic reforms, allocations to peasants were largely non-heritable. For example, under the equal-allocation (*jün-tian*) system of the Wei (A.D. 385–550), Sui

(A.D. 580–618), and early Tang (after A.D. 618) dynasties, all land belonged to the emperor but was assigned to a farmer when he reached the productive age of 18. Unless it was silk land, it would be taken away when a farmer was 65 years old for reallocation (Twitchett 1970, p. 9). Silk land was made heritable to induce farmers to invest in mulberry bushes.

Fourth, the relationships between landlords and tenants often did not fall easily into categories of private property versus feudalism but were *sui generis*. The first Song emperor (A.D. 960) rewarded his followers with vast estates, known as *chuang yüan*. These land-owners developed paternalistic relationships with their tenants, often adopting them and subjecting them to parental discipline, and peasants became transferable with the land. But there were still many free peasants who owned land that was alienable.

Fifth, land reforms were subject to reversal because of military uncertainty. Wang Mang, who usurped power from the Han dynasty (A.D. 9–23), confiscated land that had become concentrated under the early Han (221 B.C.–A.D. 9) and awarded approximately five acres to every youth of 16 years, to be returned when he reached 65. Wang Mang restored the well-field system and declared all land to be the "king's fields" and, hence, inalienable. Three years later, after peasant uprising caused by bad harvests, these reforms were reversed. The An-Lu Shan rebellion (A.D. 756) allegedly marked the end of the *jün-tian* system of the Tang, as peasants fled to other places, abandoning their lands.

In 1069, the Song emperor's chief counsellor, Wang An-Shih, insti-tuted a series of reforms reminiscent of those of Wang Mang, although they did not include land redistributions. The reforms consisted of low-interest loans to farmers, ever-normal granaries, new land sur-veys to correct tax inequities, and the commutation of corvée labor into money taxes. But these reforms, undertaken in an atmosphere of general hostility, could be enforced only because of the emperor's support. After he died, his successor was of a different mind and the reforms were weakened; Wang An-Shih was demoted.

Sixth, reforms to distribute land to peasants were generally made to increase both the imperial tax base and the security of the dynasty, not to improve peasant welfare. Tai Zong, the first Ming emperor (A.D. 1368), wanted to repopulate the North after its devastation by the Mongols. He confiscated estates wholesale from landlords accused of collaborating with the Mongol (Yüan) dynasty (A.D. 1280–1368) and then rented the new land to peasants. He also out-lawed private slavery and established a land register to monitor estate formation. Vacant lands in the North were granted to military officials for protection of the frontier.

Finally, as lands were redistributed following a change of dynasty, peasants associated with one lord might be driven off their properties. In 1127, when the Juchen drove the Song out of Yen-Ching (modern Beijing), they confiscated peasant land and reduced its tenants to slavery (Chou 1974, p. 118). During the southern Song dynasty (A.D. 1127–1279), many manors were confiscated from disgraced officials and were held by the emperor.

Nevertheless, after the Ming dynasty (1368–1644), farms became smaller. With inheritance, peasant farms were cut up. Contracts between lords and peasants were increasingly made, and sometimes security of tenancy was agreed upon. A two-tier system developed in which the tenant owned the surface and could alien it, and the landlord owned subsoil rights. Tenants began to manage farms, and financial contracts for rent became more widespread (Elvin 1973, p. 224).

Even so, the manorial economy increased. New lands opened up and garrison lands that were not intended as private became estates of the powerful. Although the land register of the Ming dynasty did monitor holders of large estates, it nevertheless provided a means by which more sophisticated operators could, by registering, steal land from peasants who were less skilled in legal procedures. Again, peasants commended themselves and their lands to landlords, and many estates grew in size.

By the 18th century, however, fragmentation with inheritance was leading to smaller farms. In 1681, the Manchus (Qing dynasty, 1644–1911), fearful of tenants who might murder their landlords, outlawed the sale of tenants with farms. By the 20th century, China had become a land of small farms. Out of 16,786 farms studied in 22 provinces, Buck (1937, p. 197) recorded an average size of 5.36 acres in the wheat region and 3.09 acres in the rice region, with a standard error of mean of .115 acres for the Yangtze wheat-rice region (p. xi; not given for other regions). Perkins (1969) also stressed the small size with low deviation. Buck found that "somewhat less than three-fourths of the land is owned by the farmer himself and one-fourth is rented" (p. 194), with seven-eighths owned in the wheat region and three-fifths owned in the rice region. He concluded: "The extent of farm tenancy in China is no greater than in many other countries and, therefore, is not a problem peculiar to China."

Why should tenancy in pre-1949 China be so much greater in the South than in the North? Usually, tenancy was explained by farmers going into debt during a famine and, unable to repay, relinquishing

171

their farms to creditors but remaining as tenants, paying 40 to 50 percent of the crop as rent. Many of these creditor/landlords were other farmers, though some were urban investors. Yet, if famine is the explanation, should it not apply equally well in the North and the South? Both Perkins (1969) and Tawney (1932, p. 37) concluded that the North differed from the South in that farming prospects were so poor that starving farmers could not find creditors to feed their families. Thus, they did not lose their land. "If conditions were hard enough," Perkins (1969, p. 100) remarked, "they lost their lives instead."

At the time of the 1949 revolution, therefore, Chinese agriculture was carried out mainly on small-scale private farms, with virtually no tenancy in the North and no excessive amounts in the South, although rentals might be deemed abusively high. Thus, the land reform of the People's Republic of China differed markedly from those of other regions, such as Latin America or the Middle East, where the aristocracy held the land.

Today, the government of China is once again taking steps toward decentralization. In March 1988, constitutional protection was accorded to private enterprise, and the right of people to buy and sell the right to use land (*New York Times*, 26 March 1988) was assured. Because farmers own only the right to the land and not the land itself, however, their position is reminiscent of ancient China's prescription that private property was always subject to imperial sanction. As China takes steps toward liberalizing the use of land, we must ask: Will this decentralization last, or will it be reversed again, with the sovereign power retaining the ultimate property right?

Japan

During the sixth and seventh centuries, Japanese property rights were strongly influenced by the Chinese. In the Taika ("Great Change") reforms of A.D. 604, the supremacy of the emperor was recognized (Asakawa 1903, pp. 73–74). Lands were confiscated from the great families, and the Chinese equal-allocation (*jün-tian*) system was adopted. As in China, the equal-allocation system broke down in Japan as the emperor gave large tracts to his military defenders and as peasants commended their lands to the gentry. But the manorial system (*sho*), which developed from the eighth century on, differed from that of China in three important ways.

First, the emperor became weak relative to the landed aristocracy. Neither the emperor nor the shogun possessed direct access to the peasants, as the Chinese emperor did. Japanese peasants served under their lords alone, who served under the emperor or shogun. Having to work through intermediaries reduced central-government's command over peasant property, compared to that of the Chinese emperor.

Second, the aristocracy proliferated, even with respect to the individual *sho*. A given estate might carry at least two aristocratic claimants: a noble patron (*honke*) and a proprietor (*ryoke*) (Asakawa 1918, p. 83). By the 10th century, two other aristocrats would also claim rights to the same land: an owner (*jishu*) and a non-noble lord (*ryoshu*) (Kiley 1974, p. 120). By the 12th century, a middle-level manager (*azukari dokoro*) had been added, and still other titles proliferated at lower levels (*gesu, sosuitushi, kumon, tadokoro*) (Mass 1974, pp. 4–5). By the 13th century, the shogun had assigned the provincial governor (*zuryo*) to serve as tax farmer. Under the first shogunate (1192), provincial governors (*shugo*) and estate stewards (*jito*) were appointed (Duus 1969, pp. 48–51).[1] These authorities had different functions. Some decided who would have lower rights to the land; others determined what would be produced; still others decided what rents and taxes would be paid and to whom and who was responsible for defense. But the division of functions was not always clear, estates differed on how they were managed, and the authorities frequently rivaled and sometimes fought each other.

Third, by the eighth century all claimants to landed functions, including peasants, held rights (*shiki*) that they could buy and sell and that could not be confiscated. There were peasant-*shiki*, proprietor-*shiki*, and managerial-*shiki* at different levels.

Fourth, by the 14th century, towns dominated by merchants were gaining political independence from central authorities. Peasants could improve their social and economic status by becoming members of these towns (Jacobs 1958, p. 88). It is not clear why the Japanese should not only develop but respect the peasant-*shiki*, but some conjectures are in order. First, the military weakness of the emperor diluted his capacity to intervene. Second, the large number of rival overlords made it possible for peasants to switch allegiance from one to another in exchange for security of tenure. Suppose that Overlord A rivaled Overlord B. The peasants, despite their weakness, might hold the balance of power between the two. By allying with one rather than the other, they might lever their own power upward, validating it by the award of *shiki*. There is also the third possibility

---

[1]For all these titles, the English terminology is only approximate.

that moving to towns provided peasants with an alternative to remaining farmers.

During the 11th and 12th centuries, warrior peasantry formed groups (*bushidan*), both to serve overlords and to protect their own rights. These groups were the precursor of a political force at the peasant level. In about 1200, a new balance of power began to emerge, consisting of the shogun (from 1192), the regents in charge of the shogun (the Hojo family, from 1199), the emperor (and sometimes an anti-emperor), town authorities, the landed and non-landed aristocracy, and the officials and armies associated with these groups. Among these were the *bushidan*, who used their power to create lower-level bargaining assemblies.

As Japan slipped into a military anarchy during the 14th and 15th centuries, under the weakening Ashikaga shogunate, a contract feudal system was formed that was similar to that found in Europe in the 10th to 12th centuries. The feudal estate became the principal focus of government. Village associations bargained for their land rights, which became well established. Neither feudal lord, nor shogun, nor emperor had the power to deny these rights to the landed peasantry.

This was the situation at the beginning of the Tokugawa shogunate (1603). During the Tokugawa centuries, Japan launched an unprecedented economic development, spurred on by several politico-social developments. First, part of the peasant/warrior class grew into a merchant class. Towns were established, carrying their political identities, which passed regulations favoring production and commerce. Without enough power to exact heavy tribute from the merchants, the landed aristocracy (*daimyo*) borrowed from them instead. The resulting indebtedness raised the merchants to the level of a new force in the balance of power. Second, peasant associations known as *ikki* evolved out of the bands of *bushidan* (Davis 1974, pp. 221–47). Their power grew not only from their rebellions but also from their capacity to bargain with agents of the *daimyo* and the shogun. Third, private property rights in land, manufacturing plants and equipment, and financial instruments became established in law. Fourth, decentralized governments with their own law courts evolved at the provincial and village levels (Duus 1969, pp. 77–78; Smith 1970, p. 3). The balance of power was preserved by a diversified court system that enforced contracts and settled disputes at many levels.

It is a reasonable hypothesis that the modern economic development of Japan is founded on politico-social relationships that emerged during the 8th to 12th centuries. Those relationships were consolidated during the military chaos of the 13th to 15th centuries and were strengthened during the Tokugawa period. Among them were the unassailable rights (*shiki*) of different groups to land; the ability of merchants and farmers to decide what they would produce, how they would produce it, and at what prices they would offer their output for sale; their ability to retain the profits; and their ability to own the property, whether real or personal, tangible or intangible, and to make contracts enforceable by law. Although higher authorities frequently tried to usurp these rights, the balance of power was such that they never fully succeeded in doing so.

Northwestern Europe

European historical experience parallels that of Japan more closely than that of China. As the Roman Empire disintegrated, its system of absolute ownership (*dominio*) fell apart. Most small holders commended themselves and their lands to gentry able to defend them, demanding secure rights to their tenancy similar to the *shiki* of the Japanese. In this way the European system of contract feudalism grew. But it was still a diversified system. Many tenants had no rights and held their land only at the pleasure of the lord, while small holders outside feudal domains held land in *dominio* or as allodial property (private lands with no lord).

In northwestern Europe (England, the Low Countries, the Netherlands including Flanders, and northwestern Germany), a contract feudalism was already developing in the 11th century that was similar to the Japanese system in the 16th and 17th centuries. This form of contract feudalism had several characteristics.

First, peasants enjoyed contractual rights with respect to their lords: The lord performed obligations with respect to the tenants (defended them, provided security of tenure), and the peasants performed obligations for the lords (providing food and services). Such contracts were far from equal. The lord's rights were much greater than those of the peasants, and peasants were often coerced into the relationship.

Second, village organizations grew on European domains, similar to the Japanese, and peasants negotiated collectively with their lords (Hilton 1978, pp. 9, 216; Genicot 1966, pp. 733–34; Brenner 1976, p. 55; Wunder 1978, p. 55; Payne 1973, p. 165).

Third, law courts were established on the European domains. Although the courts were under the nominal jurisdiction of the lords, they were operated by bailiffs, frequently of peasant origin (Hilton 1978, p. 9). Peasants were even known to sue their lords in the

175

manorial courts, and occasionally they won their cases (Berman 1983, p. 533). Thus, a peasant might be able to enforce his contractual agreement with the lord.

Fourth, autonomous towns were growing in Europe by the 11th century, forming a political force of their own (Barraclough 1979, p. 148; Gregg 1976, p. 90). As in Japan, towns provided an alternative opportunity for peasants. Serfs would become free if they remained in a town for a year and a day.

Fifth, a complex set of laws concerning property developed over the centuries (Berman 1983). As output and trade increased during the 15th and 16th centuries, European courts faced two main problems with respect to land law. One was to convert common lands to individual property, and the other was to convert family land into individual land. The first problem was tackled through the enclosure movement, by which village common lands were divided among the owners in proportion to their holdings of private land. The second problem was addressed through the courts, in which decisions tended to favor individual alienation of land rather than family entails.

Sixth, like the Japanese peasants, by the 12th century European peasants were not directly subject to their kings or emperors but to their feudal lords. Hence, central government could not reach them as easily as the Chinese emperor could reach his peasants.

Seventh, European peasants were subject to different overlords—emperors, kings, princes, and officials of the church—whom they could play off one against another.

While all of these elements of private property were developing, the Europeans were also fashioning legal and monetary systems and decentralized governments, which were complementary institutions favoring economic development.

Why did all these movements occur more in *northwestern* Europe than in southern and eastern Europe? The most likely hypothesis is that the peasants in northwestern Europe held greater leverage over their lords than did their counterparts in Spain and Italy or in eastern Germany and the Slavic lands. Because of increasing land shortages in the crucial 11th to 13th centuries, it would have been more difficult for lords to replace or discipline rebellious peasants than it was in land-abundant areas to the east and south.

In short, although peasants were social and political inferiors to their overlords in northwestern Europe, they were nevertheless part of a growing balance of power. By allying themselves with more powerful classes in disputes with other power groups, the peasants were able to lever their negotiating power upward, much as Japanese peasants did. The result was the abolition of slavery, the abolition of serfdom, the commutation of feudal dues into money rent that was later converted into taxes, and the ownership of land by peasants themselves.

Conclusion

The relationship of private property to economic development cannot be proved in the sense of a mathematical problem that has a solution. Indeed, a system of private property does not appear by itself to be an impulse to development. Were this all that were necessary, by the 19th century China might have been the most developed area in the world, recapturing the place it had held in the 7th-century Tang dynasty and in the 11th-century Song dynasty.

In addition to private property, the following elements appear to be essential to economic development. First, the peasants must participate in a balance of power along with other groups in a pluralist society. This does not imply that peasants must be organized into groups as powerful as either their government or private industry, only that they must have the bargaining power with which to defend their rights. Second, a system of enforceable law must develop, through which these property rights are secured. Third, property rights in land must evolve into other kinds of property rights, including rights to financial instruments (claims on real assets, both land and other) and to intangible property, all of which must be freely tradable. Fourth, the groups must hold enough political power so that the government is unable to confiscate their rights without serious social upheaval. For example, no government in the most advanced industrial countries (northwestern European, United States and Canada, Australia and New Zealand, and Japan) has the power to infringe on private property rights except in very limited cases (through zoning or eminent domain for highways and a few other projects of transcending national importance). Too many legal and cultural institutions would prevent it from doing so.

While China's advancement toward private property rights, in both land and business, is to be commended in the interest of economic development, one great barrier remains. The power of the central government—its sovereign right to command property—remains just as strong as it did in the days of the Empire or the Republic of 1912–49.

China has a history of reforms in property rights and other institutions that have been reversed because they were not grounded in political power from below, springing up independent of governmental grace. In many respects the present reforms are much different from those of the emperors, but one similarity remains: The ultimate ownership of land still vests in the government. As in the dynastic reforms, what the government gives, the government or its successor can take away. Only if peasants and private businesses are able to enforce their rights in law courts and only if private property becomes so politically and socially demanded that the normal functioning of the economy depends on its preservation, as has been the case in Western societies and in Japan, can one be sure that the present reforms will last.

References

Asakawa, Kanichi. *The Early Institutional Life of Japan: A Study of the Reform of 645 A.D.* Tokyo: Shueisha, 1903.

Asakawa, Kanichi. "Some Aspects of Japanese Feudal Institutions." *Transactions of the Asia Society of Japan* 46 (1918): 77–102.

Ban Gu. *The History of the Former Han Dynasty.* Baltimore: Waverly Press, 1955.

Barraclough, Geoffrey. *The Origins of Modern Germany.* New York: Paragon Books, 1979.

Berman, Harold J. *Law and Revolution: The Formation of the Western Legal Tradition.* Cambridge: Harvard University Press, 1983.

Brenner, Robert. "Agrarian Class Structure and Economic Development in Preindustrial Europe." *Past and Present,* no. 70 (February 1976).

Buck, John L. *Land Utilization in China.* New York: Nanking University, 1937.

Chang, Parris. *Power and Policy in China.* University Park: Pennsylvania State University Press, 1975.

Chou, Chin-Seng. "An Economic History of China." Occasional Paper no. 7. Bellingham: Western Washington State College, 1974.

Davis, David L. "Ikki in Late Medieval Japan." In *Medieval Japan: Essays in Institutional Theory.* Edited by John W. Hall and Jeffrey P. Mass. New Haven, Conn.: Yale University Press, 1974.

Duus, Peter. *Feudalism in Japan.* New York: Alfred A. Knopf, 1969.

Elvin, Mark. *The Pattern of the Chinese Past.* Stanford, Calif.: Stanford University Press, 1973.

Fairbank, John K.; Reischauer, Edwin O.; and Craig, Albert M. *East Asia: Tradition and Transformation.* Boston: Houghton Mifflin, 1978.

Genicot, Leopold. "Crisis: From the Middle Ages to the Modern World." In *Cambridge Economic History of Europe.* Vol. 1: *The Agrarian Life of the Middle Ages.* Edited by M. M. Postan. Cambridge: Cambridge University Press, 1966.

Gregg, Pauline. *Black Death to Industrial Revolution: A Social and Economic History of England.* New York: Barnes & Noble, 1976.

Hilton, Rodney H. "Agrarian Class Structure and Economic Development in Pre-Industrial Europe." *Past and Present,* no. 80 (August 1978).

Hsu, Cho-Yun. *Ancient China in Transition: An Analysis of Social Mobility.* Stanford, Calif.: Stanford University Press, 1965.

Jacobs, Norman. *The Origin of Modern Capitalism and Eastern Asia.* Hong Kong: Cathay Press, 1958.

Kiley, Cornelius. "Estate and Property in the Late Heian Period." In *Medieval Japan: Essays in Institutional Theory.* Edited by John W. Hall and Jeffrey P. Mass. New Haven, Conn.: Yale University Press, 1974.

Li, Yu-Ning, ed. *Shang Yang's Reforms and State Control in China.* White Plains, N.Y.: M. E. Sharpe, 1977.

Mass, Jeffrey P. *Warrior Government in Early Medieval Japan: A Study of the Kamakura Bakufu, Shugo, and Jito.* New Haven, Conn.: Yale University Press, 1974.

Pan Ku. See Ban Gu.

Payne, Stanley G. *A History of Spain and Portugal.* 2 vols. Madison: University of Wisconsin Press, 1973.

Perkins, Dwight. *Agricultural Development in China, 1368–1968.* Chicago: Aldine Publishing, 1969.

Smith, Thomas C. *The Agrarian Origins of Modern Japan.* Stanford, Calif.: Stanford University Press, 1970.

Tawney, R. H. *Land and Labour in China.* London: George Allen & Unwin, 1932.

Twitchett, Denis C. *Financial Administration Under the T'ang Dynasty.* 2d ed. London: Cambridge University Press, 1970.

Wu, Ta-K'un. "An Interpretation of Chinese Economic History." *Past and Present,* no. 1 (February 1952).

Wunder, Heidi. "Peasant Organization and Class Conflict in East and West Germany." *Past and Present,* no. 78 (February 1978).

COMMENT

PROPERTY RIGHTS AND DEVELOPMENT: THE MORAL DIMENSION

Jo Ann Kwong

In his paper, John Powelson concludes by describing the importance of an economic system in which property rights are clearly defined, enforceable, and tradable. It is clearly useful to reiterate the fact that a system of private property rights establishes the elements for an efficient economic order. But it is equally important to emphasize that such a system also establishes a framework for a moral order.

Virtues of a Free Market

Much of the debate among Chinese planners focuses on providing a reasonable standard of living for the Chinese people, while meeting certain goals regarding fairness and equity. Market-oriented economies present a dilemma for planners—these economies can efficiently provide goods and services, yet the concept of private property typically conjures up images of selfishness, greed, profit seeking, and other elements that are believed to weaken moral character. I argue that a market system, resting on private property rights, provides the framework for creating a moral social order. While morality obviously cannot be coercively imposed by any type of institutional system, a market system does, in fact, foster voluntary cooperation, provide freedom of choice, reward responsibility, foster accountability, and create wealth by making people better off through voluntary exchange. It becomes easier to embrace the efficiency of the market if these other virtues are recognized.

The author is Director of Public Affairs at the Atlas Economic Research Foundation. She thanks Peter J. Hill for his insightful discussions of the relation between markets and morality.

Freedom of Organizational Choice

In many societies, capitalism is widely associated with the individual acting out of self-interest, often in conflict with the best interests of society. A capitalist free-market society, however, is simply a system that is based on private property rights and that allows people to voluntarily enter into exchange with each other. The system is noncoercive—people trade only if they want to, presumably because both buyer and seller are made better off through the exchange.

With freedom of choice to interact, people have greater flexibility in arranging their affairs. In contrast, people living under rigid, planned economies have far fewer opportunities. Centrally planned decisions leave little choice for those who are affected. In China's experimentation with the optimal size of the labor unit, for example, the peasants—who compose the backbone of the labor force—have had little say in the state's decisionmaking. They have been mobilized into mutual-aid teams, producer cooperatives, and advanced cooperatives. With the call to mobilize labor within villages, peasants were ordered into village-sized cooperatives. When the state wished to mobilize labor for larger projects, it ordered the development of communes. When problems with internal commune management and individual work incentives arose, it then became "expedient" to reduce the size of the communes for the sake of administrative convenience.

In addition to limiting individual freedom and flexibility, each successive organizational trial was tremendously costly. Costs were incurred as the state made investments to establish the new structures, tinkered with ways to readjust further, and failed to take into account the importance of incentives. These types of costs are evident, for example, in the first phase of China's collectivization effort. The infusion of surplus labor was expected to increase agricultural production. With little incentive for workers to be productive, however, agricultural production actually fell.

Under a system of private property rights, however, all organizational forms that have been experimented with in China remain available to people if they so choose. Property owners can voluntarily organize in communes, collectives, or other systems that they believe would improve their production or provide the way of life that they prefer. In the United States, for example, many American farmers have voluntarily pooled their resources to form agricultural cooperatives. The Amish population, concentrated largely in Pennsylvania, constitutes an entirely self-sufficient agricultural community that operates without electricity or automobiles. The Hutterite communities in the western United States and Canada also live in collective agricultural communities. These alternative arrangements are possible because a system of private property rights allows freedom of organizational choice, as long as such freedom does not violate the equal rights of others.

Incentives and Fairness

Unlike collectivized government experiments, the market system encourages individuals to act responsibly. Because they bear the costs of failed experiments, people have the incentive to carefully plan their actions and adjust the process to minimize losses and maximize gains. And because they reap the benefits of successful experiments, people are encouraged to be resourceful, to consider alternative arrangements that will improve their situation, and to continually look for ways to readjust their activities to be more productive. Arrangements that improve the situations of individuals will, in the aggregate, improve the situation of society as a whole. Under capitalism, therefore, the entrepreneurial incentive operates to increase the wealth of a nation, as opposed to the myth that capitalism necessarily drains social wealth.

The entrepreneurial incentive not only leads to situations in which society is made better off but also prevents the work incentive problem that plagues collectivized arrangements. The Chinese experimentation with the responsibility system, the point system, and so on were all intended to link reward with effort. Without clear rewards, however, people generally do not work beyond the minimum required. Because the private market system relies on the voluntary exchange of work for pay, it inherently links reward with effort, thereby eliminating the need to set rewards externally.

As a result of its built-in mechanism for rewarding effort, the private market system also can be very fair. People who choose to work harder or to be more innovative are made better off. Such a system is not limited only to people with money or with a certain class status. Anyone who provides goods or services that others want will be rewarded. In addition to being fair, a market-based system creates an environment in which people, acting out of self-interest, provide for the needs of others. People who produce goods that nobody wants will not succeed in a market economy.

A further argument for the fairness or equity of the market system is that it does not require leaders to coerce other people to do things. In the Chinese system, the ruling elite—not free-market signals— tell people what to do. Those in charge of the command system, therefore, are in a position to extract national wealth. Indeed, it is a well-known fact that China's leaders have living standards that are far above those of ordinary workers. It is also recognized that political power, not economic contribution, is the key to personal wealth in a state-run economy.

The preferred positions of the leaders are especially evident in their expressed resistance to change. Fearing that they will lose power and become "more equal" to the peasants, leaders and other government officials predictably oppose reform.

Economic Systems and Wealth Creation

Wealth is created when exchanges occur that leave both buyer and seller better off. Economic systems that simply transfer wealth, rather than create it, detract from the potential wealth of society. For example, when land is taken from one group and given to another, wealth is transferred. In contrast, when private property rights are established and protected, wealth is created as people engage in transactions to maximize the value of their holdings.

There are tremendous costs to economic systems that stifle the creation of wealth. In China, central planning prevents specialization and exchange in line with the principle of comparative advantage. Centrally imposed quotas fail to take account of differences in opportunity costs, and people are often prevented from using localized knowledge to efficiently produce goods and services. As a result, many activities are forgone that would increase consumer satisfaction and enhance national wealth.

Similarly, the creation of wealth has been stifled in China by state policies that prevent migration from rural to urban areas, while these same policies fix prices of rurally produced goods. The suppression of freedom of choice reduces the opportunities of people to combine resources to efficiently produce goods and services in the places and forms that are needed. In fact, because of China's program of sending urban youth to the countryside, there has been a substantial net reverse migration, despite demands for urban labor. This interference with the free flow of labor has further promoted inequity by creating a rising disparity between rural and urban incomes. The Chinese trend toward liberalizing rural agricultural prices can help alleviate the migration problems by opening up more opportunities in the rural areas. Furthermore, by increasing workers' flexibility to respond to market prices in rural areas, the disparities between rural and urban incomes can be reduced.

Conclusion

The market has a moral dimension as well as an efficiency dimension. Powelson points to the importance of private property rights for an efficient market order. While the definition, enforcement, and transferability of property rights are critical for economic well-being, they are also essential for a moral economic order—one based on freedom of choice rather than on government coercion.

Property rights must be clearly defined to give individuals a clear idea of what actions they can take regarding resources, that is, what they can and cannot do with their property. A complete specification establishes the rights to ownership, the restrictions on these rights, and the penalties for violation of the restrictions. Furthermore, when property rights are specified as exclusive, all rewards and penalties resulting from an action accrue directly to the owner because individuals face the full opportunity costs of their actions. This structure reduces both ignorance and uncertainty with regard to ownership, leading to an improvement in the system's ability to generate information. This in turn promotes the ability of individuals to make economically efficient decisions.

The enforcement of property rights also reduces uncertainty and assures the individual as to the rights of ownership. Again, this element provides the incentive for individuals to pursue economically efficient actions.

The transferability of the rights provides the opportunity for individuals to continually move their resources to the most highly valued uses. This flow of goods from one use to another is essential for ensuring maximum efficiency when resource prices (and, thus, their value) change.

When these elements are in place, a market order can evolve. The market order provides the critical virtue of freedom of choice—people are granted the freedom to assess the full range of options available to them, and to combine capital, land, or labor in the manner that is most efficient, productive, or practical for their needs.

Although the market system requires a more limited role for the state than a centrally planned economy, government retains a very important role in preserving the freedom of choice that is so essential. The state must establish and enforce rules that protect the rights of each individual to his or her person and property. Operating under the rule of law, which is designed to be carried out impartially, fairness is more likely to be achieved. Such an institutional system provides individuals with the incentives to be responsible and accountable, to care about the wants and desires of others, and to voluntarily cooperate with others. In this process, the free market helps to create a social and moral order—as well as a spontaneous economic order—in which the actions of individuals create wealth for society and foster harmony among its members.

COMMENT

REFORMING CHINA'S PROPERTY SYSTEM
Chen Weishu

The enlightening paper by John Powelson touches on the most important core of China's economic reform, that is, property rights. The property rights issue is one that provokes extensive and heated discussions, but the angle from which Powelson approaches the issue differs from that taken by most people in China's theoretical circle. That is why I find his paper of interest.

The Basic Issues

Three basic issues in Powelson's paper deserve attention. *First*, in China, the sovereign authority has always held the right to confiscate or transfer private property. This characteristic distinguishes China's property system from those of Japan and northwestern Europe. Even today, since 1949, China's centralized property system of state ownership has a touch of the vestiges of China's history and tradition. This condition reminds us that the background of China's economic reform is not only related to the Stalinist model but also to the centuries-old Chinese tradition. Therefore, to understand the complexity and appropriateness of the current reform, one must have a knowledge of China's long history. One should also recognize, as Powelson does, that ownership encompasses a bundle of rights and that the security of these rights depends on the balance of power among the pluralist political and social groups. Decisions about production, marketing, pricing, dividend distribution, retained earning, asset usage, and contracts are all affected by the *effective* ownership arrangement.

Second, in China, the rise and decline of rulers have always been accompanied by changes in the system of property. Reforms have often been reversed only to be renewed at a later time. In the present

The author is Associate Professor and Deputy Chairman of the Department of World Economy at Fudan University.

reform, we should be on guard against the danger of overthrowing the new and rational system that is taking shape. The real base for preventing the reversal lies in the building up of extensive public support by allowing independent property ownership. If the fate of property rights is still manipulated by the sovereign power or by a handful of people, then the danger of a reversal will always exist.

Third, as Powelson points out, in addition to property rights, other conditions are also essential for economic development—especially a system of laws that safeguard property rights.

Some Elaborations

Although I generally agree with Powelson's analysis, I find that the above-mentioned issues need further elaboration.

The idea of control by sovereign authority does not fully capture the essential feature of China's property system, either in the past or at present. This idea, however, may reflect distinctive Chinese characteristics when compared with Japan and Europe. Since the disintegration of the well-field system in the dynasties of Xia, Shang, and Zhou, three kinds of property systems regulating the use of land coexisted throughout the long period of China's feudal society: state ownership, ownership by peasants, and ownership by landlords. These three systems supplemented each other and formed different combinations at different times. The period from the Warring States (or Zhan Guo) to the middle of the Tang Dynasty was the early stage of China's feudal society and was characterized by an equal allocation of land. At that time, the ownership by landholding peasants was quite common. The royal court imposed restrictions on land and commerce in order to control the merger of land. The landlords were not very strong, so they often sided with landholding peasants to fight against the state ownership of land.

The failure of Wang Mon's royal-field system clearly demonstrated that the full control of land ownership by the sovereign will not work. Thereafter, private ownership of land gained a secure position. The period from the middle of the Tang Dynasty to the Ming and Qing Dynasties was the later stage of China's feudal society and was characterized by the merger of land and the private ownership of state land. The royal court encouraged the merger, buying, and selling of land. The enclosure and occupation of land became the order of the day. The conflict between the peasants and landlords led to a new coalition as the royal court came over to the side of the rich and the powerful.

188

Judging from the cycle of a single dynasty, one can see that each time chaos followed a war, the newly established dynasty would confiscate land and give it to those who supported the new regime. During the later stage of each dynasty, the royal court generally did not directly interfere with private property. It was free to buy and sell land. However, during the declining stage, when there were internal disorder and external intervention, the royal court was unable to occupy the private land directly.

The period from 1911 to 1949 was a chaotic era full of wars and hostilities. There was no unified and efficient central government; therefore, it was very difficult to control land and private property. However, when the People's Republic of China was established, private ownership of land was abolished and land became the collective property of the peasants. Although relative stability returned, the government has interfered with the management and administration of land, which has produced harmful effects and has become the target of economic reform.

With respect to economic development, the favorableness and applicability of the decentralized power system cannot be lumped together. We ask: Why could China, with long-standing centralized power, bring about the most prosperous economy in the world in the dynasties of Sui, Tang, Song, and Yuan? Why did the tide of government intervention in the economy and nationalization engulf the whole world after the Great Depression and World War II? Why could China, the Soviet Union, and other countries with central planning have such rapid growth in 1950s and 1960s? And why could government still have and use property rights in many sectors in the developed market economies? These questions deserve further attention.

Since the late 1970s, privatization has occurred in many countries. This trend is due, in part, to the important role played by the theory and ideas of Milton Friedman. China's economic reform is aimed at making the transition from an administrative economy commanded directly by the central government toward a market economy with indirect control by the central government. The movement toward a market economy or marketization in China, however, is not due to eternal faith or truth. It is due to the changes in the specific social and historical conditions—such as changes in science and technology; changes in the industrial structure; changes in the cost of energy; greater concern over environmental damage; and, in particular, the closer international linkage among trade, finance, and production.

The modern system of decentralized ownership differs markedly from the private property system at the time of Adam Smith. Today, the predominant form of ownership is not sole proprietorships but, rather, joint-stock companies. Although corporate assets are legally private property, their use is restricted to a great extent by the common will, in accordance with the benefits of the society or groups. Indeed, government regulation of corporate property has become commonplace. As such, it can be argued that, in a sense, corporate assets have really been transformed from private to social ownership.

The nature of ownership or property is defined with reference to the rights to possess and use property, the right to capture the consequent rewards, and the obligation to bear responsibility for losses. In the modern property system, property rights have a dual character. They represent a set of ownership rights held by natural persons while at the same time the corporation itself is treated as a legal person having certain rights and responsibilities. In this kind of system, no one is able to directly control the assets of large corporations. Nor can any individual gain direct control over the tangible assets (e.g., the buildings and equipment) represented by his stock certificates. What he can do is take part in elections or sell his shares. Therefore, the joint-stock ownership of property must be carefully distinguished from the direct private ownership that was prevalent during the time of Adam Smith. It is no longer appropriate to differentiate between public and private ownership without considering the unique features of joint-stock companies.

Finally, a property rights system should be conductive to economic development. However, that does not mean that the ownership arrangements should be conducive only to improving economic efficiency. The development of a social economy includes the improvement of both the ecological environment and quality of life, in addition to efficiency and economic growth. The whole world is now faced with the threat of energy shortages, environmental damage, grain shortages, over-population, poverty, debt, and nuclear war. These are the global problems that transcend differences between races and nations. The interdependent nature of these problems needs to be recognized by all countries. Accordingly, all nations should attempt to improve their property rights systems.

A New Path

Powelson's historical comparison of the property systems in China, Japan, and northwestern Europe provides a useful reference point for China's economic reform. In reforming China's property system, however, one cannot simply adhere to the traditional choice between a centralized system of property rights and a decentralized system.

Instead, China will have to search for a new path—one that will lead to a property system that avoids the past errors of both East and West.

9

PRIVATE PROVISION OF GOVERNMENT SERVICES
Gabriel Roth

Meaning of Private Provision

The private provision of services can be carried out in a number of different ways. Where there are many buyers and many sellers, conventional markets can be organized to enable customers to seek the best values from competing suppliers, while suppliers can attempt to make the best possible deals with competing customers. However, there are at least five other ways in which goods or services can be provided by private suppliers: (1) through contracts from public agencies, (2) through monopoly franchises, (3) through management contracts, (4) through vouchers, and (5) through consumer cooperatives.

Contracts from Public Agencies

Even where government is responsible for a sector, such as roads, all or some activities of this sector can be contracted out to private firms. For example, in numerous countries, private contractors maintain roads and buildings. These contractors are selected as a result of bidding on work specifications prepared by the road or building authorities. Similarly, in seven U.S. cities and in London and other U.K. cities, private companies are paid to provide bus services. The city of La Mirada, California (population 42,000), contracts out more than 75 essential services and has only 75 full-time employees. Also in the United States, the private Corrections Corporation of America operates prisons for state governments. Instead of public provision (for example, by state-employed personnel), the government determines specifications for contracting out and provides public financ-

The author is a Consulting Civil Engineer and Transport Economist in Washington, D.C. He was formerly with the Economic Development Institute of the World Bank. A fuller treatment of the subject of his paper is given in *The Private Provision of Government Services in Developing Countries* (Roth 1987).

ing of private provision. The variety of public services contracted out in the United States is illustrated by the examples shown in Table 1.

Monopoly Franchises

Where natural monopoly or decreasing costs require that an area be supplied by a single organization, a private company can be appointed by a public authority to provide services, on a monopoly basis, at specified standards and tariffs. In France, for example, water is often provided by private companies that compete among themselves for the rights to provide water to different cities. Because of the long life of the required equipment, such contracts are usually given for a period of 20–30 years. Monopoly franchises for the supply of electricity were common in many countries and still play a major role in the United States. (But franchising need not be monopolistic. It is possible, for example, to franchise a number of competing taxi firms in the same area.)

Management Contracts

In the case of monopoly franchises, it is customary for the company awarded the franchise to make the required investments. Another possibility is for the public agency to retain responsibility for the service but to arrange for private management. One such example is provided by the Botswana telephone service, which is managed by Cable and Wireless PLC, a U.K. firm. In the United States, many urban bus companies are municipally owned but are managed by private management firms.

Vouchers

Vouchers represent an array of systems that enable consumers to get free or reduced-cost goods or services while retaining the power of choosing among competing suppliers. In the United States, vouchers are best known in the form of food stamps that enable poor people to receive subsidized food without the authorities having to open special low-price food shops. At the end of World War II a successful U.S. application in education (the G.I. Bill) gave cash grants to discharged soldiers whereby they could receive an education at any approved higher educational establishment of their choice. A variant of the voucher system is currently used in Chile to enable children to go to primary schools chosen by the parents, with the government paying the bill. Housing vouchers are used in Britain and in the United States to enable low-income people to obtain rented accommodation at free-market rents.

TABLE 1

PRIVATELY SUPPLIED MUNICIPAL SERVICES

Large Urban Governments in the United States

Dallas
Building Security
Engineering
Delinquent Tax Collection
Janitorial
Parking Management
Parks Maintenance
Recreation Services
Solid-Waste Collection
Street Lighting
Street Resurfacing
Workers Compensation Claims Management

Houston
Building Security
Recreation Facility Management
Sewage Disposal (via regional authority that
    contracts with private firm)
Solid-Waste Collection
Solid-Waste Disposal
Tax Collection
Vehicle Repair

New York
Golf Course Management/Operation
Parking Ticket Processing
Recreation Facility Management
Street-Light Maintenance

Phoenix
Building/Grounds Maintenance
Building Security
Bus System Management & Operation
Janitorial
Landfill Operation
Parking Lot Operation
Street & Traffic Light Maintenance
Solid-Waste Collection
Street Sweeping

Philadelphia
Convention Center Management/Operation
Golf Course Management/Operation
Homeless-Shelter Operation
Parking Enforcement
Parking Management
Vehicle Repair/Maintenance

TABLE 1 (con't)

PRIVATELY SUPPLIED MUNICIPAL SERVICES

Large Urban Governments in the United States

Kansas City
Auditing
Laundry
Solid-Waste Collection
Window Washing

Los Angeles County
Asphalt Resurfacing
Building/Grounds Maintenance
Building Security
Fleet Management/Maintenance
Golf Course Management
Janitorial
Management Audits
Records Storage
Solid-Waste Collection
Street Resurfacing
Street Sweeping

San Diego
Appraisal Services
Architectural & Engineering Services
Emergency Medical Service
Management & Financial Audits

San Francisco
Animal Control
Convention Center Management
Solid-Waste Collection
Police Patrol

San Jose
Janitorial
Parking Management
Solid-Waste Collection
Street Cleaning
Water Supply
Waste Recycling

SOURCE: Reason Foundation's Local Government Center and the University of Miami's Law and Economics Center (1988).

Consumer Cooperatives

Consumer cooperatives—which range in size from a few dozen members to hundreds of thousands—are self-governing, voluntary organizations run by their members. Unlike shareholders' companies, which distribute surpluses in proportion to share ownership, consumer cooperatives distribute surpluses to members in proportion to their purchases. Designed to serve the interests of their members, consumer cooperatives are particularly acceptable in monopoly situations (for example, village electricity), where consumers may not be able to benefit from competition among suppliers.

Meaning of Government Services

For purposes of this paper, "government services" means any services provided by government in China, be it the central government, a provincial government, a municipal or local government, or a government agency such as a railway corporation, a port bureau, or an electric power administration. These government services have two main characteristics: (1) The quantity and quality of the service or goods provided are determined not by what consumers are prepared to pay but by what governments determine is appropriate to provide, and (2) the prices that are charged for the goods and services produced are determined not by consideration of profit or loss but by political or other considerations.

Advantages of Private Provision

Before discussing the advantages of private provision of government services, or at least of some government services, it is important to mention one consideration that is not a factor in the discussion: This paper is not suggesting that people who work in the private sector are more clever than those who work in the public sector, or that they work harder or more effectively, or that they are in any way superior to people who work in government. In the context of China, which invented the system of competitive examination whereby the brightest children from across the country were brought into government service, such a statement would be particularly inappropriate. The case for the private sector has to be made on different grounds. The most important arguments in its favor are (a) that private markets for voluntary transactions among many buyers and sellers, taken as a whole, have a better information base than government; and (b) that private companies can go backrupt when they perform badly while government agencies cannot.

The idea that private markets have better information than government may sound strange; the explanation lies in the fact that the future is unknown, and that private businesses have many forecasts while government, in general, has only one. The point can be illustrated by the failure of the Indian Railways Board to come anywhere near a correct forecast for its coal traffic some 25 years ago. When a high-level commission of inquiry criticized the railway board for having failed to forecast correctly, the board defended itself by claiming that it had used the official government forecasts that were embedded in the 5-year plans. The commission was not satisfied and reported that the board should have made its own forecasts. One cannot help wondering how many agencies in planned economies are in a position to ignore official forecasts and to substitute their own.

If, as is usually the case, the prices of governmentally supplied services are determined by political decisions rather than in competitive markets, the suppliers and consumers affected do not have the information that freely negotiated prices reveal. For example, farmers who are able to plant different crops are not able to choose the one for which their customers are prepared to pay the most. The difficulty of the state getting information was noted in China in 1984 by the Central Committee, which stated: "Since social demand is very complex and in a state of constant flux, since the conditions in enterprises differ in a thousand and one ways, and since the economic links between enterprises are complicated, no state institution can know the whole situation fully and cope with everything in good time" (Prychitco 1987).

The ability of firms to go bankrupt is probably the most important aspect of private enterprise. Everybody will agree that government agencies design and implement useful works, such as the 80,000 kilometers of interstate highway in the United States, possibly the greatest and most expensive ($50 billion) public works program ever executed anywhere.

Closing an enterprise is quite another matter. If operated by the private sector, technical change forces the contraction of some activities and the expansion of others, such as the switch from typewriters to microcomputers in the United States today. But governmental activities, which are buttressed by political interest, are much more difficult to close, and we all have our favorite examples of projects that have outlived their usefulness and whose main purpose is support of the workers and administrators employed by them.

Given these important advantages of private provision—and there are others that need not be mentioned here—one might ask whether there is any role for government in providing goods and services. The answer to this question is clear: There are important roles for

198

governments; not all goods and services can be provided by private markets.

Why Government May Have to Provide Services

The economic literature describes five situations of potential "market failure" in which private markets cannot necessarily be relied on to provide the most appropriate pattern of services in an efficient way: (1) where there are natural monopolies; (2) where increased production is associated with decreasing costs; (3) where there are substantial externalities, which are not reflected in the accounts of private suppliers; (4) where it is difficult to charge for a service, or to exclude those who do not pay; and (5) where there are merit goods.

Natural Monopolies

Some services can be supplied only by means of a factor of production that cannot be duplicated. For example, the water supply for a city may derive from just one source. In these circumstances a private owner of the water source would not be subject to direct competition and would, therefore, be in a position to exploit those dependent on the service by charging prices considerably in excess of his cost of extraction and distribution. In this kind of situation, there are advantages in having the service provided by a public agency, which is politically responsible to the beneficiaries. On the other hand, there would also be disadvantages if public provision led to higher costs of production and a reduced rate of innovation. A judgment has to be made as to which is the lesser of two evils (or failures). In some situations, alternatives such as regulation or franchising may deserve consideration.

Decreasing Costs

The efficiency of productive enterprise, measured as the ratio of output to costs of input, can often be increased by enlarging the scale of production. This increased efficiency can happen for many different reasons: Specialized equipment (such as a machine tool), which cannot be justified for a small productive unit, might be installed; workers specializing in a narrower range of activities could become more proficient; or inputs could be bought more cheaply in large quantities. If economies of scale are so great that the industry can support only a few firms, or even only a single firm, there is a danger of monopoly power. This situation may call for government regulation or ownership, but we must bear in mind that these alternatives have disadvantages as well as advantages.

The early history of urban transport provides an example of a decreasing cost industry. When electrically powered vehicles (trams or streetcars) provided mechanized transport, one large generating system could power many vehicles; additional vehicles could be accommodated at a comparatively small increase in power costs. This fact provided a strong case for establishing large, single enterprises to operate urban transport. This tradition of organizing urban transport in large centrally directed fleets has continued even in cities where electrically powered transport systems have been replaced by individually powered, diesel-engined buses, which are not necessarily cheaper to operate in large numbers.

Externalities

Cases frequently occur when buyers and sellers who exchange goods and services create costs or benefits (externalities) for people not directly involved in the exchange. For example, factories or automobiles can cause pollution (negative externalities); beautiful gardens or people are a source of pleasure to passers-by (positive externalities). Economists used to argue that, in the absence of government action, there is overproduction of goods and services involving negative externalities, and underproduction of those involving positive externalities. Various remedies were suggested including taxes to discourage negative externalities and subsidies to encourage positive ones.

Activities relating to education and public health are often associated with positive externalities, insofar as people benefit if their fellow citizens are better educated and healthier. It is, therefore, often suggested that these services should be financed or subsidized by government, or even provided by public agencies, and not left to the private marketplace.

Inability to Charge, or to Exclude Nonpayers

Some goods and services have to be provided to a group as a whole and cannot be subdivided for the benefit of particular individuals. Typical examples are national defense, street lighting, and radio or TV broadcasting. Economists have named goods and services of this kind "pure public goods." Whatever level of service is provided is available to everybody, regardless of the extent to which individuals choose to avail themselves of the service. Furthermore, there is no way in which individual use can be charged for or in which nonusers can be excluded from nonpayment. (For example, a radio broadcast can be picked up by any radio in the area.) Because of the impossibility of charging, or of excluding nonpayers, the private market would not find it profitable to supply pure public goods; hence (it is said), the government has to act to ensure their provision.

Merit Goods

Economists use the term "merit goods" to describe those goods and services that society considers to have special merit and that, if left to private markets, could be produced in insufficient quantity. Health, education, and housing are often thought of as merit goods, at least up to a certain minimum level. Other examples are school lunches and water fluoridation programs. Merit goods may be associated with the positive externalities mentioned earlier, but this need not always be the case; the idea of merit goods is not that third parties would benefit from the provision of such goods, but that the people who receive them would themselves benefit to a greater extent than they believe. Because people would not voluntarily buy sufficient merit goods, it is suggested that those goods should be provided free by public agencies. An alternative possibility is to finance or subsidize provision by the private market.

These five cases are the main market failure situations described in the economic literature to show where the provision of goods and services in uncontrolled private markets may not be satisfactory. Services that do not fall within any of the above categories can generally be provided satisfactorily by competing firms or individuals. Table 2 shows how these situations might apply to the government services discussed below—education, water supply, electricity supply, urban transport, telecommunications, and roads. Obviously, situations vary from place to place and from one period to another: Water supply might be a monopoly in Hong Kong but not in Shanghai; formal education might be considered a merit good in some societies but not in others. The relative roles of the public and private sectors change, and the division of activities between them may have to be reviewed accordingly.

Furthermore, the possibility of government failure, as well as market failure, must be considered. The private market may be faulty, but the government remedy may be worse. The need is, therefore, to choose, not among alternative hypothetical "ideal" cases, but among alternative institutional arrangements as they would actually work in practice.

Examples of Government Services that Are Provided Privately

The number of government services provided privately is immense. Hundreds of examples, ranging from firefighting to airport

TABLE 2

"MARKET FAILURE" CHARACTERISTICS OF SOME GOVERNMENTAL SERVICES

	Education	Water Supply	Electricity Supply	Urban Transport	Tele-communications	Roads
Natural Monopoly	No	Sometimes	No	No	No	No
Decreasing Costs	No	Some	Some	No	Some	Some
Externalities	Yes	Yes	No	No	No	No
Difficult to Charge	No	Not easy	No	No	No	No
Merit Goods	Yes	Possibly	No	No	No	No

management, have been recorded in which private operation is associated with improved service or reduced costs. All I can do in this paper is take a few important sectors, comment on the applicability of the criteria listed in the previous section, and describe some roles played by the private sector.

Education

Education is not a service characterized by natural monopoly, nor are the scale economies involved in teaching of a kind that justifies government involvement. Education is not a "pure public good" as defined above, because it can be imparted to individuals and charged for.

However, education does have two characteristics that can be said to justify public intervention: It is associated with externalities that many consider to be important; and, at least insofar as education of children is concerned, it can be said to be a "merit good" in that beneficiaries might not recognize its importance.

But the fact that education is associated with important benefits is not sufficient reason for it to be provided by government. Government can finance education in various ways and can still leave its provision to private educational establishments. Both in its early history and recently, China has amply demonstrated that education can be provided privately, even by poor people.

Education in China has traditionally been accorded great respect; the Chinese invented competitive scholastic examinations, and the winners received the top jobs in government service. Despite this history, education in China was mainly private; Confucious reportedly declared that he would teach anybody who bought him a meal, implying that he did not mind how much he was paid, so long as the principle of payment was accepted. A visitor to China in the 19th century noted that

> there are numerous primary schools in China supported by the people of a neighborhood who choose to send their children. There are no schoolhouses, schools being commonly held in a spare hall or room belonging to a private family, or in part of the village temple. There is no village tax nor any aid from government received for the support of schools. Each parent must pay the teacher for the instruction of his children.

An early 19th-century estimate from Kwantung suggested that in rural districts 50 percent of the men could read, as compared to the estimated 80–90 percent within the city of Canton. The knowledge of arithmetic sufficient to carry on business was also widespread (Rawski 1979).

Villagers in China would frequently get together and invite a teacher to set up classes. Popular almanacs included contract forms, which suggests that engaging a teacher in this way was a common practice. The expenses of operating a school were not very great; students' desks were often furnished by their parents, so furniture was not a necessary cost to the school. Teachers' salaries had to be paid, but they could be quite low. Because government officials were selected from the ranks of scholars, and because scholars could bring honor and wealth to their villages, encouraging the education of its talented members was in the interest of every community. In some areas (as in the early American colonies), parents were punished if they refused to pay school fees for bright boys when they could afford to pay. And when parents could not afford the fees, scholarships were available.

In the absence of direct government funding, schools were established by local officials, by local elite families, or by guilds or groups of villagers. A vital task in establishing a school was to secure the funds needed to allow it to open year after year. Schools were often endowed with money, land, or buildings, and the use of land as a permanent source of income for schools was particularly important in China. School lands differed from privately owned plots in that they could not be sold freely. Schools obtained land from donations from private citizens and officials, who transfered confiscated plots, untaxed land, or temple holdings to schools. The lands were then rented out to tenants who paid rent either in cash or in kind; funds thus obtained were used to defray salaries and other expenses. It is noteworthy that a similar funding method is used today in Africa: When the private Kamuzu Academy was recently established in Malawi, 250 acres of tobacco land were donated to it, as a permanent source of income.

In more modern times, schools set up by Chinese immigrant communities in Southeast Asia—in Indonesia, Malaysia, the Philippines, Singapore, and Thailand—clearly demonstrate the viability of private education for children of all age groups and income classes following the migration of Chinese people (some very poor) to those countries during the first half of this century. Private tutorial groups providing a classical education for a small number of select children have been common in Chinese societies throughout history. But, in the 20th century, immigrants established new schools designed to offer a modern, Chinese-style education to all Chinese youth: boys and girls, rich and poor.

In some countries, such as Singapore, these Chinese schools receive governmental help. But in the Philippines, Chinese schools, until they were banned in 1976, were privately financed. Furthermore, children attending these schools in the Philippines received a much more demanding education because Chinese schools were allowed to operate only on the condition that they taught the normal, Filipino curriculum in addition to the Chinese curriculum. The usual way in which Chinese schools met this requirement was by offering the Filipino curriculum in the morning and the Chinese in the afternoon. The quality of this Chinese education may be gauged from the fact that those who completed it were eligible to enter Chinese-speaking universities (Orr 1977).

Water Supply

Of all public services, providing piped water is the one with which the private sector is least involved. It may be no coincidence that water is also a sector in which there are very serious problems. For example, according to World Bank data, in 1980 only one-third of households in China had access to safe water. Can the private sector help to remedy this situation?

While water vending—the sale of water by carriers—has been common in all countries throughout history, distribution of piped water for profit by the private sector is unusual. Many criteria for public provision apply to water: There can be a natural monopoly in the extraction of water; increased production and distribution over a wider area can be associated with decreasing costs; substantial externalities can be associated with the supply of safe water, and also with the safe removal of sewage; and water can be a merit good in the sense that some people might not appreciate the advantage of safe water. On the other hand, piped water cannot be considered a pure public good in the technical sense, because it is possible to charge for piped water, although it may not be easy to do so.

As we consider the role that the private sector might play in providing piped water, it is useful to distinguish among three different aspects of the problem: (1) the distribution of water for domestic consumption; (2) the extraction of ground water from wells for domestic consumption and also for agriculture and industry; and (3) the diversion of water from rivers for domestic consumption, agriculture, and industry.

Distribution of Water for Domestic Use. The private provision of water for domestic services is common in France. To avoid the cost of separate distribution systems, municipalities use bidding processes to select firms that have exclusive contracts to supply a municipal area. The two most common arrangements are the "concession" system and the "affermage" system.

In the concession system, the public authority contracts out to a single, private operator for both a construction and an operation concession. The concessionnaire finances, constructs, and operates (at its own risk) all facilities for supplying drinking water. When the concession contract ends, the concessionnaire must return the system to the public authority in perfect condition, which means that during the contract the concessionnaire must replace worn-out equipment and must recover its invested capital.

To realize a return on its investment, the concessionnaire sells water to consumers in accordance with the concession contract. That price takes account of economic trends during the life of the contract—inflation, economies of scale, taxation, legislation, and so forth. Therefore, the concession contract does not specify a single price but rather a set of rules enabling the sale price to be calculated each year.

The concession contract also fixes the level of service to be provided by the concessionnaire: the water quality and source; the quantity of water to be supplied without charge to the public authorities (standposts, sewer flush, fire hydrants, and street cleaning); obligations and terms of connecting up consumers; and so forth.

To enable the amortization of the concessionnaire's investment to be spread over a long period, concession contracts are generally for a long term, usually 30 years. A long-term contract tends to reduce the price to the consumer.

In the "affermage" system, the public authority handles construction of the system by itself and awards contracts to a single private operator (the "fermier") for the system's operation and maintenance, collection of charges, and relations with the consumers. This is an operating concession only.

As under the concession system, the fermier discharges the assigned tasks at its own risk. This means the fermier must discharge those tasks according to its contract and is compensated only by selling the water. The contract sets the sale price.

To enable the public authority to amortize its initial investments, the water price customarily includes a surcharge that is collected by the fermier for the authority's account and is then paid to the authority. Through the contract, the authority retains title to the system.

Extraction of Ground Water. Ground water, which is obtained from wells, is a major source of water. In the western United States it accounts for more than 40 percent of consumption, and this proportion has been increasing steadily for the past 40 years. In many areas these resources are being depleted faster than they are being replaced: One reason is that ground water is a common resource, so individuals with access to it have no incentive to economize in its consumption. As in the case of people seeking firewood on public land, individuals realize that anything they leave behind will be taken by others.

The private sector has already developed an answer to the problem of multiple drilling into a common pool—a solution that was not worked out for water, but for oil. Because the petroleum mining industry developed legal and contractual mechanisms that enable several drillers to extract oil from the same reservoir, the private sector is enabled to extract oil in the United States, in the Middle East, and in some other countries. If similar arrangements could be made for water, which would give those who seek it clear, transferable, and enforceable property rights, then the extraction of ground water might be considerably improved.

Diversion of River Water. Oil does not flow in rivers, and there do not appear to be any systems that enable individuals to own property rights in river waters. In some countries, such as the United Kingdom and the United States, the rights to water are owned by those whose property is alongside the river. This arrangement generally means that no one owner can extract water from the river without the permission of all other landowners, which in practice means that water has to be allocated by administrative and government rules rather than by commercial contracts that are based on private ownership. This may be the reason why there are comparatively few cases of water being transferred in large quantities from where it is abundant to where it is scarce. If this problem has not yet been solved in China, it would seem worthy of early investigation. If a legal framework could be set up enabling water to be owned and sold, its usefulness would be enhanced many times over (Anderson and Leal 1988).

Electricity

Electricity can be charged for, so it is not a pure public good, nor is it a merit good. And it does not have significant externalities. But electricity transmission and distribution may be said to have the characteristics of natural monopoly, in that it might, under certain circumstances, be more costly to have more than one system. Thus there can be good economic reasons for electricity transmission and distribution to be carried out by the public sector, or at least to be strictly controlled by it. But the same cannot be said about electricity generation. Many private companies generate electricity for their own industrial use, and there is no reason why they should not simultaneously generate power for sale to private entities or to a public sector transmission and distribution system.

Moreover, privately generated electricity need not be produced only as a by-product of other activities. In India, the Tata Electric Companies have had a long history of generating power for public use. They own their own generating stations with a total installed capacity of more than 11,000 megawatts. In the United States, Virginia Power, the utility responsible for providing the people of Virginia with electric power, announced in March 1988 that it was willing to buy all of its future power needs from private contractors. The projects offered to Virginia Power involved a variety of different types of power sources, including plants that burn coal or wood, plants that burn municipal wastes, and cogeneration plants that would be set up at industrial sites and that would produce electricity for Virginia Power and steam for other purposes. As a result of the announcement, private companies offered to install enough capacity to generate 20,000 megawatts of electricity, the equivalent of about 20 large-scale power plants that could light 2 million homes. This offer was far more additional power than was needed, and Virginia Power expected to be able to buy what it required at very favorable prices (*Washington Post* 1988).

People sometimes suggest that only rich countries, such as the United States, can afford the luxury of having a variety of generating stations producing power and that less-affluent countries should have their power generated in a few large plants situated in carefully selected areas. Is it not possible that this suggestion mixes up cause and effect, that people in the United States become affluent because laws are passed that encourage a variety of activities, and that planning processes in the so-called command economies prevent individuals from becoming affluent? We should note that many small hydropower generating stations in California use microhydro generators made in China. An uninformed observer cannot help wondering whether entrepreneurs in China have as much freedom to use Chinese generating equipment as do entrepreneurs in California.

Urban Transport

Although none of the market failure characteristics apply to urban transport, the conventional wisdom in many countries is that this service cannot be provided in cities at a profit, that it must be supplied by publicly owned or franchised monopolies, and that such services have to be slow and costly. This view is particularly prevalent in North America and Western Europe; people living in Asia, Africa, and Latin America know that it is possible to provide public transport without subsidy—at acceptable standards and at prices that most people can afford. How is this done?

Four characteristics are associated with viable urban transport systems: (1) private ownership, (2) small vehicles, (3) small operating units, and (4) route associations that are part of many successful operations.

It is not easy to isolate these characteristics, because they tend to be associated with one another (for example, private operators run small fleets of small vehicles), but there is evidence to illustrate the effects of each.

Private Ownership. The availability of public funds to cover losses results in two major handicaps to publicly operated systems: the inability to hold down costs and the inability to resist political pressures to provide unremunerative services. These difficulties may be illustrated by the case of Bangkok.

In the early 1970s, Bangkok had 24 franchised bus companies, all of which provided service for a basic fare of about US$.04. The biggest company, the Nai Lert, managed by Khunying Loesak (later Minister of Transport), was consistently profitable. In 1976, following recommendations by European consultants, the government decided to amalgamate the 24 companies and to create the Bangkok Metropolitan Transport Authority (BMTA). The plan was carried through despite the protests of Khunying Loesak and many other operators. Shortly after the buses were taken over by the city, fares were raised by 20 percent and yet the system began operating at a deficit. By 1979, the BMTA was losing the equivalent of over US$25 million a year, while an estimated 7,000 privately owned minibuses were running at a profit. Improved wages to bus crews and reduced use of vehicles seem to be the main reasons for the change from profit to loss. By 1984, the bus fare had risen to double its 1976 level and the BMTA had accumulated debts equivalent to about US$185 million.

Evidence from Australia, the United Kingdom, and the United States confirms that publicly owned transport operators have higher costs than privately owned ones, even when providing similar services, because they have less flexibility in making the best use of their resources and because they pay more to their employees. In transport, as in other fields (education, medical services, and housing), the discipline of having to live within one's budget applies a constant downward pressure on costs, a pressure that is all too easily relieved by the availability of subsidies from public funds.

A study undertaken by the World Bank (Feibel and Walters 1980) showed that in a number of cities (for example, Calcutta, Bangkok, and Istanbul), the cost of private bus services was between 50 percent and 60 percent of the costs of publicly owned concerns. Although employees of private bus companies earn less, on the average, than their public counterparts, those private employees in the three cities earned average or above-average wages. Wage costs per bus-hour under private ownership are likely to be much lower than costs in the public sector because of less-restrictive labor contracts and because of lower absenteeism and redundancy.

The study found little evidence to support the conventional allegation that private services are less safe than public ones. In addition, the charge that private operators "skim the cream" by serving only the most profitable routes does not seem to be supportable. In Calcutta and Istanbul the public system gets first choice of routes; in Bangkok the private minibuses serve the narrow and unpaved side roads on which regular buses cannot operate.

People often suggest that levels of service deteriorate on routes taken over by private operators. This contention is not supported by the evidence. In Calcutta, passengers using routes taken over by private operators enjoyed bus services that were more evenly scheduled, were marginally more comfortable, were less subject to breakdown, and were considered to have a better general appearance and performance. In Istanbul private minibuses had a faster operating speed than public buses. In general, private operators are more readily inclined to adjust to changing demands than are public enterprises.

Size of Vehicle. One of the established (but questionable) principles of operating public transport is that large vehicles are more economical to operate than small ones. The reason given for this principle is that, with labor costing more than two-thirds of all bus operating expenses, it pays for a bus company to have large vehicles. Even if those buses are full for only a fraction of their working lives, large vehicles avoid additional labor costs that would be required to meet peak demand with small vehicles. This reasoning, though perfectly logical, may be questioned on two grounds.

The first ground is that capital cost *per seat* seems to increase with the size of the vehicle. For example, while operators in San Juan, Puerto Rico, once paid $25,000 for a minibus seating 17, they now pay $200,000 for a full-sized bus seating 50. Thus, a full-sized bus can cost almost three times as much per unit of passenger capacity as a minibus. (Incidentally, the same pattern is evident if the operators move up to a rail car: A vehicle seating, say, 150 passengers can easily cost $1 million.) The main reason for this escalating per seat cost is that small vehicles (such as minibuses) can be mass produced and bought off the shelf, while large vehicles tend to be made to special order and assembled as separate units.

The second ground favoring the small bus is more subtle, but may be more important. For a given route capacity, small buses provide more frequent service than large ones and, therefore, involve less waiting time per passenger. This factor might not matter to a franchised operator who has to bear the costs of his crew but not the waiting time of his customers; hence, monopoly operators prefer big vehicles. However, where competition is allowed, people who provide public transport respond to the needs of the passengers, most of whom dislike waiting for buses. One way to reduce waiting is to use smaller vehicles to provide more frequent service. It is significant that when private bus operators took over the municipal service in Buenos Aires in 1962, one of their first actions was to replace large municipal buses with smaller ones. The small bus has other advantages: Because it holds fewer passengers, it is easier to fill with people starting at one point and wishing to travel to another. Thus, the small bus stops less frequently and for shorter periods than large buses, and, being more maneuverable, the small bus can often make its way more quickly along congested roads.

However, small buses are not a panacea suited to all circumstances. Where the demand for travel is heavy enough to sustain even big buses at high frequency, as in Calcutta and Shanghai, they may well provide the most economical solution. The choice of vehicle size is a decision that, under competitive conditions, is best left to the operators.

Size of Operating Unit. Much evidence suggests that large bus fleets incur financial losses under the same conditions that small operators make profits. Although operators the world over are reluctant to admit to making profits, the pressures to obtain permits to provide service, plus the prices at which permits in some cities change hands (or are hired out), are sure indications of profitability. This situation may be illustrated by the case of Calcutta.

Calcutta is one of the largest, most densely populated, and poorest cities in the world. It supports a population of some 10 million in an area that covers less than 600 square miles. Private buses first appeared in the city toward the end of the 19th century but were banned in 1960 when all bus services were vested in the Calcutta State Transport Corporation. The CSTC suffered from managerial and financial problems and in 1966 was paralyzed by strikes. In response to public demand before the 1966 elections, and to its need for ready cash, the government of West Bengal sold permits that allowed 300 private buses to be put into operation. These vehicles made a profit, even though they charged the same fare (equivalent to about US$.05 per mile) as the money-losing CSTC and had inferior routes. By the late 1970s, some 1,500 full-sized private buses were operating in Calcutta in addition to about 500 private minibuses. During the 1980s, unsubsidized private buses accounted for about two-thirds of all bus trips in Calcutta. Meanwhile, the CSTC, which operated similar routes at the same fares, had to be subsidized to the equivalent of US$1 million a month by a government that was desperately short of funds for other purposes.

The success of the Calcutta private bus operators has been attributed to three factors:

- Keeping vehicles on the road. As soon as a private bus breaks down, it is repaired, often on the road, and the parts, if necessary, are bought on the black market. The CSTC, in contrast, must go through formal channels to obtain spare parts, and only half of its buses are generally on the road.
- Fare collection. The private bus crews (who are paid a percentage of the revenues) make greater efforts to collect the fares than do CSTC employees. Fare evasion is estimated to be 25 percent on CSTC buses, whereas it is negligible on private buses.
- Higher labor productivity. Private buses use fewer staff members than the CSTC, which employs 50 employees per bus and thus has one of the highest staffing levels in the world.

The reasons for financial viability of the small transport firm, be it a mover, a taxi driver, or a bus operator, are well known and typical of other types of small businesses in the service sector. Owners are willing to work longer and less-regular hours than would a paid bus driver in a large fleet. They will clean their own vehicles or enlist the help of family members. They will appreciate the need for regular vehicle maintenance. They will not have their own depot but will service their vehicle on the street or at a local garage. Their record-keeping will be minimal. They will make a greater effort than a paid driver to collect fares from passengers and to ensure that the amounts collected do not get lost on the way. An extra driver can be employed if two shifts a day have to be run. Some facilities, such as two-way radio service, can add to earnings without owners relinquishing control of their vehicles.

The Route Association. Another factor in the success of private buses in Calcutta is the route association. These associations were formed voluntarily and spontaneously by private owners. Each owner retains control over the operation and maintenance of his own vehicle and receives the fares collected on it. The associations have rules to govern relationships among members; for example, vehicles must run on time. This promptness is important because a bus running late tends to pick up more passengers than a bus running on time, at the expense of the following bus. Owners of buses that do not run on time are fined by the association. It has been reported that the fines are, in some instances, proportional to the delay (at a specified rate per minute) and are paid directly to the owner of the following bus.

The precise organization of a route association varies from city to city. Any group operating a route has an interest in limiting its numbers and also in ensuring that its members work harmoniously with one another. Therefore, conditions must be imposed on entry (possibly an entrance fee). In many cities (Buenos Aires, Manila, Calcutta, and Hong Kong) route associations compete with one another so that no group has a monopoly over an entire route. There have been reports of infighting among competing groups of operators, but route associations generally work well, serving both the public and their members.

But can the private provision for public transport, by itself, offer the promise of urban mobility at levels desired by travelers? So long as the road network is operated as a "free good" by the public sector and so long as the private sector is unable to expand urban road networks to the extent that road users are willing to pay for them, one cannot envisage any rational solution to the problem of traffic congestion. (Some ideas on this subject are discussed later in this paper.)

Telecommunications

Although telecommunications might be characterized by decreasing costs (the matter is debatable), it is, of all public services, the one that is the easiest and most profitable for the private sector to provide. But there are still vast areas where people have to wait years for telephone connections, where service is frequently provided only when bribes are paid, and where economic development is hindered by the lack of adequate communications. The fault lies in the refusal of governments to allow the private sector to provide telephone connections to those prepared to pay prices appropriate in a competitive market.

Most telecommunication systems today are centrally controlled as government monopolies, but telecommunication systems were actually developed by the private sector during the late 19th century. In the United States, service was provided by thousands of companies—some large, some small—that voluntarily adopted common standards enabling a national interconnected network to be formed. Even today, more than 1,500 separate private telephone companies in the United States provide local service, and some 40 companies provide long-distance service. Europe, which is equivalent in population and size to China, has dozens of different telephone networks, all interconnected. Almost all are public sector oganizations. Private sector providers are found in the United States, in some of the Caribbean islands, and in a few countries in which telecommunications have recently been privatized, such as Malaysia and the United Kingdom. Competition, in the sense of consumers being given a choice in telephone service, exists only in the United States for long-distance calls. Telephones owned by local cooperatives can be found in Finland, Bolivia, and Chile.

How could the private sector be brought in to improve telecommunication in China? If such an idea were to find favor, the government should do two things:

- It should specify the technical standards that would enable systems provided by different suppliers to interconnect. The kind of standardization that is required is in the compatibility of signaling levels, of transmission characteristics, of voltage levels, and of other aspects of communications.
- Arrangements would have to be worked out for sharing revenues. If different elements of the system were provided by different suppliers, a call from one city to another could result in expenses to two local networks and to at least one long-distance supplier. To enable this kind of system to operate commercially, there must be rules determining the allocation of telephone revenues.

If these two conditions were met, one can envisage the establishment of many private networks, both local and long distance, with equipment being supplied by both Chinese or foreign manufacturers who could also train local people in the installation and operations of telephone networks, large or small. There seems to be no reason that a system that enabled people in the United States to obtain telephone service at the end of the 19th century should not enable people in other countries to do so at the end of the 20th. The problems today are less formidable than 100 years ago because equipment is cheaper and lighter, and because the lessons of the past are available to all those who wish to bring forward the future.

Roads

While telecommunications might be one of the easiest of government services for the private sector to provide, there is no doubt that providing roads is one of the most difficult. Why should this be so?

Roads are not pure public goods in the sense that those who do not pay for their use cannot be excluded; on the contrary, use of roads by motorized vehicles involves payments that can be both heavy and unavoidable. Roads are associated with substantial externalities, but so are telephone and electrical networks, which have been provided privately in many countries. An examination of the literature suggests that the private provision of roads is inhibited by three factors: (1) difficulty of obtaining necessary rights-of-way, (2) difficulty of road providers being paid, and (3) competition from governmentally provided free roads.

Difficulty of Obtaining Rights-of-Way. The possibilities of private road provision are frequently dismissed on the grounds that only by the use of "eminent domain" (which means the power of government to appropriate land for public use) can the required right-of-way be obtained. This objection, though important, can be met in three ways.

- In many cases a right-of-way is available alongside existing roads, railways, or canals.
- The power available to the private sector to purchase or lease land is often underestimated. Private entrepreneurs have the option of choosing different routes. In the case of pipelines, for example, people who wish to build them frequently identify alternate routes and negotiate separately with different groups of owners, settling with the group that comes up first with an acceptable arrangement. In this way, competitive pressure is brought to bear on landowners to make offers that would-be buyers of the right-of-way can accept.
- If all else fails, the entrepreneur can go to government and seek compulsory powers to use the land for a road. This approach was frequently used in the railway age, with the private sector giving up neither the rewards of successful investment nor the risks of unsuccessful ones.

Difficulty of Collecting Payment. Because the private sector, unlike the public sector, cannot operate indefinitely at a deficit, the assurance of payment for a successful enterprise is critical. Three approaches to this problem are conventional toll collection, "shadow tolls," and automatic toll collection.

While toll roads provide the best-known examples of private involvement in highways (for example, the World Bank is financing the Beijing-Tianjin-Tanggu toll expressway in China), conventional toll roads (which require users to throw coins into boxes or to pay attendants) have serious disadvantages. The restrictions of access impose substantial costs, both to users and to providers, so these

215

roads are appropriate only where distances are large and traffic is heavy. More fundamentally, these roads have been criticized for diverting traffic from less-congested to more-congested roads, which results in an inefficient use of the road network. The role of conventional toll roads is, therefore, limited.

Users of motorized vehicles can, without difficulty, be made to pay for use of roads, without stopping, by means of fuel taxes acting as "shadow tolls." In all countries revenues from these taxes go to the central government, and in some countries a proportion of the revenues so raised is routed to special funds dedicated to road improvement. The U.S. Highway Trust Fund is a well-known example. However, in all countries the moneys in these funds are distributed on the basis of administrative and political criteria; they are not usually available to fund provision of private roads. If taxes were made thus available, by, for example, distributing the revenues to different road authorities (private or governmental) on the basis of traffic counts, any agency or company responsible for road maintenance or construction could receive payment proportional to traffic. Similarly, revenues obtained from licensing heavy vehicles could, in theory, be distributed over the road network in proportion to the use of the network by such vehicles. I do not know of any country where such a system of shadow tolls is in use.

As an alternative to shadow tolls that are based on traffic counts, the technology is now available for automatic toll collection, which enables road users to be charged for road use without their vehicles having to stop at toll gates. One technology requires vehicles to carry electronic units that act as "electronic number plates." These special plates identify the owners to roadside electronic scanners and enable monthly bills to be sent out, similar to telephone bills. In the United States, the possibilities of using this method to charge heavy trucks for road use in Oregon and other states have been studied for some years. Key elements of the equipment needed for this kind of pricing were evaluated in Hong Kong during a large-scale pilot test in 1983–84 where the system performed well. Other automatic systems are being tested in California and Texas. Once installed, such systems could easily be adapted to enable private road suppliers to be paid in the same way that telephone companies such as MCI can charge for telephone use in the United States.

An important attribute of these electronic systems is that they do not have to be compulsory; it is possible to envisage "VIP lanes" installed on existing toll facilities that would enable vehicles carrying the identifying units to pass through the toll gates without stopping. For example, such a system has been designed and is to be installed in 1991 at the toll collection points serving the Dulles Toll Road in the Washington, D.C., area The widespread adoption of such devices would enable private providers of roads to be paid without having to put up conventional toll plazas. It would also enable new urban expressways to be built by private firms whenever the potential profit justified the investment.

Competition from Free Roads. The history of toll roads indicates that competition from free roads (or "freeways" as they are called in the United States) constitutes a major obstacle to the private provision of roads. To expect a private investor to risk his or her money on a road that requires payment from users, when parallel roads do not require such payments, is to expect a great deal. It is as if supermarket firms were invited to set up supermarkets next to government shops selling food at reduced prices.

However, the shadow toll described earlier could, in fact, deal with this problem to some extent because, if adopted, it could put users of roads, public or private, on an equal basis. To return to the supermarket analogy, the shadow toll would put all road users in the position of customers with food stamps who could shop around at different supermarkets and buy from whichever supplier they favored. In the case of roads, the monies would be paid to the suppliers on the basis of traffic counts. The source of revenues could be dedicated highway funds, fed from the proceeds of fuel taxes, but this arrangement need not be an essential part of the scheme. There would undoubtedly be problems with the traffic counts, as it would be in the interest of every road supplier to magnify the number of vehicles on its roads. But it should be possible to devise an acceptable counting method, for example, by the use of air photographs taken on a sample basis.

It is possible to imagine consortia of banks, civil engineering contractors, and other interested groups getting together to provide, manage, and maintain roads, where justified by traffic. Private sector elements willing to provide or maintain roads could include associations of property owners, associations of road users, and others.

Conclusion

This paper does not suggest that every government service can be provided by the private sector. If rival private sector organizations were to try to provide national security or to enforce law and order, the result could be anarchy. Also some services such as broadcasting or street lighting, by their nature, must be provided to everybody and it is, therefore, virtually impossible to charge directly. For some services, such as measures to prevent the spread of disease, a society may not tolerate the right of an individual to go untreated. But even where services have to be provided on a community basis, in many cases the actual operation is contracted out to private suppliers. And there are cases, such as education, where public financing might be considered appropriate, though the service itself can be provided competitively by schools or teachers that meet governmental standards. Thus we see an enormous scope for the private provision of government services in all societies, not only to ensure that services respond as closely as possible to the needs of the individuals, but also to free the resources of government to concentrate on the activities that only government can provide.

References

Anderson, Terry L., and Leal, Donald R. "Going with the Flow: Expending the Water Markets." *Policy Analysis*, no. 104, 26 April 1988. Cato Institute, Washington D.C.

Feibel, Charles, and Walters, A. A. *Ownership and Efficiency in Urban Buses*. World Bank Staff Working Paper no. 371, Washington, D.C., 1980.

Prychitko, Daniel L. "Modernizing Markets in Post-Mao China." *Journal of Economic Growth* 2, no. 3 (1988): 31–42.

Orr, Kenneth. *Appetite for Education in Contemporary Asia*. Canberra: Australian National University, 1977.

Rawski, Evelyn S. *Education and Popular Literacy in Ch'ing China*. Ann Arbor: University of Michigan Press, 1979.

Reason Foundation's Local Government Center and the University of Miami's Law and Economics Center. "Savings A.S.A.P.: Alternative Service-Delivery Assessment Project: An Analysis of the City and County of Los Angeles." Report Prepared for the Southern California Tax Research Foundation, November 1988.

Roth, Gabriel. *The Private Provision of Government Services in Developing Countries*. EDI Series on Economic Development. New York: Oxford University Press for the World Bank, 1987.

"Virginia Power Is Swamped with Offers of Electricity." *Washington Post*, 24 March 1988, p. B1.

COMMENT

THE "SOCIALIZATION" OF PUBLIC SERVICES
Zhou Mingwei

China's Reform Movement

China's economic reform process has been an important factor in developing an awareness of the different approaches and ideas in economic management. When people experiment with and apply some of these "new" ways of running the economy, they begin to appreciate them. The most obvious example is the market mechanism.

The practical needs and pressures that emerged during this reform period often constituted an impetus for our people to learn directly from the experiences of the more-developed countries, particularly in the area of economic management. In this regard, Gabriel Roth's paper has a very positive significance for our reform.

For the past 40 years or so, people in China, especially urban residents, have been suffering from the poor quality of telecommunications, transportation, housing, and other urban services. People are hoping for a miraculous solution and naturally become excited when there seems to be one. But many of the solutions that have proved effective in developed countries may not prove effective in China today.

Roth points out that virtually every country in the world has problems with urban services. But solutions continue to come up mostly through better and more effective management, and gratifying results have been seen in public services. I take this as a fact in the more-developed countries. Similarly, even in China better services are available in terms of higher efficiency, smiling faces, and fewer "no's" in the emerging private sector (i.e., joint ventures with foreign capital, enterprises on the shareholding basis, and individually owned businesses). This improvement, I believe, must have a lot to

The author is Deputy Director of the International Programs Office at Fudan University.

do with the fact that the quality of service is directly connected with the interests affecting the individuals or individual groups involved.

Some Fundamental Issues

Granted that reward and incentive should work, why is it that many of the solutions that are viable and effective in the more-developed countries can hardly be copied in China? It is partly because we need to look deeper than the level of direct material reward. In other words, we need to look at the transfer of public services, such as telecommunications and transportation, into private hands not just as an economic procedure but also as something more basic. We need to consider the degree to which people participate in managing their social, economic, and public affairs, and the degree to which people exercise their democractic rights in a congenial political system. For example, allowing greater participation in the political process (democratization), providing for the development of a sound legal system, and allowing greater competition in the selection of managers would help ensure better public services.

It is not that the Chinese government takes no interest in utilizing the strengths of private individuals and groups, at home and overseas, to improve public services. In fact, the government has encouraged such initiatives. But so far the results are minimal and unsatisfactory. Some of the failures did not come from the fact that we did not put to use some of the methods and techniques used in other countries. Rather, the failures came from lack of active participation on the part of the people in the social and economic management that affects them directly, and from the inadequacies of the present political and legal system. There are, of course, other important factors such as the different cultural traditions and the conditions found in China's much less-developed economy and technology.

The Link between Political Reform and Economic Reform

To enable the people to exercise their democratic rights in social management, the first and foremost thing to do should be a gradual turning over to the workers of the right to ownership (in the broadest sense of the word), the right to operation, and the right to management. When the rights accorded to each and every citizen are respected and exercised, the general participation in political and social life can be realized. For the people, political democracy finds expression in the exercise of democratic rights in economic life. It follows that to ensure that more and more people take part in or provide public service is not just a matter of economic or managerial concern. It is first of all, or at least simultaneously, a matter of political concern. This fact makes it more urgent for us to forge ahead with reforms in the political system while reforms in the economic system are moving forward.

For the effective exercise of people's rights in economic and political life, a sound legal system is absolutely necessary. It is hard to imagine a stable government without the practiced procedures of a sound legal system, by which people can guarantee their interests while participating in social and public affairs. Few people would trust and work efficiently for a government that does not have a legal system to guarantee legitimate interests.

The lesson we seem to have learned is serious. The constant shift or change of policies and the frequent interferences by illegitimate forces with the political rights of the people have created a situation where only short-term interests are valued and rewarded, only to make the provision of public services all the more inefficient. When the relevant policies and regulations change so often, and where the legal system is far less than perfect, it makes little sense to sign long-term contracts with the government for the provision of public transportation or running water.

The "Socialization" of Government Functions

The last point I wish to make concerns the socialization of the functions of the government. The government generally performs two basic functions: political and social, which throughout the whole period of human civilization do not often seem to grow at the same time. It seems true that with the progress of civilized society, the political function of government tends to decrease while the social function increases.

But history has shown that no attempts have ever been successful to superimpose the government machine, however strong it may be, upon a society to take care of all its social needs. The futility of this endeavor should be no surprise once one recognizes the impossibility of trying to mold the different and various needs and interests of millions of people into a predetermined pattern. Whenever governments have tried such an experient, the results have been economic, social, and political stagnation.

Centralization as the Root Cause of Mismanagement

In China, the root cause of the mismanagement in public services is to be found in the highly centralized and significantly inadequate political system. Without the necessary democratization of political life, which will take account of the preferences of the people, there is little hope of improving public services.

There has been a gross misunderstanding in China that the socialist economic pattern should be one with rigid, highly centralized management, and it was not to be changed. This belief in central planning and a monopoly of political power actually constituted a serious impediment to China's modernization, and the rigidity of the system led to dissatisfaction and complaints from the people. For example, the rigidly centralized political system has given government workers an incentive to provide only pleasing information to their superiors while ignoring objective economic laws. Moreover, since state enterprises respond to government plans rather than to the market or to social needs, there is little threat of bankruptcy. So despite the fact that the Chinese government did try to improve public services by investing human and material resources and by setting up more government organizations, the success has been minimal.

The Real Meaning of Socialization

Unlike China, the industrialized Western countries have allowed a far wider scope for the private sector in supplying public services, some of which were formerly considered solely government services. This change is what I call the "socialization" of public services. Society has acquired more and more complicated needs, but the stronger democratic tradition in the West, the higher level of education, and the relatively abundant material life have all contributed to the participation of individuals in all kinds of social activities. What seems to be even more important is that once the ownership of the means of production is vested in the people rather than in the government, then economic affairs and public affairs become basically private affairs, as opposed to the government's business. Many of the so-called public services themselves should not be the government's business in the first place. In this regard, simply attributing the cause of inefficient public services to political centralization does not seem accurate enough.

The socialization of government functions can be regarded as a key feature of China's reform process. However, it will take some time to eventually realize economic democracy and the devolution of political power to lower-level institutions. It took the West centuries to reach where it is today. For China, a country with thousands of years of feudalistic and centralized rule, the socialization of public services—to achieve a reasonable level of satisfaction for the people—will not occur overnight.

10

ECONOMIC GROWTH AND REFORM IN CHINA'S PROVINCES, MUNICIPALITIES, AND REGIONS

Thomas R. Dye

Introduction

In his Report to the Thirteenth National Congress of the Communist Party of China in 1987, General Secretary Zhao Ziyang restated China's goal of developing a strong socialist economy that is based on the principle of commodity exchange and the law of value (Zhao 1987). Among the important reforms endorsed were the separation of party from government functions and the separation of government from enterprise functions. The general secretary observed that under economic reform the general principle describing relationships between the state and the enterprises was "the state regulates the market and the market guides enterprises." He endorsed the "Decision on Reform of the Economic Structure" adopted by the Third Plenary Session of the Twelfth Central Committee in 1984 as "the theoretical basis for our reform of the economic structure." The Twelfth Central Committee argued convincingly that the separation of governmental functions from enterprise functions would encourage enthusiasm and initiative in these enterprises, inspire healthy competition, and establish a dynamic socialist economic structure (Communique 1984).

The wisdom of separating party from government and governmental functions from enterprise functions is widely acknowledged. In this paper, I will discuss the wisdom of decentralizing governmental functions. In referring to the political structure, Zhao (1987) called for "delegating powers to lower levels." The Twelfth Central Committee, likewise, recommended simpler and more decentralized governmental administration, less centralized bureaucracy, and increased autonomy and responsibility for provinces, municipalities, and regions (Communique 1984).

The author is McKenzie Professor of Government and Director of Policy Studies at Florida State University.

The issue of centralization versus decentralization has arisen often in the Chinese experience. Indeed, this experience has given rise to the frequently cited observation that "Centralization leads to rigidity, while decentralization results in chaos; when the economy becomes chaotic, it reverts to centralization, and when it becomes rigid, it reverts to decentralization."[1] Certainly, decentralization of government authority without first separating governmental and enterprise functions would accomplish very little. If enterprises were not permitted to manage their own affairs, it would make little difference whether governmental controls were imposed by the central government or by provinces and municipalities. But if enterprises are truly responsible for their own production, supply, and marketing, as well as their own wages and prices and their own profits and losses, then decentralization of the provision of public goods and services will serve the goals of economic efficiency, innovation, and growth.

My observations derive from the study of the system of American federalism. Despite many troublesome interventions by the national government, the American states and their local subdivisions have proven to be much more efficient providers of domestic public goods and services than the national government. State and local governments provide almost all of the nation's public education, from elementary and secondary schools to colleges and universities. These governmental units are principally responsible for the nation's police, fire protection, sewage and solid waste disposal, public health and sanitation, transportation facilities, streets, and highways. State and local governments also provide most of the nation's parks, recreational and cultural facilities, and prison and hospital facilities.

There are 82,341 local governments functioning in the United States: 50 states, 3,041 counties, 19,076 municipalities, 16,734 townships, 14,851 school districts, and 28,588 special districts. Collectively, they spend about 10.4 percent of the gross national product, while the national government spends about 24.5 percent. In aggregate terms, the role of the national government appears to overshadow that of state and local government. But if expenditures for defense, interest on the national debt, and outlays for social security are subtracted from the national government's budget, what remains in the national budget for all domestic programs is only about 8.4 percent of the gross national product. Thus, state and local governments in the United States carry the major burden of domestic governmental programs.

---

[1] Quoted, for example, by He Jianzhang (1979) and Xue Muqiao (1979).

Separating Governmental and Enterprise Functions

Economic reform in China requires careful consideration of the appropriate functions of provincial and municipal governments and their subdivisions (see Figure 1). These governments are called on to "serve the enterprises," rather than interfering with their operations or "making enterprises completely dependent upon them" (Communique 1984).

How can the appropriate functions of provincial and municipal governments be determined? We must recognize that some important goods and services cannot be provided by independent enterprises under a pricing system. Both capitalist and socialist economies encounter practical difficulties in applying the law of value to some goods. These are "public goods": goods that enterprises cannot provide through markets because nonpaying consumers cannot be excluded from their benefits. Public goods are defined as services, activities, or functions that are nonexclusive in character—once they are provided to anyone, no one can be excluded from their benefits. These goods cannot be provided on the market because "free riders" who do not buy these goods could enjoy them as much as buyers. For instance, provincial and municipal governments or their counties must provide police and fire protection, road and street repair, sanitation and garbage disposal, and other public goods that cannot be easily sold in a market. Consumers would be tempted to become free riders—individuals who would receive the benefits of public safety, good roads, and sanitary conditions without contributing to their costs.

Other public or nonmarket goods include education, because the whole society benefits from educating the young, not just the young themselves or their parents. The benefits of an educated population "spillover" to all citizens in the form of improved productivity, less social dependency, and greater prosperity for all. Similarly, many cultural, recreational, and social welfare activities benefit the entire community, not just those who directly participate. Welfare services for people who are too old, too sick, or too disabled to contribute effectively to a market-based economy are also public goods. We all might be willing to make private charitable contributions to assist these people, but if we do so individually and voluntarily, there is the temptation for others to free ride on our contributions. The free riders will benefit from seeing the old, the sick, and the disabled assisted without themselves contributing to the cost of the assistance. Finally, provincial and municipal governments might provide goods and services that constitute natural monopolies," such as water, elec-

225

FIGURE 1
LOCAL GOVERNMENTS

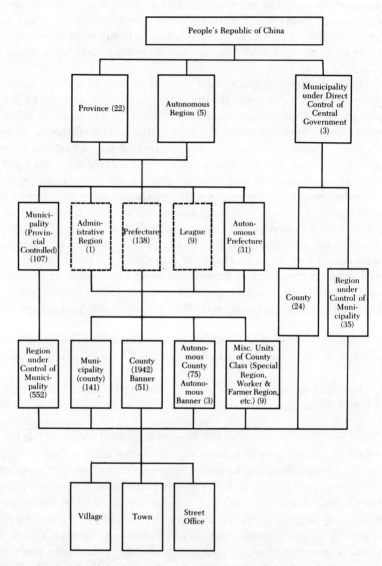

NOTE: The number of administrative units of county and above are 1983 statistics. Administrative region, prefecture, and league are not the top level of administration, but are the executive bodies of the province and autonomous region. Street office is controlled by the region under the municipality.

SOURCE: Ministry of Foreign Economic Relations and Trade (1985).

trical supply, and sewage disposal—where large capital investment serves an entire community and small competing enterprises cannot operate efficiently.

The central problem in providing public goods is determining their true value. The absence of a market with competitive prices makes information about the true value of public goods and services difficult to assess. Theoretically, we can posit a rule: No public goods should be provided if their costs exceed their benefits, and officials should opt for a level of public goods that provides the greatest benefits over costs. Practically, however, governments and government officials lack the necessary information to determine the true value of public goods.

Even if socialist policymakers are motivated to make decisions on the basis of maximum societal benefits and minimum societal costs; even if the policymakers are rational, far-sighted, public spirited, and comprehensive in their judgment; and even if they are not distracted by outside pressure, bureaucratic lobbying, or narrow self-interests, they still lack the information necessary to implement the maximum social gain rule for determining the optimum level of public goods and services. If policymakers err, it is not their fault. They have no way of knowing society's true preferences, and no accurate mechanism exists for weighing preferences or for finding the preferred balance between benefits and costs.

Markets provide this information to producers of *private* goods and services. Despite many imperfections, markets make known to producers the preferences of consumers. Price movements signal their tastes, the intensities of their desires, and their willingness to sacrifice all other goods for any particular product. The market continuously records this information whenever people choose to buy goods and when they choose not to buy. The market mechanism ensures that goods will not be produced if their costs exceed their value to society.

There is a natural tendency for public officials to oversupply public goods and services. It is natural for public officials to expand their budgets and personnel, to acquire additional prestige and authority, and to provide more direction and regulation than is required. This tendency is true of all government officials, whether in socialist or capitalist systems. And it is true of officials in provincial and municipal governments, as well as those in central governments. The problem, therefore, is to construct a system of incentives to counterbalance the natural expansionist tendencies of public officials.

227

Encouraging Responsible Local Government

Centralized government constitutes a monopoly over the provision of public goods and services throughout an entire nation. Monopoly government has no direct way of determining the efficiency of its activities. In contrast, decentralized provincial and municipal governments, with independent responsibility for determining appropriate types and quantities of public services, allow us to compare performances among governments. Multiple governments offering different packages of services and costs to both citizens and enterprises within their jurisdictions provide comparative information to everyone about what public services can be offered at what costs.

If a provincial or municipal government performs well—that is, if it provides enterprises within its jurisdiction with quality public services at low costs—its enterprises should be able to develop more rapidly and show larger profits than enterprises in jurisdictions whose governments perform poorly. Admittedly, the information conveyed by competition among government units is imperfect, and government policies are only one of many potential influences on the growth of jobs, industry, and investments. Nevertheless, some information is better than none. Centralized, monopoly government receives little comparative information about the appropriate types and levels of public goods.

Responsible provincial and municipal government requires that all costs of public services provided by these governments be derived from revenues that the governments collect. If revenues are divorced from expenditures, then the services of these governments are separated from their costs. This separation is an invitation to irresponsible government.

If the central government provides all, or any significant portion, of the revenue of provincial and municipal governments, then the relation between the benefits and costs of public services provided by these governments is distorted. Provincial and municipal governments will be prompted to provide more public services than required for efficient operation of their jurisdictions, and they will continually press the central government for even higher levels of subsidies. In the United States, the national government currently provides about 18 percent of the revenue of state and local governments through a complex system of grants in aid. This figure is slightly less than its high of 22 percent in the 1970s. There is ample evidence that these revenues cause American local governments to oversupply public goods and services. Central government subsidies provide the wrong information to local governments, thus obscuring the true costs of public services.

By requiring provincial and municipal governments to raise their own revenues, those governments are given a direct stake in the success of the enterprises in their jurisdictions. If local government revenues are derived exclusively from taxes on the profits of local enterprises, then those governments will have a direct interest in the profitability of local enterprises. Increases in local government budgets, employment, and services, as well as growth in the status and prestige of local government officials, will depend on the success of their local enterprises. Thus, provincial and municipal officials will be given a direct incentive to assist enterprises within their jurisdictions in achieving high rates of growth.

Provincial and municipal governments might be encouraged to experiment with taxes other than enterprise and individual income taxes. In the United States, five states—Florida, Texas, Nevada, Washington, and Wyoming—have no income taxes at all. Some other states have low flat-rate income taxes (e.g., 3 percent) or modestly progressive rates (e.g., 2–5 percent). Forty-five states have sales taxes on consumer items (usually 5–6 percent), which are collected by retail merchants. Overall, income taxes provide about 11 percent of state and local government revenue; sales taxes provide 19 percent, property taxes 19 percent, all other taxes 5 percent, user charges 15 percent, federal aid 18 percent, and all other revenue 13 percent. But each state can vary the mix of taxes it employs, as well as the rates and degrees of progressivity. There is some evidence that heavy reliance on income taxes and steeply progressive rates hinders economic growth and encourages individuals and firms to move to other states. Some states that lowered tax burdens in recent years experienced a strong economic revival.[2]

The central government itself, by delegating more authority to local governments, will reduce its own share of tax revenues from enterprises. Provincial and municipal governments with authority to tax enterprises at whatever levels they choose will directly confront the tasks of achieving efficiency, creating incentives, and encouraging initiative and hard work. If they set tax rates too high or adopt progressive taxes that penalize the most profitable enterprises, they risk impeding economic development in their jurisdictions. If they set tax rates too low, they cannot provide the essential infrastructure of transportation, energy, water, law enforcement, and social services required for productive enterprise. Of course, local governments will make mistakes in judgment—usually in the direction of oversupplying public goods and overregulating enterprises. But comparisons of

---

[2]On the relation between tax rates and economic growth, see Vedder (1990).

economic performance among provinces and municipalities allow both central and local government officials to observe the results of different economic policies. Mistakes can be more easily observed among multiple competitive governments than under one centralized monopoly government.

Mobility of capital and labor contributes to economic growth and efficiency. Permitting and encouraging enterprises and individuals to move about the country in search of the highest return on their capital and labor improves the overall efficiency of the national economy. Moreover, the mobility of capital and labor provides additional incentives for provincial and municipal officials to offer the best packages of public services at the lowest costs. Decentralized government, combined with mobility of capital and labor, can create a "quasi-market" for public goods and services. Mobile enterprises and individuals can choose to locate in provinces and municipalities that promise the best services at the lowest costs. Many other factors besides the performance of local governments will affect locational decisions. These factors include transportation facilities, energy availability, labor-force characteristics, access to raw materials, and so forth. But provincial and municipal government performance would be an additional consideration in the locational decisions of freely choosing enterprises and individuals.

Competition among provinces and municipalities to attract mobile capital and labor would compel these governments to improve services and reduce costs. It would force governments to make better estimates of the requirements of enterprises, both to attract new enterprises to their jurisdictions and to keep existing enterprises from moving away. New enterprises would have the option of locating in the province or municipality that promises the best package of public services at the lowest possible tax level.

Competition among provinces and municipalities also provides a rough guide to the true preferences of enterprises and citizens for government activity. Competition allows central government officials, enterprise managers, and individual citizens to compare governmental performances—to observe what services are offered at what costs in various provinces and municipalities. This comparative information is valuable in itself, but mobility of enterprises would give the system its driving force. Enterprises would be able to register their policy preferences by moving into or out of their government jurisdictions, or simply staying put. Central government officials can watch the growth of various provinces and municipalities over time. Local government officials can evaluate their own performance compared to the performance of other local governments. Loss of capital over time, a decline in productivity and income, a loss of jobs, and a decline in the revenues of government would signal decisionmakers that they should search for alternative government policies.

Observing Economic Output by Province, Municipality, and Region

Evaluating the performance of any government requires accurate and reliable data. Enterprise managers and individual citizens, as well as central government officials, must enjoy ready access to census data, national income accounts, and government tax and expenditure data. Moreover, if the performances of autonomous provinces and municipalities and their governing officials are to be evaluated, accurate and reliable data must be provided for each province, municipality, and region over time.

In recent years the People's Republic of China has made great progress in developing and publishing economic statistics. But data by province, municipality, and region are not always provided. Ideally, comparable data on all provinces (including Taiwan, Hong Kong, and Macao) would provide the best opportunity to evaluate economic performances.

An important argument for decentralized government is that it permits local policies to conform to local conditions. In a centralized system, one national policy is established for all, leaving little flexibility to adapt to local differences. The greater the variation in local conditions across a nation, the more appropriate decentralization of government becomes.

China's provinces, municipalities, and regions exhibit a great deal of variation in levels of economic development (see Table 1 and Figures 2 and 3). According to the data provided in the *Almanac of China's Economy, 1985* for the year 1984, variation in per capita total social product ranged from a high of \$2,243 in Shanghai to lows of \$209 in Xizang, \$207 in Guanxi, and \$205 in Yunnan (See Table 1 and Figure 2). The coefficient of variation (a standardized measure of variation: the standard deviation divided by the mean) for per capita, total social product among mainland provinces, municipalities, and regions is 0.91.[3] If Taiwan and Hong Kong are included in the computation, variation in levels of development is even greater; the coefficient of variation for all of China's provinces is 1.45.

Variation in per capita industrial output among provinces and municipalities is even greater. Per capita industrial output ranged

[3]It is interesting to compare this coefficient to the coefficient of variation for per capita personal income among the 50 American states, which is 0.14.

TABLE 1

PER CAPITA SOCIAL OUTPUT AND INDUSTRIAL OUTPUT BY PROVINCE, MUNICIPALITY, AND REGION, 1984

	Total Social Output		Industrial Output	
	Per Capita (US$)	Change, 1983–84	Per Capita (US$)	Change, 1983–84
Beijing	1,661	15.33	1,158	10.46
Shanghai	2,243	10.11	1,932	9.70
Tianjin	1,267	0.00	984	9.70
Anhui	281	43.98	113	15.18
Fujian	306	21.15	135	20.81
Gansu	276	10.54	152	11.22
Guangdong	393	19.00	196	26.53
Guizhou	—	—	78	17.90
Hebei	342	15.67	167	16.49
Heilongjiang	490	8.36	304	9.30
Henan	—	—	—	—
Hubei	413	19.02	230	14.88
Hunan	284	11.02	117	− 10.87
Jiangsu	580	20.72	344	19.42

Jiangxi	—	—	—
Jilin	488	19.53	265	15.50
Liaoning	716	11.74	494	11.83
Zinghai	319	9.40	126	13.93
Shaanxi	—	—	—	—
Shandong	374	15.46	187	12.47
Shanxi	401	17.59	233	16.72
Sichuan	257	14.25	119	15.17
Yunnan	205	15.24	95	15.33
Zhejian	491	28.40	253	24.69
Guanxi	207	6.35	86	9.85
Neimongol	286	5.18	129	9.05
Ningxia	—	—	—	—
Xinjiang	339	11.22	139	11.91
Xizang	209	20.59	27	8.16
Taiwan	3,010	8.90	1,505	10.30
Hong Kong	5,889	8.50	1,778	16.10

NOTE: All the RMB figures have been converted to U.S. dollars at the rate of 3.2 yuan per dollar, which prevailed from 1983 to 1984.

SOURCE: *Almanac of China's Economy, 1985.*

233

FIGURE 2

RANKING OF PROVINCES, MUNICIPALITIES, AND REGIONS
BY SOCIAL OUTPUT PER CAPITA, 1984

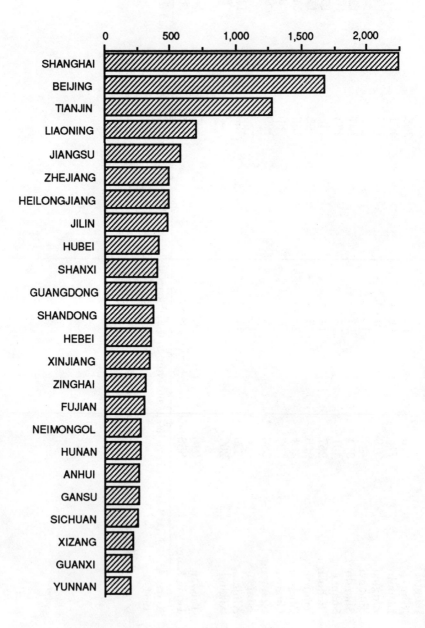

FIGURE 3

RANKING OF PROVINCES, MUNICIPALITIES, AND REGIONS
BY INDUSTRIAL OUTPUT PER CAPITA, 1984

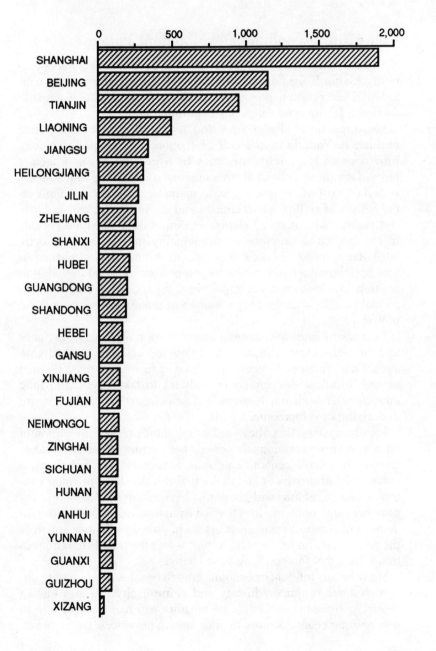

from a high of $1,932 in Shanghai to a low of $27 in Xizang. The coefficient of variation for industrial output was 1.30. If Taiwan and Hong Kong are included in the analysis, the coefficient of variation is 1.27.

Comparing Economic Development Policies

A major advantage of decentralization in government is the opportunity it affords for policy evaluation. Multiple governments, with independent power to pursue alternative economic policies, provide surrogate laboratories for policy experimentation.

Measurement of change over time is critical to successful policy evaluation. Variations in *levels* of economic development among provinces and municipalities may be a product of many factors beyond the direct control of governments, such as availability of raw materials, cost of energy, access to markets, cultural limitations on the supply of skilled labor, climate and environment, and so forth. But variations in *rates of change* in output over specified periods in any particular province or municipality may be more directly attributable to government policies. Observing rates of change in total social product and industrial output over specified periods—in separate provinces and municipalities that pursue different developmental policies—facilitates evaluation of the effectiveness of these policies.

To measure rates of change in output in each of China's provinces and municipalities, one must first develop accurate and reliable annual data for several years. The time span studied must be long enough to allow developmental policies to take effect, and long enough to smooth out temporary fluctuations that might obscure underlying developmental trends.

Ideally, systematic policy evaluation entails close observation of output measures for adequate periods both before and after the introduction of specific economic reforms. Evaluation also entails close comparison of provinces and municipalities that have pursued various economic reforms with those that have not, as well as comparing provinces and municipalities that have pursued reform with different degrees of comprehensiveness. As such, policy evaluation involves the careful measurement of both short-term effects and alterations in trend lines that forecast long-term change.

Many factors influence economic growth besides government policies. Natural resources, history and culture, physical and human capital, geography, and even the weather can play a major role in determining economic growth rates among provinces. But with sufficient observations of economic output before the introduction of reform in any particular province or municipality, as well as sufficient post-reform observations, it may be possible to control for many factors specific to each province or municipality. Sorting out the specific economic effects attributable to specific economic policies is never an easy task, but decentralization of government creates a natural laboratory.

Since the great Sichuan experiment in economic reform began in 1978, the People's Republic of China has taken the lead in economic policy experimentation at the provincial level (Shambaugh 1982). The Sichuan experiment may have been centrally directed and many adjustments may have been ordered by the central government (Lee 1986), but the principle of experimentation by province was vindicated.

Decentralization must mean more than just flexibility in the implementation of central government policies. While it is undoubtedly true that decentralization makes government more manageable, provincial and municipal governments must be more than just administrative arms of the central government. Rather, they must have significant and autonomous responsibility for the economic progress of their jurisdictions. It must also be recognized that all provinces will not develop in the same fashion or at the same rate. A rigid commitment to "equal development of all provinces" would undermine local initiative and responsibility (see Pye 1981, chap. 5).

Policy diversity throughout all of China's provinces provides a unique opportunity for the world to observe and compare different approaches to economic progress. Comparative analyses across national economic systems are very difficult because of the many cultural and historical differences among people. But comparative analyses of China's provinces can isolate differences in economic performance among people with common cultural and historical backgrounds (see Rabushka 1987). The effects of different government policies can be more easily identified against this common background. For this reason, governments and peoples throughout the world are intensely interested in the results of China's experiments in economic reform.

References

Almanac of China's Economy, 1985. Beijing: Economic Management Publishing House, December 1985.

Communique of the Third Plenary Session of the Twelfth Central Committee, 20 October 1984. "Decision on Reform of the Economic Structure."

Reprinted in *The People's Republic of China: A Documentary Survey*. Edited by Harold C. Hinton. Washington, D.C.: Scholarly Resources, 1984.

He Jianzhang. "Problems in the System of Planned Management of the Economy of Ownership by the Whole People in Our Country and the Direction of Reform." *Jingji Yanjiu*, no. 5 (1979): 35–45. Reprinted in *Chinese Economic Studies* (Summer 1980).

Lee, Peter Nan-Shong. "Enterprise Autonomy in Post-Mao China." *The China Quarterly* (March 1986): 19–44.

Ministry of Foreign Economic Relations and Trade. People's Republic of China. *The China Investment Guide*. Beijing: China Development Press, 1985.

Pye, Lucian. *The Dynamics of Chinese Politics*. Cambridge: Oelgeschlager, Gunn & Hain, 1981.

Rabushka, Alvin. *The New China: Comparative Economic Development in Mainland China, Taiwan, and Hong Kong*, Boulder, Colo.: Westview Press, 1987.

Shambaugh, David L., ed. "Zhao Ziyang's 'Sichuan Experience': Blueprint for a Nation." *Chinese Law and Government* (Spring 1982).

Vedder, Richard. "Tiebout, Taxes, and Economic Growth." *Cato Journal* 10 (Spring/Summer 1990): 91–108.

Xue Muqiao. "An Inquiry into the Problems Concerning Reform of the Economic System." 1979. Reprinted in *Chinese Economic Studies* (Winter 1983–84).

Xue Muqiao. "Socialism and Planned Commodity Economy." *Beijing Review* (17 August 1987): 14–19.

Zhao, Ziyang. "Advance along the Road to Socialism with Chinese Characteristics." Report delivered at the Thirteenth National Congress of the Communist Party of China on October 25, 1987. In *Documents of the Thirteenth National Congress of the Communist Party of China (1987)*, pp. 3–77. Beijing: Foreign Language Press, 1987.

THE PROBLEM OF
DECENTRALIZATION IN CHINA
Wang Xi

I am very honored to have this opportunity to comment on Thomas Dye's paper. Several years ago, I was privileged to read his work *Who's Running America,* and I strongly recommend it; it is a very illuminating work and the Chinese edition is now available.

Dye's paper, backed by very detailed statistical figures, presents a very clear analysis. In my view, his paper is the best I have read on the topic of decentralization in China. I do feel, however, that there are some insufficiencies in his paper, at least on two points. First, he only mentions the positive aspects of decentralization and, second, he does not specifically discuss what the decentralization of power would mean in China. These two inadequacies, however, typically appear in papers by Western observers of China's economic reform, and I would like to elaborate on them.

In commenting on China's reform movement, Western observers usually advocate the following: (1) reduction or total abolition of government intervention; (2) reliance on Adam Smith's invisible hand of market competition to determine prices, foreign exchange rates, and wages; (3) decentralization of power; (4) privatization; and (5) rapid change—preferably to do something like what Ludwig Erhart did in West Germany when he abolished exchange-rate controls overnight, or what Margaret Thatcher did in Britain when she simply announced the end of exchange controls.

I understand that our Western friends are extremely concerned about economic reform in China. But I somehow have the feeling that the ideas they are proposing scratches an itch outside our boot, to use a Chinese proverb. The problem is that Western observers appear to have missed the real itch.

The author is Professor of Economics and History at Fudan University and Deputy Director of the Center for American Studies.

In the preface to his *Principles of Economics,* Alfred Marshall, the leader of the neoclassical school of economics, wrote: "Economic conditions are constantly changing, and each generation looks at its own problem in its own way." If we substitute "each country" for "each generation," then it is easier to understand why Westerners appear to be scratching an itch outside China's boot—they are not taking into full account the differences between China and other countries.

Distinguishing Features of China's Reform

China's economic reform has three distinguishing features. First, China is making a transition from a centrally planned economy to a social market economy in which planning still exists. Second, this change, plus the speed of change, has been rather rapid. Third, because China has undergone a very fundamental change, and because the reform has proceeded relatively quickly, there have been some unavoidable dislocations. These dislocations have been manifested by an increase in the price of commodities, a shortage of some raw materials, and the fact that some people have been using the shortages to speculate and to enrich themselves. In these circumstances, during the transition process, some government intervention is believed to be necessary. But, in this case, government intervention should be aimed at ensuring that the transition is ultimately successful.

Centralization versus Decentralization

Centralization versus decentralization of power is a centuries-old issue about governmental functions. At the very time the United States was founded, Americans met with this issue, and they had been debating it for a long time before it was finally settled in principle by the Constitution. Under the powerful federal government, individual states have autonomy within the limits prescribed by the Constitution. However, the extent of their autonomy—or, in other words, the extent to which the federal government can interfere in their internal affairs—remains a controversial issue. Therefore, "big government" versus "small government" has often been an issue in presidential elections. Some long-standing issues, such as the issue of public ownership or privitization of the postal service, have not been solved even today. In short, the issue of centralization or decentralization of government authority is still under debate.

When we discuss decentralization of power, we have to address the question of Chinese history and culture. Over the last couple of centuries, when a dynasty was stable and prosperous, the imperial power was highly centralized; but catastrophe and chaos ensued when the imperial power declined and was not able to be centralized. Even in modern times, after Sun Yat-sen overthrew the Qing Dynasty in 1911 and established the Republic of China, the above phenomenon still existed. The separatist warlord regimes led to wars and foreign invasions, which caused great sufferings for the Chinese people. With the memory of this situation still fresh, people tend to regard the centralization of power as an important condition for the stability and prosperity of the country. This psychological factor often has significant effects on the decisionmaking of the government, especially on the issue of centralization versus decentralization.

After liberation in 1949, China's urgent tasks of economic development pushed the Chinese government in the direction of centralization. China developed an unprecedentedly powerful central government built on the Soviet model. Because China has had a centrally planned economy for a long time, most Chinese tend to think of the high degree of centralization as totally justifiable. China is a big country with vast territory. Different regions, as Dye mentions, exhibit a great deal of variation in levels of economic development. It is very difficult for economically backward regions to increase the pace of their development without outside aid; thus, they have to depend on the support of the central government. As such, the central government needs to have authority over financial control and centralized redistribution.

Soon after the liberation, China faced the task of reconstruction. Some large projects in defense and economic development were beyond the capability of local governments and, therefore, had to be financed by the central government. They included the public goods mentioned by Dye. One current example is that neither the Shanghai municipal government nor the Jiangsu provincial government have the financial wherewithal to sustain the budget of Fudan University. The funds can come only from the central government. Consequently, many faculty members are concerned about the decentralization of power; because, if decentralization occurs, Fudan's budget is going to be in trouble. Last year I was at Michigan State University and I was surprised to learn that every year the state government allocates more than $500 million to Michigan State University and the University of Michigan. No province in China has such financial ability to provide public goods. Rather, the central government has to provide the funds for all China's key universities. Expenditures on such public goods need centralized financial control.

Negative Effect of Overcentralization

The negative effect caused by overcentralization, however, has become more and more obvious. Overcentralization tends to be an obstacle in the following obvious ways: It hurts the initiative of local governments; it increases the burden on local governments; and it prevents the implementation of economic reform in line with local conditions.

For example, Shanghai is an area of high revenues, but it has to hand over half of its revenues to the central government for redistribution among poor areas. For a very long time Shanghai has been short of funds for self-development. Its outdated industrial equipment and installations were not replaced and the essential infrastructure (such as subways, underwater tunnels, telecommunications, and housing) was not constructed. Shanghai's products are gradually losing their competitiveness. If things go on this way, Shanghai will be reduced to backwardness. There is no doubt that Shanghai needs to retain more autonomy over its finances, foreign trade, and foreign economic relations, including the right of issuing bonds overseas.

Obstacles to Decentralization

The old concepts are undergoing a change. As early as the days of Mao Zedong, the issue of centralization versus decentralization was noticed. After more than 40 years of swinging between centralization and decentralization, the Chinese have come to agree on the principal idea that power should be decentralized. Without decentralization, the reform and open policy cannot be carried out effectively. There are, however, four basic obstacles to decentralization.

The greatest obstacle to the present decentralization in China lies in the ambiguity on the part of the government about the definition of authority. As a result, the central government tends to strictly interpret how power should be decentralized, while local governments tend to loosely interpret existing law with the aim of maximizing local interests.

Even though there is support for decentralization, there is concern that once power is decentralized, chaos will result. The problem is that decentralized power does not have a clear definition prescribed by law. The central government is often in a position of losing control.

Second, bureaucracy and corruption are also thwarting the process of decentralization. Local governments tend to make use of their decentralized power to strengthen the local bureaucratic system. Some individuals are then able to abuse power for their own benefit or group interests. This outcome, in turn, reduces efficiency and creates new disorder.

Third, the long-standing habit of sticking to old practices is holding back decentralization. For example, the long-standing habit of government administration of enterprises has fixed people's way of thinking. In the event that enterprises are separated from government administration, people are unlikely to readily adapt themselves to the new situation, either mentally or in practice.

Fourth, decentralization involves the entire political system. On the one hand, with respect to administration, power is subdivided between the central government and local governments, and between the government administrators and enterprises. On the other hand, the party organizations on different levels, which parallel the corresponding levels of administration and enterprises, are still centrally controlled from the top to the bottom. The best method of coordinating the two contradictory directions of decentralization and centralization needs to be found out in practice. Here I agree with Steven Cheung's view that "China has reached a point when piecemeal tactics are not likely to be effective in advancing her economic reforms" (Cheung 1989, p. 593).

The Uncertain Future

Despite all this, the central government has not hesitated to take measures to implement decentralization. Recently, an essential step has been taken. Through legislation, the Chinese government has permitted privately owned economic entities to exist and develop within the limits prescribed by the law. The government also has established the principle of separating land ownership from the right of land use, permitting paid transfer of the right to use state land. This change involved amending the Constitution. The National People's Congress has passed the amendment and the State Council has promulgated the regulations implementing the law. This change in property rights will instill more vitality into China's economy. Its far-reaching significance cannot be overestimated. Another development has been the creation of the Special Economic Zones (SEZs). These zones have the most favorable environment for decentralization, as witnessed by the rapid development of private enterprises in the SEZs.

The problem China is facing today is not whether central authority should be decentralized; general agreement has already been reached on this issue. Rather, with decentralization going into effect, the problem today is how to deal with the rise in the prices of raw materials, the persistent inflation, the inefficiency of state enterprises, and the lag in real wages. It was thought that the expected price increases, occasioned by decontrolling the prices of certain goods, would be stabilized by supplying more goods after the economic efficiency of enterprises was raised—the so-called "digestion by enterprises." Now, however, it seems that this road will get nowhere. If so, what shall we do next?

References

Cheung, Steven N. S. "Privatization vs. Special Interests: The Experience of China's Economic Reforms." *Cato Journal* 8 (Winter 1989): 585–96.

Dye, Thomas R. *Who's Running America? The Reagan Years.* 3d ed. Englewood Cliffs, N.J.: Prentice-Hall, 1983.

PART III

ECONOMIC REFORM AND FOREIGN RELATIONS

11

THE IMPACT OF CHINA'S REFORM AND DEVELOPMENT ON THE OUTSIDE WORLD

Xu Zhiming

A historic transformation has been taking place in China over the past decade. China's economy, politics, and society have experienced structural changes, and there have been quiet changes in its ideology and values. Along with other Asian-Pacific countries, China has showed impressive economic strength and potential as the world's largest developing country. It is not too early to conclude that while reform is certain to change China's destiny, China's reform will also have a significant effect on the outside world.

China's Movement

The shifting panorama of the Chinese reform is perplexing to those who are watching it. Indeed, the decade of reform is full of pros and cons, compromises and backlashes. Even today there is no clear agreement about where and how the reform should be directed. Ancient history and cultural heritage give pride to China, but they also give rise to a complicated social structure. A variety of conflicting interests interfere with one another to strike an "inert balance," and thus set the precondition for the content, goals, measures, and ways of social progress.

The difficulties of the reform and its implications were not readily apparent until after the reform curtain had been raised. By 1988, the reform was seen not simply as a make-shift revision or modification but as a sweeping transformation of China's socioeconomic system. Many believed that China was on the eve of a great change. The reform movement, which began in 1978, resulted from the changed domestic and international environment, which altered the leadership's perception of the factors that affect China's national security and social stability. With the end of the Cultural Revolution and the

The author is Visiting Professor at the Chinese Academy of Management Science, Guest Research Fellow at CITIC International, and a Ph.D. Candidate (Econ.) at the University of Manchester.

normalization of ties with the United States, China was ready to make economic growth its main priority and to increase its people's standard of living. This change in priorities paved the way for economic reform.

Ever since the economic reform began, however, it has been constantly challenged by the old system. Intentionally or not, the party and governmental organs have served as a drawback to the market in its contest with central planning. The formidable vested interests are alarmed and resentful because they fear that they will lose influence and power with the demise of central planning. In such a situation, political reform becomes the most crucial factor in deciding the fate of economic reform. It is clear that the future path of the reform will depend on the obstacles that stand in the way of such reform. Until recently, China's reform was picking up new meaning in theory and practice along its way of execution.

Where should China's reform go? Reality testifies that the stumbling block to China's reform is not simply the old system or a certain social group, but the dominant social values of the old vintage. The people and the old system may fade away with time, but the old values remain. One of the tasks of the reform is to free people from ideological beliefs that are inconsistent with China's realities and level of development. These ideological elements, however, do not constitute a real threat to China's future, since they were introduced into China relatively recently and, therefore, are easier to modify or even reject if they clash with national interests. They become more disturbing, however, if they are integrated with the old values, which are likely to acquire more justification in a new mantle, and thus become more difficult to get rid of. This is why China's social transformation will have to start with economic and political reform. Unless progressive social values are created to dominate the whole social development, it will be hard for China's reform to advance.

Over the 1978–88 period, plurality became increasingly apparent in the process of reform. On the one hand, the reform led to a focus on higher economic growth, which helped to create and consolidate new orders in various economic and political fields. On the other hand, the reform quietly set the stage for social change that, in turn, had a positive influence on political and economic reform. If these two trends were to persist, China's reform would be likely to accomplish its real mission, that is, to rebuild not only China's economy but also its society and splendid civilization.

Of course, since 1989, the reform movement has stagnated. Already in 1988 there were frictions between the pro-reform elite and their common followers, between the radical reformers and the prudent

rulers, and between those who aspired to the future and those who
wanted to keep their vested interests intact. These frictions were
fueled by inflation and urban unrest over deteriorating economic
conditions. The whole situation exploded with the events of May-
June 1989, and the reform came to a standstill.

China must wisely and clearly notice that, over the past decade, it
has been making at least two main mistakes, which have caused
today's problems. First, since the beginning of the reform, a pragmatic idea—roughly expressed as "to cross a river by touching the
stones on the riverbed"—has been running through the entire reform
strategy and measures. This pragmatic attitude may have been useful
in helping to launch the reform, but it is of little benefit in resolving
China's fundamental problems. It also brings about frequent changes
in the macro-policies of the government. Such policy uncertainty and
lack of adherence to principles cause social instability; people tend
to focus only on the short-run consequences of their actions rather
than on the long run. Second, the facts prove that when special
interests prevail, it is difficult to promote economic reform and social
stability. As there is no permanent major beneficiary from the reform,
a firm supporting force cannot be established for the reform. Consequently, once any kind of fluctuation happens in China, the reform
will reach a crisis stage.

It is important, therefore, for China's leaders and reformers to show
a greater boldness and resoluteness in promoting future reform. We
must throw off the traditional system completely. We cannot go on
believing that there is a social revolutionary road that satisfies everyone, otherwise China's reform will not be able to get rid of the current
situation of pacing back and forth with no consistent progress.

The Path of Development

Which development model should China choose? This is the primary question. China is different from other developing countries,
and factors limiting China's range of options include ideological
ones, the power structure, and dominant values—in addition to those
of an economic and social nature.

The two key components of China's development model, as it
evolved over the past decade, are dubbed "invigoration" and "opening." Invigoration demands that the old development model of central planning be changed. Under the old economic model, the economic decisions of society were controlled by the state, and it was
assumed that prompt and accurate planning would achieve maximum
output with minimum input. The effort was a failure since central

planning turned out to be unable to allocate resources rationally and to activate people's enthusiasm. As a result, economic activities lacked both efficiency and vigor. The new model was intended to redress the situation by developing a market mechanism within the framework of the planned system and, thereby, add a private sector to the previously monolithic public sector. Under the new system, all economic relations necessary for development were to be created by the market. Insofar as it was allowed to operate, the new development mechanism—the market mechanism—has been quite successful.

The second feature of China's new development model—opening—demands that a complementary relationship be established between China's economic development and that of the rest of the world, so that China can realize greater benefits from the international division of labor and resource allocation. This opening, or open-door policy, is more than a simple utilization of foreign capital, technology, and resources; it is also more than the use of foreign markets or the introduction of foreign competition to stimulate the domestic market. Development demands more than that from opening, because in order to develop, a real open economy is needed instead of a symbolic opening; and China's market, resources, and productive capacity must plunge into the world economic flow to create more market and development opportunities. China's opening is still at a primary stage, and its development still largely depends on its own domestic economy. Notwithstanding the differences of opinion on the aforementioned two key components of the new economic model, there is no denying that the new model has exerted a profound impact on China's economy. During the entire 1979–88 period, China experienced rapid economic growth, with real GNP growing on average by more than 9 percent per year. But many defects remain in the mixture of the old and new models now in practice. With the market economy grafted to the planned economy and state ownership, the state can still decide the scale and direction of development. This mixed system not only restrains the role of the market economy, but also misrepresents economic realities.

The disadvantage of the mixed economic model was revealed by the problems of China's economic performance in 1988, during which a high growth rate coexisted with a high inflation rate. This situation caused the top leaders to blame the market mechanism, to freeze prices, and to reemphasize the planning model. But this policy reversal was a major mistake; it was not the market that was chaotic but the mixed system in which planning dominated the market.

China's rapid economic growth coupled with high inflation in 1988 illustrate two points. First, the introduction of the market mechanism invigorated the development of China's economy. However, a deep crack between the market system and the planning system still exists. Second, there is a serious imbalance in the domestic economic structure, especially in the area of transportation, as well as in the supply of energy and raw materials. The rigid supply system and the inefficiency of state-owned enterprises have been major impediments to development, and the use of bank credit to cover enterprise losses has led to inflation.

In light of the present situation, China has two choices. It can either continue the process of introducing the market mechanism and more fully open its door to the outside world, or it can restrain the market and strengthen the planned economy. It is clear that if China chooses the market model, it would not only speed up development but also create a beneficial condition for breaking up the bottlenecks that are an integral part of central planning.

It was really a pity that in 1988 China's leaders did not finally get rid of the shadow of the planned economy. Instead, they chose some "old measures," which were similar to those employed in the traditional Soviet-style planned economy, to handle the "new problems" they faced. By reintroducing price controls and stalling experimentation with new forms of ownership, the leaders who chose the old ways also chose to leave a heavy burden for the future.

The longer China waits to abandon the mixed economy and to move toward a market system, the greater will be the clash between the two systems. A thoroughgoing transition to a market economy is required if China's economic system is to mature. Thus, what is needed are privatizing, developing a universal and better domestic market, and linking the domestic market to the foreign market. Although this transition process will be difficult, it must be completed if China is to come of age and join the global economy.

China's Impact on the Outside World

As a giant with one-fifth of the world's population, China is surely in a position to have a profound impact on the outside world. For nearly 30 years (from the 1950s to the late 1970s), however, the impact that China should have had on the outside world was limited by China's choice to remain isolated from the West. During that time, China had to depend on playing the part of a strategic giant and then exerting its influences on world issues through international forums on the global strategic balance. It is very obvious that, from a long-term point of view, this approach has few benefits for either China or the outside world.

After 1978, the reform and the openness of China provided the necessary preconditions for changing the above situation. The overall adjustment of both domestic and foreign policies during the reform and openness in China, as well as favorable developments in the rest of the world, created an opportunity for China to participate in world issues in many ways, especially in economic matters. In addition, the reforms set the potential for China to become a real superpower in the foreseeable future.

The initiation of economic reform meant that the motives and ways for China to influence the outside world were completely different from the previous ones. Prior to the reform, China influenced the outside world by taking a position of self-reliance and by emphasizing its deterrent force. After the reform, however, China proceeded more frequently from its requirements for economic development and on the basis of international cooperation. In this way, China hoped to bring about greater profits both for itself and for other countries.

Over the past decade China's reform movement clearly symbolized a new stage for world development. China's pragmatism and the success of its agricultural reforms and Special Economic Zones (SEZs) represent one of the options to be followed by all socialist countries seeking to leave behind the old system of planning and to adopt a market economy. The most obvious example is the Soviet Union who followed China's lead. Emanating from China, reform has become a global trend—even though China has now backtracked, at least temporarily.

According to the World Bank's *World Development Report 1987*, China's GNP was U.S.$322.5 billion in 1985, making China the eighth largest economic power in the world and the largest one in the developing world. There is no doubt that China will continue to grow, but the rate of growth will depend on the choice of development model and on China's openness to the outside world. In my opinion, it is absolutely necessary to establish a rational price system, guided by the market mechanism, for the success of China's future; financial and ownership reform are also necessary.

Whether or not China's leaders will take these steps, however, is uncertain. If they do, China will realize its full growth potential and we can expect the following effects on the world economy. First, China's development will promote the multi-polarization of the world economy, thus enhancing the position of the developing countries in the North-South dialogue. Second, with greater industrialization, more rapid technological progress, and improved management, China will gradually gain status as a world economic power. Once China reaches its potential as an exporter, its productive capacity and low cost of production will change the configuration of world economy. Finally, notwithstanding its relatively low living standard and consumption level, China's large population and great potential for development and opening will make it a huge market for foreign commodities and capital, thus easing the trade conflicts that now exist.

Of course, China must extend its active economic influences on the outside world, not only in degree but also in scope. China must strengthen its economic contacts with Japan and the four Asian "tigers" (i.e., Hong Kong, Taiwan, South Korea, and Singapore). If China can spread its influence in these countries, a stable core would be established for accelerating the entire region's prosperity. Although it is too early to conclude that the 21st century will be the Pacific century, we can be sure that economic cooperation within the Pacific Rim will be a driving force for world economy. Thus, it is very important for China to become an active economic partner in the Pacific Rim economic miracle, as well as to seek more paths for cooperating with the United States and Japan on the basis of enhancing mutual confidences. China also must seek to establish closer economic ties with Europe, so that a solid foundation can be created for a prosperous, stable, and peaceful Eurasia.

12

THE CHINA–HONG KONG CONNECTION
Yun-Wing Sung

A notable feature of China's open-door policy is the pivotal role played by Hong Kong. The Chinese view Hong Kong as a window or a bridge to the outside world. They value this window so much that they have promised, in the Sino-British joint declaration, to preserve the capitalist system in Hong Kong for 50 years after 1997. Capitalistic, free-wheeling Hong Kong has become the linchpin in opening up the socialist and rigidly regimented Chinese economy.

Hong Kong is China's foremost partner in commodity trade, tourist trade, direct foreign investment, and loan syndication. Since 1979, Hong Kong has contributed two-thirds of all direct foreign investment to China and 80 percent of China's tourist earnings. In 1989, China's exports to Hong Kong totaled 48 percent of all Chinese exports; imports from Hong Kong made up 32 percent of all imports. Hong Kong also plays an important role in trans-shipment. Besides trade and investment, Hong Kong facilitates China's open-door policy in many indirect ways, serving as a contact point, a conduit of information and technology transfer, and a market and production training ground.

A distinctive feature of China's open-door policy is its regional approach. China opened its coastal areas first, with Hong Kong playing an important role in the regional orientation of the open door. Guangdong and Fujian provinces, where the four Special Economic Zones are located, are close to Hong Kong and have enjoyed special autonomy in trade and investment since 1979. Guangdong is adjacent to Hong Kong, and 80 percent of Hong Kong's inhabitants have their ancestral roots there and speak Guangdong dialect. A substantial part of Hong Kong's investment and trade is directed to Guangdong. Direct foreign investment in Guangdong amounted to 70 percent of the national total, and Guangdong surpassed Shanghai in 1986 to become the largest exporter in China. Hainan Island, formerly part of Guangdong province, was opened in 1983 and was given provincial status in 1988.

The author is Senior Lecturer in Economics at the Chinese University of Hong Kong.

Hong Kong's Pivotal Role

As one examines the role of Hong Kong in China's trade, it is important to distinguish among trans-shipment, entrepôt trade, and direct trade. Trans-shipment means that goods are consigned directly from the exporting country to a buyer in the importing country, though the goods are transported via an entrepôt and may be temporarily stored at the entrepôt for further shipment. Trans-shipped goods may change their mode of transportation at the entrepôt. Chinese goods, for example, are carried by train or coastal vessels to Hong Kong, where they are consolidated into containers. Trans-shipped goods are not usually regarded as part of the trade of the entrepôt, and they do not clear customs because they represent only goods in transit.

Unlike trans-shipment, entrepôt trade is indirect; imports for re-exports are consigned to a buyer in the entrepôt and the buyer takes legal possession of the goods after clearing customs. These imports may then be processed before being re-exported. Processing may include packaging, sorting, grading, bottling, drying, assembling, decorating, diluting, or even minor manufacturing processes, such as the pre-shrinking of gray cloth. According to the official definition imposed by Hong Kong, any manufacturing process that permanently changes the shape, nature, form, or utility of the basic materials used in manufacture makes the product a domestic export—that is, it is an export manufactured in Hong Kong—qualifying the good to be classified as originating in Hong Kong.

Direct trade includes domestic exports and retained imports. If one follows the definition imposed by the Hong Kong government, retained imports are the difference between total imports and re-exports, and the re-export margin (estimated to be around 25 percent) is ignored (Sung 1987, p. 33).

The role of Hong Kong in China's open-door policy can be summarized under four main functions: (1) financier, (2) trading partner, (3) middleman, and (4) facilitator (Figure 1).

Financier

Hong Kong has a share in direct foreign investment in China that is as high as two-thirds. The share held by Hong Kong in China's external loans is quite small, though it rose from 0.6 percent in 1983 to 9.4 percent in 1989. This share is low partly beause Hong Kong does not extend official loans to China. In 1987, however, China-backed companies began to raise funds in Hong Kong's stock market through share placements (*South China Morning Post* 18 June 1987), and there are signs that China may rely more on Hong Kong's stock

FIGURE 1

HONG KONG'S ROLE IN CHINA'S OPEN-DOOR POLICY

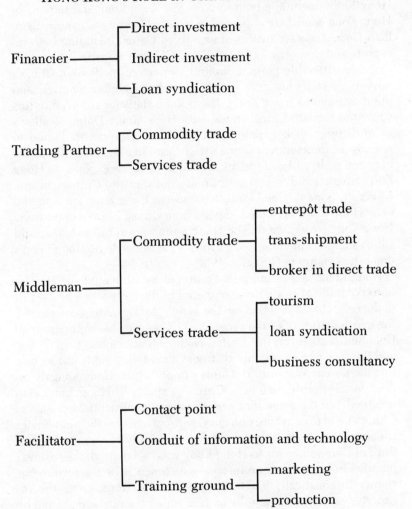

market in the future. Hong Kong also plays a leading role in syndicating loans to China. The share of China's external loans syndicated in Hong Kong rose from 16 percent in the 1979–82 period to 31 percent in 1987.

Trading Partner

When referring to Hong Kong as a trading partner, we refer to direct trade only (entrepôt trade is covered under the middleman

257

function). China's trade statistics do not distinguish between direct and indirect trade. Moreover, China's statistics of total imports from Hong Kong (including both imports via Hong Kong and imports of Hong Kong goods) are appreciably lower (26 percent lower in 1986) than Hong Kong's statistics of exports to China (including both re-exports and domestic exports). From Chinese statistics, it appears that a considerable portion (around 35 percent in 1986) of China's imports via Hong Kong can be attributed to the country of origin and the remainder to Hong Kong. Hong Kong statistics are used in this paper to calculate China's trade with Hong Kong. Doing so allows us to distinguish between direct trade and entrepôt trade and to remedy the deficiency of China's statistics. Time lags and differences between f.o.b. and c.i.f. prices are ignored, China exports via Hong Kong are assumed to be Hong Kong's re-exports of Chinese origin, China's exports retained for internal use in Hong Kong are assumed to be Hong Kong's retained imports from China, China's imports via Hong Kong are assumed to be Hong Kong's re-exports to China, and China's imports of Hong Kong goods are assumed to be Hong Kong's domestic exports to China.

Hong Kong was an important entrepôt for China until 1951. The entrepôt trade of Hong Kong withered in the early 1950s as a result of the centralization of trade in the hands of state trading companies, the re-orientation of China's trade to the Comecon bloc after the 1949 Communist takeover, the United Nations trade embargo on China, and the U.S. ban on all imports from China following China's entry into the Korean War in 1951. China's imports from Hong Kong dwindled to negligible amounts. China's exports to Hong Kong also declined, but the amount of exports was still substantial because of China's need to earn hard currency, particularly after the Sino-Soviet rift of the late 1950s. Before 1979, however, only one-quarter to one-third of China's exports to Hong Kong was re-exported; the rest was retained in Hong Kong for internal use. Since 1979, the picture has changed dramatically. Of China's exports to Hong Kong, the re-exported portion grew rapidly and exceeded the retained portion by 1984. From 1977 to 1989, China imports via Hong Kong grew 349 times and imports of Hong Kong origin grew 793 times. Hong Kong re-emerged as a major entrepôt for China, and China became a major market for Hong Kong products.

In the late 1960s and early 1970s, Hong Kong was the largest final market for Chinese exports (excluding Chinese exports via Hong Kong). The Hong Kong market was overtaken by the Japanese market in 1973 and by the U.S. market in 1987. But Hong Kong still accounted for more than 9 percent of China's exports in 1989. China continues to regard Hong Kong as its largest market, since Chinese trade statistics disregard the substantial re-exports of Chinese products via Hong Kong. Domestic exports of Hong Kong to China have grown from negligible amounts to US$5,548 million in 1989. In 1984, Hong Kong became the third largest supplier of goods to China after Japan and the United States. Part of the reason for the rapid growth of Hong Kong's domestic exports is Hong Kong's investment in processing and assembling operations in China. Hong Kong firms supply these operations with raw materials and components, some of which are made in Hong Kong. Since 1987, China has regarded Hong Kong as its largest supplier, since Chinese trade statistics regard a substantial part of the re-exports of Hong Kong to China as imports from Hong Kong.

China's exports that are retained in Hong Kong have been stagnating since 1984, and their share of China's total exports has declined sharply. China has been unable to capture the higher end of Hong Kong's market, which has been dominated by Japan. Given Hong Kong's increasing affluence and the Japanese dominance in vehicles, capital goods, and quality consumer durables and consumer goods, the future of Chinese products in Hong Kong is not very bright (Sung 1986, p. 86).

Service trade, mostly tourism, is also important. Hong Kong accounts for about 60 percent of tourist arrivals and 70 percent of tourist expenditures in China. Chinese tourists visiting Hong Kong have also grown rapidly, but the trips are usually paid for by Hong Kong relatives of Chinese tourists.

Middleman

Hong Kong plays the role of middleman both in commodity and services trade, including tourism, financial services, and business consultancy. A middleman creates opportunities for trade and investment by lowering transaction costs. In commodity trade, Hong Kong is an important entrepôt as well as the center of trans-shipment for China. The value of trans-shipped goods is not available because they do not go through customs, but their weight is known. From 1983 to 1989, trans-shipment of goods to China via Hong Kong increased 13.2 times; trans-shipment of goods from China to Hong Kong increased 2.7 times. In 1988, trans-shipment of goods to China weighed about 21 percent of China's imports from Hong Kong; trans-shipment from China weighed about 31 percent of exports. This evidence implies that a significant portion of China's trade is trans-shipped via Hong Kong. Hong Kong trading firms also perform an important brokerage role for China's direct trade, amounting to US

$15 billion or 7 percent of China's total trade in 1988. Hong Kong is also the foremost gateway for China tourists. In addition, many foreigners join package tours of China organized in Hong Kong, and the percentage of foreign tourists visiting China via Hong Kong has been increasing since 1982, rising to more than 70 percent in 1989.

Loan syndication can also be viewed as a middleman function performed by Hong Kong. In recent years Hong Kong has become the center for raising 80 percent of China's syndicated loans (excluding soft loans and non-syndicated loans). Hong Kong is also the foremost center for China consultancy services.

Facilitator

In addition to its role as financier, trading partner, and middleman, Hong Kong facilitates the open-door policy in many intangible ways. It serves as a contact point, being the foremost base for China's trade and investment for both foreign and Chinese companies. Hong Kong is an important conduit of market information and technology transfer. It also provides a market and production training ground for China. Some skills can be learned only through practice in a free-market environment, and Hong Kong provides a dynamic and convenient training ground. To utilize Hong Kong as a market and production training ground, China had invested close to US$6 billion in Hong Kong by 1985 (*The Economist* 11 May 1985), exceeding the amount of Hong Kong's direct investment in China.

The Theory of Intermediation

Since the inauguration of the open-door policy, China has established diplomatic, commercial, and transportation links with the rest of the world. Paradoxically, Hong Kong's role as middleman is becoming more prominent—and an increasing share of China's commodity trade, tourist trade, and loan syndication is handled through Hong Kong. To explain this paradox, we can construct a theory of intermediation that has strong predictions for entrepôt and services trade. Because of a lack of data on services trade, however, the predictions for entrepôt trade will be discussed in more detail.

The usual explanation of entrepôt trade in terms of transportation cost is faulty because it ignores the importance of transaction costs. It is useful here to classify re-exports into those that are processed and those that are pure. Processed re-exports refer to re-exports that have been physically treated (packaged, sorted, and so on); pure re-exports have not been changed in any physical way.

Pure re-exports are difficult to account for theoretically because re-exports involve higher costs than trans-shipment (other things being equal) owing to two factors. First, re-exports have to clear the customs of an entrepôt twice, whereas trans-shipped goods do not have to clear the customs of the entrepôt at all, making for fewer delays and lower storage costs. Second, trans-shipped goods are insured and financed only once, whereas re-exports have to be insured and financed twice, first when they are imported into the entrepôt and then when they are re-exported. While transportation costs determine trans-shipment, pure re-exports are determined by both transportation costs and transaction costs; processed re-exports involve processing costs as well.

Our theory of intermediation includes an explanation of the need for intermediation. It also includes an analysis of the economies of scale and agglomeration in supplying trading services, since these economies increase the efficiency of intermediation.

Intermediation can be accounted for by the existence of transaction costs. When Townsend (1978) constructed a model in which intermediaries emerge endogenously, he assumed that establishing a bilateral trade link between economic agents involves a fixed transaction cost. Thus, an exchange structure in which everyone is linked to everyone else (the Walrasian model) is generally inefficient. Efficient structures minimize the number of bilateral trade links and necessarily involve intermediation. Increasing the number of households in a trading coalition decreases risks but increases the number of links and transaction costs. A trade-off is involved, and Townsend used a core equilibrium concept to show how to arrive at equilibrium.

The existence of economies of scale in intermediation enhances the demand for the middleman, since small firms will not be able to trade efficiently. Yamamura (1976, pp. 184–85) argued that significant economies of scale exist in the production of trading services, since the production of these services usually involves large fixed costs and small or declining marginal costs. In the production of market information, which is part of intermediation, he argued that considerable costs are involved and that the same market information is useful in many transactions.

Traders tend to agglomerate in a city, suggesting that there are significant external economies involved. This implies that once a city acquires a comparative advantage in trade, the advantage feeds itself, as more trading firms will come to the city, making the city even more efficient in trade.

There are, in fact, external economies on both the demand and supply sides in trade. External economies on the demand side operate through search; an increase in the number of potential trading partners makes trade easier. Economic theory suggests that agglomeration should be most prevalent in the trading of heterogeneous goods under conditions of low search and travel costs (Stuart 1979, p. 17). A rise in heterogeneity increases the need to search in a marketplace with many sellers. A decline in travel costs will shrink cost differentials between marketplaces and will lead some buyers to shift from small, local marketplaces to larger, more distant ones.

External economies on the production side are also important in trade. Hicks (1969, pp. 47–49) observed that an increase in the number of merchants in the trading center will permit specialization and division of labor, not only by lowering costs, but also by lowering risks. The larger the number of traders, the easier it is to acquire information and the easier it is to arrange multilateral contracts or to develop specialized contracts such as insurance and hedging. Lucas (1985) stressed the importance of agglomeration, especially in service industries, because people in the same trade can interact and learn from one another. He called this "externality of human capital."

Application to Entrepôt and Services Trade

Our theory of intermediation predicts that a decline in travel and communication costs will lower the fixed cost of transaction, and the fraction of world trade handled through intermediation will decline. Declining travel costs, however, also raise the attractiveness of large trading centers relative to small ones, and the fraction of world trade handled through large trading centers may not decline. The secular decline of the fraction of world trade handled through intermediation is quite evident. For instance, before the modern era, goods usually changed hands many times in long-distance trading. Chinese-European trade was usually handled by Indian and Arab middleman, but they lost their livelihood with the advent of modern communications. Large entrepôts, including Hong Kong, Singapore, Gibraltar, Bahrain, and Puerto Rico, continued to thrive, as did the large Japanese trading companies that handle a substantial portion of Japan's foreign trade (Yamamura 1976).

The share of Hong Kong's re-exports in world exports increased from 0.73 percent in 1938 to 1.47 percent in 1989 (the share declined from 1951 to 1973 due to China's isolation). To remove the erratic China factor, we can look at Hong Kong's re-exports from market economies to other market economies. The share of these re-exports in world trade rose from 0.11 percent in 1968 (the first year in which such data were available) to 0.28 percent in 1989. This evidence shows that an increasing fraction of the trade among market economies is handled through Hong Kong in the form of entrepôt trade, which confirms our theory on the efficiency of large trading centers.

Our theory predicts that product heterogeneity increases search costs and the demand for intermediation. Manufactures are usually more heterogeneous than crude materials, which may explain the different fortunes of entrepôt trade in Hong Kong and Singapore. Hong Kong's re-exports were dominated by manufactures as early as 1948 (the first year that data were available), and Singapore's re-exports were dominated by crude materials (chiefly tin and rubber) until 1974 (Sung 1987, p. 28). The share of Hong Kong's re-exports in world exports rose continuously after the early 1960s, but the share of Singapore's re-exports in world trade fell from 1.8 percent in 1951 to 0.25 percent in 1975 because Malaysia and Indonesia tried to cut out the Singaporean middleman. From 1975 onward (the year that manufactures exceeded crude materials in Singapore's re-exports), however, the share of Singapore's re-exports in world trade increased, reaching 0.45 percent in 1984, reversing a 24-year downward trend; the proportion of manufactures rose to two-thirds of Singapore's re-exports in the same year (Sung 1987, p. 29). Moreover, the share of China's trade in manufactures (both exports and imports) handled via Hong Kong in the form of entrepôt trade is much higher than the corresponding shares of China's trade in agricultural products or crude materials (Sung 1987, pp. 43–44), again confirming our theory.

Our theory also predicts that the demand for intermediation will be higher in the services trade than in commodity trade because the "products" of services tend to be tailored to individual requirements and are more heterogeneous than commodities. This view is consistent with the limited data on services trade, as China's reliance on Hong Kong middlemen in loan syndication and in tourism is even more pronounced than in commodity trade.

Intermediation and Decentralization

Since China's adoption of an open-door policy in 1979, it is easier to trade directly with China. The fixed cost of establishing a direct trade link has declined, which should lead to a rise in direct trade relative to indirect trade. In 1979, however, China started to decentralize its foreign trade system by replacing vertical channels of command with horizontal links. The supervision and coordination costs of command have decreased, but transaction costs have increased, creating a hugh demand for intermediation. Before 1979, establishing trade links with 10 trading corporations would have ensured a complete coverage of China's trade. By 1984, the number of trading corporations had increased to more than 1,000, making it prohibitively costly for an individual firm to establish trade links with all Chinese trading corporations. Intermediation emerges to economize on the fixed cost of establishing trade links, and the demand for intermediation is channeled to Hong Kong because of its comparative advantage in entrepôt trade. (It should be noted that China's foreign trade decentralization came in two waves, in 1979 and 1984.)

The market composition of China's indirect trade via Hong Kong and the change over time of these markets in dependency on Hong Kong's entrepôt trade confirm the overwhelming importance of trade decentralization on intermediation (Sung 1987, pp. 41–43). Countries with long histories of trading with China found it worthwhile to pay for the fixed cost of establishing trade links, and they are less dependent on Hong Kong than are new entrants. Political recognition and trade pacts also lower dependency on Hong Kong, but the decentralization of China's trading system in 1979 and 1984 increased the dependency of both old China hands and new entrants on Hong Kong's entrepôt trade. For instance, the dependence of Canada and the United States on Hong Kong for China's exports decreased in the early 1970s when they established political and commericial links with China, but the trend was reversed in 1979. Since 1984, the dependence of all of China's major markets (Japan, the United States, Singapore, West Germany, the United Kingdom, Canada, and Australia) on Hong Kong for China's exports increased substantially. Similarly, since 1979 all of China's major suppliers (Japan, the United States, West Germany, the United Kingdom, France, Italy, and Singapore) became more dependent on Hong Kong for their exports to China.

The rapid jump in the share of China's loans syndicated in Hong Kong in 1987 appears to be related to the decentralization of China's financial system. Starting from early 1987, selected provincial governments and enterprises were allowed to raise foreign loans without central approval. Decentralization appears to have a determining effect on intermediation.

Hong Kong's Prospect as a Middleman

Both theoretical and empirical analyses indicate that the prospect of Hong Kong in China trade is bright. China plans to further decentralize its economy, which implies a further multiplication in the number of trade links and a greater demand for intermediation.

At present, Chinese import and export firms compete with Hong Kong firms, but many of these Chinese firms are inefficient state enterprises hampered by administrative controls. In the very long run, with successful economic reforms, efficient, profit-maximizing Chinese trading firms may emerge. Given economies of scale and economies of agglomeration in the production of trading services, however, Hong Kong does not have to fear competition from Chinese trading firms.

Even in the very long run, Shanghai is likely to be the only Chinese city capable of challenging Hong Kong's position in intermediation, but Shanghai's transport and communication facilities lag considerably behind Hong Kong and its services industries are rudimentary. China's commodity trade will shift toward less bulky and more heterogeneous goods, which will enhance the demand for intermediation. The open-door policy led to the development of services trade and investment in addition to the traditional commodity trade, and this will enhance the need for intermediation because the "products" of services tend to be more heterogeneous. Moreover, the secular decline in travel and transportation costs imply that Shanghai's locational advantage will be less important and that proficiency in trading skills will be more important.

The Chinese are establishing many trading companies in Hong Kong, indicating that they recognize the established efficiency of Hong Kong in trading. Some Hong Kong traders fear competition from Chinese trading companies in Hong Kong, but the situation is not a zero-sum game because of economies of agglomeration. The arrival of Chinese trading companies should further enhance the position of Hong Kong as a trading center.

Hong Kong as a Spur to China's Reform

It has been repeatedly stressed that, in the long run, the viability of China's open-door policy depends on the success of economic reforms. Hong Kong plays a crucial role in China's reform drive, especially in the reform of China's external sector. The dynamism of the Hong Kong market directly activates market forces in China, and the best example is the growth of a black market in foreign exchange in China. The presence of a black market forces planners to devalue the Renminbi and to create a thriving gray market for foreign exchange. The presence of Hong Kong also exerts pressures on China to decentralize its trade, since many localities and enterprises have been able to trade with the outside world covertly through their Hong Kong connections.

Hong Kong is an efficient, flexible instrument for promoting China's trade and investment, but China has not mastered its use of this instrument. Given the efficiency and versatility of Hong Kong as a promotor of China's trade and investment, irrational policies in China will be manifested quickly in the Hong Kong market, and Chinese planners can avail themselves of the rapid feedback mechanism of the Hong Kong economy to gauge the rationality of their policy in trade and investment.

In the long run, the most important role Hong Kong can play in spurring Chinese reform is by demonstrating the efficiency of a free-market economy. China can choose to utilize, to learn from, to adapt, or even to destroy Hong Kong's market model, but China cannot ignore it.

References

Hicks, John R. *A Theory of Economic History*. London: Oxford University Press, 1969.

Lucas, Robert. "The Mechanics of Economic Development." Marshall Lecture, Cambridge University, Cambridge, 1985.

Stuart, Charles. "Search and Spatial Organization of Trading." In *Studies of the Economics of Search*. Edited by S. A. Lippman and J. J. McCall. New York: Elsevier-North Holland, 1979.

Sung, Yun-Wing. "The Role of Hong Kong and Macau in China's Export Drive." Working Paper no. 85/11. National Centre for Development Studies, Australian National University, 1985.

Sung, Yun-Wing. "The Role of Hong Kong in China's Export Drive." *Australian Journal of Chinese Affairs*, no. 15 (1986): 83–101.

Sung, Yun-Wing. "A Theoretical and Empirical Analysis of Entrepôt Trade: Hong Kong and Singapore and Their Roles in China's Trade." Paper presented to the 16th Pacific Trade and Development Conference on Trade and Investment in Services in the Pacific Region, Wellington, New Zealand, 25–29 January 1987.

Townsend, R. M. "Intermediation with Costly Bilateral Exchange." *Review of Economic Studies* 45 (1978): 417–25.

Yamamura, Kozo. "General Trading Companies in Japan: Their Origins and Growth." In *Japanese Industrialization and Its Social Consequences*. Edited by Hugh Patrick. Berkeley: University of California Press, 1976.

COMMENT

THE ROLE OF HONG KONG IN CHINA'S REFORM
He Gaosheng

Yun-Wing Sung has written an elaborate paper describing the role of Hong Kong in China's reform, development, and opening to the outside world. His analysis of the economic relationship between mainland China and Hong Kong is heuristic and gives us much food for thought. I would like to make some comments on his arguments while offering some of my personal observations.

Hong Kong's Contribution to China's Development

By quoting a series of statistics, Sung identifies four roles of Hong Kong in China's foreign economic relations and trade: a financier, a trade partner, an intermediator, and a facilitator. These are the roles Hong Kong has played and will continue to play in the future.

The development of economic relations between China and Hong Kong since the founding of the People's Republic of China can be divided into two stages: first, the stage from 1949 through 1978, which was characterized by contacts in the field of commercial trade; and second, the stage that began in 1979, when China started to restructure its economic system and to open its door to the outside world. Since then more and more Hong Kong entrepreneurs have swarmed into the mainland for industrial investment in joint ventures. In recent years the dealings and cooperations have further expanded into financial areas. It is a logical trend that the development of commercial, industrial, and financial ties between the two economies have stimulated even more intermediators and facilitators in business exchanges.

Despite the unfortunate events of May-June 1989, I think the future remains strong for trade relations between Hong Kong and the

The author is Director of the Office of the Shanghai Economic System Reform.

mainland. The key to future prosperity, however, is for China to adopt Hong Kong's policy of stability and prosperity. With its social stability and economic prosperity, I believe Hong Kong will play an even larger role in China's future reform, development, and opening to the outside world.

Hong Kong as a Model for China

Hong Kong is now operating as a free port and pursuing a market economy under a capitalist system. Such a system should be sustained in Hong Kong. The purpose of China's economic reform has been to bring the market mechanism into play and to establish a new economic system under which "the state regulates the market and the market guides enterprises," while public ownership plays the dominant role in the economy.

But is it possible to combine public ownership with the market mechanism? Some overseas economists hold that it is impossible. But according to our initial practices, I believe it is possible. Of course, further experiments and practices are necessary for us to get a better combination of the two. In restructuring our economic system, we should study and make use of the successful experience in economic administration of other countries including the United States. Surely we should study and use the valuable lessons and effective tools of Hong Kong in its economic management and development. Hong Kong will be an object of our constant studying and learning.

However, China should not mechanically imitate Hong Kong's economic structure, because there are many differences between the two economies. In accordance with the actual conditions on the mainland, we must pursue a new structure of the Chinese-style socialist commodity economy.

Shanghai's Road to Reform

Shanghai is an important part of China's economy and its economic health is essential to China's future. As China's largest port, Shanghai also has important ties to Hong Kong. The following five-point economic reform package has been proposed to help invigorate and revitalize Shanghai's economy:

1. Restructure the existing ownership system so that public ownership, while playing a major role, will develop hand-in-hand with other types of ownership. The chief way to achieve this goal is to convert most of the government-owned enterprises

into shareholders' organizations but with the public as the major shareholder.

2. Separate enterprise operation from government administration so that enterprises can make their own management decisions and take full and real responsibility for their own profits and losses.

3. Foster and perfect a market system so that the prices of most products can be determined by free-market forces.

4. Restructure macroeconomic administration and institute a new system of regulation to manage the national economy by a combined use of economic levers, legal means, planning tools, and some necessary administrative activities so as to foster stable economic growth.

5. Reform the political system in an orderly fashion so as to separate the Chinese Communist Party from the operation of government, strengthen the legal system, improve and decentralize the regulatory functions of government in economic affairs, and streamline administrative organizations to eliminate bureaucracy and establish an honest and efficient government.

Relations between Shanghai and Hong Kong

Sung suggests that in the future Shanghai may well be a challenger to Hong Kong. Such a view is of course an encouragement for us. Shanghai is China's largest economic center and was once the biggest financial center in the Far East. But for nearly 30 years (1949–78), Shanghai's functions as an economic center were reduced by the rigidity of the system of national economic planning. It was not until the reform movement and decentralization, which started to gain momentum in 1979, that Shanghai regained its economic functions. We are now making every effort to reconstruct Shanghai into a modern international metropolis and business center. In the days to come, there surely will be competition between Shanghai and Hong Kong, but there also will be many opportunities to learn from each other and to cooperate with each other.

Both Shanghai and Hong Kong have their characteristics, advantages, and weaknesses. The attitude we in Shanghai take is to learn from the strong points of others so that we may offset our weaknesses. If pressures exist, I think Hong Kong exerts a greater one upon Shanghai. Such a pressure should be taken as a kind of accelerator or promoter. I believe that as Hong Kong becomes more prosperous and Shanghai develops into a modern international metropolis, all of China will benefit. Such a development will be encouraging and it will also be pleasant news for our many friends around the world.

COMMENT

THE INTEGRATION OF HONG KONG AND CHINA
John G. Greenwood

Yun-Wing Sung has written a thorough and workmanlike paper describing the economic relationship between Hong Kong and China in its many forms. He explains how the mainland Chinese view Hong Kong as a window or bridge to the rest of the world. He shows how the relationship between the two economies has developed in trade, tourism, investment, and loan syndication. He argues that Hong Kong has played a pivotal role for China as a trans-shipment center, as an entrepôt, and as a direct trading partner. He classifies Hong Kong's role under four main headings: as a financier, as a trading partner, as a middleman, and as a facilitator of trade and investment. He quotes some impressive statistics to show how Hong Kong has played a dominant role in China's development since the announcement of the Four Modernizations in 1978, and he seeks to encapsulate this multifaceted role in a theory of intermediation.

Sung develops his theory of intermediation to explore the paradox of Hong Kong becoming more prominent as a middleman during the past decade in contrast to the case of Singapore, whose role in handling Malaysian and Indonesian goods between 1951 and 1975 declined progressively, though it has subsequently risen again. One factor to which he attributes Hong Kong's success as a middleman is the decentralization of China's trade that occurred between 1979 and 1984, enhancing Hong Kong's role as an entrepôt. He predicts that greater decentralization of the Chinese economy will enhance Hong Kong's role as an entrepôt even further in the future.

This argument seems to me entirely sensible and reasonable. However, it is hardly surprising that Hong Kong's entrepôt role should have grown as much as it has considering the prolonged period of

The author is Chairman of G. T. Management (Asia) Limited and Editor-in-Chief of the *Asian Monetary Monitor*.

enforced or artificial separation between Hong Kong and the mainland during the years between the United Nations' embargo on trade with China and the start of the open-door policy in the 1970s. In fact, I believe it is more appropriate to talk about the Hong Kong economy becoming increasingly *integrated* with the economy of southern China than to talk about Hong Kong acting merely as an entrepôt. Hong Kong is a large city with numerous specialist services such as finance, banking, transportation, and the high value-added services associated with the manufacturing process such as design, marketing, and so forth.

Hong Kong's Integration with China

In recent years Hong Kong has seen a trend toward the employment of large numbers of Chinese mainlanders in factories north of the border, either in the Special Economic Zones (SEZs) or in China proper, so that today it is estimated that Hong Kong–owned factories employ more people in China than they do in Hong Kong, where the number of people in the manufacturing sector is approximately 860,000. This integration of the Hong Kong economy with the rest of China is comparable to the integration of New York or Manhattan with the surrounding economies of Massachusetts, Connecticut, New York State, Pennsylvania, and New Jersey. Just as New York was once a center for the textile and garment industry and that industry has now moved out to the Carolinas, so Hong Kong's low value-added industries are currently being moved out toward the low-wage cost areas in China, and Hong Kong is concentrating on high valued-added services such as garment design, the provision of fashion parades for buyers from overseas countries, the packaging and marketing of garments, and so on. Accordingly, the description of Hong Kong as an entrepôt will, I believe, prove to be only a passing phase. Ultimately, Hong Kong will become fully integrated with the economy of southern China, performing the kind of specialist function that one would expect of any large city that also has the only deep-water port in the region.

The Degree of Future Integration

The real question, it seems to me, is whether China can leave Hong Kong well enough alone to encourage or enhance the integration of the two economies over the next decade or two. The concern and anxiety that the people of Hong Kong have shown is already apparent in the outflow of financial capital and increasingly of human capital, which we call the brain drain. The answer will depend largely on political developments in China and on the attitude of Chinese opinion leaders toward Hong Kong. I shall therefore concentrate the rest of my comments on some aspects of current Chinese attitudes toward Hong Kong, which I have learned from visiting Chinese scholars.

Chinese Attitudes toward Hong Kong

As you may know, in the wake of the Sino-British Agreement of 1984, numerous associations for the study of the Hong Kong economy were formed all over China. I have met with several representatives of those associations when they have visited Hong Kong and they have frequently conveyed the view that Hong Kong has some special attributes to offer China that can be learned and imported into the mainland from Hong Kong. In particular, these Chinese economists emphasize the desirability of importing *management* and *technology* from Hong Kong. This notion appears also to underlie the basic rationale for the creation and existence of China's SEZs. The four SEZs, as I understand the concept, were intended to provide a kind of workshop to which employees from state and municipal corporations all over China would be sent to study Western management and technology in joint ventures with foreign companies. The idea was that, having learned these skills in the SEZ, these individuals would return to their provinces and transmit their new skills to their colleagues and employees, and as a result modern methods of management and technology would gradually percolate back into inner China.

A Flawed View of Management and Technology

Unfortunately, this concept contains a fundamental flaw. Both management and technology are attributes or skills that are themselves responses to a whole set of market incentives and opportunities. It is unlikely that they would have emerged independently without the framework of a free-market economy. It is therefore questionable how far they can be imported into China and applied without China's making fundamental changes in its institutional arrangements. Let me illustrate my point with two examples from Hong Kong. The first is taken from my own industry, namely investment management. In the investment management business we employ skilled investment managers, investment analysts, economists, marketing staff, accounting and computer staff, and so on. Many of these individuals work with computers that have state-of-the-art software, providing financial information and enabling them to conduct rapid and sophisticated analysis of newly announced financial data. The basic business of investment management is the

273

investment of individual or institutional savings and pensions in a variety of financial instruments such as bonds, equities, and deposits in order to maximize the return, and we derive our income from a fee that is based on value of funds under management. We would not employ all of these skilled individuals in a whole range of activities unless we thought that each of them individually was going to contribute to increasing the returns to our funds under management or otherwise serving the needs of our customers and, hence, enhancing the income of the firm.

Now contrast our business with the management of a government-run pension fund, such as the Central Provident Fund (CPF) in Singapore. The CPF employs a mere handful of people and virtually all of the proceeds of the contributions from employees and employers in Singapore are invested in Singapore government bonds. Aside from a few accountants there is virtually no technology required for this business. As a result, the returns from the CPF have been no better than the returns on government bonds and there is certainly no technological progress resulting from competitive pressures in this industry in Singapore.

Another example concerns the postal system in Hong Kong. In Hong Kong, as in many other countries, the postal system is owned and operated by a government department. As a result there has been very little technological innovation in the postal service over the past 100 years, and aside from a few improvements in sorting techniques, the industry operates very much as it did a century ago.

Again contrast that situation with developments in the private sector. In the private sector in recent decades we have seen the emergence of companies specializing in the delivery of private packages and documents both within countries and between countries. Among the best known of those companies are Federal Express in the United States and DHL and Skypak in Britain, Hong Kong, Australia, and elsewhere. These companies normally guarantee delivery within 24 hours within a country and delivery within 48 hours to almost any part of the globe. Furthermore, as companies attempt to overcome the inefficiency of government-run mail systems, we have seen, in recent years, the development of facsimile machines and computer-based information networks that enable written messages to be transmitted by telephone line or data line virtually instantly around the world. The incentive to do this has been the prospect of profits to the makers of facsimile machines and computers, and to the owners or operators of international telephone lines and satellites. It is inconceivable that this set of technological developments could have occurred in the government sector.

Adopting the Building Blocks of Hong Kong's Economic System

What are the key elements of these two examples? There are three components that are common to both. First, private ownership of both industries has stimulated the introduction of sophisticated management and improvements in technology. Second, there is free-market pricing in terms of the setting of wages, the setting of product prices, and the prospect as a result of profits to the owners of these businesses. Third, in both areas competition has stimulated improvements in the service to consumers. China can perhaps import management and technology at some levels and for some period of time, but China cannot expect these skills to develop and percolate in a vacuum, for example, in the absence of an appropriate institutional framework—namely, the existence of private ownership, free markets, and competition among producers.

Suppose China does import these skills (management and technology) over the next decade but that the open door remains partially or fully closed as a result of the events of May-June 1989 or other events. What will happen? If the door were fully closed, I would predict that the level of technological progress remains nearly static thereafter, rather like the well-documented history of the Indian textile industry after Imperial protection was extended to it in the 1920s. Whereas India's textile industry had been one of the most successful and innovative in the world before World War I, after the war the industry atrophied. India was overtaken by Japanese and other textile producers, and today the Indian textile industry produces roughly the same quantity of material and garments as it did in the 1920s. India's technological level is very backward by world standards, and profits in the industry are maintained only by protectionist policies (see Saxonhouse 1985). As this example illustrates, it was the absence of competition together with some degree of price control, not nationalization, that caused the demise of the Indian textile industry. But today, in the case of China, there is a massive requirement to privatize industry and commerce, to abolish price controls, and to allow free competition in a whole range of markets.

In conclusion, Hong Kong's economic success, its high level of technology, and its skilled management depend fundamentally on the following processes: the protection of private property rights; the ability to set prices freely (i.e., to allow the market to allocate resources to where the needs are greatest); and the existence of competition, which ensures that goods are produced at the cheapest cost and which continuously spurs innovation and risk taking. None

275

of these processes can occur continuously under government or state ownership, under price control, or in the absence of competition. China's best hope for modernization is not to import management and technology as such but to import (or at least learn from and adapt) the basic institutions that have made management and technology such a prominent feature of the Hong Kong economy in the eyes of Chinese economists. The greatest degree of integration between Hong Kong and China will be achieved if China adopts the basic ingredients or building blocks of Hong Kong's economic system. If China attempts merely to import the products of Hong Kong's system, the result will be far less successful and far less capable of supporting self-sustained economic growth.

Reference

Saxonhouse, Gary. "Determinants of Technological Choice: The Indian and Japanese Cotton Industries." In *Japan and the Developing Countries*, pp. 135-55. Edited by K. Ohkawa and G. Ranis. Oxford: Basil Blackwell, 1985.

13

EAST ASIAN ECONOMIC SUCCESS: IMPLICATIONS FOR CHINESE AND U.S. FOREIGN POLICY

Edward A. Olsen

When the post–World War II era dawned in Asia, few would have had the temerity to predict that by the 1980s the Western world would be speculating about the "Pacific Century." Immediately after the war, Japan was in ruins, witnessing the results of its wartime adventurism and paying the bitter price of failed policies. China, a major victim of Japanese wartime exploits, was in the throes of a civil war. Korea, a different type of Japanese victim, was enduring the dislocations of being liberated from colonialism by two powers whose policies led to the division of that long-suffering nation. The Southeast Asian nations were experiencing different forms of decolonization. Only the Philippines seemed to have relatively bright prospects because of the United States' firm commitment to relinquish its colonial role and help its former colony get back on its feet after the devastation of the war. The rest of Southeast Asia was a backwater.

In the more than four decades since the end of World War II, the Far East has experienced tremendous change. That transformation has included political, military, and cultural facets, but no other area has witnessed as dramatic a complex of changes as the economic sector. Not all of the Far East has experienced rapid economic change for the better; some areas have lagged behind. The reasons for this slower pace of development have to do with cultural differences that influence the ways in which nations approach work, characteristics of their political cultures that shape the institutions that guide and regulate economies, disparate opportunities for advancement caused by differing levels of foreign support, historical factors that shaped the manner in which nations began their postwar development, and ideological factors that led the various nations to march toward development to the beat of distinctly different drummers. The examples

The author is Professor of National Security Affairs and Asian Studies at the U.S. Naval Postgraduate School.

of relatively slow development range from the idiosyncratic approaches of Burma and North Korea to the fitful experimentation of China and the enervating sluggishness of countries like Indonesia and the Philippines.

Confucian and Marxist Values

When Westerners examine the modern economic success stories of Asia from a broad perspective, the most important characteristic has appeared to be their common link to cultures with Confucian roots. Consequently, Japan and the so-called new-Japans—South Korea, Taiwan, Singapore, and Hong Kong—share certain values that stem from Confucian traditions. For years, it seemed as though it might have been the Japan-like bent of those societies that was the secret to their success. Both South Korea and Taiwan imbibed Japanese entrepreneurial values during their colonial experiences and may have had their respective work ethics influenced by Japanese values. Both of those countries consciously emulated Japan's development model in an adaptive fashion, molding it to meet their specific needs. On a much smaller scale, Singapore and Hong Kong also modeled their export-led economic successes after Japan. But all of those societies shared with Japan certain values inherited from Chinese civilization and adapted to their own purposes. Briefly stated, those values emphasize a work ethic, individual honesty in dealing with others, a respect for law and order, and conformity within a hierarchical society. Group-oriented Confucianism contributed to both Asian socialism and Asian capitalism, which does not necessarily share Western capitalism's confidence in the efficacy of individualism.

The three major exceptions to the Confucianism-linked theory of modern economic success were the People's Republic of China, the Democratic People's Republic of Korea, and North Vietnam (and later the unified Socialist Republic of Vietnam). All were seen in the West as having allowed their Marxist ideological proclivities to get in the way of what many Westerners and representatives of the East Asian success stories believed was the superiority of the non-Marxist approach. The non-Marxist perceptions of Vietnam and North Korea as failures remain intact in that their dogma appears to preclude their prospects for joining the ranks of East Asia's success stories. Both have expressed interest in that alternative approach, and each has taken tentative steps in that direction. Vietnam has moved more rapidly than North Korea, but neither has effectively pursued free-market experiments.

The situations regarding China, however, has changed significantly. Although Westerners and non-Marxists in East Asia remain uncertain about precisely what amalgam of Confucian-rooted Chinese traditions and Marxism-Leninism is shaping the economic successes of the People's Republic of China, these observers have had to reassess their views about the causes of those successes. If China is able to transform itself and add its name to the list of success stories in the region—without forgoing its claims to being a "socialist" state that aspires to communism—then the criteria for the East Asian economic success model will have to be revised. The distinction is more than a mere semantic fine point. Should China prove capable of adapting free-market theory and institutions to an amalgam of Sino-Marxist political cultures, it will have created a distinctly different variation of existing East Asian economic models.

There are skeptics in the capitalist world who doubt that this can be accomplished. They think either China will fail because it will be unable to overcome the obstacles imposed by ideology or it will succeed by following a form of Confucian command capitalism (similar to Japan and the "new Japans") that cloaks itself in Marxist garments. The Chinese routinely dismiss such skepticism by noting that the notion of "Marxist dogma" is an oxymoron because Marxism contains within it the ability to adapt to new circumstances. This view rarely persuades the skeptics.

Be that as it may, there is a reasonable chance that over time the People's Republic of China will become one of East Asia's economic success stories. This possibility promises to add a new sense of urgency to the question of how the United States should cope with the issues raised by the emergence of East Asia's economic powerhouses. It also raises questions about how key Asian countries, including China, might cope with the United States' responses to the changing economic mix in the region.

In order to evaluate these questions, we must first address the ways in which the East Asian economic "miracles" occurred and assess their impact on the United States and the People's Republic of China. Then we can explore what might happen because of economic changes in East Asia and estimate what the United States and China might do in response. Having done that, I will offer some normative prescriptive advice about what the United States should do. Although those recommendations will have implications for China's foreign policy options, there will be no specific suggestions in that regard. Arriving at solutions should rightly be the domain of Chinese analysts, not Americans.[1]

[1]For an alternative view of these issues, see Lardy (1987).

Role of the United States

The United States was intimately involved in the creation of the East Asian economic success story. Although there could have been no success without the self-motivation of the people involved, the United States clearly helped the processes of economic growth by providing the capital, technology, and markets as the "seed money" and the catalytic factors that stimulate growth. Had Japan not experienced a relatively benevolent and generous U.S. occupation (that is, had the United States been vindictive or had the Soviet Union been the occupying power), it is easy to imagine how differently postwar Japan might have evolved. Japanese nationalists prefer to think that the innate abilities of the Japanese people would eventually have led Japan to rise to the top of the economic heap, but that ethnocentric view remains problematical. Even if one grants that perspective some validity, it seems certain that Japan would not be as powerful economically as it is had it lacked U.S. assistance. The hundreds of millions of dollars the United States committed to Occupied Japan's economic recovery were invaluable to Japan's survival. Moreover, by initiating constitutional reform in 1947, the United States laid a solid basis for personal and economic freedom (Johnson 1983, pp. 719–20). Consequently, one can justifiably claim a significant American role in the emergence of postwar Japan as an economic dynamo.

The American role in the economic renaissance of South Korea and Taiwan was far more explicit than its role in Japan, even though in the Japanese case the United States was a victorious occupier and in South Korea and Taiwan it was a friendly benefactor. In the early stage of their development, neither South Korea nor Taiwan enjoyed enthusiastic U.S. support. During the late 1940s the United States was not strongly committed to South Korea, despite the crucial American role in creating the Republic of Korea. Americans, then, were actively disengaging from Korea. American enthusiasm regarding Taiwan was similarly subdued. The United States' fruitless support for Chiang Kai-shek's Republic of China and the "loss" of China to the victorious Communists had seriously soured many Americans regarding the Taiwanese government.

Americans did not visualize either South Korea or Taiwan as potential economic or military powers. It was only when Americans perceived that those two countries were facing a threat from communism that the United States increased its willingness to assist those countries in their development efforts. Were it not for inter-Korean and inter-Chinese armed tensions that were considered detrimental to U.S. interests in the Far East, the United States' commitment to facilitating the economic development of South Korea and Taiwan would have been much weaker. The ways in which U.S. interests in South Korea and Taiwan were transformed from marginal to major are closely related to the tremendous shift in the United States' stake in Japan midway through the occupation era.

Altered Motives

After the war, the United States' occupation of Japan quickly shifted from a negative punative phase, through a holding-action phase designed to keep Japan's head above the waters of postwar devastation, and into a restorative phase intended to bring about an economic renaissance. The last phase was the crucial one, because it positioned Japan to take advantage of its human resources and to cultivate opportunities that the United States made available within the group of nations then being assembled into an alliance network. Although a once-powerful Japan had economic potentials that were self-evident, the crucial factor in this phase was that U.S. actions were *not* taken for economic purposes.

These policies were made clear by the efforts of the U.S. occupation authorities to keep Japan's head above water, to not allow its vulnerable population to become susceptible to communist inroads, and to foster an economy strong enough to sustain the U.S.-created Japanese defense forces. Those efforts were underscored by the widely noted concerns of Secretary of State John Foster Dulles that Japan might have difficulty producing anything that postwar Americans might want to buy, apprehensions that would subsequently be tinged with irony. Strengthening Japan's economy was a means to an end—namely, making Japan resilient enough to prevent it from succumbing to Soviet-led communism. In short, the United States' purposes were geopolitical: It wanted to prevent a vacuum in Japan into which the Soviet Union might step. At the outset, then, U.S. strategic motives drove Japan's economic agenda.

Something similar occurred in South Korea and Taiwan. The United States was relatively unenthusiastic about the prospects for each country's economy until a strategic motive emerged. After 1950 and the eruption of the Korean War, the American desire to cultivate anti-communism in Asia spread and solidified the United States' commitment to South Korea and Taiwan. American economic assistance to each country was less concerned with the then far-fetched prospect of fostering economic powers than it was with bolstering two allies so that they would not collapse in the face of an armed adversary. American policymaking toward South Korea and Taiwan was dominated by U.S. military interests, and U.S. economic assistance and diplomacy reinforced those strategic interests. American commercial interest in either South Korea or Taiwan was minimal until the mid-1960s.

During the 1950s, the military-oriented posture remained intact in South Korea and Taiwan because neither country made phenomenal progress. Both had low economic growth rates, and the Americans considered those countries to be poor prospects. South Korea, in particular, was considered a "basket case" that would require American assistance for decades. At best, U.S. economic policy toward both allies was a tenuously calculated effort to give them each a bit of breathing space so that they could become more self-reliant economically and develop the economic wherewithal to defend themselves. Japan was different. Primarily because it did not have to contend with an armed counterpart state and it possessed a reservoir of advanced skills from its Imperial stage, Japan had a substantial head start in its economic redevelopment. It used the United States' largesse of the 1950s, the opportunities the Korean War had fortuitously placed on its doorstep, and the relatively minimal pressures on it to step up its own self-defense efforts as opportunities to accelerate economic growth. By the end of the 1950s, Japan had gained an edge over its neighbors that it has kept to this day.

The 1960s and 1970s witnessed significant changes in South Korea and Taiwan as Seoul and Taipei demonstrated the ability of a tightly disciplined, military-backed regime to instill enough purpose in its people to overcome the effects of inertia, stagnation, and corruption. Taiwan, South Korea, and the very different enclaves of capitalism in Singapore and Hong Kong made tremendous progress during those two decades. Their economic growth rates mushroomed, and each gained fame as a "miracle" that other developing countries might emulate. Derogatory descriptions, such as "basket case" or aid-consuming "rat holes," were forgotten as American and other Western commercial interests rushed to become part of the action. The successes of the 1950s, 1960s, and 1970s built on each other, culminating in the 1980s with a decade that marked Japan's emergence as a center of world trade and finance and with the "four dragons" in its shadows as major actors in world economic affairs.

During those years, something subtle occurred that Americans should have noted but did not. The original strategic rationale for U.S. support of Japan and the other two allies—to give them time to get on their feet defensively and economically—was surpassed to a surprising degree. If a projection had been in the 1950s of the levels of wealth that might be sufficient for Japan, South Korea, and Taiwan to ensure their own security, the numbers proposed would have been of a magnitude that was reached in the 1960s or 1970s. In short, the strategic rationale was overtaken long ago by events, and another— usually understated—rationale succeeded it: The United States supports and helps sustain its economic partners militarily because they are so important economically.

This transition is barely acknowledged in the United States or Asia because it has been so gradual and is still not complete. It may never be possible to put a definitive terminal date on the process, but it is crucial to the future of U.S.-Asian relations. While the United States waits for those newly prospering allies to assume more fully their own security burdens, it also now has reason to fear the conquest of these economic centers by an adversary. At some point during those years the United States' relationship with its East Asian allies and trade partners traversed a major watershed. The logic of the prevailing arrangements was quietly turned upside down.

Successful Results

By 1988, the United States was the trade and strategic partner of two major allies in East Asia. In the case of Japan, the United States is the primary economic partner of the world's second largest economy, whose leaders may aspire to supplant the United States as number one in the world.[2] In the case of South Korea, the United States is the partner of the world's fastest growing economic dynamo. South Korea has transformed itself from a poverty-ridden, war-torn, client-state into a prosperous nation whose people enjoy a well-balanced distribution of wealth and whose leaders have largely rid themselves of the "client-state" mentality. South Korea, with a $120 billion economy, has become the world's 12th-ranking trading nation and is the United States' 7th-ranking trade partner. Its transformation was the result of hard work and skillful management by South Korea's people and leaders. The impact of South Korea's rapid economic progress on its relationships with the United States, however, is truly "miraculous" when one considers how much has changed since the 1950s (see Olsen 1988).

In these two cases, the United States' policies produced successes that are wildly beyond the imagination of what was initially anticipated. Taiwan enjoyed comparable economic successes, though the political circumstances of U.S.-Taiwan interaction have been altered

---

[2]A number of Americans, including the author, believe Japan is close to achieving this partial role reversal. Some Americans think it already has happened. See, for example, Prestowitz (1988).

in ways that neither side adequately foresaw in the 1950s. Taiwanese economic growth, with strong U.S. support, was predicated on solid American political support for the Republic of China. The strategic needs of the United States required a shift in Washington's diplomatic and political relations with all of China. Regardless of those changes, the U.S.-Taiwan economic relationship has continued to prosper, even as the larger U.S.-People's Republic of China (PRC) set of relationships took root and flourished. Elsewhere in the East Asian Confucian realm, the same general approach toward modernization that enabled Japan, South Korea, and Taiwan to grow economically also created cultural conditions that allowed Singapore and Hong Kong to succeed.

U.S.-China Relations

Since the normalization of U.S.-PRC relations and the emergence of Chinese economic reforms, something comparable to previous East Asian economic development experiences has occurred in China but against a strikingly different background. Although American motives vis-à-vis China can hardly be equated with the earlier anti-communist drives behind U.S. policy, there have been comparable security incentives. Both China and the United States had an interest in seeing China become more prosperous, stable, and free of debilitating dependencies. By becoming a participant in the quest for prosperity, China has become a more secure country. The PRC-Taiwan question remains unresolved, but that too seems to be relatively stable as Beijing and Taipei improve their communication and lessen tensions.

The United States and Japan helped promote China's economic progress by facilitating China's access to large markets. The United States, in pursuit of its own interests, also remained as a strategic backstop in Asia, coping with the Soviet Union in ways that benefited China and relieved some of the strategic pressures that Beijing felt. China was being threatened by the Soviet military presence to the north, northeast, and west, and China eventually felt that pressure from the south and southwest as result of Soviet policies toward Vietnam, India, and Afghanistan. The United States' global maritime presence helped to offset those pressures. Unlike other East Asian cases, however, China was able to reciprocate strategically by pursuing its own military interests versus the Soviet Union in ways that complemented U.S. interests. China's continental military power was massive, if not particularly advanced, and served to tie down

Soviet ground and air forces in a way that complemented the United States' off-shore focus in the Pacific.

In this sense, the United States also enjoyed some "breathing space," allowing Washington to adjust to the growth of Soviet forces in the Asia-Pacific region. Alignment with China permitted the United States to confront the Soviet Union with a new correlation of forces. China, unlike any of the other East Asian development cases, pursued its own strategic interests in a way that immediately offered the United States a level of mutually beneficial geopolitical harmony. Moreover, China displayed enthusiasm for this task while U.S. allies in Asia were more reluctant. China's enthusiasm for those tasks diminished in the late 1980s, but it still remains more self-motivated than the United States' allies in Asia.

From a comparative perspective, there are facets of China's economic development process that are important for U.S. policy in East Asia because of their parallels with Japan, South Korea, and Taiwan. In short, they are the ways in which China has emulated aspects of the development model fostered by Japan and adapted by South Korea and Taiwan. Just as South Korea and Taiwan have been reluctant to acknowledge too candidly the extent to which their development experts were influenced by the Japanese, China has been wary of admitting how much it follows those who went before. Neither South Korea nor Taiwan want to denigrate their indigenous innovations and contributions by stressing the role of a model, especially one borrowed from their former colonial ruler, but the parallels are too obvious to be convincingly denied.

Similarly, China has difficulty postulating a Japanese-style model. It has even more difficulty acknowledging that what Taiwan has accomplished might be considered worthy of emulation, though the "Learn from Taiwan" slogan has been used periodically since the late 1970s. China has been least ambiguous about the utility of South Korea's successful "model." Regardless of the practitioners' willingness to admit the degree of cross-emulation that is evident to Westerners, the key result of all of these East Asian nation-builders has been the creation of a range of countries that pose roughly similar challenges to the United States.

Economic Success and Frictions

As Americans assess the results of U.S. postwar policy toward East Asia, there is much for which we can be proud and grateful. U.S. policies helped foster an economically strong and resilient array of allies and friendly states. Most Americans appreciate the ways in

285

which much of East Asia has pulled itself out of the trauma of war and poverty. Similarly, most Americans appreciate the economic contributions East Asia makes to the well-being of other nations of the world and, most pointedly, to the United States. This is a result few Americans anticipated in the early postwar years. However, not all the results of East Asia's economic performance have pleased Americans. In a sense, American unpreparedness for the scale of East Asia's economic success and the United States' laggard competitiveness have produced a profound consternation among some Americans who believe that U.S. policies toward Japan and the Asian dragons may have been *too* successful.

That notion is difficult to argue in the abstract because rational Americans do not begrudge the successes of our trading partners. The view that prosperity is a zero-sum game went out with mercantilist economics. There can be many winners in international economic relations. More important, there is no doubt that U.S. economic problems must be solved at home, not overseas. Nevertheless, U.S. domestic reform efforts depend in part on the ability of the United States to export more successfully than it does now. Consequently, there is a pressing need to achieve thorough market opening among the United States' East Asian trade partners. The problem with the successes achieved by those trade partners concerns American perceptions that the search for prosperity is a game that East Asians have been playing on a field that is not level and that favors them and their quasi-mercantilist forms of economic nationalism at the expense of the United States. Many Americans believe that the U.S. commitment to free trade has not been sufficiently reciprocated by Japan, South Korea, and Taiwan, which do not allow Americans the sort of access to their markets that they enjoy in the United States. Their voices are heard in the halls of Congress, in U.S. labor unions, and in the American Chambers of Commerce.

These feelings by Americans are the cause of the acrimonious trade frictions that have troubled U.S.-Japan, U.S.-ROK, U.S.-Taiwan, and—to a lesser extent—U.S.-ASEAN relations. Clearly, there is great unhappiness in certain American circles about the neo-mercantilist attitudes of some in East Asia, which led to sluggish market opening, persistent nontariff barriers, and complaints that American demands (that East Asia engage in free and fair trade) are unfair. Economic frictions have aroused considerable animosity on both sides of the Pacific and have caused upsurges of anti-Americanism and nationalism in East Asia. In the United States, protectionism has raised its head again. Although markedly toned down from earlier and harsher versions, the 1988 trade law is commonly perceived as another step toward protectionism. It is important to recognize that economic frictions have enormous political consequences that assume a life of their own and that strongly influence economic choices.

Contagious Frictions

Concurrent with this sort of questioning of the wisdom of past and present U.S. economic policy toward East Asia, which has produced serious concerns about East Asia's ability to challenge the United States, a minority of Americans are asking equally serious questions about the security portion of the original U.S. objectives. The United States' goal was to provide breathing space so friends and allies could regain their equilibrium sufficiently to fend for their own security. Implicit in those arrangements was a sunset clause in which the United States was supposed to disengage as our allies regained their prosperity. The latter has happened, but not the former and some Americans are asking, "Why not?"[3] This question focuses most sharply on U.S.-Japan security relations, but it is also relevant to U.S.-South Korea relations.

In short, U.S. frustration in its major trade relationships with East Asia's capitalist states has spilled over into U.S. attitudes toward American ties with the others. This process of contamination or cross-fertilization arouses enormous resentment among the countries that receive the spillover. Collectively, this frustration has fostered a sense of negativism that does not auger well for the future of U.S. ties with its long-established East Asian trade partners. Although it is not as evident, American economic frustration is also spilling over into U.S. security ties with its East Asian capitalist allies. Because of a palpable sense of anxiety about the long-term wisdom of the United States—as a superpower with an economy that is becoming weaker relative to that of the countries it protects—persisting in a strategic role that may be outdated by changed economic circumstances, Americans across the political spectrum are questioning whether that role should be perpetuated.[4]

This is the fundamental context into which U.S.-PRC relations must be placed. All of the problems extant in U.S. relations with

---

[3]In addition to congressional reports over the years (see, for example, the U.S. House of Representatives, Armed Services Committee, August 1988, "Report on Burden Sharing"), the studies by Bandow (1987) and Krauss (1986) illustrate these concerns.

[4]Two excellent examples are conservative economist Melvyn Krauss' *How NATO Weakens the West* (1986) and liberal historian Paul Kennedy's *The Rise and Fall of the Great Powers* (1987).

Japan, South Korea, and Taiwan loom on the horizon of U.S.-PRC ties. The various American criticisms of these trade partners can be easily transferable to China, which is a low-wage competitor, is politically authoritarian, and seeks free access to Western markets while restricting foreign access to its market. China already experiences some of this spillover and must anticipate more in the future.

Even if China had been part of the original wave of East Asian economic "miracles," it is doubtful that the United States could have absorbed enough of its potential production to have done for it what it did for Japan, South Korea, and Taiwan. China's potential production levels are so large that it is difficult to conceive of the American economy being able to be the almost exclusive consumer of such products. While economic theory holds that the U.S. economy has a limitless ability to absorb whatever China (or any other external source) produces—so long as the quality and price are attractive—political reality does enforce constraints. The United States alone simply cannot do for China what it once did for its much smaller neighbors, and in an age when foreign economic competition was not a serious challenge to U.S. power. Even though China has belatedly jumped on board the East Asian development train, it cannot expect to traverse the same terrain as its predecessors.

Chinese Development in a New Context

If China is to develop economically in ways that are proportional to its more successful neighbors, it must do so in an atmosphere radically different from that experienced by those neighbors. The United States is unlikely to play the sustaining roles that it did for those neighbors, although it almost certainly will play a supportive role. Instead, the United States will be joined by Japan, the "new Japans," Western Europe, and possibly the Soviet Union, which collectively might be able to absorb enough of China's exports to sustain export-led development. That approach, plus a greater emphasis on development based on domestic sectors of the economy than was true of its prosperous neighbors, seems likely to be the ingredient of China's prospective economic success.

This scenario raises some troubling questions. How might the United States and China react to the reality of Japan actually becoming "Number One"? That adjustment, if it becomes necessary, is unlikely to be easy for either country. It will also not be easy for the Soviet Union, which now finds itself falling further behind the Euro-American "West" and the East Asian "West." Will Moscow be capable of dealing competently with either? Will the USSR be able to help China, even if Moscow wants to? Conversely, what might Moscow need from either "West"? In short, the Soviet Union's prospective economic, political, and military roles in the Far East are in flux, and it is difficult to be confident about the impact of that process on China's developmental aspirations or on U.S.-Chinese relations. The Soviet Union could prove helpful for China, but there is little reason to be sanguine about that possibility. Finally, the prospects for China as a truly massive power cannot be considered bright. Its large population, poverty, and ideological ambiguity are more likely to be hindrances than assets.

As the United States and China contemplate the prospects for China's broader participation in a Western-oriented international trading system, Washington and Beijing should be realistic. Despite many factors that should have dissuaded them, some Americans remain enraptured by the "Great China Market." Accordingly, there are popular fantasies about a billion-plus consumers, each buying one U.S.-made widget, thereby enriching American widget-producers. Other countries also share that vision, notably neighboring South Korea. China is also envisioned by some Americans as an alternative to Japan and the "New Japans." Some of these prospects no doubt will be realized because the Chinese market certainly is "great" and it can supply some products more cheaply than its neighbors can, but it is unrealistic to carry such thoughts too far.

For better or worse, the United States is now economically wedded to Japan in ways that would make a divorce very messy and traumatic. The two countries are incredibly interdependent industrially, financially, and as consumer markets. Americans now require Japanese funding, investment, technology, and markets. It is true that the United States could more easily survive the disruption of those ties than Japan could, but their severance would unquestionably be traumatic for the United States. American national interests would also be severely damaged if Japan's capabilities and financial resources were to be realigned with an adversary of the United States.

Therefore, the United States must view its broader Asian relationships, including those with China, in terms that are predicated on the U.S.-Japan cornerstone. Americans may not prefer this approach, and the Chinese almost certainly do not favor it. Nonetheless, it remains a reality of late 20th-century life and is sure to shape the next century. The United States cannot, and should not, want to choose between Japan and China. Both are important, but Japan has become an integral element in global economic decisionmaking that makes it necessary for Washington to mesh its views with Tokyo's as it contemplates what is proper policy. Japan has enormous clout, and its voice will be expressed in areas that affect its interests. There is no doubt that Washington will listen to Japan's views on Asian trade, investment, finance, banking, and a diverse range of political and strategic issues.

It is becoming increasingly difficult to separate the corporate interests of U.S. and Japanese firms that act as supranational forms of multinational firms. Further, their interests influence the views of each nation. Consequently, U.S. policy toward Asia is necessarily filtered through its connection to Japan. In this context, the United States cannot prudently consider China as an alternative to Japan. There is a danger implicit in such thinking, namely, that the United States will opt to put itself in Japan's "camp" at China's expense. It would be too easy for the United States and Japan to cluster together hegemonically as prosperous nations in order to fend off those nations that are still seeking to improve their economic positions. That choice would be disastrous for all three countries. The point is not that the United States would be "pro-Japanese" but that it should work with Japan in ways that will enable the combined efforts of the West to shore up China's self-help efforts as the best way to ensure peace, prosperity, and stability in Asia.

Future U.S.-China Relations

The United States cannot do for China what it once did for some of China's neighbors. There is too much strategic and political ambiguity by both the United States and China for earlier circumstances elsewhere in Asia to be replicated. Perhaps most important, the world has changed far too much for the United States to respond in the same ways it did in the 1950s and 1960s. In addition, the American people are unlikely to sanction such an effort; they are more interested in their leaders making the United States more competitive than in fostering more competition, particularly in Asia.

While this cannot be good news for China, it is not necessarily bad news either. The United States still seeks peace and stability in international affairs. Once it could take the lead unilaterally in the pursuit of peace and stability, but now it requires the assistance of increasingly prosperous allies and trade partners. This is where China stands to benefit. Most of the United States' capitalist trade partners in Asia have the wherewithal to join with the United States as it encourages China's participation in the Western economic system. Most already do this for commercial reasons. As motivation that approach is ample, but it would be preferable if the United States in cooperation with Japan fostered a different perspective on these economic activities. They should be viewed as the contemporary equivalents of the geopolitically oriented approach the United States followed in the 1950s. What is needed is a post–Cold War developmental surrogate for the anti-communist objectives of the past. The United States and the PRC may agree to disagree about the goals of communism, but there can be a meeting of minds about the means each state uses to pursue prosperity.

If the West and Japan can be confident that China's path to communism will lead it through peaceful development, then the developmental surrogate will be self-evident. That should be the overriding goal for U.S. foreign policy as it deals with an economically emergent China. With that perspective preeminent, the United States should be able to cope successfully with pressures to deal with China in the same ways that it does with other East Asian trade challengers. Some general treatment seems inevitable, but the significantly different independent strategic role China plays in a much earlier phase of its modernization experience should make it eligible for special handling. In other words, because China is a great military power and plays an independent geopolitical role, it cannot be treated like the United States treated its smaller neighbors when they were economically weaker.

China must be rendered a status that fits its unusual combination of strengths and weaknesses. So, even as the United States pressures China (and Japan, Taiwan, South Korea, and the ASEAN states) for enhanced market opening, Washington must bear in mind the unique strategic role China plays and modify its trade pressures accordingly. Reconciling these issues will not be easy, especially in light of the United States' need to coordinate its policy with Japan's. Nevertheless, both Washington and Tokyo seem to share a security interest in seeing China make headway against longstanding obstacles to its prosperity and progress, which should reduce its incentives to pursue any policies that might jeopardize peace and stability in the region.

The United States should also be realistic in another vein. American culture tends toward optimism, and Americans tend to discount the cautionary advice from the Japanese, who suggest that China may never overcome its problems sufficiently to catch up with its neighbors. While not falling victim to negative-minded self-fulfilling prophesies, the United States should also prepare itself for the possibility that China will not succeed and for what that could mean for Asia, the Soviet Union, and U.S. policy. Similarly, American impatience should not lead the United States to prematurely judge the rate of Chinese economic success. Slow success or temporary setbacks should not be equated with failure. What the United States and other concerned parties can do is to provide ample incentive for China to do what is necessary to prevent that failure.

References

Bandow, Doug. "Korea: The Case for Disengagement." Cato Institute *Policy Analysis* no. 96 (8 December 1987).

Johnson, Paul. *Modern Times.* New York: Harper and Row, 1983.

Kennedy, Paul. *The Rise and Fall of the Great Powers.* New York: Random House, 1987.

Krauss, Melvyn. *How NATO Weakens the West.* New York: Simon and Schuster, 1986.

Lardy, Nicholas R. *China's Entry into the World Economy.* Lanham, Md.: The Asia Society and University Press of America, 1987.

Olsen, Edward A. *U.S. Policy and the Two Koreas.* San Francisco and Boulder: The World Affairs Council of Northern California and Westview Press, 1988.

Prestowitz, Clyde V., Jr. *Trading Places: How We Allowed Japan to Take the Lead.* New York: Basic Books, 1988.

COMMENT

CHINA'S MARKET, U.S. COMPETITIVENESS, AND SOCIALISM
Chen Qida

In reading Edward Olsen's paper, I discovered a great deal of common ground between us. His views on the following points are basically in agreement with mine: the American strategic motive in East Asia, the Sino-U.S. common interest in China's prosperity and stability, the cross-emulation between East Asian economies, the economic contributions East Asia makes to the well-being of other parts of the world (especially the United States), the re-emergence of protectionism in the United States, the supporting role (as distinguished from a sustaining role) that the United States is to play in China, the possible disastrous consequences if the United States and Japan were to join hegemonically at China's expense, and the need for a developmental surrogate for the anticommunist objectives in the West's economic relations with China.

However, there are also several points on which I disagree. Many of these points are not necessarily Olsen's; rather, they are reflections of a section of the American public. On such occasions, what people usually do is to agree to disagree. But I think perhaps it would be better if we can finally agree to agree after clearing up some misunderstandings or non-understandings through fruitful exchange of ideas. Here I would like to put forward three questions for discussion: (1) How is one to estimate the capacity of the Chinese market? (2) How is one to view the competition the United States now faces in East Asia? (3) How is one to look upon the relation between Marxism and economic success?

Estimating the Capacity of the Chinese Market

Olsen advises both Washington and Beijing to be "realistic" in estimating the capacity of the Chinese market. According to him, the

The author is Senior Fellow and Director of the Third World Studies Program at the China Institute of Contemporary International Relations in Beijing.

"Great China Market" and the talk of "a billion-plus consumers" are only "fantasies." I agree that we should be realistic, for over-optimism often leads to pessimism when things fall short of expectations. In view of the present low level of the purchasing power of the Chinese people, the "Great China Market" is really not so great, and the "billion-plus consumers" are not big consumers. Still, the Chinese market and a billion-plus consumer are not mere fantasies.

Although the Chinese market is not so great at present, it is not small, either. This is a point that Olsen himself admits. According to the statistics of the World Bank, China's imports amounted to $43.17 billion in 1986, ranking first in the Third World and tenth in the whole world. And what is more, the Chinese market experienced rapid growth during the last decade as China's economy grew. Leaving aside the probably too optimistic forecast of the recently published report of the American Commission on Integrated Long-term Strategy, which rates China's GNP as second in the world by the year 2010, Olsen acknowledges that "there is a reasonable chance that over time the People's Republic of China will become one of East Asia's economic success stories." If that is so, there is little doubt that China's plan to re-double its foreign trade to the tune of $160 billion a year by 2000 will be fulfilled or even over-fulfilled. And if we take a long-term view, the prospect would be still brighter. When China attains her goal of becoming a medium-level developed country by the mid-2000s, with per capita GNP of over $4,000 a year, the size of her population will become a very important factor. At that time, the one billion-plus consumers, or even one billion and a half consumers, will become something really fantastic.

In assessing the Chinese market, we should also take into consideration the structure of its imports. An examination of China's merchandise imports, for example, shows that in 1986, according to the statistics of the World Bank, machinery and transport equipment accounted for 31 percent of the total, other manufactures for 56 percent, and all other items (food, fuels, and other primary commodities) for only 13 percent. This clearly shows that there is ample room for complementarity between China and the Western-developed countries in merchandise trade. Looking to the future, China's demand for capital and intermediate goods will continue to rise along with the progress of the "four modernizations."

China's capacity for foreign investment is also of interest in assessing the scope of China's market. It should be noted that China's open-door policy has placed more emphasis on foreign investment than on foreign credit. The coastal development strategy, for instance, opened China's door not only to foreign traders but also to foreign investors. In order to attract foreign investment, China took a number of steps over the 1978–88 reform period—chief among these was a commitment to increase the role of the market. Compared with other East Asian countries or areas, China's investment conditions were rated among the best. For one thing, labor costs in China are only one third of those in South Korea or Taiwan, and only one-tenth of those in Japan. With China's enormous manpower reserve, labor costs will be comparatively low for a long time to come.

The policy reversal that began in late 1988 and the events of May-June 1989, however, have led to a shrinkage of foreign investment in China. Yet, it can be conjectured that with the further development of China's market mechanism and the further improvement of its infrastructure, China may well become one of the most attractive markets for foreign investment.

It should be recognized, of course, that the creation of a "Great China Market" requires international cooperation. The more other countries, especially the Western developed countries, import from China, invest in China, and transfer technology to China, the greater the Chinese market will become. Of course, even if foreign investors take an attitude of "wait and see," the Chinese market will grow all the same, only at a slower pace. So, if our American friends really want to have a "Great China Market," and to have it sooner, there is much they can do to help to bring it about. What is urgently needed is for them to take concrete actions, and the sooner the better.

U.S. Competition in East Asia

According to Olsen, Americans are now "more interested in their leaders making the United States more competitive than in fostering more competition, particularly in Asia." American assistance to Asia and Europe in the post–World War II years is regarded as having fostered competition against the United States. Not only that, Olsen notes that the resultant "U.S. frustration in its major trade relationships with East Asia's capitalist states has spilled over into U.S. attitudes toward American ties with the others," including China.

I don't think this is Olsen's own thinking, for he writes: "The view that prosperity is a zero-sum game went out with mercantilist economics. There can be many winners in international economic relations." But since it is referred to as "American people's" thinking, I want to say a few words about it.

First, what is the real cause of the decline in U.S. competitiveness? According to Olsen, the American perception is that in East Asia "the search for prosperity is a game that East Asians have been playing on a field that is not level and that favors them and their quasi-mercantilist forms of economic nationalism at the expense of the United States." I grant that "Japan, South Korea, and Taiwan . . . do not allow Americans the sort of access to their markets that they enjoy in the United States," but I think this is only one side of the story; these are only the external factors. What is more important are the internal factors, which can be found only in the United States itself.

According to a report of *The Straits Times* (23 April 1988), during a hearing held by a subcommittee of the U.S. House of Representatives on April 21, 1988, a former State Department official, Robert Hormats, said in his testimony that America's ability to meet competitive challenges from the Newly Industrializing Economies (NIEs) would depend heavily on the quality of U.S. domestic policies to promote investment, research, and education. "Unless the United States moves soon to strengthen its performances in all three [areas], our competitive position will inevitably slip," he said. Here Mr. Hormats tried to find out the internal causes of America's declining competitiveness instead of attributing its troubles to other countries. I think this is a practical and realistic attitude. Or let us go a step further. Competition is a good tradition of the American people. American civilization itself is a product of competition. There is utterly no need for the United States to be afraid of competition. On the contrary, only through competition can America restore her leading competitive position.

Second, as was acknowledged by such influential U.S. publications as *Newsweek* and the *Asian Wall Street Journal*, the trade imbalance between the United States and its East Asian trading partners is greatly exaggerated.[1] It is simply incorrect to regard, as is now done in official statistical reporting, all goods exported to the United States from East Asia—including those produced by U.S. multi-nationals based in East Asian countries—as these countries' exports to the United States. As Olsen himself admits, "It is becoming increasingly difficult to separate the corporate interests of U.S. and Japanese firms that act as supernational forms of multinational firms." So we can safely say that at least a considerable part of the U.S. deficits in her trade with these countries are not deficits in the true sense of the word. Moreover, as Olsen rightly points out, "most Americans appreciate the economic contributions East Asia makes to the well-being of other nations of the world and, most pointedly, to the United States." So, I really cannot see ample reason for the United States to begrudge its trading partners in Asia so much.

[1]See, for example, Meyer, Powell, et al. (1987).

Third, granting that America is now facing strong competition in East Asia, what is the best way to handle it? All indications show that there is a strong tendency in the United States to resort to protectionism. Even President Reagan, who had time and again pledged to free trade, signed the mammoth U.S. trade bill. I do not think such protectionist legislation is good for the long-run health of the U.S. economy. Protectionism can protect only stagnant productivity and is bound to lead to retaliation, and then to a new round of trade wars, in which there will be no winner.

As to the so-called spillover effect, I have to say that it would be harmful not only to China but to the United States. I appreciate Olsen's statement that "both China and the United States had an interest in seeing China become more prosperous, stable, and free of debilitating dependencies." In view of this, I believe it is the wish of both China and the United States that we work to strengthen our trade and cultural relations.

The Relation between Marxism and Economic Success

Talking about the "superiority of the non-Marxist approach," Olsen writes that there are "many skeptics in the capitalist world" who doubt whether China is able to "add its name to the list of success stories in the [East Asian] region—without foregoing its claims to being a 'socialist' state that aspires to communism." According to Olsen, these skeptics "think China will either fail because it will be unable to overcome the obstacles imposed by ideology or it will succeed by following a form of Confucian command capitalism . . . that cloaks itself in Marxist garments." In other words, they think that Marxism and economic success are incompatible, and that China must make a choice between the two.

I do not think skeptics' doubts are entirely baseless, because most countries claiming to be socialist have not done well with their economic development, nor had China until she made the historic policy decision in 1978 to restructure her economy and to open up to the outside world. But generally speaking, people who entertain such doubts have two misunderstandings about Marxism. The first is that they mistake the Soviet model, or the Stalinist model, for the sole and orthodox model of socialism. To be sure, the Soviet model was regarded as such a model once, but not now, still less in the future. Socialism is bound to have various models in the course of its development in different countries with different historical, economical, political, and cultural backgrounds. The Soviet model has already proved unsuccessful. That is the very reason why President Gorbachev initiated "perestroika" and why China decided to embark on economic reform and to build "socialism with Chinese character-istics," which allows play for market forces but retains predominantly social ownership.

The second misunderstanding of the "skeptics in the capitalist world" is that they mistake Marxism for some fixed dogmas. But just the opposite is the case. Marxism demands itself always to develop with the times, that is, with the new development of the objective world as well as with the new experiences of man's practices. In the final analysis, the only criterion of true Marxism is whether it can liberate productive forces from under the yoke of the out-of-date old production relations and, thus, promote the development of produc-tive forces. If it cannot, it cannot be called true Marxism, but only pseudo-Marxism. Of course, China as a socialist state will adhere to the ultimate goal and fundamental principles of Marxism, but that in no way means that China must also adhere to everything Marx wrote more than a century ago, or that China cannot draw on the good experiences of capitalist countries.

I think this is the correct understanding of Marxism, and this is also exactly what China is doing, or is trying to do. Just as the Chinese have to make a new assessment of capitalism, the Westerners also have to make a new assessment of socialism. Capitalism today is not the same as it was during the days of Marx, Engels, or even Lenin. Nor is socialism today the same as it was during the days of Stalin, or even Mao Zedong. Such being the case, I am confident that Marx-ism and economic success will "live together" in China. And so will the socialist and capitalist systems in the world, which will co-exist and develop together for a long, long time to come. During the process, there will be cooperation as well as competition between them.

References

Meyer, Michael; Powell, Bill; et al. "The Phony War: Six Trade Myths—Half-Truths Cloud the U.S.-Japan Relationship." *Newsweek*, 13 April 1987.
"U.S. Firms 'Must Do More to Cut Deficit.'" *The Straits Times*, 23 April 1988. The World Bank. *World Development Report 1988*. New York: Oxford University Press for the World Bank, 1988.

14

THE UNITED STATES, CHINA, AND THE SOVIET UNION: MANAGING A COMPLEX TRIANGULAR RELATIONSHIP

David M. Lampton

Introduction

To speak of "managing" the evolving relationships among the United States, China, and the Soviet Union implies a degree of control by and cooperation among those countries that is unrealistic to presuppose, and I do not. Domestic political and social events in each country frequently (and perhaps usually) will produce foreign policies that only minimally take into account the needs or desires of the other two countries. As well, the vagaries of the international economy will be a perpetual wild card, as will be the actions of other countries such as Japan, the Koreas, and the states in the Persian Gulf. Moreover, many would say that we should conceive of international relations less as "management" and more as governments restraining their own actions in order to allow economic logic to bring order to the international system.

If the use of the word "management" is so simplistic, why have I employed it here? "Management" is one useful way of thinking about the possibility of a new era in relations among these three countries, because a good manager takes into account a number of factors in trying to produce the most favorable outcomes at the least resource cost. A good manager defines the *context* in which he is operating, the *objectives* that he has (or the problems to be overcome), and the *policy alternatives* available to achieve those ends.

Although neither the United States, China, the Soviet Union, nor any other state makes policy in this clinical and cerebral way, it is an essential exercise for leaders to think in these terms at some point in the foreign-policy process. This paper seeks to identify the new and continually evolving context in which the three nations are operating,

The author is President of the National Committee on U.S.-China Relations, Inc. The views expressed in this article should not be construed as representing those of the National Committee, its members, or sponsors.

the primary challenges facing our leaders in this new era, and some policy alternatives that must be considered as the future becomes the present.

The Context for Sino-American-Soviet Relations

There are many important dimensions of change in the international setting for relations among the United States, China, and the Soviet Union. First, the currently prevailing leadership group in Moscow seems to be embarked on an effort to fundamentally change internal political and economic systems and incentives in the Soviet Union. However, the Soviet Union has provided few immediate economic benefits of reform to its people, and the reform process must overcome deeply rooted Stalinist institutional forms. The Soviets, unlike the Chinese, have tackled the more sensitive area of political reform first; but while Gorbachev has made progress in consolidating his position, his political longevity is by no means assured. In short, the prospects for reform in the Soviet Union must be assumed to be uncertain.

Moreover, debates continue in Moscow over whether or not "class struggle" should remain central to the formulation of Soviet foreign policy. In mid-1988, Foreign Minister Shevardnadze concluded that, "the struggle between two opposing systems is no longer a determining tendency of the present era." This view has not been accepted by Yegor Ligachev, a ranking Kremlin leader who continues to argue for international class struggle.

Political systems, however, are not only institutions with lives of their own; they are also held together by sets of ideas that both legitimate the institutions and are legitimated by them. Neither institutions nor ideas die easily.

Second, the post–World War II era is over. Most fundamentally, the economic preeminence on which American influence and military might rested has diminished in comparative terms. This is most starkly seen in an examination of foreign-owned assets in the United States, which now exceed the total value of American-owned assets abroad (*New York Times* 28 August 1988, p. E5). The Bush administration will have as its primary tasks the initiation of policies that will bring government spending into closer alignment with revenues, the reduction of America's global trading imbalances, and the stimulation of added productive domestic savings and investment.

There are several ways in which these tasks might be accomplished, but China, the Soviet Union, and other countries will probably face an America trying to slow imports, seeking to accelerate exports, pushing vigorously for access to markets (including those in China and the Soviet Union), and protecting its technological edge.

In the military domain, the perception in many quarters of a declining Soviet threat, combined with the new affluence of past beneficiaries of the American military "umbrella," will create increasingly strong pressures for encouraging friends in Asia (Japan and South Korea) and Western Europe to assume a greater share of military expenditures. The House of Representatives' Burden Sharing Panel is simply one manifestation of this trend. Concisely, burden sharing, market access, and protecting technological competitive advantage will become increasingly potent concepts in the American foreign policy debate.

Third, the prospects for reform in China and, therefore, continued economic growth and involvement in the world trading system, although seriously set back by the tragic events of May-June 1989, appear promising—provided there is a return to openness and bold economic thinking. Nonetheless, under any set of leadership or policies, considerable uncertainties exist—uncertainties that derive from inflationary pressures, price distortions and corruption, rapidly rising expectations, population growth, inequalities, popular demands for security amid change, and so forth.

Therefore, over the next decade we can expect to see a China that is vigorously promoting its economic interests abroad and pushing for the most favorable technological and financial treatment from the international system. We can also expect a China that will eschew allowing military and security entanglements to further complicate its development tasks. China's "independent foreign policy," Beijing's avoidance of any hint of "alliance" with the United States after 1982, and China's recent assertions that its improved relations with the Soviet Union will never assume the character of an alliance are manifestations of the desire to ensure that international conflict does not get in the way of development.

Further, as China's economic growth and global involvement increases, China's actions at greater distances from its shores will concern other states, particularly the United States and the Soviet Union. With China's growing global power and influence will come increasing demands from others that this power be used in noninjurious ways, whether it be nuclear or missile technology transfers or weapons sales.

Fourth, the startling economic success of many areas in Asia has been accompanied by demands for changes in the political system, for altered budgetary priorities, and, in some cases, for increased nationalism. The demands for internal political changes and a more

301

nationalistic posture in dealing with other countries create some domestic instabilities and more assertive stances in foreign policy.

Taiwan, with about US $75 billion in hard currency reserves, is a major international economic force. In Taipei, we see demands for political liberalization and more self-confidence in dealing with others, whether the People's Republic of China or the United States. With Japan's increased economic power, we see a willingness to consider a gradual expansion of its defense spending and military capabilities, debates over the appropriate levels for consumption versus saving, and more involvement abroad in both the economic and security realms.

Fifth, both China and the United States are improving relations with the Soviet Union in the areas of trade, cultural exchange, and reduction of tensions.[1] As both China and the United States are improving relations with the Soviet Union, there is a need to reconceptualize the rationale for Sino-American relations. Both countries must also be careful to ensure that improved ties to Moscow do not inadvertently weaken support for Sino-American relations. With the strategic rationale being somewhat less important, the economic and cultural dimensions become more central to stable and mutually beneficial Sino-American ties. Because economic and cultural relations tend to be more politically laden in both countries' domestic politics, the task of managing Sino-American ties is becoming increasingly complex.

In a nutshell, the *context* in which the "management" of Sino-Soviet-American relations will occur has the following features: uncertainty over whether fundamental changes in Soviet behavior will occur and whether or not domestic stability will be maintained; cautious optimism about the long-term direction and durability of reform in the People's Republic of China; an emphasis on economic issues in almost all countries in the Pacific Basin; much greater multipolarity in Asia; desires among the major powers to reduce military expenditures and entanglements while some of the newer players (particularly Japan and South Korea) will increase their military capabilities; increased nationalism; and greater domestic instabilities as some countries (including China) initiate reforms and others accommodate themselves to the rising demands of emergent middle classes. All of this will make the management of Sino-Soviet-American relations more complex.

---

[1]For a discussion of the improvement of Sino-Soviet relations, see Lampton (1986).

Challenges and Policy Implications

In this setting, five challenges present themselves to foreign policy leaders in the United States, China, and the Soviet Union. The way these are handled will have important policy implications.

The Challenge of Balance and Stability

A fundamental challenge facing China, the Soviet Union, and the United States in "managing" their relationship in Asia in the above context is: *How can China, the United States, and the Soviet Union maintain regional military stability and balance at potentially lower American force levels, with more independent (and stronger) actors, amid rising nationalism and increasingly vigorous economic competition?* Processes are under way in the Soviet Union, Japan, China, and South Korea that will produce increased military strength. At the same time, conflicts over offshore resources and territory persist and may become more intense. We must forthrightly ask: Do American forces play a stabilizing role? If so, at what strength and in what locations? If American forces are to be reduced, what corresponding reductions or adjustments are the Soviets prepared to make? What would (and should) be Japan's response in the new situation? To address these questions, there is a need for multilateral forums in which these issues can be candidly discussed.

Because the problem of balance and stability is becoming increasingly multilateral in character, the traditional desire of China, the United States, and the Soviet Union to address issues bilaterally will increasingly have to be supplemented by multilateral discussions.

The Challenge of Soviet Reforms

This brings us to a second challenge, principally to the United States and China as they think about trends and possibilities in the Soviet Union: *Is it in the interests of the United States and China, singly and together, for Gorbachev's efforts at reform to succeed?* What are the policy implications of the answers to this question? A cynic might say that a perpetually weak Soviet Union is the best we can hope for, tragic as that may be for the Russian people. One argument, for example, has it that a Soviet Union that perceives itself to be weak is a cautious Soviet Union. If that is true, it might be folly to help Moscow's leadership become more economically confident.

We can assert three things with near certainty as we think about this question. First, increased Soviet economic power will produce increased capabilities that could be used constructively or destructively. The road that the Soviet Union will travel depends on future leaders and domestic forces, which are unpredictable. Risk is inherent in this choice, and there are no guarantees. Second, neither China nor the United States will be the principal determinant of the choices that leaders in the Soviet Union might make; U.S. influence operates at the margins. Third, if the United States or China adopts a policy of not taking the Soviet attempts to change seriously or if we play obstructionist roles, we almost ensure the belligerence of future Soviet generations whether the reform efforts succeed or fail.

I believe that the prudent course lies in adopting a supportive stance toward Soviet efforts, continuing to demand real changes in Soviet foreign policy behavior and force posturing, and being exceedingly cautious with respect to infusions of high technology and large amounts of capital until there are some military changes. Until then, there is much room for cultural and educational exchange, increased trade, and small- and medium-scale joint venture undertakings. But it is premature to alter the balance of military forces in the region or to think about bold capital investment, joint-venture, or technology-transfer undertakings.

In the more distant future, if the Soviet Union changes its force postures, both China and the United States should be willing to become more involved in efforts to transform the Soviet economic system, hopeful that increasing economic welfare and social complexity in the Soviet Union will promote pluralism and political changes that will give less support to military adventures. In this environment, discussions about necessary American force levels in the region would probably make sense.

The Challenge of Developing U.S.-China Relations

A third challenge that China and the United States face in thinking about the Soviet Union is: *How do our changing relations with Moscow affect our bilateral relationship?* When the new relationship between the United States and China was crafted, strategic (meaning anti-Soviet) considerations were paramount in the minds of President Nixon and Chairman Mao. Today, the cultural and economic components of our relationship are comparatively more important. Whatever the advantages and disadvantages of having a strategic basis for our relationship may have been, it did provide a seemingly compelling rationale to ignore, or at least downplay, some of the irritants that characterize a relationship when economic, trade, and cultural/political issues rise in importance—issues such as human rights.

Although the strategic benefits that derive from our relationship remain very real, we are making the relationship inherently more vulnerable to the vagaries of domestic politics as we improve relations with Moscow and focus on economic, trade, and cultural issues. As a result, China policy will increasingly be influenced directly by Congress and the pulling and hauling of interest groups.

It is precisely because China policy has become connected to an inherently more political set of institutions and issues as the strategic rationale diminishes in the minds of many that it is important how and at what pace each country improves its relations with Moscow. If China were to suddenly improve relations with Moscow in the context of deteriorating Soviet-American relations, it would damage Sino-American ties. I presume that China would be worried by a similar dramatic improvement in Soviet-American relations in a setting of increased Sino-Soviet tension, or deteriorating U.S.-China ties. But, if both countries gradually move to improve ties with Moscow, fully mindful of the interests of the other, this should be manageable.

The Challenge of Consultation

As a nation's economic and technological level increases, so does its capacity to act in the world, to influence events at increasingly greater distances from its shores. Therefore, the challenge is: *How can we develop ongoing forums and methods of consultation that will minimize the instances where the exercise of power or influence by one party is inimical to the U.S.-China relationship?* Looking to the Sino-Soviet-U.S. relationship, such consultative mechanisms need to be developed as well.

For instance, many Americans have not fully appreciated the technological capabilities of the People's Republic of China. As a result, it was with considerable surprise that Americans suddenly realized that their forces in the Persian Gulf were threatened by Chinese-made weapons. Chinese ballistic missile sales to Saudi Arabia were of even deeper concern because of the risks of introducing long-range weapons into a region where hostile states share borders. Similarly, American actions have held important consequences for China. The same kinds of ties and interactions also bind both countries to the Soviet Union.

More broadly, the world must come to terms with what a strong and modern China and Soviet Union mean for all of us. Further complicating the management task, countries in the Pacific Basin will have a greater impact on the environment as they modernize. Therefore, as modernization occurs in China and other countries, we can expect to see increased concerns in the United States and Japan about carbon dioxide and chemical discharge rates. Mechanisms must be developed to discuss these issues and reduce conflict.

The Challenge of Timing

A final challenge in managing the Sino-Soviet-American relationship is: *When in the process of the hoped-for reduction in strategic weapons in the Soviet and American arsenals, does China need to enter the negotiating process?* China's strategic and regional nuclear capabilities are growing and are becoming increasingly diversified and sophisticated (see, for example, Tow 1988).

Given the geographic position of the Soviet Union and the natural "worst-case analysis" logic of planners in both the Kremlin and Washington, as the United States and the Soviet Union move toward fewer nuclear warheads and delivery systems, it will be increasingly difficult for each side to agree to further reductions without involving China in the negotiating process.

Both the Soviet Union and the United States need to have a clearer sense of China's goals in building a nuclear force. More precisely, will China be willing to enter talks on strategic force reduction without commitment by the superpowers to the goal of eventual and total disarmament?

Conclusion

Where do we go from here? First, both China and the United States are set on a course of seeking improved relations with the Soviet Union. This search need not damage ties between Beijing and Washington, as long as relations among all three powers are improving and improving at about the same rate. Second, both China and the United States should not assume that Gorbachev will succeed in his efforts either to hold power or to durably change Soviet internal and external policy, though the likelihood of a total policy reversal in Moscow is remote, whether Gorbachev remains in power or not. Nonetheless, both countries have an interest in the success of his endeavor, and they should be prudently helpful, cooperating in small ventures at first and becoming more involved as they gain confidence.

With respect to Sino-American ties, as the strategic (anti-Soviet) rationale for that relationship recedes, both countries need to reconceptualize the basis for their relationship. Although there are still important strategic benefits to strong U.S.-China relations, economic and cultural links will become increasingly important. As this occurs, we can expect the number of abrasions that naturally accompany expanded economic and cultural ties to increase. Our task is to develop a relationship in which these abrasions can be constructively addressed. The rise of American human rights concerns vis-à-vis China and the growing congressional anxiety over a trade deficit with China are two indicators of what lies ahead.

References

Lampton, David M. "China's Limited Accommodation with the U.S.S.R." *AEI Foreign Policy and Defense Review* 6, no. 3 (1986): 26–35.

Tow, William T. "China's Modernization and the Big Powers." In *China's Global Presence*, pp. 173–74. Edited by David M. Lampton and Catherine H. Keyser. Washington, D.C.: American Enterprise Institute, 1988.

COMMENT

CHALLENGES FACING SINO-AMERICAN-SOVIET RELATIONS
Lu Yimin

It is a pleasure for me to comment on David Lampton's interesting paper dealing with Sino-American-Soviet relations. Lampton offers insights into contemporary international relations by presenting the major challenges facing China, the United States, and the Soviet Union. The questions he poses are sensitive and the analyses he makes are enlightening. I would like to contribute to the discussion of his paper by giving a few personal remarks.

A New Orientation for Sino-American-Soviet Relations

A proper understanding of the "management" of Sino-American-Soviet relations requires an appreciation of the continually changing international situation. Lampton does a good job in singling out the key dimensions of the rapidly evolving context for the triangular relations. These dimensions cover a wide range of changes in current world affairs: perestroika in the Soviet Union, economic reform in China; decline of economic and military power in the United States; presence of the newly industrializing countries (NICs); and the emerging bilateral relations among China, the United States, and the Soviet Union in the areas of trade and cultural exchanges.

Even though problems prevail, there are encouraging signs for Sino-Soviet-American relations. Events such as the signing of the Intermediate-Range Nuclear Force (INF) Treaty, the establishment of formal ties between the European Economic Community (EEC) and the Council for Mutual Economic Assistance (CMEA), the Soviet decision to withdraw troops from Afghanistan, the newly found free-

The author is Director of International Exchange Programs and Associate Professor of Political Science at Fudan University.

doms in Eastern and Central Europe, and, most significantly, the end of the Cold War have set the basis for an improved triangular relationship.

The present world is a changed world, different from what it was 20 to 30 years ago. East-West confrontations are being replaced by dialogue; cold war is being replaced by detente; in North-South relations, closed-door policy and economic stagnation are being replaced by open-door policy and economic development. Within the Western countries, monopoly and plunder are being replaced by competition and cooperation. A unified world market has been created and cultural exchanges extended on a global scale. Although the threat of war is still looming, we have every reason to believe that "today the economic interdependence of the nations of the world and economic cooperation as well as competition among them are steadily increasing" (Li Peng, as premier of China's State Council, in *Beijing Review*, 25 April–1 May 1988), and that domestic reform and international detente among the superpowers have become the main trends of the global order.

What, then, is the implication of the current international situation for Sino-American-Soviet relations? In my opinion, although difficulties remain, the present situation offers a new setting as well as a new orientation for the Sino-American-Soviet triangular relationship. In other words, triangular relations should be oriented toward peace and development—the two fundamental issues on which the evolution and future of the overall world situation and international relations depend.

Principles for a Stable Triangular Relationship

Looking at present Sino-American-Soviet relations, we must acknowledge that they are complex, volatile, and sensitive. Every change from one side will affect the bilateral relations of the other two sides. As such, prudent management is required and certain principles should be set for the three countries to follow.

Three basic principles can be ennumerated. First, the management of the relations with one party should not be conducted at the sacrifice of relations with the other party; for example, China's or America's changing relations with Moscow should not be inimical to Sino-American bilateral relations. Second, the management of the relations should be conducive to economic development of other countries. We not only hope for a better economy for the United States but also support President Gorbachev's efforts at reform in the Soviet Union. Third, the management of the relations should create favorable conditions for maintaining regional and global stability. China, the United States, and the Soviet Union should not fall short of expectations cherished by peoples of the world.

New Challenges in a Changing World Order

The Information Revolution and the Growth of Multipolarism

The world has entered a revolutionary era. Rapid development of knowledge, high technology, and global communications has profoundly altered perceptions and behavior both within and among societies. These changes will create new challenges as well as greater opportunities for international cooperation and development. China has begun to transform its economic system since 1978, and the United States and the Soviet Union have begun to shift their efforts from military to economic and technological endeavors. All three countries desire a stable world environment with fewer confrontations and conflicts. Therefore, in the coming 10 to 20 years, economic and technological relations will be the dominant part of the triangular relationship. Bipolarism will be replaced by multipolarism as Japan, Western Europe, and various NICs make further economic progress. Of course, the management of the global balance by the United States and the Soviet Union will still be of crucial concern to all nations. But U.S.-Soviet influence will diminish as will the importance of the Sino-American-Soviet triangular relationship.

The Challenge of Nuclear Disarmament

The final challenge Lampton mentions is that concerned with nuclear disarmament. After many years of negotiations, the United States and the Soviet Union finally signed the INF Treaty for eliminating medium-and-short-range missiles. This treaty represents the first step toward reduction of nuclear weapons. It thus received great attention and warm welcome all over the world. Like many other countries, China has evaluated the treaty and hopes that it will be implemented in earnest.

At the same time, China realizes that the task of disarmament has a long way to go. According to statistics, there are still 50,000 nuclear warheads in the world, of which the United States has 26,000 and the Soviets 22,700. The two countries possess more than 97 percent of the world's total nuclear weaponry. Yet, the nuclear weapons covered by the INF Treaty constitute only a very small portion, merely 3–4 percent of the nuclear arsenals of the two countries. Even if they can reach agreement and reduce by half the number of strategic nuclear weapons, their nuclear arsenals will still account for approximately 90 percent of the world's total—enough to destroy the earth several times over.

It is hoped that improved Sino-American-Soviet relations will expedite arms control and disarmament. China would like to contribute to that goal and has always advocated comprehensive and thorough disarmament. China has never participated in the arms race; its avowed purpose in possessing a tiny number of nuclear weapons is self-defense. The Chinese government has repeatedly stated its clear-cut and firm position that at no time and under no circumstances would China be the first to use nuclear weapons.

As to the question of when China needs to enter the negotiating process of the hoped-for reduction in strategic weapons, this question reminds me of a well-known parable about a disarmament conference among animals. The animals, having decided to disarm, convene in order to discuss the matter. The eagle, looking at the bull, suggests that all horns be cut off. The bull, looking at the tiger, says that all claws should be clipped. The tiger, looking at the elephant, is of the opinion that tusks should be either pulled out or shortened. The elephant, looking at the eagle, thinks that all wings should be clipped. Then the bear, glancing around at all his brethren, says in tones of sweet reason: "Why all these halfway measures? Let us abolish everything—everything but my fraternal and all-embracing hug."

The implication of this parable is self-evident. China opposes those disarmament negotiations that degenerate into an arms race; China supports all genuine efforts for nuclear disarmament. China unequivocally and consistently holds that the ultimate goal of nuclear disarmament should be the complete prohibition and thorough destruction of all nuclear weapons. The United States and the Soviet Union, as superpowers, bear a special responsibility. They should take the lead in putting an end to the testing, manufacturing, and deploying of all types of nuclear weapons. Only after this is done will the necessary conditions be created for the convention of a broadly represented international conference on nuclear disarmament with the participation of all the nuclear powers. By then, China will no doubt take an active part in that process and make its due contributions.

15

CHINA AND AMERICA IN A CHANGING WORLD ORDER

Ted Galen Carpenter

One of the most difficult challenges facing U.S. and Chinese officials in the coming decade is to ensure that their countries maintain a cordial, productive relationship amidst the multifaceted political and economic changes taking place in the Pacific Basin and throughout the world. This will not prove to be an easy task for either government. At the same time, there are no intractable quarrels or prospects for a collision of vital interests between the two nations that might pose a lethal threat to the current relationship. Even the strains that have occurred following the Beijing government's suppression of the pro-democracy movement, although serious, should not necessarily cause permanent damage to Sino-American ties. That episode, however, underscores the need for mature statesmanship to contain and resolve various contentious issues that may develop in U.S.-China relations as we approach the 21st century.

Of the various changes in the regional and global geopolitical context, three are especially important: the foreign policy implications of the reforms now taking place in the Soviet Union; the decline of U.S. military and economic dominance in the world; and the rise of significant regional powers, especially in Europe and the Pacific Rim. All of these changes must be taken into account by foreign policy officials in China and the United States.

Implications of Soviet Reforms

On balance, it is probably in the interests of both China and the United States that Mikhail Gorbachev be successful in his campaigns for perestroika and glasnost, because a less-aggressive and expansionist country is likely to emerge from the process. Nevertheless, Beijing and Washington should realize that successful reforms will also produce a more capable competitor for political and economic

The author is Director of Foreign Policy Studies at the Cato Institute.

influence in the Pacific Basin and elsewhere, and that outcome could significantly complicate the foreign policy agendas of both governments.

Indeed, we are already witnessing the effects of a far more sophisticated Soviet foreign policy. Gorbachev's dramatic address at the United Nations in December 1988, highlighted by his promise to make unilateral reductions in the size of the Soviet armed forces, was a striking example—foreshadowing his acceptance of the political revolutions that swept Eastern Europe. His speech at Vladivostok in July 1986 advocating closer economic ties with Pacific nations was an even earlier indication that Moscow had made a significant shift in its foreign policy priorities. The new Soviet strategy placed less emphasis on helping to install and maintain compliant Leninist clients, concentrating instead on improving ties with a variety of noncommunist regimes (Carpenter 1987).

There were ample reasons for such a change. Superficially, it appeared that the Soviet Union had scored significant geopolitical gains during the 1960s and 1970s, with the establishment of clients in Cuba, Vietnam, Angola, Ethiopia, and other nations. But Moscow discovered that such "victories" entail enormous and seemingly endless financial drains. Fidel Castro's Cuba consumes an annual Soviet subsidy approaching $5 billion, while Angola and Vietnam absorb more than $1 billion each. An even worse situation developed in Afghanistan where the USSR foolishly committed its own military forces in an effort to stave off the collapse of a pro-Soviet regime.

The realization has apparently dawned on Soviet leaders that Moscow's network of Third World Leninist clients constituted a liability rather than an asset. Moscow's tendency to employ clumsy subversion techniques to install such clients also served to alienate other nations, arousing suspicion of Soviet intentions and serving to isolate the USSR from the rest of the global community. It was this realization that led one Soviet commentator to assert that "clear-cut notions about the Soviet Union's true national-state interests were lacking" throughout the Brezhnev era. Those interests were not served by "the pursuit of essentially petty, pro forma gains connected with top-level coups in certain developing countries. Our true interest was in ensuring a favorable international atmosphere for profound transformations in the Soviet Union's economy and in its social and political system" (Dashichev 1988, pp. 4–5).

In the past several years, evidence of the new Soviet strategy has become pervasive. The decision to withdraw from Afghanistan was a clear indication of the Kremlin's desire to distance itself from dependent regimes that lack viability. Moscow's barely concealed

pressure on pro-Soviet governments in Angola and Vietnam to negotiate an end to conflicts in their respective regions are other examples
of a desire to stanch the financial hemorrhage caused by ill-advised
Third World commitments. The establishment of diplomatic relations and commercial agreements with Kiribati, Vanuatu, and other
Pacific island nations, the proposal for a mutual U.S.-Soviet with-
drawal from military installations in Vietnam and the Philippines,
and the concessions leading to the INF treaty are all manifestations of
the Soviet Union's concerted strategy to curry favor with nonsocialist
countries.

The most important development, however, was Moscow's aquies-
cence in the political and economic transformation of Eastern
Europe. That step effectively removed the West's principal griev-
ance against the Soviet Union, which had animated the Cold War for
more than four decades. By allowing its East European neighbors to
determine their own political and economic systems, Moscow has
evidently opted to join the broader global community rather than
attempting to continue dominating a limited sphere of influence.

In that context, it is also pertinent to note that while the USSR has
sought to ease the conflict with its longtime Cold War adversary,
even more attention has been paid to other major powers (Hough
1988). Indeed, Gorbachev's troop reduction gesture seemed to be
aimed primarily at reducing tensions in Europe and along the border
with China, since Soviet conventional forces scarcely menace the
United States. Moscow is also making a determined effort to improve
relations with South Korea and Japan. Soviet-South Korean relations
have become surprisingly cordial in recent years (Kim 1988). The
vast expansion of Soviet-ROK trade from virtually nothing a few years
ago to more than $600 million in 1989 (and more than $1 billion
anticipated in 1990) is one indication of that thaw. The historic sum-
mit meeting between Gorbachev and ROK President Roh Tae Woo
in June 1990 symbolized Moscow's determination to cultivate ties
with South Korea and to distance itself from its long-time ally, North
Korea.

Efforts to achieve a rapprochement with Japan have been somewhat more cautious, but that goal is undoubtedly on the Soviet
agenda. The Kremlin has even hinted that it might be willing to
return the Japanese "Northern Territories" seized after World War
II, a gesture that is in stark contrast to Moscow's long-standing refusal
even to discuss the issue. The territorial issue has been the principal
stumbling block to improved Soviet-Japanese relations throughout
the post-war era; a solution to that problem could lead to progress
in other areas, perhaps even a "marriage" of Japan's technological

315

capabilities with the vast natural resources of the USSR—an arrangement that would serve the economic interests of both countries (Kim 1986).

All of these initiatives seem motivated by a desire to divide the various members of a potential anti-Soviet coalition as well as project a more benign image of the USSR to the outside world. They may also reflect an attempt to ease global tensions to a degree that would permit the reduction of the bloated military sector that so burdens the Soviet economy (Corcoran 1990). Gorbachev's speech on January 6, 1989, announcing a 14 percent cut in the military budget to ease his government's fiscal woes certainly suggests that such concerns are a factor. But whatever Moscow's motives, Washington and Beijing must realize they are now confronting a more subtle, adept Soviet foreign policy, and that policies designed to counter the bullying tactics and the clumsy expansionist probes of Gorbachev's predecessors will no longer suffice.

A More Disengaged U.S. Foreign Policy

A second crucial change in the global geopolitical environment is the decline of U.S. military and economic preeminence. Historian Paul Kennedy has sparked a vigorous debate about the concept of "relative decline" and whether it applies to the United States. According to Kennedy, the United States faces the daunting challenge of all earlier great powers: "Whether in the military/strategical realm, it can preserve a reasonable balance between the nation's perceived defense requirements and the means it possesses to maintain those commitments; and whether as an intimately related point, it can preserve the technological and economic bases of its power from relative erosion in the face of ever-shifting patterns of global production." He is pessimistic, concluding that "the United States now runs the risk, so familiar to historians of the rise and fall of previous Great Powers, of what might be termed 'imperial overstretch': that is to say, decisionmakers in Washington must face the awkward and enduring fact that the sum total of the United States' global interests and obligations is nowadays far larger than the country's power to defend them all simultaneously" (Kennedy 1987, pp. 514–15).

Kennedy's opponents respond with two points. Some contend that the United States is not like earlier "amoral" great powers because it has solid moral and ideological foundations. Secretary of State George Shultz, for example, assailed "false prophets" of decline and asserted: "Great nations have suffered decline but they were imperial, or absolutist, or dominated by tradition-bound classes. Our nation is none of these" (Shultz 1989, p. 4) Others argue that the republic is actually ascending in power, not declining.

The first contention scarcely deserves attention, since moral virtue—or the lack of it—is only marginally relevant to objective indices of national power. America may indeed embody the important values of limited government and respect for individual rights, and in that sense it is certainly more admirable than most previous great powers. But if it pursues foolish external policies that exhaust its economic strength and create bitter internal political divisions, it will not avoid the consequences of such profligacy.

The second criticism must be taken more seriously. Critics of Kennedy's thesis note that GNP is now considerably higher in the United States than at the dawn of the Cold War and that U.S. military power is likewise greater (Luttwak 1987, Huntington 1988–89, Nye 1990). They are correct on both points, but the policy conclusion they draw from that observation—that the United States can continue to pursue a global interventionist strategy without undesirable domestic consequences—is dangerously erroneous.

Such advocates of a hyperactive foreign policy misconstrue the concept of relative decline; it is not that the United States has grown weaker in absolute terms, but that other nations have grown so much stronger—especially in the economic realm. At the end of World War II, the United States accounted for an astounding 50 percent of global GNP, and the figure was only modestly below that level in the early 1950s. Today, the figure is less than 25 percent and falling. That shift translates into a reduction of Washington's ability to dominate the world scene. Governments that once routinely deferred to U.S. policy preferences on a range of political, economic, and security issues, no longer do so. The process is most evident with America's NATO allies, who now frequently defy Washington on such matters as Middle East or Central America policy (Krauss 1986, Layne 1987), but Japan, South Korea, and other long-time U.S. allies in the Pacific Basin are demonstrating increasing independence as well.

The decline of U.S. preeminence is also creating irresistible domestic incentives to reduce the scope of America's global security commitments. In particular, the persistent federal budget deficit (still hovering around $150 billion per year) is causing thoughtful Americans of diverse political persuasions to question whether the United States can continue subsidizing the defense of wealthy allies, several of whom are now on a sounder fiscal footing than is the United States. Critics note that while the United States spends 6.1 percent of its GNP on the military, NATO's principal frontline state, West Germany, spends less than 3 percent, and America's most important security partner in the Pacific, Japan, barely 1 percent. Measured on a per capita basis, the disparity is equally apparent. The United States spends $1,190 each year on the military, West Germany $574, and Japan an anemic $236. (Department of Defense 1990, pp. A17, A40.)

The initial report of the burden-sharing panel of the U.S. House of Representatives reflects the growing sentiment for a curtailment of overseas military commitments, albeit in somewhat diluted form. Annoyance with U.S. allies permeates the document, and there is an implicit assumption that those nations are free riding on the U.S. security guarantee:

> The Panel believes that the current situation—high levels of U.S. defense spending and much lower levels of allied defense spending—is not fair to the U.S. Although the Panel predicts that the allies are likely to favor the retention of the status quo (since a high level of U.S. defense spending provides them with a no-cost insurance policy if our threat assessment turns out to be right and their assessment wrong), the Panel believes that the allies should not expect to "have it both ways" [U.S. Congress, House Committee on Armed Services 1988, p. 18].

But the embryonic reassessment of global security commitments now taking place in the United States is likely to go beyond limited burden-sharing considerations. Indeed, more far-reaching proposals for a significant devolution of U.S. defense responsibilities are already becoming respectable among foreign policy experts. Such proposals have surfaced with respect to NATO (Krauss 1986, Calleo 1987, Layne 1988, Steel 1990); South Korea (Goose 1989, Bandow 1989–90, Corbin 1990); and ANZUS (Bandow 1989). Increasing public and congressional resistance to the financial burdens entailed by the network of U.S. security commitments has already brought a halt to the massive military buildup of the Reagan years. And sentiment is building for significant troop reductions in Western Europe and East Asia.

The more conciliatory image now being projected by the Soviet Union will almost certainly provide impetus to that trend. It has been the perception of a Soviet expansionist threat and the need to neutralize it that have been the raison d'être for the presence of U.S. forces in allied countries on the perimeter of the USSR. The belief on the part of the American public that such a threat no longer exists will make it extraordinarily difficult for U.S. officials to justify the continuation of that troop presence.

A New Multipolar World

The third crucial change in the global political environment–a logical corollary of the second—is that the economic success of Japan, South Korea, and other Pacific Rim nations, as well as the countries of Western Europe, will eventually translate into more assertive foreign policies. The United States is already encountering that phenomenon in its relations with various allies. As noted above, it is most pronounced with regard to the European members of NATO, but it is also reflected in such events as New Zealand's decision to deny port access to U.S. warships with nuclear weapons (Carpenter 1986, McMillan 1987) and South Korea's recent efforts to achieve a limited rapprochement with North Korea. The highly nationalistic, often mercantilistic, economic policies being pursued by some Pacific Basin governments over the vehement objections of the United States provide equally graphic examples.

Such episodes cause considerable consternation in U.S. policy-making circles, but they merely underscore the transition that is taking place from a world that has been starkly bipolar politically, economically, and militarily, to one that is multipolar in all three realms. Various regional powers in Europe, the Pacific Basin, and elsewhere have their own policy agendas, and increasingly they have the ability to implement them regardless of Washington's preferences. It is pointless to blindly defy such trends; the pertinent challenge confronting officials in both Washington and Beijing is how to adjust to a multipolar world and position their countries to prosper in that new global environment.

For the United States, the principal problem is to reduce its security commitments in an orderly fashion while maintaining its extensive economic relations throughout the world. There are two possible dangers to that objective. One is that fiscal constraints and rising public resentment against "ungrateful" allies may cause a rapid, largely uncoordinated divestment. That action would not only damage diplomatic relations with previously friendly countries, it would create serious regional power vacuums. It might be added that the longer U.S. policymakers seek to preserve an outmoded set of burdensome security commitments, the more likely that change, when it finally comes, will take the form of an abrupt, acrimonious repudiation of obligations rather than a gradual devolution of defense responsibilities.

The other danger is that the effect of reducing or severing security ties with allies will spill over into economic relations. Potent protectionist sentiments have been building in the United States for years—

319

partially in response to exclusionary policies adopted by other governments—and the Pacific Basin countries are frequent targets of that wrath. There is, to be sure, more than a slight measure of hypocrisy in U.S. complaints about East Asian protectionism, since the United States has scarcely been a paragon of free trade in recent years (Richman 1988). Nevertheless, such sentiments are likely to create serious tensions in U.S. relations with countries throughout the Pacific region.

It would be a tragedy if the necessary and desirable reduction of U.S. security commitments became a pretext for the adoption of autarchical and xenophobic measures, but that danger certainly exists. Again, the orderly devolution of defense responsibilities, explicitly based on a recognition that the world has changed sufficiently to warrant a lower U.S. military profile outside the Western Hemisphere, is the best method of preventing such developments. By taking action *before* intra-alliance disagreements concerning military issues poison economic and political relations, U.S. leaders could credibly portray the shift to a new strategy as something more profound than retaliation against recalcitrant allies. They could also stress the importance of maintaining strong diplomatic and economic ties with former allies now that the military links were being severed, and the American people would be more likely to respond favorably to such reasoning.

Challenges Facing China

For China the task of adjusting to a multipolar geopolitical environment is somewhat more complex. Not only must the People's Republic of China (PRC) become accustomed to a more-restrained U.S. political and military role, but it must realize that various regional powers will become more active and assertive. In the case of the Pacific region, for example, it can be anticipated that Japan will eventually play political and military roles commensurate with its status as an economic power of the first rank (Morse 1987–88). And the Soviet Union is also likely to take a greater interest in Pacific affairs in an attempt to advance its political and economic influence.

These changes pose both dangers and opportunities for China. The principal danger is that the retrenchment of U.S. military commitments in the Pacific Basin will increase China's vulnerability to pressures from other strong states in the region, especially the Soviet Union and Japan. Such pressure would not necessarily take the form of crude military coercion as occurred earlier in this century, although even that possibility should not be ruled out. As Chinese leaders know all too well, previous Soviet regimes were quite willing to employ the USSR's military power in an effort to intimidate the PRC. The danger on that score from Japan is more long term and problematical since it would first require an accelerated rearmament effort by Tokyo, including overcoming entrenched domestic opposition to the acquisition of a nuclear capability. But even without resorting to the military option, the Soviet Union or Japan—or both nations acting in concert—might be tempted to employ economic and political pressure against China to advance their aims. They might also adopt policies toward neighboring East Asian countries that would undermine Chinese interests in the region.

The above speculation is not meant to imply that such coercive policies are inevitable. But one consequence of a multipolar system replacing the Pax Americana that has dominated the Pacific Basin since the end of World War II is that strong regional states have far greater latitude to pursue their own objectives, whether those objectives are benign or malignant. Given its geographic position, China dare not assume that the objectives of its powerful neighbors will be benign.

China has the delicate and important task of remaining on good terms with both superpowers. It must avoid being identified too closely with the security interests of either the United States or the Soviet Union. In the 1950s, the PRC was perceived by most Western leaders as little more than a junior partner of the USSR, and consequently earned the enmity of Washington and its allies. The bloody conflict between U.S. and Chinese forces in Korea and the proliferation of military incidents throughout the remainder of the decade— any one of which could have exploded into a catastrophic war—are reminders of what both countries must strive to avoid in the future.

Conversely, during the mid- and late-1970s, Moscow often saw the PRC as a de facto U.S. security partner, and that perception was hardly conducive to a needed improvement in Sino-Soviet relations. To the contrary, it fostered Soviet fears of encirclement and deepened the Kremlin's already potent animosity toward China. Conversely, U.S. officials began to take the PRC for granted, sometimes openly boasting about "playing the China card" in the Cold War rivalry with the Soviet Union.

The proper alternative to an unhealthy "tilt" toward one superpower or the other is clearly not a return to the diplomacy of undifferentiated hostility that Beijing often practiced in the 1960s. That strategy led only to a dangerous degree of isolation and alienation from the world community. A more prudent approach is the one that Chinese leaders followed throughout most of the 1980s—equidistance between the two superpowers. It is no coincidence that after several years of that strategy, China's relations with both the United States and the Soviet Union are generally cordial, a phenomenon that had not occurred previously since the 1949 revolution.

Maintaining that delicate balance will not be easy for China in the 1990s. The PRC still has numerous grievances toward the Soviet Union—not the least of which is the existence of territorial disputes along the lengthy border between the two countries—that could jeopardize the current thaw in relations. There are fewer potentially disruptive issues involving China and the United States. Even the once contentious issue of Taiwan no longer appears to have the potential to poison Sino-American relations. There are two possible exceptions to this benign scenario. A serious source of friction would exist if the United States adopted exclusionary trade measures, since China would be victimized by such practices. The other threat to the relationship would be if Chinese officials continue their attempt to make the United States (or more generally, "Western influences") a scapegoat for the anti-government demonstrations that erupted in May and June 1989, or if they continue the brutal reprisals against internal dissidents that have already damaged the PRC's reputation in the eyes of the American public.

As the United States adopts a lower military profile in the Western Pacific, the likelihood of conflict over security issues recedes to the vanishing point. Indeed, the United States and the PRC are likely to have compatible rather than conflicting security objectives in the Pacific Basin in the forseeable future. Even the ongoing improvement in U.S.-Soviet relations should not unduly strain Sino-American ties. Similarly, the United States can afford to view the evolving detente between the PRC and the Soviet Union without alarm (Manning 1989).

The necessity of preserving constructive relations with the two superpowers is obviously important, but there are other, equally crucial tasks facing Chinese leaders. To preserve its own safety in a multipolar world, China must be able to meet Japan and the Soviet Union on an approximately equal footing in terms of two vital indices of national power: military and economic. Militarily, that means the continued modernization of the People's Liberation Army (PLA) as well as the preservation—indeed, in the absence of further U.S.-Soviet strategic arms reductions, perhaps even the enhancement—of China's modest independent nuclear deterrent.

China's nuclear status may complicate strategic arms negotiations between the United States and the Soviet Union. Certainly the two superpowers cannot pursue those negotiations without reference to the capabilities of secondary nuclear powers such as the PRC and France. At the same time, the two nuclear giants must be sensitive to the legitimate security concerns of those nations, and that may involve a relative strengthening of French and Chinese capabilities vis-à-vis the United States and the Soviet Union. In that context, it should be noted that the credibility of the PRC's nuclear deterrent could be enhanced either through a larger Chinese strategic arsenal or through major reductions in the arsenals of the two superpowers. The latter would seem to be the preferable option, since it would prevent another expensive and potentially destabilizing nuclear arms race, but that choice rests primarily with Moscow and Washington.

Greater economic strength is also necessary if China is to operate effectively in a multipolar context. Indeed, a robust economy is the foundation of any viable national security strategy—a point that is sometimes lost on U.S. leaders in their enthusiasm for maintaining expensive military commitments around the globe. For China, the emergence of a multipolar world underscores the urgency of accelerating, not slowing, the pace of economic reform. It is also important that China expand its economic ties to other nations, rather than pursuing the chimera of "self-sufficiency." Increased receptivity to trade and investment opportunities involving Japan, South Korea, the ASEAN members, the Soviet Union, the United States, and other countries will benefit all the parties concerned and contribute significantly to the modernization of China's economy. Moreover, extensive economic links have the important collateral effect of reducing the danger of political and military conflicts; there is a major disincentive to attack neighboring countries who are important trading partners. That point may be especially pertinent with respect to China's relations with Japan and the Soviet Union.

In addition to accelerating the pace of economic reform, it is essential for the PRC to adopt a program of political reform. As the tragic events of May and June 1989 demonstrated, the existing political system is dangerously out of touch with the aspirations of the Chinese people. A sullen, angry population, kept in check only by ever-increasing applications of brute force, can never serve as the foundation for China to play a vigorous and constructive role in the world. Instead, repression in the political arena will undermine the hard-won economic gains, sow dangerous divisions within the country, and destroy the legitimacy of the PLA (as the most visible instrument of repression) in the minds of the people. The result will be to weaken China as a nation and as a geopolitical actor, a development that would not advance the long-term security interests of either the PRC or the United States.

The success or failure of China's foreign policy cannot be separated from the success or failure of domestic economic and political reform. Only by unleashing the creative energies of the Chinese people and respecting their fundamental rights can China attain the strength that will be needed in the coming years. The PRC has an opportunity to play a vigorous and constructive role as a great power in East Asia and throughout the western Pacific; indeed, China has the potential to become a global superpower later in the 21st century. But more substantive economic and political reforms—and healing the wounds of the bloody confrontation that occurred in the spring of 1989—are a prerequisite.

Conclusion: Adjusting to a Multipolar World

The emerging multipolar global environment will test both the wisdom and the ingenuity of foreign policy officials in China and the United States. Yet there is little reason to mourn the passing of the old bipolar system. Too often in pursuing their Cold War objectives, the United States and the Soviet Union showed a callous disregard for the interests and welfare of other nations. On a few occasions, the intense superpower rivalry came perilously close to plunging the entire planet into a nuclear cataclysm. Even the two superpowers, despite their exercise of far-reaching influence, did not ultimately benefit from bipolarity. Maintaining dominant positions within their respective power blocs during the past four decades has exacted an enormous economic and social toll on both nations.

The one benefit of bipolarity is that it did impose a degree of stability—albeit a dangerously fragile one—that probably reduced the number of major conflicts between regional powers. It is that aspect of bipolarity that will be the most difficult to replace. In a multipolar system, the probability of a conflict escalating to a global conflagration is diminished because not every local or regional quar- rel will draw in the superpowers; there is a greater opportunity to confine such conflicts to the original belligerents. At the same time, since the superpowers will no longer exercise hegemony within their security networks, the likelihood of conflicts between regional powers may increase. That is the inherent dilemma of a multipolar environment.

There is little doubt that the adjustment to multipolarity will be the most difficult in Europe, given the unusual number of medium- size regional powers. But the Pacific Basin also has the potential to be a volatile region, since China, Japan, the Soviet Union, the United States, and other nations all have important economic and security interests there. U.S. and Chinese officials must seek not only to minimize Sino-American conflicts, but also to defuse contentious issues involving each of their countries and the other major powers. The Pacific Basin can become an arena for the peaceful resolution of disputes and the coexistence of diverse societies, thereby setting a valuable example to the rest of the world. It will be the supreme test of Chinese and American diplomatic skill to help bring about that result.

References

Bandow, Doug. "ANZUS: A Case of Strategic Obsolesence." In *Collective Defense or Strategic Independence?: Alternative Strategies for the Future,* pp. 121–32. Edited by Ted Galen Carpenter. Lexington, Mass.: Lexington Books, 1989.

Bandow, Doug. "Leaving Korea." *Foreign Policy* 77 (Winter 1989–90): 77–93.

Calleo, David P. *Beyond American Hegemony: The Future of the Western Alliance.* New York: Basic Books, 1987.

Carpenter, Ted Galen. "Pursuing a Strategic Divorce: The U.S. and the ANZUS Alliance." Cato Institute Policy Analysis no. 67 (27 February 1986).

Carpenter, Ted Galen. "How Now to Counter Moscow?" *Wall Street Journal,* 13 October 1987.

Corbin, Marcus. "Mission Accomplished in Korea: Bringing U.S. Troops Home." *Defense Monitor* 19, no. 2 (1990). Washington, D.C.: Center for Defense Information, 1990.

Corcoran, Edward A. "Perestroika and the Soviet Military: Implications for U.S. Policy." Cato Institute Policy Analysis no. 133. (29 May 1990).

Dashichev, Vyacheslav. "The Search for New East-West Relations." *Literaturnaya gazeta,* 18 May 1988. Reprinted in *Current Digest of the Soviet Press,* 13 July 1988.

Department of Defense. *Report on Allied Contributions to the Common Defense,* April 1990.

Goose, Stephen D. "U.S. Forces in Korea: Assessing a Reduction." In *Collective Defense or Strategic Independence?: Alternative Strategies for the Future,* pp. 85–102. Edited by Ted Galen Carpenter. Lexington, Mass.: Lexington Books, 1989.

Hough, Jerry F. "Gorbachev's Anti-Americanism." *New York Times,* 11 November 1988.

Huntington, Samuel P. "The U.S.—Decline or Renewal?" *Foreign Affairs* 67 (Winter 1988–89): 76–96.

Kennedy, Paul. *Rise and Fall of the Great Powers: Economic Change and Military Conflict From 1500–2000.* New York: Random House, 1987.

Kim, Roy. "Warming Up Soviet-Japanese Relations?" *Washington Quarterly* 9 (Spring 1986): 85–96.

Kim, Roy. "Gorbachev and the Korean Peninsula." *Third World Quarterly* 10 (July 1988): 1267–99.

Krauss, Melvyn. *How NATO Weakens the West.* New York: Simon and Schuster, 1986.

Layne, Christopher. "Atlanticism Without NATO." *Foreign Policy* 67 (Summer 1987): 22–45.

Layne, Christopher. "Continental Divide—Time to Disengage in Europe." *National Interest* 13 (Fall 1988): 13–27.

Luttwak, Edward N. "Why Do the Mighty Fall?" *Washington Post*, 27 December 1987.

Manning, Robert A. "Chinese-Soviet Detente: Not to Be Feared." *New York Times*, 31 January 1989.

McMillan, Stuart. *Neither Confirm Nor Deny: The Nuclear Ships Dispute between New Zealand and the United States.* New York: Praeger, 1987.

Morse, Ronald A. "Japan's Drive to Pre-eminence." *Foreign Policy* 69 (Winter 1987–88): 3–21.

Nye, Joseph S., Jr. *Bound to Lead: The Changing Nature of American Power.* New York: Basic Books, 1990.

Richman, Sheldon L. "The Reagan Record on Trade: Rhetoric vs. Reality." Cato Institute Policy Analysis no. 107 (30 May 1988).

Shultz, George P. Address Before the Citizens Network for Foreign Affairs, 9 January 1989. State Department Press Release no. 03.

Steel, Ronald. "The Superpowers in the Twilight of NATO." In *NATO at 40: Confronting a Changing World*, pp. 3–14. Edited by Ted Galen Carpenter. Lexington, Mass.: Lexington Books, 1990.

U.S. Congress. House of Representatives, Committee on Armed Services. "Report of the Defense Burdensharing Panel." 100th Cong., 1st sess., August 1988.

PART IV

THE ROAD TO CHINA'S FUTURE

16

THE ROOTS OF CHINA'S CRISIS
Nien Cheng

Socialist Ideals and Communist Realities

Both my late husband and I went to the London School of Economics in the 1930s, and we became very liberal, or left wing. When I read a book on the Soviet Union by Sidney and Beatrice Webb, I thought, "How wonderful and idealistic socialism sounds." However, I was shocked by Stalin's show trials in 1937, so I never joined the British Communist party.

My late husband was a diplomat in the Nationalist government. At the end of 1948, after serving in Australia during World War II, we returned to China. Conditions there were very bad. During China's eight years of waging a war of resistance against Japanese aggression (1937–45), 20 million Chinese people had lost their lives. Millions more were impoverished. The economy was in a terrible state, with runaway inflation and shortages of daily necessities. We thought the Kuomintang would never be able to pull China together.

The communist underground was actively circulating propaganda materials. One of them was an essay by Mao Zedong, "On the United Front Government," in which he advocated democracy and the unity of every sector of Chinese society in order to rebuild China. It greatly appealed to us and to our friends, many of whom were professors with Ph.D.s from universities in the United States, Britain, Germany, France—Western democratic countries. We all decided to stay in China.

At the London School of Economics we had learned about socialism, the planned economy, and state ownership, which to young people sounded very equitable and fair. But there was no mention of class struggle, which was the most important thing to Mao and the Chinese Communist party, so we were unprepared for the realities of communist rule.

Nien Cheng is the author of *Life and Death in Shanghai*. This article is an expanded and revised version of an article carrying the same title that appeared in *Cato Policy Report* (1989). The article is based on two lectures the author gave at Cato Institute functions: the first in August 1989 and the second in January 1990.

Between 1949 and the end of the Cultural Revolution, Mao launched no fewer than nine major political movements as well as several minor ones. And during each political movement a large number of Chinese people were wrongfully accused of crimes and thrown into prison. I was one of them. In 1966, at the beginning of the Cultural Revolution, I was accused of being a spy. I could not have become a spy even if I had wanted to; I had no access to confidential government information. Many innocent people were thrown into prison or labor camps, and many lost their lives.

Periodically the communists would encourage people to express their opinions. The biggest fiasco was the Hundred Flowers campaign in 1956, during which everyone was urged to offer constructive comments about the shortcomings of the Communist party. The following year all the people who had said anything were seized and punished. Most of the victims were educated people—intellectuals. After that there was almost complete silence in China, and all cultural activities stagnated.

Now once again there has been a crackdown on the student movement. This episode has to be viewed on two levels: as a power struggle within the party leadership and as a spontaneous expression of discontent on the part of the Chinese people.

China's Present Crisis

The Power Struggle

Early in 1989, there were hints of an impending power struggle that might result in the ouster of Zhao Ziyang, who had been China's prime minister at the beginning of the economic reforms. When Hu Yaobang was ousted as general secretary of the Communist party because he had refused to repress the December 1986 student demonstrations, Zhao Ziyang became general secretary and Li Peng became prime minister.

Deng Xiaoping had entrusted both Hu and Zhao with carrying out the economic reforms. Contrary to the general understanding outside China, Deng never intended China to go the whole way and adopt a market economy—that is, abandon socialism. He wanted to preserve the socialist sector—government-owned factories and so on—and have only a small capitalist sector to supplement it. Of course, that's an unworkable idea.

The reason Deng wanted to apply market economies' methods to the management of the socialist sector is that at the end of the Cultural Revolution China's productivity was at an extremely low point, and the prestige of the Communist party was at an all-time low. Deng wanted to improve the people's standard of living a little and pull China together economically.

But in the course of implementing Deng Xiaoping's policy, Zhao Ziyang and Hu Yaobang both realized that it was impossible to keep half of China's economy under state planning and half of it free. For one thing, the state-owned enterprises got their raw materials from government agencies at very low subsidized prices, and side by side with that arrangement was a free market for the same materials at prices five to eight times as high.

In such a situation, the opportunity for corruption is tremendous. Anyone who had access to government-supplied raw materials could sell them on the free market. Some of the factories could afford to pay their workers without producing anything at all. Everything was based on personal relations. Factory managers without connections were obliged to buy raw materials on the free market. Of course, the children and associates of senior government officials were at a great advantage because they had connections. There was a great deal of corruption, and the economy was in a constant state of confusion.

Zhao Ziyang and Hu Yaobang realized that China must go the whole way and adopt capitalism. On the other hand, the old guard, leaders who are now in their eighties, would not give up socialism. But neither could they oppose Deng Xiaoping; he is too strong and has too much personal prestige in the party. So what they hoped to do is destroy the men who implement the economic reforms. First they got rid of Hu Yaobang, and then they turned on Zhao Ziyang. Naturally, because of his position, Zhao had a great deal of power. Deng Xiaoping felt that Zhao was too ambitious and independent, so he sided with the old guard.

As Simon Leys, who is a great writer on China, noted in a recent article, whether a Chinese leader is a hero or a scoundrel from the point of view of the people depends on whether he has been ousted or is in power. Hu Yaobang was not very popular when he was in power, but when he died, having been ousted, the students all turned out to eulogize him. Their pro-Hu demonstration on April 15 was also a typically Chinese way of making a statement. The demonstrators were not only paying tribute to Hu but saying "We support Zhao Ziyang," because Hu and Zhao represented the same viewpoint. Of course, later Zhao refused to be a party to the decision to suppress the student demonstrations by force. That is the background of the power struggle.

Popular Discontent

As for the Chinese people's discontent, consider what happened when Poland relaxed its price controls: All the basic necessities became much more expensive. The same thing happened when Zhao released a few items from price control. People on fixed salaries, such as professors, had a hard time making ends meet. By May 1989, the official figure for inflation in China was 26 percent, but the unofficial estimate put it at over 40 percent.

The main reason for the Chinese people's discontent is not that they cannot exercise the freedom of speech or assembly, criticize the government, or choose alternative candidates for the People's Congress. The reason for their discontent is basically economic—their living standard has declined. The discontent is not confined to urban areas. Because the government does not have enough money to pay the peasants for their grain and other products, they are being given IOUs. With the inflation rate so high, in no time at all an IOU is worth nothing.

When the students first demonstrated in Tiananmen Square, all they meant by "democracy" was freedom of the press; a student union that was freely elected, not controlled by the government; and an end to corruption and nepotism. Of course, they also wanted more control over their lives. Young people in China know that when they graduate from college, it is the government that will give them jobs. They know that if the government gives them jobs in, say, Tibet, that is where they will have to go. They are not free to make such basic choices as where to work, where to live, and how many children to have. The government intrudes in people's lives to a great extent.

Obstacles to Thoroughgoing Reform

When property is in the hands of the state and all the important economic decisions are left to the state, individuals become subservient to the ruling elite and economic decisions become the subject of political influence. In such a political-economic order, incentives to produce necessarily suffer. This has been the experience in China.

Take the case of Chinese agriculture, for example. Even though China's agricultural reform enlarged the opportunities of farmers to use the land at their disposal, it did not extend full ownership rights. The communes were abolished and individual farming was allowed on a family basis. However, farmers were not allowed to own the land they farmed. They merely sign a contract with the government for a number of years. As such, they have little incentive to reinvest their money to improve their farms. Instead, they use the money for other purposes.

Likewise, in the cities, the reform allowed for small-scale industries, but those entrepreneurs who earned profits were not allowed to expand their businesses—because they were limited to small-scale firms to supplement the nationalized industries. Since entrepreneurs cannot own, develop, or invest their profits, they have no real incentive to innovate or be overly productive.

Of course, there are many other problems. But, in my view, the limits placed on ownership and the insistence on adhering to "half and half"—that is, to a socialist economy and a market economy existing side by side—are the two most serious stumbling blocks to a thorough and speedy transformation of China's economy and any real improvement in the standard of living.

A third stumbling block or obstacle for those who want to move toward free markets is psychological. After more than 40 years of communist rule, the Chinese people have become shortsighted and lazy. The discretionary nature of government policy—with shifts from left to right and right to left—has made individuals highly uncertain about the future and has impaired their ability to plan their own lives. In addition, the lack of private ownership rights and the inability of individuals to capture the rewards for hard work or to suffer the consequences of failure have reduced incentives to work. Under the doctrine of the "iron rice bowl," jobs have been guaranteed, firms are seldom allowed to go bankrupt, and incomes have been equalized to a high degree and maintained at level that has allowed most people to get by. In such an environment, people have lost their sense of responsibility and there is little incentive to take risks.

The lack of a rule of law in China over the past 40 years has had a deep psychological impact as well. China is a society where everybody feels obligated to break the government's rules because they are so detestable and calculated to make the people's life so unpleasant. There is little respect for property because it is state owned, and the people's attitude is—"If I can get away with not obeying the rules, it is my duty to do so."

How do you educate people to obey the law? The only way you can succeed is if that law applies to the senior officials and their families as well. As long as there is a privileged class in China that cannot be touched by law no matter what its members do, one cannot expect the people to obey the law.

The Choice between Socialism and a Market System

In 1987, I wrote: "Unless and until a political system rooted in law, rather than personal power, is firmly established in China, the road to the future will always be full of twists and turns" (Cheng

333

1988, p. 543). The events of May-June 1989 further illustrate the importance of separating economic decisions from political control and establishing a stable rule of law in China. The only way the Chinese can succeed and really improve their economic situation is, of course, to insist on economic reform and to liberalize the price system—despite the pain and hardship the transition will temporarily cause. But the leaders and the party members must be the first to set an example. They should convince the people that the costs of reform are short-lived, while the expected benefits are large and permanent. They should express the notion that "We all have to go through the transition process together." If the leaders and party members take this approach, real reform will be possible, and everything will be better. At present, the leadership cannot do this because they have lost their credibility in the eyes of the people. However, if a new leadership comes, then economic reform can also come about.

In conclusion, China is faced with the choice between socialism and a market system; a mixed system is doomed to failure. The obstacles to China's development can be removed only if China goes all the way toward a private market system with constitutional protections for both economic and civil liberties. China's crisis is a crisis of confidence; the people are in a half-awakened state of mind. The old regime has lost its legitimacy but a new regime has not emerged to fill the vacuum, and there has been no clear commitment to the path of markets and freedom of choice.

To regain consciousness and emerge from the semi-conscious state that now envelops China will take time. But reality requires that China recognize the death of communism. Reality also requires that China embark on thoroughgoing reform or face the prospect of being left behind in the wake of the liberal revolution that is now sweeping the globe.

References

Cheng, Nien. *Life and Death in Shanghai.* New York: Penguin Books, 1988.
Cheng, Nien. "The Roots of China's Crisis." *Cato Policy Report* 11, no. 5 (September/October 1989): 1, 10–11.

17

A FREE-MARKET CONSTITUTION FOR HONG KONG: A BLUEPRINT FOR CHINA*

Alvin Rabushka

China's leaders understand the basis for Hong Kong's stability and prosperity. In particular, they recognize that the adoption of Hong Kong's institutional and policy mix would go a long way toward promoting growth on the mainland. The central message of this paper is that the provisions of Hong Kong's Basic Law, which may be regarded as a free-market constitution, can serve as a blueprint for economic reform in China. Likewise, the market-oriented economies of the other Pacific Rim "dragons"—Singapore, Taiwan, and Korea—also provide valuable lessons for China, some of which will be examined along with the Hong Kong model.

Hallmarks of Hong Kong's Economic Success

In contrast with the vacillating economic strategies and policies that prevailed in mainland China between 1952 and 1978, which often reflected ideological struggles over the proper objectives and means to implement socialism, Hong Kong maintained an extraordinary degree of stability in its political and economic institutions. Founded as a free port in 1841, Hong Kong has an economy today that depends on export-oriented light manufacturing industries along with a myriad of servicing industries within a free-port, free-enterprise environment. Highly developed banking, insurance, and shipping systems complement its industrial sector.

A rundown of Hong Kong's fiscal and economic policies reveals a portrait of life that encompasses the following: balanced budgets (almost always in surplus), avoidance of public debt, an economy ethic in government that strives to avoid wasteful spending, an aversion to central planning, minimum intervention in or regulation of the private sector, commercial provision of public economic services, a constitutional and legal framework that protects private property

*Reprinted from *Cato Journal* 8 (Winter 1989): 641–52, with revisions.
The author is Senior Fellow at the Hoover Institution at Stanford University.

and a whole range of personal freedoms, free trade, free movement of capital, avoidance of subsidies to industry, minimally intrusive general business requirements (it takes little time or money to open a business), a free market in labor, and a system of low rates and low overall taxation. In short, free trade, free markets, low taxes, nonintervention, and personal liberty are the hallmarks of Hong Kong's economic success.

The Future of Hong Kong

Hong Kong has experienced several noticeable episodes of political and economic instability since 1949. The two most dramatic occurred in 1966–67 as a spillover of the Cultural Revolution on the mainland and in 1982–84 during the Sino-British negotiations over the future of Hong Kong. As political confidence in the future waned during the talks, the colony experienced a run on the Hong Kong dollar and a sharp decline in stock and property values. The signing of the Joint Declaration in 1984 restored a measure of stability to Hong Kong and the economy quickly resumed its upward economic path. Apart from external political shocks, Hong Kong's resilient capitalistic economy has successfully weathered international recessions, trade quarrels, oil shocks, and internal disputes. Its free-market economy has enabled Hong Kong businessmen to adjust quickly to changing external circumstances.

China's political leaders and economic analysts are well aware of Hong Kong's achievements. They are also aware of the institutions and policies in Hong Kong that have made the territory's remarkable prosperity possible. More than 700 Chinese firms, encompassing banking and finance, travel, shipping, city, provincial and national organizations, insurance and oil companies, and special economic zone organizations, among others, have steadily expanded their direct investments and business activities in the colony, now running into the billions of dollars.[1] In addition, tens of thousands of mainland personnel have been dispatched to Hong Kong to learn how to do business in a market-based economy. The Bank of China group is believed to be the second largest holder of deposits in Hong Kong after the Hongkong and Shanghai Banking Corporation.

[1]These estimates, obtained from the *Far Eastern Economic Review* (23 June 1988, pp. 64–66), reflect a variety of sources including Beijing's own calculations, local Hong Kong university professors, and the U.S. State Department's Foreign Commercial Service. The total capital investment of Chinese-funded enterprises in Hong Kong is estimated to range between U.S. $7–12 billion.

Chinese political leaders have also learned, especially from the crisis of confidence that erupted in 1983 when the Sino-British talks appeared to be going poorly, that political confidence in the future of Hong Kong is extremely fragile and, if shattered, threatens to destroy its stability and prosperity. A prosperous Hong Kong is deemed essential in China's developmental plans to provide hard currency earnings, to provide access to trade and technology, and to serve as a proxy for the absence of a major Southern port city.

Since 1982, when China publicly announced plans to resume sovereignty and administrative authority over Hong Kong on July 1, 1997, when Britain's 99-year lease on the New Territories is scheduled to expire, Chinese authorities have repeatedly stated their primary objective of preserving stability and prosperity in Hong Kong. To maintain stability and prosperity, Deng Xiaoping advanced the novel doctrine of "one country, two systems," in which socialism on the mainland and capitalism in Hong Kong would peacefully coexist within one sovereign China.[2] In particular, China guaranteed that Hong Kong would be allowed to retain its capitalist way of life for 50 years after 1997 until 2047.

The Basic Law: Lessons for China

Under the provisions of the Sino-British Joint Declaration, Hong Kong is to receive its own mini-constitution. Upon the resumption of the exercise of sovereignty over Hong Kong, China agreed to establish a Hong Kong Special Administrative Region (HKSAR), which would retain a high degree of autonomy in all matters except defense and foreign affairs. The National People's Congress (NPC) of the People's Republic of China will enact and promulgate a Basic Law by 1990.

In April 1985, the NPC established a drafting committee for the Basic Law of the HKSAR, which comprised 59 members, among whom 23 were from various sectors in Hong Kong. To ensure that the drafting committee received a wide range of public opinion within Hong Kong, it set up a consultative committee of 180 persons reflecting the various sectors and strata in Hong Kong. In April 1988 the drafting committee issued a draft Basic Law, on which it solicited

[2]Chinese officials hope that the successful application of the "one country, two systems" doctrine in Hong Kong would provide a mechanism for the gradual unification of Taiwan with the mainland on a similar basis. That is, socialism in China and capitalism in Taiwan could peacefully coexist within one sovereign political system. Failure of the "one country, two systems" experiment in Hong Kong would make it virtually impossible to extend the same doctrine to Taiwan, thereby thwarting reunification.

opinions from the general public during May-September 1988. Following amendments and revisions, a second draft Basic Law was issued in February 1989, on which consultation was held during the balance of the year. A final round of revisions was made in early 1990 and the Basic Law was promulgated by the NPC in 1990.[3]

The Basic Law contains a statement of general principles, along with chapters that enumerate the relationship between the HKSAR and Chinese central authorities, the fundamental rights and duties of Hong Kong residents, political structure, the economy, social services, external affairs, interpretation and amendment of the Basic Law, and a variety of supplementary provisions. It also contains a preamble that states that the mainland's socialist system and policies will not be practiced in Hong Kong.

To the best of my knowledge, the Basic Law for the HKSAR is unique among contemporary national constitutions in one respect: It enshrines general principles and concrete policies to preserve individual economic freedom. It does so because Chinese authorities recognize that the preservation of economic freedom in Hong Kong is critical to its continued stability and prosperity. The list of economic liberties is in addition to a standard list of civil rights that normally appears in a constitutional document. A review of the economic provisions in the Basic Law for the HKSAR provides lessons that China can bring to bear upon its own development.

Importance of Private Property Rights

Perhaps the most fundamental individual economic right of all is itemized in Chapter I in the Basic Law, which sets forth general principles. Article 6 (of Chapter I), in particular, protects rights of private ownership of property in accordance with law. Article 104 (in Chapter V) stipulates that compensation for lawful deprivation of private property shall be based on real market value and be promptly paid in convertible forms of payment. Private property rights are the keystone of Hong Kong's market economy and their preservation is

---

[3]This process has been politically charged. Some advocates of direct democracy in Hong Kong assert that a coalition encompassing local big business, the colonial government, and Chinese authorities has conspired to minimize the extent of political reform in Hong Kong to ensure that when China takes over in 1997, it will retain an iron grip over the HKSAR's new political structure. Opponents of rapid democratic reform argue that direct democracy imperils Hong Kong's stability and democracy and that democratic reforms need to be introduced gradually. This paper, however, focuses almost exclusively on questions of economic policy, not political structure, and therefore the political structure of Hong Kong is not discussed.

Throughout this paper, citation of specific articles in the Basic Law refers to the February 1990 final version.

essential in maintaining Hong Kong's capitalistic system. By way of contrast, China is in the very preliminary stages of injecting property rights into its socialist economic system. Prior to 1982, individuals could not own land, which belonged to the state. Revisions to the constitution in 1982 allowed for the development of "individual" economy and gave citizens the right to own houses and inherit private property. Rural economic policies, begun in 1978, have created a de facto system of property rights in agriculture, in which peasants can inherit or trade 15-year leaseholds to specific plots of land, and agricultural output has sharply increased in response to these new individual incentives made possible by a system of property rights in agriculture. State or collective ownership remains the primary form of urban and industrial ownership. To improve industrial efficiency, China will have to make major strides in creating and enforcing a system of private property rights in urban land, business ownership (other than very small enterprises that are currently private), and a variety of financial assets.[4] China's attempts to reduce and phase out urban food subsidies will have to encompass the government's control over housing, jobs, and other amenities. Since Chinese urban residents have enjoyed housing and food subsidies for decades, phasing out subsidies and moving to a system of private ownership will be extremely difficult.

Maintaining a Rule of Law

Private property flourishes only within a framework of the rule of law. Article 8 stipulates that the laws in force in Hong Kong, including common law, customary law, and legislation, shall be maintained. Retention of the existing legal system serves to protect private property rights. In particular, the British legal system, arising from the common law, is especially concerned with protection of private property. Confidence in the legal system requires an independent judiciary, which is provided in the Basic Law; it shall have jurisdiction on all affairs arising within Hong Kong, except cases relating to defense and foreign affairs. China, in contrast, lacks a fully articulated legal system that would permit contract disputes to be resolved with some measure of certainty. As well, the judiciary is more an arm

---

[4]Several delegations of Chinese economists from academic institutions, the State Council, the Chinese Academy of Social Sciences, and the Economic Structure Reform Commission have visited Stanford University. They have indicated that the topic of reforming ownership rights of property is an issue in internal debate along with the important task of price reform. The debate centers around the speed with which some measure of private property rights can be injected into the industrial urban economy. There is growing recognition that price reform without property reform will not yield the maximum gains in economic performance.

of the government that seeks to implement state policy rather than settle disputes among individuals on a totally impartial basis. China will need to forge ahead with the development of a national commercial legal system that serves both the Chinese and international business communities and with the development of a court system that applies the law impartially.

Fundamental Rights and Duties

Chapter III of the Basic Law enumerates fundamental rights and duties of the residents: equality before the law; the right to vote; freedom of speech, association, assembly, and trade unions; the prohibition of unlawful search and seizure; freedom and privacy of communications; freedom of movement; freedom of occupation; freedom of academic research; the right to legal counsel; and so forth. These rights are virtually identical with those enumerated in Chapter II of China's own national constitution and thus offer nothing new in terms of economic principles. In reality, most Hong Kong residents have enjoyed these rights relatively free from government interference. In China, these rights have often been suppressed. Few Chinese subjects have enjoyed freedom of occupation, movement, and academic research on sensitive topics, though the situation has improved in recent years. Freedom of occupation and movement, in particular, are important to moving labor to where that economic resource can be used more efficiently.[5]

Economic Policies for Stable Growth and Prosperity

To preserve prosperity in Hong Kong and to maintain the region's capitalist economy, the Basic Law Drafting Committee members, of whom the majority are mainland Chinese schooled in the socialist system, have enunciated a set of economic policies that govern the conduct of public finance and taxation, money and finance, external trade and economic relations, industry and commerce, land leases, shipping, and aviation. These policies are regarded as the keystone of Hong Kong's prosperity. Indeed, knowledgeable Chinese recognize that these policies are generally conducive to fostering a climate for economic growth. The issue in China is how to overcome the political obstacles and historical conditions that prevent rapid implementa-

---

[5]Since 1949, the government in China has generally assigned most jobs. Chinese are attached to work units, which carry housing, ration coupons, and other benefits. Few Chinese are free to leave their jobs and take up others without official permission, nor can employers summarily dismiss employees. China will need to develop free labor markets, as exist in Hong Kong, to gain maximum benefit from its large labor force.

tion. These economic policies are set forth with remarkable clarity in Chapter V of the draft Basic Law.[6]

Public Finance and Taxation. Two themes have historically governed the conduct of Hong Kong's public finances. First, low rates of direct taxation stimulate work, saving, and investment, thereby fostering high rates of economic growth. Moreover, in Hong Kong's open economy, deficit financing is inappropriate since any increase in public spending can leak overseas. Balanced (surplus) budgets are considered the norm of sound fiscal policy. Second, the size of the public sector must be kept small to prevent it from crowding out the private sector.

Article 107 stipulates that the HKSAR shall practice an independent tax system, taking the low tax policy previously pursued in Hong Kong as reference, which means that any expansion in public sector spending must come either from the fruits of economic growth or by substituting spending in one program for another. Article 106 links Hong Kong's low tax system with a budgetary policy that requires a balancing of revenues and expenditures. To ensure that the public sector does not grow in relative terms, the policy also stipulates that the rate of increase of taxes or spending shall be commensurate with the growth rate of the gross domestic product. These provisions ensure that the government will remain limited in its scope and size, which means that the creation and distribution of income is left in private hands.

In general, China has pursued a conservative fiscal policy, mindful of the fact that inflation destroyed the political basis of support of the Nationalist Party. Until recent years, China's command and control economy had little need for a formal system of taxation, since nearly the entire economy was under public ownership in which the government supplied all inputs and collected all receipts of industry. As China moves in the direction of injecting market forces into its economy, it will replace its system of allocating and collecting funds by a system of taxation based on salaries and profits.[7] It must gradually

[6]It is somewhat ironic that a socialist system is setting forth specific economic rights in a constitution that will apply to a portion of its own territory considering that no Western industrial capitalist democracy contains similar measures in its own constitution.

[7]Chinese venture capitalists have complained that rates of taxation on business profits have risen from 55 percent to nearly 80 percent in the past few years, thus adversely affecting incentives. As well, a steeply graduated personal income tax with a top marginal rate of 60 percent was enacted in 1987, ostensibly to capture a share of the windfall benefits that accrued as prices were deregulated. Nonetheless, it seems counterproductive to tax heavily the class of investors, self-made entrepreneurs, and skilled workers upon whose efforts China's growth depends. Hong Kong's top marginal tax rates, in comparison, range between 15 percent and 16.5 percent for personal income and profits, respectively.

reduce the scope and size of the public sector to ensure that resources are used efficiently either in private hands or under autonomous management. The lesson that Hong Kong provides is that low rates of taxation and limited government supply strong incentives to individuals.

Money and Finance. Hong Kong is an international financial and banking center. Indeed, the financial services sector is the most rapidly growing part of its economy, now contributing nearly one-quarter of gross domestic product. The Basic Law addresses the features of money and finance that foster a prosperous financial sector in Hong Kong.

To begin with, the Basic Law requires in Articles 110 and 111 that the HKSAR shall continue to practice its historical monetary and financial policies. In particular, this calls for the following provisions: no exchange controls shall be imposed in the HKSAR; free flow of capital within, into, and out of the region; free entry into financial business and financial markets; and maintenance of an independent, freely convertible Hong Kong currency, which shall be 100 percent backed by a reserve fund.

The contrast with China could not be more striking. China lacks even rudimentary domestic capital markets. Exchange controls severely limit access to foreign currency. The Renminbi, China's national currency, is not freely convertible into foreign currencies by Chinese or foreigners, nor is it backed by any foreign currency or commodity. The banking and financial services sectors are not open to free internal or external competition. The state exercises disproportionate control over the allocation of credit and investment, though it is moving away from grants and subsidies to the use of interest rates. Before China can deploy its scarce capital efficiently, it will have to create capital markets in which the supply of credit and capital is carefully matched with those individuals and organizations that can use them most efficiently.

Trade and Industry. Articles 113 and 114 of the Basic Law ensure policies of free external and free internal trade. The HKSAR shall continue to do business on the basis of external free trade, and to that end the free movement of goods, intangible assets, and capital shall be maintained. All investment shall be protected by law. The region shall remain a free port, true to its historical founding principles dating back to 1841.

Once again, the contrast with mainland China is marked. Foreign trade has largely been governed by the Ministry of Foreign Economic Relations and Trade. Recent progress has been made in granting various enterprises the right to buy and sell in world markets with fewer restrictions than in the past, but China is a great leap away from any semblance of free external trade. Similarly, the bulk of industrial output is still generated by state-owned enterprises or collectively owned enterprises in accordance with state directives.

The remaining provisions in the draft Basic Law pertaining to economic policy maintain existing land use rights, retain the territory's existing system of private shipping business, and continue the existing system of civil aviation management and Hong Kong-licensed air carriers.

No article in Section V specifically deals with the subject of business regulation, which potentially affects the costs of doing business in Hong Kong in the form of fringe benefits, environmental controls, and so forth. The general principles in Chapter I state that the existing capitalist system and way of life shall not be changed for 50 years, which implies that the general policy of nonintervention in the private sector shall be maintained. The existing system also eschews subsidies to consumers or business firms. There is, curiously, a specific provision to maintain the existing social welfare system, but its chief hallmark is that it consumes a relatively modest share of national income and does not typify the vast schemes of costly welfare programs found in the Western democracies.

A Free-Market Constitution

The Basic Law Drafting Committee was not content to rest with a statement of general economic principles. It believed that confidence in Hong Kong's future required a detailed specification of economic institutions and policies in the form of a free-market constitution. The chief features of this "constitution" include private property, the rule of law, freedom of occupation and movement, low taxes, a limit on the scope and size of government, free movement of capital, a convertible (fully backed) currency, free entry into any line of business, unregulated prices, free trade, and the retention of a free port. These provisions were judged to be the *sine qua non* of Hong Kong's stability and prosperity.

One is tempted to suggest that China turn over the management of its economy to the Hong Kong government. But a good substitute for that recommendation is for Chinese economic planners to study the Basic Law for the HKSAR, which was written by a China-dominated committee, in which its own members displayed their understanding of Hong Kong's free-market economy. Of course, the drafters were not encumbered with an official ideology of socialism for the HKSAR, which hampers efforts at market-oriented reforms on the mainland. It would be vastly more difficult to copy Section V of the Hong Kong Basic Law into China's own constitution, even though policymakers are grappling with the means of injecting reforms that create equivalent incentives. The critical fact, however, is that Chinese officials clearly recognize the policies that are conducive to prosperity, and in doing so implicitly recognize the need for a free-market constitution.

Lessons from the Other Dragons

Singapore, Taiwan, and Korea differ from Hong Kong in many respects, and numerous books and articles have been written stressing the uniqueness of each country's developmental experience. However, one can discern a common mix of institutions and policies that propelled each into the ranks of industrial modernity within the short span of a generation.

Singapore, Taiwan, and Korea each endured major wartime disruption, each lacked abundant natural and financial resources, and each was a poor country with a low standard of living. All three initially embarked on a program of import-substitution behind a protective wall of tariffs and quotas. All sought foreign aid. Growth under this initial strategy was at best moderate.

External circumstances prompted the leaders of all three countries to switch strategies from an import-substitution policy for a limited domestic market to the development of labor-intensive, manufactured goods for export to world markets. International price competition replaced domestic subsidies and tariffs; private firms decided what to produce and where to sell. Government relaxed its grip on the economy and allowed the marketplace to determine the pattern and scope of economic development.

What were the major ingredients that went into a successful strategy of growth? To begin with, emphasis was placed on the private sector for the creation of jobs and the distribution of income and wealth. Although the government in each country played a role in allocating credit, building infrastructure, and guiding development, by and large, the private sector was the primary engine driving growth. This strategy required a system of private property rights that would protect both domestic and foreign investors.

Another critical factor was reform of the exchange rate system to ensure that each country's currency was not overvalued. An overvalued currency cheapens imports, makes exports more expensive thus hampering their growth, and invariably leads to a balance-of-payments crisis.

Other important factors included stabilizing the labor market to give foreign and domestic investors confidence that strikes and labor agitation would not distort investors' calculations of profitable investments. All three governments adopted a number of measures to encourage national savings and capital formation, and each country quickly developed extremely high rates of capital formation. In every case, tax incentives were used to encourage foreign and domestic investment, which included such devices as tax holidays, accelerated depreciation, duty-free export processing zones, credits for exports and research and development, special low rates of tax, preferential treatment in the form of low rates imposed on interest and dividends, and exemption of capital gains from taxation. A final emphasis was the need to hold down spending on social programs until high rates of economic growth provided sufficient revenues to finance a growing list of government programs out of growth, rather than at the expense of growth. As well, each country tried to run its utilities and government economic enterprises on a commercial basis in which services were priced to reflect full opportunity costs, rather than depend on heavy subsidies.

Conclusion

The standard of living of the four dragons—Hong Kong, Korea, Singapore, and Taiwan—has caught and surpassed a number of European countries. Moreover, the dragons enjoyed near double-digit growth rates in the late 1980s. In my view, the single most important factor that accounts for their economic success is that each country affords its residents a considerable measure of economic freedom. This factor translates into a well-defined and enforced system of private property rights, an effective legal system that protects the individual's economic and political liberties, reliance on private enterprise for the creation and distribution of income, and the maintenance of economic policies that motivate and reward individual behavior.

China itself would no doubt like to become the fifth dragon and has taken a series of bold measures to that end. Careful study and application of the economic institutions and policies that propelled the four dragons from third-world to first-world status provide a clear set of measures that can assist China in its effort to modernize.

Chief among these measures are the principles and economic policies incorporated into Hong Kong's free-market constitution, as set out in the Basic Law. By applying this blueprint to the economic reforms in China, the basis will be established for a new Chinese order characterized by individual freedom and prosperity.

COMMENT

FREEDOM AND REFORM IN ASIAN-PACIFIC ECONOMIES*
Richard Y. C. Wong

A commentator is expected to find faults with what the author has to say, but I find myself in substantial agreement with what Alvin Rabushka has written. My comments, therefore, are largely directed at certain omissions in Rabushka's paper, whose inclusion I think would make his case for economic freedom convincing. In particular, I believe Rabushka's argument would be enhanced by taking a more thoroughgoing comparative institutions approach, and that his treatment of the Basic Law would benefit from a closer examination of the implementation problem and those provisions that clash with economic freedom.

A Comparative Institutions Approach

The Asian Pacific region provides many useful examples of economies that are great successes or dismal failures. Much can be learned from comparing and contrasting the different institutions and policies adopted by these countries as they developed over time. A comparative analysis of the varying economic growth experiences of these countries would provide useful lessons for China.

The major omission in Rabushka's paper is that he does not make full use of such comparisons, although he does so to some extent elsewhere (see Rabushka 1987). Here, he simply concentrates on some of the success cases. A useful comparative analysis, however, must contrast success with failure and bring out the essential differences between them.

Rabushka does distill from the success stories, based primarily on the experience of Hong Kong, a number of policies that he regards

*Reprinted from *Cato Journal* 8 (Winter 1989): 653–56, with revisions.

The author is Director of the Hong Kong Centre for Economic Research and a Senior Lecturer in Economics at the Chinese University of Hong Kong.

347

as essential for economic success. These policies include the protection of economic and personal liberties through the creation of a sound legal framework, the maintenance of a competitive price system, and a tax system conducive to saving and investment. The problem, however, is that Rabushka does not spell out in sufficient detail which of the various policies are most important for China and how they can be implemented given existing constraints and opportunities.

These are difficult issues, but the experience of the Asian-Pacific countries offers some guidance. The strategy adopted by and the experience of Taiwan—and to some extent South Korea, Singapore, and post-Sukarno's Indonesia—in deregulating the economy, scaling back protectionist policies, raising suppressed interest rates, and letting the exchange rate be set close to market levels are highly relevant. Indeed, the political and economic strategies, which are pursued by these governments—with varying success and in the face of opposition—to achieve a general move toward a more open and competitive system in which prices reflect scarcity values, deserve detailed examination. The adopted strategies provide hints as to what priorities should be set and what steps should be taken in implementing a policy of successful liberalization. One general observation is that few countries began by relaxing all prices at once; instead, most tried to focus on interest rates and exchange rates.

There are also negative experiences. In the 1970s, South Korea backslid into greater protectionism and suffered from it. The manipulative industrial policies in Singapore in the 1970s paved the way for a loss in economic responsiveness during the worldwide recession in the early 1980s, which hit Singapore with unusual severity. In some countries, state monopolies simply became private ones without resulting in much improvement in economic efficiency and often generated significant social unrest because inequities and corrupt practices became more evident.

Another major issue is the extent to which these policies can be carried without the creation of new institutions and a fundamental change in the organization of the economy and even the polity. Within China there is an ongoing debate about the appropriate policy mix on the one hand and fundamental reform on the other. The Chinese authorities seem to have achieved some limited consensus regarding the need for basic reform, but the issue of pace and how far it should go remains highly contentious.

Here again the Asian-Pacific economies provide many important lessons. The case of North and South Korea (or for that matter East and West Germany) is a powerful illustration of Rabushka's claim that "economic freedom" in the Asian dragons is "the single most important factor that accounts for their economic success." In particular, the experience of the four dragons strongly suggests that modernization requires not only the adoption of sound economic policies, but also the creation of an institutional framework based on private initiative and competition.

Even within capitalist countries, where private property rights are recognized, economic policy failures are quite common and are primarily associated with the fact that highly interventionist governments often impede the process of price competition and hence the individual's economic freedom to engage in production and exchange. Arbitrary transfers and barriers to entry weaken private property rights. Marcos' Philippines, Sukarno's Indonesia, and to a lesser extent Malaysia, South Korea, and Taiwan in the 1950s were not success stories, largely because the wrong policies were pursued. A proper institutional framework is essential and will be strengthened by the consistent application of free-market policies. Interventionist policies can erode even the best-designed institutions.

The Basic Law: Its Implementation and Inconsistency

One of the most interesting experiments in the Asian-Pacific region, of course, is Hong Kong, which will have a fundamental change in its political system after 1997. Whether such a change also would bring with it a gradual change in economic policies that over time would weaken the present institutions, which allow a great measure of individual economic freedom, is a matter of great concern. The Basic Law, which would serve as the constitution for Hong Kong after 1997, may provide some limited hints of likely future events.

According to Rabushka, the fact that China is willing to enshrine many of the successful policies adopted by Hong Kong in the Basic Law demonstrates China's recognition of the value of these policies in leading to economic success. The only remaining issue for Rabushka appears to be for China to adopt these policies for her own modernization. While I think there is much truth in this, there are two fine distinctions that should be noted.

First, the challenge facing China in overcoming the political and economic obstacles blocking the path toward reform is much more formidable than merely preserving policies that have proven successful in Hong Kong. For this reason, the problem of how to implement "a free-market constitution" in China is at least as important as what such a fundamental law should include. Second, the Basic Law is

itself not an unambiguous document or "blueprint for China."
Rabushka has correctly pointed out that the Basic Law includes many
articles that aim to limit the arbitrary power of the state in economic
policymaking and to preserve individual economic freedom. But he
fails to emphasize that it also includes articles to the contrary, for
example, the provision that the state should actively promote industries. The enforcement of this provision would open the way for the
introduction of preferential and interventionist economic policies.
In many ways the Basic Law is necessarily a contradictory document.
It hopes to incorporate the interests of various parties—both within
and outside Hong Kong—whose goals are dissimilar and whose time
horizons are different.

Finally, in considering freedom and reform in Asian-Pacific economies, the role of the political system in determining economic policies needs further scrutiny. It is not sufficient to enumerate sound
policies and institutions. Why do some countries adopt "free-market
constitutions" and others do not? In answering this question, it is
necessary to go beyond Rabushka's analysis to something more fundamental within the political system. The task is obviously difficult,
and I am not sure that the experiences of the Asian-Pacific countries
have given us clear lessons on this account—much work remains to
be done.

References

Alvin Rabushka. *The New China*. Boulder, Colorado: Westview Press, 1987.

COMMENT

CHINA AND THE GROWTH-ORIENTED POLICIES OF THE PACIFIC BASIN
George Shen

Alvin Rabushka provides a useful analysis of Hong Kong's Basic Law. He points to the critical role of a "free-market constitution" in establishing a stable and prosperous economic order. He also deals with the basics of economic policy that enabled the four Asian dragons—Hong Kong, Singapore, South Korea, and Taiwan—to emerge from relative backwardness to newly industrialized economies approaching first-world status in less than three decades. His conclusion is that China should look to Hong Kong and the other dragons for guidance in setting up and implementing proposals for reform. The most important lesson is that the basic ingredient for achieving economic success is to allow individuals "a considerable measure of economic freedom." Since Rabushka devoted a major portion of his paper to Hong Kong, I would like to make a few observations on the experience of Singapore, South Korea, and Taiwan.

Singapore

The four dragons are not a homogeneous group. While South Korea and Taiwan are agriculturally based economies, Hong Kong and Singapore are basically urban centers with little or no rural population. Both "city states" started as entrepôts and upheld free trade that helped cultivate an outward-looking attitude among their peoples. Factors contributing to Singapore's success are similar to those of Hong Kong, but a number of external circumstances and domestic conditions enjoyed by Singapore during its early stage of development may merit some mention.

The main exogenous factor favorable to Singapore's economic development was sustained growth in world trade during the 1960s

The author is Chief Editor of the *Hong Kong Economic Journal*.

and early 1970s, which sparked a search for low-wage and politically stable overseas locations by multinational corporations. This factor together with the flight of capital from Hong Kong following the 1967 disturbances, the boom in oil exploration in the region, and the Vietnam War helped Singapore attract foreign capital and technology that, in turn, contributed to economic growth.

In the meantime, endogenous factors also helped Singapore's rapid industrialization. First, its geographical location enabled Singapore to develop into a distributing and processing center. Second, the government created a number of statutory bodies with specific functions to implement development policies such as the promotion of investment in the manufacturing sector, provision of infrastructure for industry, expansion of social services, and building of low-cost housing for a large percentage of the populace. These policies went a long way in creating an amiable investment environment, stabilizing prices and wages, and establishing Singapore as an attractive manufacturing center for foreign investors. In addition, Singapore introduced measures to curb population growth, ease immigration control, and upgrade the training of skilled workers. Singapore also was one of the most efficient and corruption-free governments among developing countries.

There is no denying, however, that Singapore's road to development was not all smooth sailing. There were times when numerous policy measures taken by the government were quite different from, if not contrary to, the "positive noninterference" policy that contributed to Hong Kong's prosperity. These measures had an adverse effect on Singapore's economy, as manifested by the fact that Singapore was the last of the four dragons to recover from the recession in the earlier part of the 1980s.

South Korea

South Korea and Taiwan went through a path different from either Hong Kong or Singapore. During their early years of development, both underwent land and agricultural reform and adopted a system of economic planning and import substitution with the government playing a dominant role. While land reform helped lay a sound foundation for economic development, government planning and import substitution resulted in slow growth and other difficulties, such as dependency on imported intermediate inputs, noncompetitive prices, and so on. It was not until the mid- and late-1960s that these economies switched their policy to export-oriented growth that subsequently led to a spectacular economic take-off.

The case of South Korea may be of special interest to China in a number of aspects. In particular, there was heavy government intervention aimed at encouraging the rapid development of heavy industries such as iron and steel and petro-chemicals during the first three 5-year plans between 1962 and 1976. Also, several capital-intensive, high-technology projects were launched with government support in the 1970s. However, over-intervention by the government distorted costs and prices and disrupted market functions. Hence, the effort backfired and the Korean economy experienced negative growth in 1979. The government responded by changing to a more market-oriented policy, thus putting the economy back on track.

Another example was the development of rural industries. As early as the 1960s, planners in South Korea saw the merit of rural industries not only as a means of absorbing excess labor in rural areas and of complementing import substitution but also as a potential vehicle of industrialization through the broadening of the country's industrial base. With government encouragement, rural industries started to flourish during the 1960s and 1970s. However, large numbers of the rural population continued to migrate to urban centers. In addition, many rural industries were dependent on large industries in the cities for raw materials and intermediate inputs, thus defeating the original objective of utilizing raw materials from agricultural outputs and by-products. The situation turned for the better in the 1980s, thanks to improvements in both administrative procedures and integrated programs in manpower development and technology transfer.

Lessons that may be drawn from South Korea's economic experience include the following. First, and foremost, is that the role of the market must be given full recognition. In the earlier years, the government's industrial policy had strongly favored investment in heavy and chemical industries by means of a variety of tax and financial incentives, sometimes even directly intervening in the allocation of resources through controlling banks' lending activities. The economic set-back in the late 1970s, however, convinced the government that intervention could never be a good substitute for a market mechanism both in terms of resource allocation and the provision of incentives for private enterprises.

Second, import substitution lacks adaptability to external shocks, especially for a country with limited natural resources. South Korea's switch from import substitution to an open economy, with an outward-looking development strategy, proved to be instrumental in propelling exports. It also proved more efficient in providing opportunities for private entrepreneurs to exploit the changing world economic environment.

Third, an outward-looking policy induces the inflow of foreign capital that, in turn, contributes to economic growth. At an early stage of development, South Korea learned the importance of foreign investment (whether direct or through joint ventures) to technology transfer. South Korea also learned that, in order to encourage the inflow of foreign capital, it was vital to maintain a more liberal economic policy so as to gain the confidence of foreign investors.

Fourth, the transfer of technology has a prerequisite, namely, the capability to absorb, adapt, and disseminate imported technology. The South Korean government realized that emphasis on manpower development through education and training, coupled with a policy to provide for continuous expansion of employment opportunities, plays a crucial role in economic success.

Lastly, there ought to be social and political stability. Although Korea is still a divided country and South Korea has to spend a considerable percentage of its revenues on defense—and the government has been more totalitarian than democratic—the last 30 years have witnessed remarkable social and political stability, violent student movements notwithstanding.

Taiwan

Taiwan's industrialization may be attributed to planning within a market economy and land reform. Since the first development plan in 1953, Taiwan has adopted a "loose planning concept." The essence of this approach to development is to provide economic forecasts and projections, to publicize government intentions, and to supply overall economic information to promote mutual understanding among policymakers (in public and private industries), entrepreneurs, scholars, and professionals. The plans have been conceived and executed as flexible and indicative mechanisms rather than as mandatory policy.

As to land reform, Taiwan started the first program between 1949 and 1953, which not only brought about a radical change in the tenure system to provide major incentives to farmers to raise productivity but also had a great social and economic impact through the redistribution of income and enhanced status for farmers. After the changed economic circumstances, which necessitated adjustments in agricultural production, Taiwan initiated the second phase of land reform in 1980. This phase was essentially directed toward enlarging the size of farms, providing credit, and mechanizing farms. It should be mentioned that the success of Taiwan's land policy was due to several factors, including the existence of organized farmers' associations and a rural infrastructure, the absence of vested bureaucratic interests in land ownership, the diversion of the interest of landowners to industry through government incentives, and the availability of opportunities in the industrial sectors.

Taiwan was also successful in quelling two hyperinflations. During the 1946–49 period, Taiwan succeeded in eliminating inflationary psychology. It did this by adopting monetary reforms that absorbed excess money through the manipulation of interest rates and the maintenance of a balanced government budget. When the world oil crisis led to another hyperinflation in 1974, the government adopted a multi-pronged policy that included controlling the money supply and maintaining high interest rates to promptly increase time and savings deposits, and by reducing taxes to curtail costs and to promote faster economic recovery.

Other factors that contributed to Taiwan's economic growth included the shift from labor- and energy-intensive industries to technology-intensive and high value-added ones, education and training to improve micro-level management skills, and the transfer of technology from abroad coupled with the strengthening of indigenous research and development capabilities. These measures enabled Taiwan to export high-quality, technology-intensive products at competitive prices. (It may be mentioned that South Korea once adopted a policy of distorting capital costs by providing massive subsidized credit, which resulted in Korea's factor input of export products becoming capital intensive, thus losing competitiveness. Taiwan was wise enough to have avoided this pitfall.)

Conclusion

Among the four dragons, the experience of South Korea and Taiwan may be more relevant to China than either Hong Kong or Singapore. The positive and negative experiences of planning within a market mechanism and an agriculturally based industrial economy may provide useful lessons for many developing countries, including China.

18

ECONOMIC DEREGULATION IN THE
UNITED STATES: LESSONS FOR AMERICA,
LESSONS FOR CHINA*
William A. Niskanen

Over the past decade, the federal government of the United States
has eliminated or substantially reduced the regulation of price and
entry in domestic aviation, trucking, railroads, interstate buses, ocean
shipping, long-distance communications, energy, and financial institutions. In addition, the federal government eliminated the general
controls or guidelines on prices and wages throughout the economy.

The focus of this paper is on the lessons that might be learned from
the U.S. experience with economic deregulation. For the United
States, deregulation has caused certain problems but, in general,
the net benefits have been higher than first expected. Although the
political and economic system in China is very different from that in
the United States, the American experience with economic deregulation may also provide some important general lessons for China.

Political Lessons

For a political economist, the political lessons from the U.S. experience with deregulation are the most intriguing, seeming to defy much
of the conventional wisdom. The processes that led to deregulation
of most of the above industries shared the following five general
characteristics.

First, deregulatory actions were initiated by the regulatory agencies. About the same time that economists concluded that the regulatory commissions were "captive" of the regulated industries, the
commissions began to prove them wrong. The Federal Communications Commission (FCC) was the first to declare independence,
allowing competition in telephone terminal equipment in 1968 and
progressively broader competition in long-distance communication

*Reprinted from *Cato Journal* 8 (Winter 1989): 657–68, with revisions.
    The author is Chairman of the Cato Institute and a former member of the Council of
Economic Advisers.

beginning in 1969. The Civil Aeronautics Board (CAB), following an internal staff study, began to relax price regulation of domestic airlines in 1976. The Interstate Commerce Commission (ICC) broadened the allowed bands on trucking rates in 1976 and relaxed entry controls in 1978. These and other commission actions provided tests of the effects of partial deregulation before Congress considered changes in the regulatory legislation.

Second, there was very little popular support for deregulation, even though consumers would be the major beneficiaries. Consumer satisfaction with airline and telephone service was especially high, and the general public was only vaguely aware of most forms of economic regulation. The support of general business groups for deregulation was late to develop and was broad but not deep.

Third, opposition to deregulation by the regulated firms was first broad but was not sustained. The prospect that the regulatory commissions, with presidential support, would pursue deregulation under the existing law led to the erosion of opposition to the regulatory reform legislation by the regulated firms. The strongest and most enduring opposition to deregulation was from the labor unions in regulated firms. In retrospect, it appears that both the regulated firms and their unions underestimated the extent to which deregulation would undermine the wage structure in these industries.

Fourth, the substantial reduction in economic regulation began during a period in which there was a sizeable increase in the "social" regulation of health, safety, the environment, and the uses of energy. The reduction of economic regulation, thus, did not reflect a general reaction against regulation but was a response to conditions specific to the deregulated industries.

Fifth, a number of conditions appear to have been associated with the selective success of the deregulation movement: There was a convergence of *elite* opinion on deregulation issues, including a near unanimity of economists. Both the support and the opposition to economic deregulation was bipartisan. The deregulation measures were represented as pro-consumer rather than pro-business. A developing concern about increasing general inflation broadened the support for deregulation. Some amount of deregulation was possible without new legislation. And the support of three presidents was necessary to sustain the momentum for deregulation by the commissions and to speak for the general interest.

In their recent book, *The Politics of Deregulation,* Martha Derthick and Paul Quirk (1985) reflect on the political lessons from U.S. deregulation and conclude that the deregulation measures were achieved through the politics of ideas—specifically through the fusion of expert analysis with public opinion—and suggest that the political victory of a diffuse interest over particularistic interests, though due in part to special features of these cases, was not an aberration. Rather, it shows that the U.S. political system has a greater capacity for transcending narrow interests than has generally been acknowledged.[1]

My hope is that "the politics of ideas," a concept that the Chinese may have invented, has a similar success in China.

Economic Lessons

For economists, although not for many others, the economic effects of the deregulation of price and entry in the targeted industries were less surprising. A review of these effects, however, is useful in evaluating the prospects for similar measures in other industries and other countries.

Transportation

The general effects of the deregulation of domestic transportation have been expanded service, lower rates, and higher productivity.

Since Congress approved the Airline Deregulation Act of 1978, the number of city-pairs served by more than one airline increased by 55 percent, flights to smaller cities increased by 20 to 30 percent, and service has been expanded to 140 additional airports. About 90 percent of air travelers now use discount fares, and average real discount fares declined about 10 percent on short flights and 35 percent on long flights. Airline productivity also increased. Since the CAB initiated partial deregulation in 1976, the percentage of passenger seats occupied increased from 55 to 60 percent, and airline productivity increased by more than 7 percent. On net, the effects of domestic airline deregulation appear to have increased benefits to travelers by about $11 billion and by about $4 billion to the airlines.[2]

The effects of the substantial deregulation of trucking are similar. Since Congress approved the Motor Carrier Act of 1980, the number of authorized carriers has nearly doubled, and the restrictions on the licenses of many existing carriers were removed. A recent survey found that average real rates declined about 25 percent for small

[1]Bruce K. Maclaury in his Foreword to Derthick and Quirk (1985, pp. vii–viii). This book is the best summary of the conditions that led to the deregulation of airlines, trucking, and communications.
[2]These figures were compiled from the *Economic Report of the President* (1986, 1988).

shipments, and other surveys indicate a general improvement in service.[3]

The Staggers Rail Act of 1980 authorized a partial deregulation of rail rates. Most bulk commodities are now shipped at private contract rates; average real revenues per ton have declined about 11 percent for coal and 33 percent for farm products, despite a small increase in the average distance shipped. Rail-car utilization increased about 10 percent and ton-miles per employee increased 44 percent in the first four years, substantially increasing the profitability of what had recently been a sick industry.[4]

(Experience under the Bus Regulatory Reform Act of 1982 and the Shipping Act of 1984 has been too brief to provide comparable summaries.)

Several related developments also merit attention. A concern has been expressed that deregulation of the commercial transportation industries may have compromised safety, even though the government maintained safety regulation of each of these industries. The facts are otherwise. Airline accident and fatality rates continued to decline after deregulation. Truck accidents were also lower, except in one year. Rail accidents due to track defects are sharply lower. Truck and rail deregulation has contributed to a reduction of about $100 billion in the total logistics costs of American industry, about one-third due to lower freight rates and one-third to lower inventories (Barnekov 1987).

There are a number of other conditions in the airline and trucking industries, however, that should be recognized. Several airlines and many trucking firms have gone bankrupt, finding that they were unable to be competitive under their prior labor contracts. Airlines found that they could hire qualified new employees at wages up to 50 percent lower than under the labor contracts of the existing carriers. This discovery led to a rapid increase in new airlines and in wage concessions and two-tier wage systems in the older airlines. Similarly, most of the new trucking firms pay less than the union rates of the older firms. In retrospect, it is now clear that the major beneficiaries of economic regulation were neither the consumers nor the owners of regulated firms but rather the workers and managers in these firms.

Communications

The partial deregulation of telecommunications was the result of a series of FCC decisions and a major antitrust case, without any

[3]See *Economic Report* (1986, p. 161).
[4]On railroad deregulation, see Barnekov (1987).

change in legislation. Local telephone services are still regulated, but most other services have been substantially deregulated. More than 200 firms now offer long-distance telephone and data services at substantial discount below the AT&T rates, and the market for telephone equipment has expanded rapidly. The full effects of the breakups of AT&T are yet to be realized. The separation of the regional telephone companies from AT&T was expected to reduce long-distance rates and to increase local rates, and this is what happened; in the first four years following separation, real interstate rates declined about 12 percent and real local rates increased about 12 percent (Crandall 1987). These actions have also reduced the power of the communications union, leading to a reclassification of thousands of jobs to reduce average labor costs; the union has been transformed from a militant bargainer to a promoter of AT&T's long-distance services. Although these measures have been strongly supported by business users of telecommunications services, they are not yet well received by the general population.

Energy

Oil prices were first directly regulated as part of the general price and wage controls in 1971 but were unfortunately maintained when these other controls were phased out. As a consequence of the two oil shocks, these controls became increasingly burdensome. After approval of the "windfall profits" tax on domestic oil, Congress scheduled the termination of the oil price controls for September 1981. President Reagan terminated these controls immediately after his inauguration in January 1981; after a small initial increase, real oil prices have generally declined since March 1981. Within two years, domestic oil well completion was nearly 50 percent higher than in 1980, and production (exclusive of Alaska) increased slightly, reversing a 10-year trend and despite a decline in real oil prices. The energy "crisis" of the 1970s was ended by the stroke of a pen. By 1983, the administration and Congress were considering ways to maintain the domestic price of oil.

The wellhead prices of natural gas were first regulated as a consequence of a court decision in 1954. This regulation did not impose extraordinary costs until the first large increase in oil prices in 1974. Following a severe shortage of natural gas in the winter of 1977, Congress approved the Natural Gas Policy Act of 1978, legislation that was designed as a deregulation measure but was all too clever. The act authorized the phased decontrol of all "new" gas discovered after 1977 but maintained price controls on more than 20 categories of "old" gas. This policy would have caused only minor problems if not for the second large increase in oil prices in 1979–80. The results of the controls were somewhat surprising. Consumers did not benefit from the continued controls on the price of old gas, because delivered gas prices, after a short lag, moved in parallel with oil prices. The primary effects of the controls were to increase the margins of the pipelines and distribution companies and to reduce the production of old gas, risking the loss of old gas reserves equal to 1–3 years of consumption. The substantial decline in real oil prices in the 1980s has reduced the short-run problems of the remaining gas controls, but provides a good opportunity for their removal. A comparison of the experience with oil and gas decontrol suggests that abrupt general decontrol requires more political courage but causes far fewer problems than phased partial decontrol.

One other remnant of the energy regulations implemented in the 1970s has also been abolished. In 1987, Congress repealed the Fuel Use Act, which had prohibited utilities and industrial firms from building new boilers dependent on oil and natural gas. The repeal of this act has made it possible to add capacity in smaller increments, more quickly, and with much lower environmental effects than is possible with a coal-fired plant.

Financial Institutions

For the most part, changes in financial regulation were forced by major developments in the financial markets. Commercial and savings banks had been subject to interest rate ceilings on their deposits since the 1930s. These ceilings led to severe problems only when market interest rates increased rapidly, first in the late 1960s and again in the late 1970s. Small depositors were especially harmed by these ceilings. The development of the money market mutual funds in the 1970s offered savers deposit-like accounts with market interest rates and led to an erosion of deposits in the banking system. Congress finally responded to these developments in 1980 by approving the gradual removal of interest rate ceilings by 1986. Another law in 1982 authorized banks to offer new types of accounts to both small and large depositors. These new types of accounts proved to be very popular and were estimated to increase the interest payments to depositors by $3.6 billion a year with no significant effect on interest rates to borrowers. Other provisions of the 1982 legislation permit the acquisition of a failed bank by an out-of-state bank or by a bank of a different type.

General Price and Wage Controls

In August 1971, President Nixon imposed general price and wage controls as part of a larger program that ended the Bretton Woods agreement on exchange rates. This was the first peacetime use of general price and wage controls in the United States. Although these controls seemed effective for a year or so, they only deferred the measured inflation. The consumer inflation rate increased from 4.3 percent in 1971 to 11 percent in 1974 as these controls were phased out (except for oil).

After the severe recession of 1974–75, the consumer inflation rate declined to 5.8 percent in 1976. A continued concern about inflation, however, led President Carter to impose a new system of "voluntary" price and wage guidelines in 1977; these guidelines were supposed to be enforced by public exposure and by denial of government contracts to those who exceeded the guidelines. Carter's guidelines proved to be no more effective, however, than Nixon's controls, and the consumer inflation rate increased to 13.5 percent in 1980.

The major lesson of this experience is that general price and wage controls are not sufficient to restrain inflation in the presence of a rapid increase in total demand. Although some politicians and economists continued to believe that the controls were valuable, President Reagan believed otherwise. Shortly after his inauguration in January 1981, Reagan abolished the price and wage guidelines and the office that monitored those guidelines. After another severe recession in 1981–82, the consumer inflation rate declined to 3.2 percent in 1983, and a moderate growth of total demand has maintained inflation at about this rate for five years. The major lesson that one should have learned from this experience is that monetary restraint is both necessary and sufficient to reduce inflation, sometimes at the expense of a temporary reduction of output. Moreover, price and wage controls, as with any form of economic regulation, reduce the general productivity of the economy. From 1973 through 1980, for example, U.S. output per hour increased at an annual rate of only 0.5 percent; since 1980, in contrast, productivity has increased at an annual rate of about 1.5 percent. Reagan's judgment on these issues proved to be correct: Inflation is best reduced by monetary restraint, not by price and wage controls, and the reduction of both inflation and regulation is likely to increase general productivity.

Unresolved Problems

Our government, unfortunately, has not yet addressed the complementary measures that are probably necessary to sustain the deregulation of several industries. Some change in the procedures for rationing the congested airspace and airports, for example, is probably necessary to sustain airline deregulation. Similarly, some change in the procedures for rationing the frequency spectrum is probably necessary to sustain the deregulation of communications.

The most urgent problem, however, involves the financial institutions. The combination of interest rate deregulation and the current structure of deposit insurance is not viable in the long run, because banks now have an opportunity to shift more of their risks to the insurance system; some reregulation is probable unless the deposit insurance premiums or rules are changed. The total net worth of the savings banks, by commercial accounting standards, is close to zero, and this system is very vulnerable to an increase in interest rates. Bank failures continue to increase, and the current reserves of the deposit insurance agencies may be insufficient. The administration and Congress have not been willing to address the laws, almost unique to the United States, that restrict national banking or the right of banks to own or underwrite equities in nonfinancial firms.

Federal economic regulation has been substantially reduced during the past decade, but a great deal remains to be done. American agriculture is still plagued by marketing orders that limit production or set price floors on a range of products. Regulation of the frequency spectrum has inhibited the use of some communications technologies. The potential for deregulating the uses of energy, the supply of natural gas, and the production of electricity have yet to be realized. Our financial system is still cartelized by region and type of loan. Labor regulation restricts a wide range of relations that would be preferred by both employers and employees. International air travel is still subject to both price and entry regulations, railroads are subject to archaic work rules, and shipping between domestic ports is still restricted to American ships. One should recognize that many of the effects of deregulation cannot be anticipated. The general success of the economic deregulation to date, however, strengthens the case for reducing or eliminating most of the remaining types of price and entry regulations.

Some General Lessons for China

Without a specialist's understanding of China, I am cautious about offering suggestions for economic reform. Yet, in the spirit of trying to learn from each other about issues of common interest, let me summarize two general lessons from the American experience that should apply in any country: (1) As a rule, regulation is neither necessary nor sometimes sufficient to achieve the shared goals of a national community; and (2) regulation is often the most costly means to achieve these goals, both in terms of individual freedom and economic efficiency.

Let me illustrate the application of these lessons to three major goals of contemporary Chinese policy: reducing the growth of total population, maintaining a rough balance of payments, and reducing the rate of general inflation. My understanding suggests that some policy changes could achieve these goals without the restrictions on individual freedom and economic efficiency inherent in current policies.[5]

Population

As I understand, China is now attempting to reduce the growth of total population primarily by regulating the number of children per family. Effective enforcement of these regulations, by either sanctions or social pressure, is probably sufficient to meet this goal, as indicated by the sharp decline in the crude birthrate from 1970 through 1976. But such regulation is not necessary to reduce population growth. Both the long historical record and current cross-country comparisons indicate a strong negative relation between birthrates and the levels of urbanization, industrialization, and economic development. The birthrate in all of the high-income countries is now below the reproduction rate. But it is most important not to misinterpret this evidence. The most careful evaluations of this evidence indicate that *lower birthrates are a result, not a significant cause, of economic development.* The sustained economic development of China would reduce both the birthrate and death rate by different processes, and the rate of growth of total population would gradually decline without any specific policies to affect this rate.

Moreover, to an American, a limit on the number of children per family would be an intolerable restriction on individual freedom. Some rural parents may want more children because of the greater opportunity of rural children to contribute to family income. Some urban parents are surely more caring, better parents than others. As one of three sons and now the father of three daughters, my views on this issue may be biased, but children with brothers and sisters seem less "spoiled" and more prepared for adult life than are single children. In our political system, the government must bear the burden of proving that regulation of specific activities serves some broader interest. There are no obvious reasons to restrict the freedom

---

[5]The basic source for my understanding of economic conditions and policies in China is Perkins (1988).

of each family to choose the number of children consistent with its own conditions and preferences.

The goal of reducing the growth of total population in China can probably be achieved by other policies that involve less restriction on the freedom of individual families. Education and the general availability of contraceptives have proven effective in reducing the number of unwanted births. Welfare programs and the tax code can be designed to influence the choice of family size. Such indirect policies can limit the total number of births without restricting the freedom of each family to make this choice. Such policies will lead some families to make mistakes in this choice. The very concept of freedom, however, means the right of an individual to make his own mistakes as long as they do not affect the rights of others.

Balance of Payments

Similarly, I understand that China is now attempting to achieve a rough balance of international payments primarily by limiting the net foreign exchange available to each firm. In effect, this limitation has required each firm to maintain its own balance of payments. The several effects of this constraint on the economy should be recognized. One effect has been to limit the opportunity of firms to specialize in either exports or imports, because each firm must earn about as much foreign exchange by exports as it uses to purchase imports. A second effect has been to limit foreign direct investment to a much lower level than was expected when the Joint Venture Law was approved. A third effect, given the large excess demand for imports, has been to strengthen the power of the bureaucracy relative to the market in the allocation of foreign exchange, with the consequent problems of favoritism and the incentives for corruption. The current controls on access to foreign exchange are probably the most important policy that limits the potential for increased integration of China into world markets.

Two types of policies would reduce the costs of these foreign exchange controls consistent with any desired level of the total balance of payments. One alternative would be to devalue the yuan. A substantial devaluation of the yuan, however, would probably be necessary to eliminate the excess demand for imports, given the extensive system of foreign quotas on products exported by China and the "soft budget constraint" on many Chinese firms. Most economists would support the relaxation or, preferably, the elimination of the many U.S. quotas on textiles, apparel, and other Chinese exports, but the near-term prospects for such changes are not encouraging. The soft budget constraint on Chinese firms can best be tightened by reducing government subsidies that offset the losses of individual firms. In the absence of these changes, a major devaluation of the yuan would probably be necessary.

The only effective alternative would be policies that would increase saving by Chinese families and firms or reduce the dissaving by the government. One should recognize that the current account balance of any country is the difference between saving by residents of that country and investment in that country. China, or any country, can increase domestic investment only by increasing domestic saving or by reducing its current account balance. As long as China, for whatever reason, wishes to maintain a rough balance on its international accounts, increased investment must be financed from increased saving. The major source of potential saving, as well as the best way to tighten the soft budget constraint, may be to reduce the discretionary subsidies to Chinese firms.

Inflation

For good reasons China also wants to maintain a roughly constant general price level, but the primary policy to constrain inflation has been the control of the prices of individual goods and services. Such controls have never proved sufficient to restrain inflation for a sustained period, and they cause severe misallocations and often social unrest. In some cases, the relaxation of price controls increases the measured price indices, but that is usually a statistical illusion. Price controls increase nonprice types of rationing—by queues, favoritism, bribery, and a deterioration in the quality of goods and services. A relaxation of such controls, thus, sometimes increases measured prices but reduces these other types of rationing that are not reflected in the measured price indices.

Most of the variation of inflation in China, as in other countries, is due to an increase in the money supply relative to the level of output.[6] In the long run, monetary policy is sufficient to determine any level of general prices or the general inflation rate. In addition, it is especially important to allow increases in specific prices that would increase output, whatever their immediate effect on the measured price indices. China has ample reason to be concerned about the increased inflation rate since 1984, but the most effective response would be a combination of monetary restraint and "supply-side" economic policies to increase output, not the futile and costly reimposition of controls on specific prices.

[6]See Cheng (1987) and Chow (1987).

Conclusion

The most important general lessons from the American experience with economic deregulation are the following:

- Deregulation was politically possible, on occasion even politically fashionable, despite the forceful opposition of some groups.
- Deregulation generated substantial benefits to consumers and substantial opportunities for new firms.
- Deregulation undermined the wage structure of some unions and the easy life of managers in the previously regulated firms.
- Deregulation led to a substantial increase in productivity in the affected industries and contributed to a general increase in productivity in the economy, creating benefits that were much larger than the losses.

The road to deregulation is not without rocks or detours, but it is the road to prosperity and opportunity. A government that represents the nation, rather than the interests of specific groups, will choose this road. Economic deregulation has been supported by the past three administrations in the United States. The government of China has the opportunity to choose this same road.

References

Barnekov, Christopher C. "The Track Record." *Regulation* 11 (January/February 1987): 19–27.

Cheng, Hang-Shen. "Monetary Policy and Inflation in China." Paper presented at a conference at the Federal Reserve Bank of San Francisco, September 1987.

Chow, Gregory. "Money and Price Level Determination in China." *Journal of Comparative Economics* 11 (September 1987): 319–33.

Crandall, Robert W. "Has the AT&T Break Raised Telephone Rates?" *The Brookings Review* 5 (Winter 1987): 37–44.

Derthick, Martha, and Quirk, Paul J. *The Politics of Deregulation.* Washington, D.C.: The Brookings Institution, 1985.

Economic Report of the President. Washington, D.C.: Government Printing Office, 1986 and 1988.

Perkins, Dwight Heald. "Reforming China's Economic System." *Journal of Economic Literature* 26 (June 1988): 601–45.

19

LET A BILLION FLOWERS BLOOM*
George Gilder

The first great rule of enterprise is do not solve problems, pursue opportunities. Problems are infinite and they multiply continuously; when you solve them, you are back where you began. Governments specialize in creating problems that they then generously solve for the people, creating yet more serious and more systemic problems in the process. The key to the success of China will be to spurn the problem solvers of the world and to pursue the supremely inviting opportunities that now exist.

The Age of Information

China now stands at the threshold of the greatest opportunity in human history: a new economic era promising greater wealth and achievement than any previous epoch. This chance to begin again is a great advantage for China, because China almost entirely missed the last economic era. The new era is the age of information, and the prime measure of the previous failure in China is the gap between the incomes of Chinese people in China and Chinese people in the rest of the world. By some measures, if the incomes of the Chinese people in China had grown just one-third as fast as the incomes of Chinese in other countries, China would be the world's largest economy and the world economy would be some 25 percent larger than it is.

Forget oil, gold, land, the ocean floor, or the reaches of outer space. The single greatest untapped resource in the world economy is the Chinese people. Many demographers and political scientists—and even the words of the Chinese language itself—treat the Chinese people as if they are mouths: a burden on the world's food supplies. But far more than mouths, the Chinese people are minds. The key

*Reprinted from *Cato Journal* 8 (Winter 1989): 669–75, with revisions.

The author is a Senior Fellow of the Hudson Institute and a former Fellow of the Kennedy Institute of Politics at Harvard University. His book *Wealth and Poverty* was a worldwide best seller and his current book is *Microcosm: Into the Quantum Era of Economics and Technology.*

issue of the next 25 years is whether the minds of the Chinese people in China will be emancipated on the frontiers of the new economic era.

The law of the new economy is mind over matter. A typical information product of the previous era is a book. A book is not just a paper product or a product of wood and chemical technology. A book is an information technology. That means its worth derives not from its material substance but from its informational content—not from its chemical value but from its conceptual value. A book costs about 80 cents to 2 dollars to manufacture in volume, but it sells for between 10 times and 100 times that amount depending on the value of the ideas it contains.

I want to present a new information technology. You cannot really see it, because it is a set of microchips in which the actual components are invisible. Microchips, now available in prototype, are the size of your thumbnail and can hold the contents of a large textbook. They will cost about the same amount as the book to mass-produce: between 80 cents and 2 dollars. An optical compact disk holds 600 megabytes of information—the equivalent of 600 large books. That compact disk also costs between 80 cents and 2 dollars to produce in volume and will sell for the value of the information it contains.

Microchips are the prime products of the new age, the key source of value in every computer and computer-related product. The substance of a microchip is mostly sand: the silicon in sand, the most common substance on the face of the earth. What matters again is not its substance but its contents: the idea, the design, the function.

So what does this mean for China? What this new technology means for China is that one of Chairman Mao's most cherished dreams can now come true. That dream can be summed up, perhaps, as power to the people. Twenty-five years ago, Chairman Mao tried to fulfill this dream by launching a program of steel mills in every backyard. This approach was very stupid. Steel mills are very bad things to have in your backyard. To function efficiently, they require huge economies of scale, involving many thousands of regimented workers.

The new microchip technology, by contrast, is based on economies of microscale. The smaller each device on the chip, the more powerful the machine. This fact means that, in the information age, power is constantly pulled down to individuals who command single work stations, single personal computers based on the power of the chip.

The new economy is based not on digging into the world for valuable resources, but on designing new worlds on valueless grains of sand. A single computer work station can create value in the new economy greater than a huge steel mill. A computer work station linked to a global ganglion of satellites and fiber-optic cables can transport more value in microseconds than an entire fleet of supertankers in months.

The new technology means that Mao's dream can come true not in the backyard but on the kitchen table. For example, software programs are perhaps the most important products of the information revolution. Some 80 percent of the value of a telecommunications system comes from software, and 80 percent of the value of a computer system comes from software. Even the design of a microchip itself begins as a software program. Software can be created by any individual at a work station. In the new age, power moves from the managers of large steel mills and other huge facilities to the masters of small computers.

Thus, it is easily possible to fulfill Mao's dream of industrial power distributed to the people. However, to fulfill that dream absolutely requires that China abandon Mao's other dream: the dream of central planning of an economy.

The Futility of Central Planning

The law of the microcosm—the law of the microchip—is that the power of individual work stations always grows much faster than the power of large computer systems. Gone is the long dream of the socialist that giant computers will allow planners to simulate markets and thus manage large economies. The socialist dream has been confounded at the heart of the computer itself. The power of the chip always grows faster than the power of the larger system. Today's individual personal computers are more than 100 times more cost effective than large mainframe computers.

The previous technology of the industrial era to some extent favored control. By control over territory, control over natural resources, control over industrial capital, and control over taxes and trade, governments could increase the power of nations. Governments could increase national power by increasing governmental power. The new technology, on the other hand, favors freedom. It truly fosters power to the people.

Breaking the Iron Rice Bowl

Mao said: "Let a hundred flowers bloom; let a thousand thoughts contend." This showed his incomparable misunderstanding of the powers of the Chinese people. The rule of capitalism is "Let a billion flowers bloom; let a trillion thoughts contend." I believe that this is going to happen. We are going to have an efflorescence of entrepreneurship in China that will make China the richest economy in the world within the next 25 years.

How do I know this? Because whenever and wherever you set the Chinese free, they create new wealth. China liberated agriculture and, within eight years, output tripled in rural areas; the Chinese now export rice. The new era is no different. Everywhere in the world except China, the Chinese people are in the forefront of the information age. In the United States, for example, there are thousands of crucial information companies launched by Chinese entrepreneurs.

Before the June 1989 turnaround, there were exciting signs of progress in China itself. One of the fastest-growing computer firms on earth was started just six years ago on a street in Beijing. "When you go out into the dark night," says Chinese entrepreneur Wan Ruttan, "the first thing you must do is throw out a stone to see where the road is." Wan Ruttan is the entrepreneur who began that computer company. His "dark night" was the totalitarian murk of the economy of this so-called People's Republic.

Without market prices or consumer choices to reveal patterns of scarcity or need, an economy operates in the dark. Because no one knows what is needed in what amounts, output and demand are always mismatched, and no one produces very much. Starting a firm is pretty much a matter of throwing dice—or a stone.

Nonetheless, despite the dark shadows, Wan Ruttan hit the road hard with Stone Computer Inc., generating $137 million in revenues in 1988. Within four years after its founding, Wan's firm passed all the numerous state-run computer firms to rank number one in China.

How did he do it? One young Chinese who had studied in the United States told me Wan and his ilk got rich through "greed" and "corruption." A more insightful report in *Electronic Business* magazine, however, ascribes Wan's success to his willingness, as he put it, to "break the iron rice bowl."

The "iron rice bowl" symbolizes the employment security of the Chinese: Everyone supposedly gets a job and a bowl of rice no matter how little or how ineptly he works. But in another sense, any totalitarian economy is an iron rice bowl. Designed to provide an income floor, the iron bowl always ends up imposing a rigid lid on all personal achievement and economic growth.

Wan substituted a clay rice bowl that is "stronger than iron but breaks more easily." In other words, Wan was willing to accept risk as well as rice. Accepting risk, he also created a shocking Communist scandal: a $9.5 million after-tax profit in 1987.

Everyone wants security. But if a system tries to provide security for every individual, it will create insecurity and sterility for all. The iron bowl of socialism is designed to shield the citizens from risk. But the result is to shield them from knowledge of the real dangers and opportunities in any society.

Rather than benefiting from a multiplicity of individual ventures and plans, the entire economy absorbs the much greater risk of remaining static in a dynamic world. Sooner or later, even the iron bowl is empty, and all too often it is worn as a helmet for a war of conquest or civil suppression. This cycle sums up a millennium of Chinese history.

Microstability—guaranteed jobs and incomes—comes at the cost of macroinstability: the inflexibility, weakness, and insecurity of the system as a whole. During the heyday of Maoism and the iron rice bowl guarantee, the nation's total rice production actually declined for several years. Despite all Communist claims, Harvard demographer Nick Eberstadt reports, millions of Chinese died of famine.

After the death of Mao, China began to take the lid off, allowing farmers to keep all their production and sales beyond their quota owed to the state. This system is the opposite of the iron rice bowl, a quota of food for every citizen. Instead, the state got the iron bowl—an assured quota of rice—while the farmer got freedom to keep all production beyond the quota.

In effect, the Chinese had discovered supply-side economics, imposing a zero marginal tax rate on all income beyond the government's guarantee. The result was that China began feeding itself and even exporting some rice. Output from the rural areas more than tripled, rising 246 percent according to government data. Breaking the redistributive iron bowl made China the rice bowl of the world.

The most deadly force in business life is the search for the sure thing. Only the past is ever sure. Pursuing safety first, businesses and managers end up copying the previous successes of others and often achieving obsolescence in the process. To find the road ahead—the road to future success—even in free economies, it is still necessary to throw a stone, take a risk, and break the iron bowl like Wan Ruttan.

Stone throwers, however, are not popular in the iron bowl bureaucracies. For example, the state-run Science and Printing Institute threatened to sue Wan's company for alleged violation of patents, and many bureaucrats at the government computer firms resented the triumph of Stone Inc. Wan told *Electronic Business:* "They claim it's my fault that nobody wants to buy their products. They would prefer it if I sold lower-quality products at higher prices."

Pursue Opportunity

My advice to Chinese reformers is, do not solve problems—inflation, corruption, trade deficits, inequality, poverty. You will just increase the power of government, weaken the power of the people, and create newer and worse problems in the process. Take the route of Wan Ruttan: Pursue opportunity.

Ruttan did not solve the problem of the 20 government computer companies that were far ahead of him when he began six years ago. He did not eliminate inflation, corruption, poverty, bureaucracy, or inequality. Instead he pursued his opportunity to create a new firm that would leap ahead of all the government companies. He did not try to liquidate the government firms or privatize them. He did not try to reform the financial system. He did not overthrow the communist cadres. He simply transcended them. In 1988, on that same street in Beijing, there were 170 other new high-technology companies and 1,000 more such companies applying for licenses. None of them can solve the systemic problems of China. But if they are allowed the freedom to pursue opportunity, they will ultimately transform the Chinese economy.

I would like to conclude by telling a story about problems and opportunities. Two shoe salesmen were sent deep into the boondocks of Africa. One wired back to the home office: "Get me out of here. No one even wears shoes. There is no chance for sales." The second shoe salesman wired back: "Great opportunity! Everybody is barefoot here. Send all stock; we can dominate the market."

There are still a lot of barefoot people in China. But 25 years from today I believe that China is going to be the richest economy in the world if it pursues the opportunity of freedom and profit. Let a billion flowers bloom!

References

Eberstadt, Nick. *The Poverty of Communism.* New Brunswick: Transaction Books, 1988.
Electronic Business, 18 August 1988.

INDEX

Abrams, Jim, 44n
Agglomeration, 261–62, 265
Agricultural sector: competition in,
    26; effect of communal system
    on, 154–55; markets for products
    of, 159–62, 184; performance of,
    159; privatization in, 8; reforms
    in, 157, 252, 332; as system of
    property rights, 22–23. *See also*
    Collective farms; Communes;
    Grain market; Procurement sys-
    tems; Responsibility contract
Alchian, Armen, 45, 49n, 51n
Anderson, Benjamin, 50
Anderson, Terry L., 207
Armentano, Dominick T., 77n
Asakawa, Kanichi, 173
Ashton, Basil, 154n
Assets, financial, 94–95, 98

Bade, Robin, 104
Bajt, Aleksander, 50n
Bandow, Doug, 287n, 318
Banking system, 126, 133–35; state
    control of, 9, 43. *See also* Free
    banking system
Banks: investment, 134; role in
    financial sector of, 137–46; state-
    owned, 133–34
Bankruptcy Law, 36
Barnekov, Christopher C., 360
Barraclough, Geoffrey, 176
Basic Law, Hong Kong, 337–38; as
    blueprint for China, 345, 349–50;
    economic policies of, 340–43;
    fundamental rights enumerated
    in, 340; monetary and fiscal pol-
    icy elements of, 341–42, 343; pri-
    vate property rights in, 338–39,
    343; rule of law under, 339–40,
    343
Berman, Harold J., 176

Bernholz, Peter, 94, 111, 114
Bernstein, Richard J., 70n
Bian Yi, 49
Bonds: central government,
    138–40; financial institution,
    142–43; of local governments,
    140–41, 146; Treasury, 138–40
Brenner, Robert, 175
Bresciani-Turroni, Constantino, 100
Brutzkus, Boris, 77n
Buchanan, James, 40
Buck, John L., 171
Budget deficit: financing of Chi-
    na's, 138, 146; of United States,
    317
Burden sharing, 301, 318

Calleo, David P., 318
Campbell, Colin D., 106
Capitalism, Marxism critique,
    72–76, 88
Capital market: coordination in,
    93–98; experiments with, 48;
    lack of, 43. *See also* Financial
    instruments; Financial system
Capital movements, South Korea,
    354
Carpenter, Ted Galen, 314, 319
Central bank: instability of,
    130–31; proposed role for,
    126–27. *See also* Free banking
    system; People's Bank of China
    (PBC)
Centrally planned economy: in
    China, 17–18, 240–41; effect on
    economic reform of, 222; ele-
    ments of, 181–86; information
    dissemination in, 197–98; mixed
    with market system, 18–19,
    33–34, 50, 250–51, 268, 297–98,
    334; service provision by, 228
Central Provident Fund (CPF), 274

375

Chan, Wing-Tsit, 57–58
Chang, Parris, 168
Chaos theory, 64, 88–89
Cheng, Hang-Shen, 367
Cheng, Nien, 44, 56n, 333–34
Cheung, Stenen N. S., x, 21, 22, 24–25, 45, 46, 50–54, 243
China. *See* People's Republic of China (PRC)
China International Trust and Investment Company (CITIC), 136
China Investment Bank (CIB), 136
Chou, Chin-Seng, 171
Chou, Shun-Hsin, 104
Chow, Gregory, 367n
Collective farms, 149, 153–54, 159, 162–63, 182
Communes, 154. *See also* Production team system
Communique of the Third Plenary Session of the Twelfth Central Committee, 223, 225
Complexity, modernism conception, 67–69
Confucian traditions, 278
Constitution: for market order, 53–57; for stable monetary regime, 114–18, 120–21
Constitution, Hong Kong. *See* Basic Law, Hong Kong
Constitutional economics, 39–44
Contract procurement system, 160–61
Cooperatives, 152–53; credit, 134, 147. *See also* Collective farms
Corbin, Marcus, 318
Corcorn, Edward A., 316
Council for Mutual Economic Assistance (CMEA), 309

Dashichev, Vyacheslav, 314
Davis, David L., 174
Decentralization: effect on intermediation of, 264–65; obstacles to, 242–43; question of degree, 240; rationale for, 223–37
Decentralization trend: in agricultural sector, 172; in banking sys-

tem, 134; implementation of, 243–44, 264–66. *See also* Agricultural sector; Economic reform; Financial instruments; Financial system
Democracy, Marxist conception, 74–76
Deng Xiaoping, 29, 44, 54–55, 330–31, 337
Department of Defense, 318
Deregulation experience, United States: economic effects of, 7, 359–63; lessons for China in, 364–68; political, 358–59; problems of, 363–64
Derthick, Martha, 358
Dissipative structure theory (Prigogine), 88–89
Dorn, James, 54n, 106
Dougan, William R., 106
Du, Runsheng, 157n
Duus, Peter, 173, 174

East Asia, 301–2
East Asian countries: changing nature of U.S. relations with, 319–20; cultural links among successful, 278; lessons in success of, 348–49, 351–55; U.S. relationship with, 280–90; *See also* Hong Kong; Korea, South; Singapore; Taiwan
Eastern Europe, 315
Eckstein, Alexander, 153
Economic development: in China, 285; in East Asian countries, 277–78; elements for, 177
Economic performance: in China, 21, 31, 252; of East Asian countries, 280–82; with mixed economic model, 250–51
Economic reform, 19, 34–37, 87, 334; application of new view of science for, 64–65, 82–83, 87–88; conditions for, 44–45; decentralization proposals for, 225; direction for, 17–18, 248–51; features of, 240; ideology as basis for, 39–40, 44; impact of world econ-

About the Editors

James A. Dorn is Vice President for Academic Affairs at the Cato Institute and Editor of the *Cato Journal*. He is also Professor of Economics at Towson State University and a Research Fellow of the Institute for Humane Studies at George Mason University. He has served as a member of the White House Commission on Presidential Scholars. His publications include *The Search for Stable Money* (coedited with Anna J. Schwartz) and *Economic Liberties and the Judiciary* (coedited with Henry G. Manne). Dorn holds a Ph.D. in Economics from the University of Virginia.

Wang Xi is Professor of Economics and History at Fudan University, Director of the China-U.S. Program, and General Editor of the multivolume series on Sino-American relations published by Fudan University Press. He has been awarded grants from the Henry Luce Foundation, the Ford Foundation, l'Ecole des Hautes Etudes en Sciences Sociales, and the Committee on International Relations Studies over the past five years to lecture and conduct research in France and the United States. His publications include *U.S.-China Economic Relations: Present and Future* (coedited with Richard Holton) and *International Trade and International Economic Cooperation.*